ADVANCES IN

EXPERIMENTAL
SOCIAL PSYCHOLOGY

VOLUME 24

ADVANCES IN

Experimental

Social Psychology

EDITED BY

Mark P. Zanna

DEPARTMENT OF PSYCHOLOGY
UNIVERSITY OF WATERLOO
WATERLOO, ONTARIO, CANADA

VOLUME 24

ACADEMIC PRESS, INC.
Harcourt Brace Jovanovich, Publishe
San Diego   New York   Boston
London   Sydney   Tokyo   Toronto

This book is printed on acid-free paper. ∞

Academic Press, Inc.
San Diego, California 92101

United Kingdom Edition published by
ACADEMIC PRESS LIMITED
24-28 Oval Road, London NW1 7DX

Library of Congress Catalog Card Number: 64-23452

ISBN 0-12-015224-X (alk. paper)

PRINTED IN THE UNITED STATES OF AMERICA
91 92 93 94   9 8 7 6 5 4 3 2 1

CONTENTS

Mood and Persuasion: Affective States Influence the Processing of Persuasive Communications

Norbert Schwarz, Herbert Bless, and Gerd Bohner

A Focus Theory of Normative Conduct: A Theoretical Refinement and Reevaluation of the Role of Norms in Human Behavior

Robert B. Cialdini, Carl A. Kallgren, and Raymond R. Reno

The Effects of Interaction Goals on Person Perception

James L. Hilton and John M. Darley

Studying Social Interaction with the Rochester Interaction Record

Harry T. Reis and Ladd Wheeler

Subjective Construal, Social Inference, and Human Misunderstanding

Dale W. Griffin and Lee Ross

CONTRIBUTORS

Numbers in parentheses indicate the pages on which the authors' contributions begin.

HERBERT BLESS (161), Fakultät für Sozial-Wissenschafte, Universität Mannheim, D-6800 Mannheim,Germany

GERD BOHNER (161), Fakultät für Sozial-Wissenschafte, Universität Mannheim, D-6800 Mannheim, Germany

ROBERT B. CIALDINI (201), Department of Psychology, Arizona State University, Tempe, Arizona 85287

JOHN M. DARLEY (235), Department of Psychology, Princeton University, Princeton, New Jersey 08544

CAROLYN L. FUNK (1), Department of Psychology, University of California, Los Angeles, Los Angeles, California 90024

JEFF GREENBERG (93), Department of Psychology, University of Arizona, Tucson, Arizona 85721

DALE W. GRIFFIN (319), Department of Psychology, University of Waterloo, Waterloo, Ontario N2L 3G1, Canada

JAMES L. HILTON (235), Department of Psychology and Research Center for Group Dynamics, University of Michigan, Ann Arbor, Michigan 48106

CARL A. KALLGREN (201), Department of Psychology, Pennsylvania State University—Behrend College, Erie, Pennsylvania 16563

TOM PYSZCZYNSKI (93), Department of Psychology, University of Colorado at Colorado Springs, Colorado Springs, Colorado 80933

HARRY T. REIS (269), Department of Psychology, University of Rochester, Rochester, New York 14627

RAYMOND R. RENO (201), Department of Psychology, University of Notre Dame, Notre Dame, Indiana 46556

LEE ROSS (319), Department of Psychology, Stanford University, Stanford, California 94305

NORBERT SCHWARZ (161), Zentrum für Umfragen, Methoden und Analysen, D-6800 Mannheim, Germany, and Universität Heidelberg, D-6900 Heidelberg, Germany

DAVID O. SEARS (1), Dean of Social Sciences, College of Letters and Science, University of California, Los Angeles, Los Angeles, California 90024

SHELDON SOLOMON (93), Department of Psychology, Skidmore College, Saratoga Springs, New York 12866

LADD WHEELER (269), Department of Psychology, University of Rochester, Rochester, New York 14627

THE ROLE OF SELF-INTEREST IN SOCIAL AND POLITICAL ATTITUDES

David O. Sears

Carolyn L. Funk

John F. Kennedy, in his inaugural address in 1961, said, "And so, my fellow Americans, ask not what your country can do for you; ask what you can do for your country." Ronald Reagan, as he appealed for last-minute votes in 1980, said, "As you go to the polls next Tuesday and make your choice for President, ask yourself these questions: Are you better off today than you were four years ago? Is it easier for you to go and buy things in the store than it was four years ago?" The contrast raises a fundamental question about the bases of social and political attitudes.

Self-interest is never far from front stage when we consider the ordinary individual's social and political attitudes. Yet there is much dispute about both its pervasiveness and its normative value for society as a whole. In the modern era, this dispute dates from the work of Thomas Hobbes. As Mansbridge (1990a) has noted, he began with the single assumption of self-interest, and from it deduced a world of "all against all." This appalled his contemporaries, who saw self-interest as thereby supplanting such traditional motives linked to civic virtue as honor, honesty, fidelity, and loyalty. But it was reflected in the liberal political and economic theories of the next century, such as John Locke's theories that religious tolerance and majority rule are required out of respect for the diversity of individual interests, or Adam Smith's justification of the free market in the ultimate public good of the exercise of individual self-interest.

The framers of the American constitution were torn between these new liberal ideas stressing individual interests and the older tradition of civic virtue as promoting the public good. Their solution was both to design institutions that would channel unrestrained private interests into the public interest (and guarantee individual liberties, in the Bill of Rights), and to emphasize, in Madison's

ADVANCES IN EXPERIMENTAL
SOCIAL PSYCHOLOGY, VOL. 24

terms, "the importance of virtue among both representatives and people" (Mansbridge, 1990c, p. 13).

Yet, among political theorists, the self-interest thesis has begun to dominate the idea of civic virtue in recent decades. Mainstream pluralists viewed democracy as functioning through bargaining and tradeoffs among competing interest groups, yielding outcomes that gave everyone at least a little. Marxists came to a different view, though from the same assumption: rhetoric about serving the "public interests" only camouflaged the underlying self-interested domination of large private interests over government and other social institutions.

Beginning in the late 1950s, formal economic models have increasingly been applied to democratic theory. The rational choice or "public choice" theorists derived models of all aspects of the democratic process from the assumption of self-interest. Voters vote their self-interests and congressmen simply seek reelection by satisfying their constituents' selfish interests; the notion of the "public interest" is a mere rationalization, as are notions that group solidarity or moral values might motivate social choices. Reliance upon the self-interest assumption in public choice models is justified ostensibly only for parsimony, but with time it has increasingly become an article of faith (see Mansbridge, 1990a).

This has led to a substantial revolt among social theorists. Economists such as Sen (1977), Hirschmann (1985), and Frank (1988), sociologists such as Etzioni (1988), and political scientists such as Reich (1988) and Mansbridge (1990b) have all begun to attack the rational choice formulation, often focusing particularly on the self-interest assumption.

But much of the debate has gone on at a normative rather than at an empirical level. The purpose of this article is to examine the empirical evidence on the role of self-interest in forming and maintaining sociopolitical attitudes.

I. The Idea of Self-Interest

The notion that human behavior is governed at least in part by selfish urges is a part of virtually every psychology and moral philosophy in Western thought. The great thinkers of the Christian era, such as St. Augustine, denounced the various lusts, of which lust for money and possessions (also known as greed or avarice) was one (but only one, and by no means necessarily the worst). Thomas Hobbes regarded the human being as motivated first and foremost by self-interest. Adam Smith also concluded that hedonistic selfishness was in some contexts the ruling motive of the human species: "every man feels his own pleasures and his own pains more sensibly than those of other people." But he saw self-interest as focused particularly on one motive, "augmentation of fortune." Green (1988, p. 46) aptly quotes Lord Macauley's essay on utilitarianism: "What proposition is there respecting human nature which is absolutely and universally true? We know of only one: and that is not only true, but identical; that men always act from self-interest . . . . when we see the actions of a man, we know with certainty what he thinks his interest to be" (see also Hirschman, 1977; Myers, 1983).

From this mixture of antecedants, neoclassical economics has deduced three basic psychological assumptions: the idea of rationality, that decisions are made on the basis of reasonable calculations limited primarily by the amount of information available; the idea of materialistic hedonism, or a simple pleasure–pain principle of human motivation; and the idea of egoism, that outcomes to the self weigh more heavily than outcomes to others. Today such models dominate economics. For example, Frohlich (1974, p. 57) observes that "economic models using the assumptions of rationality and self-interest have been so successful that economists . . . . have treated rationality and self-interested behavior as if they were the same." It is particularly central to the public choice school of thought: "the basic behavioral postulate of public choice, as for economics, is that man is an egoistic, rational, utility maximizer" (Mueller, 1979, p. 1).

Theories of self-interest have also been influential in the history of psychology. Its formative years were much influenced by Darwin, so accounts of human motivation were dominated by the view that humanity is basically selfish and driven by basic biological needs that ensure species survival. Freud viewed all behavior as motivated by such instinctual survival-oriented drives as hunger and procreation, operating according to the pleasure principle. Mainstream academic psychology developed a not dissimilar view. Hull's and Skinner's ideas of primary drives assumed that deprivation motivates overt activity, and that the organism learns adaptive habits when reinforced with drive reduction.

The idea of self-interest has also been common in the study of interpersonal and intergroup relations. A leading model of interpersonal relationships has been exchange theory, which assumes selfish, economic-like motives and behavior (see Homans, 1961; Thibaut & Kelley, 1959). Even research on methods of promoting cooperation in social dilemmas has typically appealed to egoistic, individualistic motives (Lynn & Oldenquist, 1986). "Realistic group conflict theory" assumes that the realistic competition between groups for scarce resources motivates ethnocentrism, hostility toward the outgroup, ingroup solidarity, punishment of deviants in the ingroup, and so forth (LeVine & Campbell, 1972). It is perhaps not unfair to say, with Campbell (1975) and Wallach and Wallach (1983), that the dominant modern psychological theories of motivation have been fundamentally egoistic and hedonistic.

II. The Social Psychology of Self-Interest

The idea of self-interest carries three separable psychological assumptions, then: rationality, materialism, and egoism. What in contemporary social psychology might give us reason to expect these tendencies to dominate the formation of political and social attitudes?

A. RATIONALITY

Psychologists have historically devoted great attention to the question of rationality. A strong and consistent body of work has assumed that human decision making is basically rational, that people make reasonable calculations of the costs and benefits of choice alternatives, and decide accordingly. The most common formal models of such processes in social psychology have centered on an expectancy–value formulation; choice is based on the product of the probabilities of various alternatives times their costs or benefits (e.g., Ajzen & Fishbein, 1980; Edwards, 1954; Feather, 1982).

Yet much of psychology has emphasized the irrational. Psychoanalytic theory highlighted the persisting effects of early experience and the influence of unconscious motives. Behaviorism focused especially on mindless conditioning and on the resistance to change of ingrained habits even in quite changed circumstances. Conflict theory highlighted the unusual power of fear and such irrationalities as displaced aggression. Gestalt theories emphasized perceptual biases introduced by the human's effort to achieve a coherent perceptual organization of the world.

In recent years, research on cognitive biases has introduced particularly potent challenges to rational choice models. An alternative to economists' traditional assumption of objective (or substantive) rationality is Herbert Simon's (1985) notion of cognitively bounded rationality—rationality bounded by the individual's cognitive limitations. The latter is based quite explicitly on modern cognitive psychology (see Dawes, 1988; Hogarth & Reder, 1987; Kahneman, Slovic, & Tversky, 1982; Lau & Sears, 1986). However, it should be noted that this critique still portrays a wholly cognitive process, merely adding in some shortcuts and guesswork as an acknowledgment that human time and energy are finite. And some cognitive psychologists explicitly challenge the pervasiveness even of irrational cognitive biases (e.g., Cheng & Novick, 1990).

B. MATERIALISM

The idea of self-interest also places materialistic motives in a superordinate role. People are thought to be most strongly motivated by the desire to acquire material goods, and money, the token for acquiring them. Where psychology has historically departed from economics has been in *not* privileging such materialistic or economic motives, relying instead on a considerably longer list of human motives. Murray (1938), for example, in an early and influential taxonomy of human needs, listed 20 of them, none particularly resembling greed, avarice, or augmentation of future wealth.

Similarly, in psychologists' comprehensive taxonomies of the functions that political and social attitudes serve for the individual, material self-interest is usually not given top billing. To be sure, functional theories always include instrumental or utilitarian functions (i.e., attitudes can be held because they promote the attainment of the individual's goals) but always several others as well, functions that have had more extensive research literatures associated with them, such as object appraisal, value-expressive, ego-defensive, and social adjustment (Katz, 1960; Smith, Bruner, & White, 1956). The same holds today for the resurgent literature on functional approaches to attitudes (see Herek, 1986; Prentice, 1987; Pratkanis, Breckler, & Greenwald, 1989; Shavitt, 1989; Young, Thomsen, Borgida, Sullivan, & Aldrich, in press). Social psychologists' comprehensive taxonomies of attitude functions include but give no special role to material self-interest.

C. EGOISM

Far more pervasive, and indeed nearly universal, is the assumption that costs and benefits affecting the self are weighed especially heavily in any decision-making process. Why should that be the case? Five general answers have been given.

1. Hedonic Needs

For hedonic reasons our attitudes should be most responsive to those pleasures and pains that affect us most strongly. For example, the considerable literature on fear-arousing communications suggests that, under most cirumstances, fear does promote acceptance of fear-reducing communications (Janis, 1967; Leventhal, 1970). Similarly, hedonic needs may produce a variety of cognitive biases: through self-serving attributional biases, people exaggerate their own responsibility for their successes and minimize their responsibility for their failures (Sicoly & Ross, 1977); through egocentric biases, people exaggerate their own contributions to collective products (Ross & Sicoly, 1979); through false consensus biases, they exaggerate the extent to which others share their own preferences (Ross, Greene, & House, 1977); and through the "illusion of control," people exaggerate the extent to which they control their own destinies

(Langer, 1975). Whether these are wholly due to motivational processes is still being debated, but it is likely that they are at least partly influenced by the need to enhance self-esteem (Greenwald, 1980; Markus & Wurf, 1987).

If hedonic needs similarly affect social and political attitudes, we could expect to find people forming policy preferences and candidate evaluations on the basis of how they will personally be affected by the policy or the candidate's actions. Those which benefit the self should be favored and those which hurt the self should be opposed. And those that affect us directly should therefore influence us more than those that affect us indirectly or that affect only others.

2. Ego Involvement

Other work has focused on the individual's psychological involvement in his or her attitude, usually with the expectation that attitudes with greater personal involvement will be stronger, more resistant to change, and more influential over other attitudes and judgments. The earliest major conceptualizations of involvement were omnibus in nature. Sherif and Cantril's (1947) notion of *ego involvement* referred to a wide variety of psychological linkages of attitudes to the ego without being particularly specific about the nature of those links. They did suspect that the strongest ego attitudes had anchors in some sense of group identity (see Greenwald, 1982), as did Converse (1964) in forwarding the related notion of the *centrality* of an attitude. A contemporary omnibus concept is attitude *importance*. In several studies, Krosnick has shown that the policy attitudes perceived by the individual as being most important have the strongest impact on candidate preferences (1988a) and are most stable over time (1988b). Not much research has yet been done on the role that self-interest plays in generating attitude importance, although people do sometimes invoke self-interest to explain their most important attitudes (Krosnick, 1990). Another contemporary omnibus concept is a sense of *conviction* about one's attitude, which Abelson (1988) describes as deriving in part from a special emotional preoccupation emerging from the self.

Later work on ego involvement has distinguished several different versions of it. The one that most closely parallels self-interest is *personal involvement* (also known as "issue involvement" or "personal relevance"), which emerges when people expect the issue to have significant consequences for their own lives (Apsler & Sears, 1968; Petty & Cacioppo, 1986). Several different lines of work have proposed that personal involvement produces more thorough and rational information processing. According to Petty and Cacioppo's (1986) elaboration-likelihood theory, it should produce closer attention to the merits of the arguments, greater persuasiveness of strong relative to weak arguments, and diminished reliance on "peripheral cues." A number of studies have provided supportive evidence (Borgida & Howard-Pitney, 1983; Howard-Pitney, Borgida,

& Omoto, 1986; Omoto & Borgida, 1988; Petty & Cacioppo, 1986; Wu & Shaffer, 1987).

A related idea is that *outcome dependency* in an interpersonal relationship (i.e., the knowledge that one's future outcomes will be partly determined by another person) will produce more thoughtful processing of information about that person, presumably because such information would be more consequential for one's interaction with him or her. For example, Berscheid, Graziano, Monson, and Dermer (1976) found that people paid closer attention to potential date partners than to nonpartners, and Erber and Fiske (1984) found that outcome dependency led people to pay closer attention to information about their partner that was inconsistent with their initial expectations (also see Harkness, DeBono, & Borgida, 1985; Neuberg & Fiske, 1987).

Personal involvement and outcome dependency have also been thought to reduce attributional and other cognitive biases that result from "top of the head" processing. Omoto and Borgida (1988) have suggested that personal involvement reduces categorization and stereotyping effects; Borgida and Howard-Pitney (1983), that personal involvement reduces the impact of more visually salient cues in favor of more systematic processing of message arguments; and Taylor (1975), that outcome dependency reduces misattribution biases.

On the other hand, personal involvement may not always contribute to rationality, since it may actually stimulate self-serving biases. Kunda (1987) found that self-serving evaluations of research evidence increased when the personal consequences of the research were more serious. Kunda presented subjects with information on the consequences of caffeine consumption for disease. Those who were most likely to be affected by such a linkage, the heavy caffeine consumers, were less likely to believe the research evidence when the disease was said to be painful, progressive, and possibly linked to cancer. When it was said to be so common that it was not even a disease, self-interested subjects showed no such special rejection of the evidence.

3. Accessibility

A concept that integrates such notions into social cognition is that of *accessibility*. A social construct such as an attitude can be more or less accessible on a chronic basis, and/or can be activated (made accessible) by exposure to the appropriate attitude object (Higgins & King, 1981). Chronically accessible social constructs are spontaneously activated in the presence of the attitude object, supposedly automatically and without conscious goals or attention or awareness, placing minimal demands on processing capacity (Bargh, 1988, 1989).

In general, a social construct should have more impact to the extent that it is cognitively accessible. In this form accessibility resembles other indicators of attitude strength, such as ego involvement, centrality, importance, and conviction.

Accessibility can have this effect in two ways. Some social constructs are strong and chronically accessible, and are likely to have strong effects on judgment and behavior whatever the context. Less strong constructs must be explicitly primed to have an effect.

Priming an accessible construct has been demonstrated in several ways to give it more impact over other attitudes, judgments, and behavior. First of all, priming a strong construct has been shown to evoke automatically the evaluation associated with it; that is, "the mere presentation of an attitude object toward which the individual possesses a strong evaluative association would automatically activate the evaluation" (Fazio, 1989, p. 157). Second, priming a particular trait construct has been shown to give it more weight in impression formation (Bargh, Lombardi, & Higgins, 1988). Similarly, Iyengar and Kinder (1985) have shown that emphasizing a particular issue in a news broadcast had an "agenda-setting" effect, in that that issue took on greater weight in determining viewers' evaluations of presidential performance. Presumably watching network coverage of that issue primed the individual's evaluations of the president's performance on it. And third, framing variations have been shown to prime different underlying constructs. For example, Kahneman and Tversky (1984; also see Quattrone & Tversky, 1988) suggest that framing choices in terms of relative gains produces risk aversion, whereas framing them in terms of relative losses produces risk seeking. Fourth, presenting issues in different terms often yields quite different attitudes. Presenting the Korean War as intended "to stop the Communist invasion of South Korea" yielded more public support than when it was simply described as "the war in Korea" (Mueller, 1973); presenting domestic spending in terms of specific program areas such as "education" or "health" produced more public support than describing it as "larger government" (Sears & Citrin, 1985); and presenting public assistance to the disadvantaged as "helping the poor" produced more support than describing it as "welfare" (see Sears & Citrin, 1985; Smith, 1987). And Beer, Healy, Sinclair, and Bourne (1987) found that presenting international relations in terms of Allied weakness prior to World War II produced recommendations for more aggressive policies toward a hypothetical international dispute than did introducing it in terms of the slaughter caused by World War I.

The link to the self-interest assumption is the hypothesis that self-constructs are generally more chronically accessible than are other social constructs (Higgins & Bargh, 1987, p. 395). There are two plausible reasons why they might be. More information may be available about outcomes and experiences that affect the self. Alternatively, the self is highly salient and may, therefore, be used as a reference point against which to judge social and political attitude objects. Either way, individual self-constructs may have particularly high levels of chronic accessibility. The consequence would be that constructs relating to the self, such as self-interest, should be weighed especially heavily in attitude formation simply because, relative to other kinds of social constructs, they are particularly likely to be evoked in everyday life.

However, Sherman, Judd, and Park (1989) point out that not all aspects of the self are equally accessible at all times, though they should have special impact when they are made accessible. For example, self-consistent behaviors are more likely when self-awareness is high (e.g., when manipulated through mirrors and other techniques). In this view, priming of self-constructs may be important, but start with no particular advantage relative to any other social construct. And, as Iyengar (1989) has suggested, in political life information about the self may generally not be very accessible, because the mass media are our primary sources of information, and their focus is on national and collective affairs rather than on matters directly relevant to our own lives.

4. Perceptual Egocentrism

That the self may have unique properties as a cognitive structure is a notion that has drawn great attention in recent years. As Higgins and Bargh (1987, p. 389) put it, the "self" may be an unusually rich and highly organized cognitive structure that can introduce egocentric influences into information processing (for other capable reviews, see Greenwald, 1980; Kihlstrom et al., 1988; and Markus & Wurf, 1987).

For one thing, the self is said to be overused as a perceptual point of reference; i.e., "the self acts as a background or setting against which incoming data are interpreted or coded" (Rogers, Kuiper, & Kirker, 1977, p. 678). The most widely researched example is the so-called *self-reference effect* by which information is especially likely to be remembered if the individual considers its relation to the self at the time of initial consideration. A large number of studies have found that such self-reference tasks do contribute to enhanced memory (e.g., Rogers et al., 1977), although its interpretation is still open to dispute, particularly concerning any special role of the self (see Higgins & Bargh, 1987; Kihlstrom et al., 1988; Klein & Loftus, 1988).

Egocentrism may also lead to overweighting the self as "the axis of cause and effect," producing various attributional biases (Greenwald, 1980, p. 604). Biases such as "the illusion of control," egocentric biases in causal attribution, and false consensus effects were cited earlier as possibly originating in hedonic needs, but they can also be interpreted as purely cognitive biases. Very similar phenomena have been reported in Jervis's (1976) accounts of misperceptions in international politics.

People may have heightened sensitivity to self-relevant stimuli, such as self-relevant adjectives (Bargh, 1982) or even the letters in their own name (Nuttin, 1985). Memory for one's own behavior is greater than it is for others' behavior or for nonsocial information (Markus & Wurf, 1987). As Higgins and Bargh

(1987, p. 395) suggest, "self-knowledge is associated with quick decisions, easily retrievable evidence, confident self-prediction, and resistance to contrary evidence" (see also Markus & Wurf, 1987, p. 317). However, as they point out, this does not necessarily privilege the self; it could be true of any belief the individual is committed to.

Finally, there is much evidence that our memory overestimates the consistency of our own past history, a phenomenon Greenwald (1980) called "ego as self-justifying historian" (also see Ross, 1989). For example, after being given the correct answers to a series of problems, people claim that they knew it all along (Fischhoff, 1975); in experiments, people "remember" their preexperimental attitudes as being more similar to their postexperiment attitudes than they were in fact (Bem & McConnell, 1970; Goethals & Reckman, 1973); and in surveys, people seriously underestimate how much their own political attitudes have changed over time (Markus, 1986; Niemi, Katz, & Newman, 1980; Reiter, 1980). For all these reasons, then, the self may have an especially prominent role in organizing our perceptual experience and therefore our thinking and judgment.

5. Direct Personal Experience

A number of quite disparate literatures have asserted that direct personal experience with an attitude object has unusually powerful effects on attitudes and judgments toward it. McGuire, in two extensive reviews (1969, 1985) of the attitude literature, suggested direct experience does have strong intensifying and strengthening effects on attitudes, citing both single imprinting-like formative experiences (such as in "born-again" religious experiences or combat experiences) and long-term direct intergroup contact. However, the former have not been rigorously researched, and the latter does not have simple effects (Hewstone & Brown, 1986; Miller & Brewer, 1984). Moreover, with rare exceptions such research has not compared direct experience with indirect experiences such as interpersonal or mass media communication.

Still, the notion that direct personal experience has unusually strong effects is a pervasive and compelling one to many researchers. Two main explanations have been offered. The most thoroughly developed theory comes from Fazio and Zanna (1981): direct experience provides more information about the attitude object, makes the attitude more salient and therefore more accessible, and is more likely to elicit behavioral responses, which (through self-perception processes) should lead to more confident inferences about one's own attitudes. In laboratory research, they found that direct experience with the attitude object produced more confident attitudes, attitudes that were more persistent and resistant to change, as well as more attitude–behavior consistency. Further experimental evidence of the attitude–strengthening effects of direct experience has been presented by Wu and Shaffer (1987).

A second explanation invokes vividness. Nisbett and Ross (1980, p. 45) define a stimulus as vivid to the extent that it is "(a) emotionally interesting, (b) concrete and imagery-provoking, and (c) proximate in a sensory, temporal, or spatial way." Directly experienced stimuli are presumably inherently more vivid than those only indirectly experienced, and have been hypothesized to have a greater influence on evaluations for that reason. However, research on vividness comparing the persuasiveness of communications presented directly (live and in person) as opposed to presented indirectly (video, audio, or written) has generally not found much difference (see Taylor & Thompson, 1982, for a review). Indeed in one study (Collins, Taylor, Wood, & Thompson, 1988), recipients believed more vivid messages were more persuasive but did not evidence more attitude change. So the belief in the greater persuasiveness of vivid messages may mainly be an illusion.

And in naturalistic settings, the special effects of personal experience are not so pervasive as originally hypothesized. For example, Tyler (1980) compared the effects of personal crime victimization and mediated, indirect experience with crime on judgments of risk. Tyler found that personal experience affected people's estimates of their own personal vulnerability, but not their baserate estimates of the overall crime rate. Similarly, media reports about such risks as firearms, drunk driving, and floods influenced judgments of risk at the societal level, but not at the personal level (Tyler & Cook, 1984). Both findings suggest direct experience may have more impact on attitudes about one's personal situation than about broad social and political issues. And Weinstein's (1989) general review of research on direct personal experience with hazards (auto accidents, crime victimization, natural disasters, and myocardial infarctions) found that in most cases, direct personal experience did not have any special effect on judgments of risk, policy attitudes, or self-protective behavior.

In short, the hypothesis that direct personal experience has especially strong effects on individuals' attitudes has been widely propagated and tested. However, it is not clear that personal experience does usually have stronger effects than indirect experience on judgments and attitudes. Nor is it clear that the proposed mediators of such hypothesized effects do: vividness seems not to have uniformly strong effects, and there are other ways to become well informed. It should be noted, however, that the vividness literature has largely focused on passive audience experiences. The notion of self-interest would seem generally to imply a more interactive type of direct experience, such as in Tyler's (1980) comparison of recent crime victims with those who have only indirect experience with crime through media reports. So these failures may not be as damaging to the self-interest hypothesis as might appear at first glance.

D. SUMMARY

Self-interest has had quite a specific meaning, then, focusing on the conjunction of egoism, materialism, and rationality. The heritage of neoclassical economics, in stressing self-interest as the dominant human motive, remains a potent intellectual force. However, the picture is more mixed in psychology. For example, social psychologists' few attempts at comprehensive taxonomies of the bases of attitudes do not put self-interest in any especially prominent position. The assumption of rationality has a strong tradition in psychology, but it cannot be said to be unchallenged or even dominant. The assumption of materialism so fondly held by neoclassical economics is not common among psychologists. The assumption of egoism, on the other hand, is quite widely shared by social psychologists, many of whom believe that attitudes or other social constructs connected directly with the self are conferred some special power; that personal consequences of an attitude object produce more rational information processing about it; that egocentric biases in information processing are manifold, pervasive, and powerful; and that direct personal experience with an attitude object confers special powers to it. The general thrust of sociopsychological research, then, would certainly seem to leave the door open for a major role for self-interest, although it does not compel it.

Having said that, two caveats are in order. First, the internal validity of much of the experimental evidence supporting the egoism assumption is more open to dispute than might be thought from the strongly phrased theories generating it. And second, there are external validity problems: most of the sociopsychological research on the self has been conducted on college students, and such late adolescents are perhaps unusually egocentric relative to individuals in other life stages (Sears, 1986). So contemporary sociopsychological research on these matters is perhaps more useful as a series of theoretical benchmarks than as a fully trustworthy guide to what we are likely to find in adults in their natural habitats. While it is plausible that self-interest might play an important, or even central, role in attitude formation, then, it is far from self-evident.

III. Alternatives to Self-Interest

Moreover, there are clear alternatives to self-interest in understanding the ordinary person's response to social and political objects. In our own work we have used a "symbolic politics" approach. This is not the place to develop the approach in detail, but some of its more central features can be outlined.

A. SYMBOLIC POLITICS

The symbolic politics approach has appeared in a variety of guises, mostly sharing several basic assumptions. People are said to acquire learned affective responses to particular symbols relatively early in life (variously placed anywhere from childhood to early adulthood). These learned responses from those formative early experiences (which we here generically call predispositions) persist to some degree into and through adult life. And they strongly influence the adult's attitudes toward current political stimuli. The strongest of these learned responses, which we have called "symbolic predispositions," are distinguished by their special persistence over time and influence over other attitudes.[1] Attitudes then reflect the affects previously conditioned to the specific symbols included in the attitude object. For example, attitudes toward "forced busing" to integrate whites and blacks would depend on affects toward such symbols as "force," "busing," "integration," and "blacks." We have assumed that the processing of such political symbols is well described by the simple cognitive consistency theories (which perhaps would be more aptly described as affective consistency theories, or transfer-of-affect theories). That is, people simply transfer affects from one symbol to another (Lorge, 1936; Osgood & Tannenbaum, 1955).

These basic ideas have undergirded research on a wide variety of problems. Research on political socialization has investigated children's and adolescents' early learning of attitudes toward such symbols as the flag, the President, stigmatized racial groups, and the political parties. Such early learning presumably yields such standing predispositions as party identification, racial prejudices, ethnic identities, basic values, nationalism, and attachment to various symbols of the nation and regime (e.g., Campbell, Converse, Miller, & Stokes, 1960; Easton & Dennis, 1969; Jennings & Niemi, 1981). The persistence of these predispositions has been investigated as a variable in its own right (see Alwin & Krosnick, 1988; Converse, 1975; Sears, 1983).

The activation of these predispositions by political symbols in the adult's environment, and their influence over attitudes toward such symbols, have received even more research attention. Longstanding partisan predispositions or basic values are activated by policy and candidate alternatives, thereby influencing the individual's preferences (Campbell *et al.*, 1960; Feldman, 1988; Sears, Lau, Tyler, & Allen, 1980). Racial predispositions are activated by black candidates and racial issues, and influence attitudes toward them (Kinder & Sears,

---

[1]It should be emphasized that both the timing of initial acquisition of these predispositions and the degree of their persistence over the life span are usually now treated as variables dependent on other factors, in contrast to the simple primacy-and-persistence assumptions made by early investigators (see Alwin & Krosnick, 1988; Sears, 1975, 1983).

1981; Sears, Hensler, & Speer, 1979). Other basic values can be activated by symbols of injustice, inequity, or immorality, and thus produce mass protest (Gusfield, 1963; Sears & Citrin, 1985; Sears & McConahay, 1973). Longstanding antagonisms toward such groups as the Communists, Nazi party, and Ku Klux Klan are evoked by debates about their rights, and influence support for extending civil liberties to them (Sullivan, Piereson, & Marcus, 1982).

There are some good reasons for expecting that symbolic predispositions might have stronger effects on sociopolitical attitudes than self-interest does. The notion of symbolic politics is that political symbols activate underlying predispositions reflexively. Put another way, such symbols automatically activate relevant and accessible social constructs (Bargh, 1989). Why might such social constructs, as opposed to self-constructs such as self-interest, be especially likely to be activated by information about societal and public affairs?

The informational environment in the public arena is dominated by communicators, principally journalists, who constantly condense its complexities into simplified symbolic terms. Put in Tulving's (1983) terms, they engage in semantic coding that consolidates the bits and pieces of real life into more abstract categories. Politicians go still further. Their principal goal is to code political symbols in terms that will evoke widespread and supportive predispositions in the citizenry. To do this they use abstract symbols ("welfare," "crime in the streets," "patriotic," "busing," "Watergate," or "Vietnam"). Such processes result in an informational environment that itself is coded in terms of abstractions corresponding to the social constructs most common among attentive ordinary citizens. This simplification has great advantages for these citizens, since it provides symbols that readily prime their most accessible attitudes and thus render meaningful the booming and buzzing confusion of public life.

In contrast, such communicators rarely help to code the rich complexity of private experience into simple symbolic terms. Individuals' personal experiences are often too proximal, complex, and individuated to lend themselves to easy generalization. As a result, personal experience becomes, as Lane says, "morselized": "[the] treatment of an instance in isolation happens time and time again and on matters close to home: a union demand is a single incident, not part of a more general labor–management conflict; a purchase on the installment plan is a specific debt, not part of a budgetary pattern—either one's own or society's. The items and fragments of life remain itemized and fragmented . . ." (1962, p. 353). People see the trees, not the forest.

In short, political dialogue is by its nature coded into abstract semantic terms. But personal experience may be morselized because it is difficult to code the rich complexity of direct personal experience into the simple symbolic terms that can readily be triggered by political symbols. As a result, the two should tend to be cognitively compartmentalized. Perceptions and evaluations of events in the public arena should tend simply to be perceived as in a different cognitive realm, separate from personal experience. Political events would have implications for one's political attitudes, and personal experiences would have implications for private behavior; but there would be relatively little cross-over.

The core of the symbolic politics process, then, is that standing learned predispositions are evoked by political symbols in the current informational environment. The dominance of symbolic predispositions may come about because of a general tendency toward reflexive affective responses to political symbols. Political symbols may come semantically coded in ways that make them easy to link to symbolic predispositions, but difficult to connect to the confusing idiosyncracies that are our daily personal experience.

B. THE PUBLIC INTEREST AND SOCIOTROPIC POLITICS

Another tradition, alluded to earlier, is that people are motivated by their sense of the "public interest" (see Reich, 1988), or, alternatively, that some people are especially "public-regarding" (see Banfield & Wilson, 1964). The most extensive empirical work on this approach has been described as "sociotropic politics": people evaluate social and political objects in terms of the general societal, rather than personal, costs and benefits they provide. For example, a voter evaluates the president in terms of whether or not he has presided over a healthy economy and a nation at peace rather than whether or not the voter has prospered and been unharmed by war (Kinder & Kiewiet, 1979). We will discuss this below since it is particularly relevant to some cases we will discuss.

IV. Self-Interest in Everyday Life

The central purpose of the remainder of this article is to assess the empirical evidence on the power of self-interest as a motive in the ordinary citizen's political and social attitudes.

A. DEFINING SELF-INTEREST

Our intention has been to define self-interest in terms that match as closely as possible both its conventional usage in intellectual history and the common-sense, person-in-the-street understanding of it. We also wanted the definition to be sufficiently restrictive that the self-interest hypothesis would be both verifiable and falsifiable. As a result, we define an individual's self-interest in a particular attitudinal position in terms of (1) its short to medium-term impact on the (2) material well-being of the (3) individual's own personal life (or that of his or her immediate family). For example, a worker with no health insurance might have self-interested reasons for supporting a legislative proposal that would mandate all firms to provide health coverage (material well-being) to their employees (own personal life) within the next 6 months (short-term impact). [For a similar definitional analysis, see Barry (1965, Ch. 10).]

We have excluded several other possibilities that we feel both fall outside the normal connotations of the term and would make its effects much more difficult to assess (and indeed in some cases nonfalsifiable). For example, we excluded "interests" that involve nonmaterial aspects of well-being, such as spiritual contentment, self-esteem, social adjustment, social prestige, or feelings of moral righteousness. The ordinary person rarely equates conformity with high spiritual or moral codes as expressions of "selfishness"; in ordinary language, self-ishness refers to egoistic materialism. And while neoclassical economics may include such matters as legitimate bases for the individual's utilities, such inclusion makes the hypothesis impossible to falsify, since any goal that people strive for would be in their "self-interest." Essentially the term would be redundant with "motive" or "goal-directed behavior."

We also excluded long-term or "enlightened" self-interest, such as a young worker's support for increased social security benefits on the basis of a perception that it will secure his or her own old age. While this falls at least close to both intellectual and person-in-the-street definitions, it makes the hypothesis excessively difficult to falsify; any attitude position could be justified in such terms, and the very lengthy time perspective involved makes any real impact on the individual difficult to assess. In any case, an attitude object's immediate personal impact should have stronger effects than its long-term prospects would, so this restriction should limit us only to a focus on the most potent kinds of self-interest.

Finally, we rule out "group interests"; i.e., interests that affect the well-being of the individual's group but not necessarily that of the specific individual. For example, we would not describe as "self-interested" the support given by wealthy Jews to Jewish welfare agencies. It is not part of everyday understanding, we believe, to identify such generous aid to others as "selfishness." However, we will return in more detail to enlightened self-interest and group interest below.

B. BOUNDARIES

Before proceeding, we should specify the boundaries of our endeavor.
Three other possible effects of self-interest fall outside the scope of this article.

One is the role of self-interest in private life; e.g., individuals' preferences about how family chores should be divided, or about boundary disputes with neighbors, or the role of economic incentives in consumer or job choices. Plainly self-interest plays a large (if hardly omnipotent) role in such choices. Second, we are not concerned with the operation of political interest groups or other political elites or their influences on government decisions. There is a substantial literature on the origins of interest groups and their means of functioning (e.g., Caldeira & Wright, 1988; Schlozman & Tierney, 1986; Walker, 1983). We would not dispute a role of self-interest there, although again it may often be overestimated and other kinds of symbolic incentives discounted (see Bauer, de Sola Pool, & Dexter, 1963). Nor would we dispute the observation that political officeholders often operate their daily lives in a self-interested manner, husbanding their energies behind activities that ensure their continuation in office and ignoring those that will not help much (Aberbach, 1990).

And third, we do not focus on self-interest as a motivator of the political *behavior* of the ordinary citizen. Here the evidence is mixed to date, with some positive evidence (as on compliance with or protest against school desegregation or programs of energy reduction; see Giles & Gatlin, 1980; Green & Cowden, 1990; Sears, Tyler, Citrin, & Kinder, 1978) and some negative (as on popular protest; see Barnes, Farah, & Heunks, 1979). For a general review, see Green (1988, Ch. 7). In practice, the ordinary citizen's participation in political life is considerably more likely to be attitudinal (or quasiattitudinal, as in casting a vote or expressing opinions to a pollster or to a friend) than it is to be behavioral (as in marching in a protest demonstration), so this restriction does not much limit the social and political importance of the phenomena under scrutiny here.

C. AGGREGATE-LEVEL DATA

There have been three general approaches to testing the effects of self-interest on political attitudes. One has used aggregate-level data to predict from broad conditions (such as national economic conditions) to mass outcomes (such as aggregate presidential vote). Numerous studies have tested the hypothesis that fluctuations in the strength of the economy are correlated with support for an incumbent government, as reflected in presidential approval, presidential vote, and support for the president's party in congressional, senatorial, or parliamentary elections (Abramowitz & Segal, 1986; Kramer, 1971; Monroe, 1979; Tufte, 1978). These aggregate-level studies have not yielded uniformly strong correlations, but they do appear to be fairly consistent for at least one economic indicator (per capita real disposable income) and one dependent variable (presidential vote; see Erikson, 1990; Owens, 1984). The typical interpretation has been that individuals were voting their own pocketbooks.

Other kinds of aggregate-level correlations have led to similar conclusions. The most racist white candidates in the old segregated South generally drew most votes from whites in areas with the heaviest concentrations of blacks (Key, 1949; Pettigrew & Campbell, 1960). The usual interpretation again focused on individual self-interest: where blacks were most numerous, they produced the most personal racial threat to individual whites, and therefore the strongest electoral support for segregation. Similarly, in a referendum on a rapid transit system in Atlanta, each precinct's votes correlated with the percentage in that precinct using the bus to commute to work, and with that precinct's proximity to the nearest proposed rapid transit station. Again the interpretation was that individuals were voting their own interests, in terms of their potential personal benefits from the system (Schroeder & Sjoquist, 1983).

In all such cases, though, the inference of individually self-interested behavior from aggregate-level data risks the ecological fallacy, and so is largely speculative in the absence of individual-level evidence. Nothing in the aggregate-level data specifies that the specific individuals most affected by the independent variable (economic conditions, large numbers of blacks, rapid transit availability) show the most appropriate attitudinal response. Unfortunately, efforts in such studies to use more proximal, but still aggregate, independent variables sometimes yield weaker findings, rather than strengthening the correlation as the self-interest hypothesis would predict. Aggregate voting in congressional contests did correlate with changes in national economic conditions over the 1970s and early 1980s. But it did not correlate with changes measured at the more proximal congressional district level, which should index more closely the individual voter's self-interest (Owens, 1984; Owens & Olson, 1980). The same is true for gubernatorial vote: over the period 1940 to 1982, it correlated with the state of the national economy more strongly than with the state of the more proximal state economy (Chubb, 1988). The national-level data may indicate, then, that individual voters are responding to well-publicized national economic indicators rather than to their own personal economic situations. A satisfactory test of the self-interest theory about individuals' attitudes, then, requires individual-level evidence.

D. DEMOGRAPHIC VARIABLES

A second approach has been based on individual-level data, using individuals' demographic variables to predict their sociopolitical attitudes. The classic example is socioeconomic class. It has long been assumed, by Marx and many others, that social class differences produce political cleavages due to self-interest; e.g., "the less privileged have supported parties that have stood for greater equality and protection against the strains of a free enterprise economy through government intervention'' (Lipset, 1981, p. 469; also see Alford, 1963; Hamilton, 1972; Lazarsfeld, Berelson, & Gaudet, 1948).

The relevant empirical research uses surveys on public opinion and voting behavior. And the classic early studies did indeed find that socioeconomic status correlated with vote preferences, therefore concluding that self-interest was an important motive. *The People's Choice* (Lazarsfeld *et al.*, 1948) reported strong correlations between social class and the vote, and in *Voting: A Study of Opinion Formation in a Presidential Campaign,* Berelson, Lazarsfeld, and McPhee (1954) explained them in terms of ''position issues'' whose motivational appeal was presumed to be ''self-interest of a relatively direct kind'' (p. 184). Similarly, in *The American Voter,* Campbell *et al.* (1960) concluded that Americans commonly responded to domestic issues in terms of ''primitive self-interest'' (p. 205) and in terms of ''fairly concrete and short-term group interest'' (p. 223), rather than ideologically.[2]

However, most demographic variables are not adequate indicators of individual self-interest, for two reasons. One is that, like aggregate-level data, they are too distal from the individual's behavior. For example, income level is negatively correlated with support for medical aid earmarked for the poor (Lupsha, 1975). But we have no assurance that individuals' relative actual potential use is responsible. This correlation could emerge if stably employed, unionized workers, with adequate health insurance, were the most politically aware and therefore most ideologically supportive of egalitarian policies, even though requiring little special government funding themselves. More proximal measures of the direct personal impact of such political issues are required if a causal role for self-interest is to be safely inferred.

A second reason is that demographic variables index not only the individual's material interests but also the residues of much earlier socialization, and therefore can reflect the symbolic politics process as well as self-interest. For example, young working women who are college graduates are unusually favorable to women's rights, such as legalized abortion and antidiscrimination laws (Sears & Huddy, 1990a). But is that because they have a special self-interest in such positions? Possibly. On the other hand, they have been exposed to more intensive socialization than other women in support of the women's movement in college, at work, and among peers. Similarly, on occasion *upper* status

---

[2]The early voting studies did have some evidentiary base other than demographics on which to assert the operation of self-interest. For example, Campbell *et al.* (1960) did infer it from the pattern of voters' attitudes and their links to the vote; e.g., party differences in domestic policy preferences, especially among those most attentive to politics, who should be most attuned to their own interests (pp. 205–208). Many people also identified the good and bad points of the parties and presidential candidates in terms of benefits to one group or another (Campbell *et al.*, 1960, Chapter 10). However, both sets of data are vulnerable to other explanations that have little to do with the self, as will be seen below.

individuals paradoxically demonstrate the greatest support for helping the disadvantaged, presumably because of more sympathetic symbolic predispositions (Shingles, 1989).

The self-interest hypothesis has fit so comfortably with the conventional wisdom about human nature that for many years it has been widely accepted throughout the social sciences. However, we would suggest that it has generally been accepted on the basis of only indirect evidence. Aggregate-level data are subject to the ecological fallacy, and demographic variables are excessively crude implicators of self-interest.

E. PERSONAL IMPACT

More appropriate, then, would be yet a third paradigm, using individual-level data that link individuals' attitudes directly to the circumstances of their private lives and perceptions of their own interests. It would use the direct personal impact of the attitude object to predict the individual's attitude toward it. Much research has been done in recent years using this third paradigm. The primary goal of this article is to canvass that literature. It centers on the research done by ourselves and our colleagues, although it is intended as a reasonably comprehensive review of the literature as a whole.

Let us begin by describing our own general research strategy. To assess the effects of self-interest upon an individual's sociopolitical attitudes, we have measured both variables in large-scale cross-sectional survey studies. A positive effect of self-interest would be reflected by a positive correlation with the presumably associated attitude. For example, we would interpret a correlation of personal unemployment with support for government-guaranteed jobs as reflecting self-interest: being unemployed motivates support for remedial government action.

1. Samples and Measures

To obtain reliable estimates of self-interest effects, we have generally used large-scale public opinion surveys with representative samples. Almost all of them have involved national samples, statewide California samples, or samples of large local jurisdictions, such as residents of Los Angeles County or the City of Los Angeles on such local matters as school busing or mayoralty elections. In one case we utilized a college student sample; this was a relatively unusual case, in which students' self-interests were much involved (a threat to reinstitute the military draft) and we were able to secure a representative sample of undergraduates at a large public university (Sears, Steck, Lau, & Gahart, 1983).

Our dependent variables have generally been of three kinds: policy preferences (such as support for national health insurance or increased spending on the public schools), evaluations of political leaders (such as level of approval of an incumbent president), or electoral preference (such as preferring an incumbent congressman to his or her opponent, or support for a tax cut initiative).

Our independent variables, measures of self-interest, have varied along two dimensions: (1) *objective,* the researcher's assessment of the individual's self-interest (e.g., parents with children in the public schools have an interest in increased school funding) vs *subjective,* the individual's perceptions of his or her well-being (e.g., people who perceive that their own finances have been deteriorating have an interest in dismissing political incumbents), and (2) *retrospective* (e.g., having recently lost one's job provides an interest in current government employment policy) vs *prospective* (e.g., expecting that an oncoming recessionary will soon cause one to be laid off provides an interest in government employment policy).

Most of our research has contrasted the effects of self-interest with those of symbolic predispositions. We have generally used only a rather small and conservatively selected set of the latter, primarily party identification, ideological self-placement, and racial tolerance. These can be shown to have been quite stable through most individuals' adult life spans, and so are unlikely to be substantially influenced by the individual's short-term material self-interest in adulthood (for the reasoning, see especially Sears, 1975, 1983, 1989).

2. Statistical Criteria

We have used several statistical criteria for assessing the effects of self-interest. A convenient starting point is the simple bivariate correlation of the self-interest index with the attitude in question, in terms of (1) its statistical significance (using the usual threshold of $p < .05$ with a two-tailed test). However, a relatively weak correlation can meet the minimal criterion of statistical significance in large survey samples, and, according to the usual rule of thumb, account for only a trivial amount of the variance in the dependent variable. So we also refer to (2) the absolute size of the correlation.

We usually have then moved to simple least squares regressions that regress the dependent variable not only on self-interest indicators but on symbolic predispositions, and often demographic controls, as well. These yield three further measures of effect: (3) statistical significance of the regression coefficient for a particular self-interest index, (4) the total variance in the dependent variable accounted for by all relevant self-interest indicators, and (5) a comparison of the amount of variance accounted for by all self-interest indicators pooled with that accounted for by all available symbolic predispositions.

We report correlation and standardized regression coefficients primarily because they are most intuitively interpretable. Some researchers would contend that relying on either is inappropriate because they confuse the strength of the effect with the amount of error, and so would prefer unstandardized regression coefficients. However, we feel that strength can be assessed only in light of error. Over a large number of cases, such coefficients should yield a fairly accurate approximation of the strength of self-interest effects.

V. The Minimal Effects of Self-Interest

The results of all our studies are tabulated in Table I. Moving from left to right, the table shows, for each study, (1) the type of self-interest (e.g., "vulnerability to busing") and the number of self-interest measures used, (2) the political attitude that serves as the dependent variable (e.g., "opposition to busing") and the number of items used, (3) the sample area and date of survey, (4) the mean bivariate correlation between self-interest and dependent variables and type of correlation used, (5) variables used in the regression equation, (6) the percentage of self-interest measures that yielded statistically significant regression coefficients, (7) the mean standardized regression coefficient for the self-interest terms, and (8) the number of coefficients on which that mean is based. These analyses were taken from previous research reports, so the procedures vary somewhat from study to study.

A. RACIAL ISSUES

Our work began as an outgrowth of analyses of whites' responses to the racial crisis in America in the late 1960s. As the Southern system of racial segregation broke down and as the Northern black population grew, whites throughout the country were increasingly faced with demands for greater racial equality in education, jobs, housing, politics, and other areas. These demands produced increasingly direct personal racial threats to a white population that had been relatively insulated from them. The self-interest hypothesis was that those direct racial threats to whites' personal well-being should turn whites against pro-black policies and candidates.

1. Black Candidates

This hypothesis was first tested with a pair of surveys done in 1969 and 1973 in an almost all-white suburban section of Los Angeles, when the incumbent white mayor, Sam Yorty, was challenged by a moderately liberal black city councilman, Tom Bradley (Sears & Kinder, 1971; Kinder & Sears, 1981). The measures of personal racial threat (i.e., self-interest) focused on (1) the danger of

TABLE I
Effects of Self-Interest on Public Opinion[a]

| Self-interest | | Dependent variable | | Survey | | Correlation (Mean) | Type | Regression | | | Source |
Type	No. of items	Type	No. of items	Sample	Year			β (net percentage significant)	β (mean)	No. of tests	
Racial Issues											
1. Racial threat	20	Oppose black mayoral candidate	1	Los Angeles suburbs[b]	1969, 1973	+.21[c]	1	11.1	+.04	(18)	Kinder and Sears (1981)
Neighborhood integration	5					+.41[c]	1	0.0	+.06	(5)	
Economic competition	6					+.21[c]	1	25.0	+.02	(4)	
Racial busing	5					+.05[c]	1	0.0	−.01	(5)	
Black violence	4					+.26[c]	1	25.0	+.09	(4)	
2. Vulnerability to busing	5	Opposition to busing	2	National[b]	1972	+.01	4	16.7	+.02	(6)	Sears, Hensler, and Speer (1979)
3. Vulnerability to busing	5	Opposition to busing	1	National[b]	1976	NA[d]	4	0.0	−.02	(4)	Sears, Lau, Tyler, and Allen (1980)
4. Vulnerability to busing	24	Opposition to busing	14	National, California, Los Angeles[b]	1964–1979	NA	4	21.1	+.03	(52)	Sears and Allen (1984)

(continued)

TABLE I (Continued)

Self-interest		Dependent variable		Survey		Correlation		Regression			Source
Type	No. of items	Type	No. of items	Sample	Year	(Mean)	Type	β (net percentage significant)	β (mean)	No. of tests	
5. Vulnerability to bilingual education; bilingualism	9	Opposition to bilingual education	7	National[e]	1983	+.02	1	0.0	+.01	(8)	Huddy and Sears (1989)
General economic issues											
6. Declining personal finances	2	Presidential performance	3	National	1983	+.04	NA	NA	NA	(6)	Sears and Lau (1983)
7. Declining personal finances and vulnerability to inflation	2	Opposition to taxes and spending	18	California	1979	NA	1	0.0	.00	(10)	Sears and Citrin (1982)
8. Vulnerability to inflation	2	Presidential performance	4	National	1983	-.03	4	NA	NA	(4)	Sears and Lau (1983)
Employment											
9. Employment problems	6	Government-guaranteed employment	2	National	1976	NA	1	33.3	+.02	(3)	Sears et al. (1980)

24

No.	Topic			Location	Year						Reference
10.	Employment problems	4	5	National	1983	+.04	NA	NA	NA	(8)	Sears and Lau (1983)
11.	Women's role in the workplace	3	5	National	1984	NA	3	16.7	NA	(6)	Sears and Huddy (1990a)
Energy											
12.	Personal impact of energy crisis	4	8	Los Angeles County	1974	NA	3	0.0	.00	(2)	Sears, Tyler, Citrin, and Kinder (1978)
Service recipients											
13.	Poor health insurance	3	1	National	1976	NA	1	66.7	+.08	(3)	Sears et al. (1980)
14.	Service recipience	13	18	California	1979	NA	1	25.0	+.03	(20)	Sears and Citrin (1985)
15.	Service recipience	4	2	Massachusetts	1980, 1981	NA	4	25.0	+.03	(4)	Lau, Coulam, and Sears (1983)
16.	Women's economic disadvantage	5	3	National	1984	NA	3	20.0	NA	(10)	Sears and Huddy (1989)

(continued)

25

TABLE I (*Continued*)

Self-interest		Dependent variable		Survey		Correlation	Regression				Source
No. of items	Type	Type	No. of items	Sample	Year	(Mean)	Type	β (net percentage significant)	β (mean)	No. of tests	
Taxes											
17. 5	Federal tax burden	Support for tax cuts	4	National	1983	+.10	NA	NA	NA	(16)	Sears and Lau (1983)
18. 2	State and local tax burden	Opposition to taxes and spending	18	California	1979	NA	1	90.0	+.15	(10)	Sears and Citrin (1985)
19. 4	State and local tax burden	Support for Prop. 2½	2	Massachusetts	1980, 1981	NA	4	50.0	+.12	(4)	Lau et al. (1983)
Public employment											
20. 1	Public employees	Support for taxes and spending	18	California	1979	NA	1	60.0	+.09	(5)	Sears and Citrin (1985)
21. 2	Public employees	Opposition to Prop. 2½	2	Massachusetts	1980, 1981	NA	4	100.0	+.14	(2)	Lau et al. (1983)
Crime											
22. 6	Vulnerability to crime	Support for law and order policies	5	National	1976	NA	4	33.3	+.03	(3)	Sears et al. (1980)

War

23.	Relatives and friends in Vietnam service	6	Opposition to Vietnam War	3	National	1968	+.04[f]	3	16.7	+.04	(6)	Lau, Brown, and Sears (1978)
24.	Vulnerability to military draft	7	Opposition to draft; support detente	11	UCLA students	1980	−.08	2	−20.0	−.05	(10)	Sears, Steck, Lau, and Gahart (1983)
25.	Concern about likely war	3	Opposition to draft; support detente	11	UCLA students	1980	.20	2	50.0	+.19	(2)	Sears et al. (1983)
	Total:	147		168			+.07		22.8	+.04	(188)	

[a] The number of items shown is prior to the development of composite scales. Correlation is Pearson r unless otherwise specified. Regression type included only self-interest terms, where possible (type 1); otherwise they included self-interest and some demographics (type 2); self-interest and symbolic predispositions, typically ideology, party identification, and racial attitudes (type 3); or all three (type 4). The standardized regression coefficient (β) is shown. Net percentage significant is percentage in predicted direction minus percentage significant in opposite direction. (Source: Sears and Funk, 1990a.)

[b] Whites only.

[c] γ.

[d] NA, not applicable.

[e] Non-Hispanics only.

[f] τ_c.

neighborhood desegregation (opposition to it, perceived likelihood of it), (2) economic threat from blacks (dissatisfaction with own economic gains compared to those of blacks, likelihood of having a black supervisor at work, likelihood of losing jobs or promotions due to preferential treatment for minorities), (3) racial busing (having children in the public schools; likelihood of minority children being bused into, or white children out of, neighborhood schools), and (4) fear of black crime (likelihood of black violence in own neighborhood; distance from a small black ghetto in the area). The symbolic predisposition used was "symbolic racism," an index of racial intolerance.[3] The dependent variable was the difference in evaluation of the two candidates.

Electoral choice was closely related to symbolic racism but not to racial threat. As Table II shows, only 2 of the 18 regression coefficients for racial threat were significant, and their average was a nonsignificant +.04 (also see Table I, Study 1). In contrast, symbolic racism had highly significant effects, accounting for 22.3 and 15.3% of the variance in candidate preference in the 2 years. Symbolic racism contributed 15.7 and 8.9% of the unique variance explained in candidate preference, whereas racial threat contributed only 3.0 and 0.0%. Racial threat failed in three other respects not shown in Table II, as well. It had only trivial effects on symbolic racism; the votes of those most vulnerable to threat were not more influenced than others by their affects toward that threat (e.g., distaste for neighborhood desegregation had no greater effect on the vote among people living close to a black ghetto or feeling their own neighborhood was likely to be desegregated than it did among those not so vulnerable); and vulnerability to these threats did not increase the impact of symbolic racism on the vote. This first study, then, gave little support to the racial threat version of the self-interest hypothesis.

2. Busing

We then focused specifically on whites' opposition to busing. The self-interest hypothesis was that being personally affected by busing (in terms of having children in the public schools, living in districts with busing happening or threatened, and/or living in all-white neighborhoods) should produce the greatest

---

[3]Symbolic racism is typically indexed with items focusing on (1) antagonism toward blacks' demands (e.g., "blacks are getting too demanding in their push for equal rights"), (2) resentment about special favors for blacks (e.g., "over the past few years, blacks have gotten more economically than they deserve"), and sometimes (3) denial of continuing discrimination (e.g., "blacks have it better than they ever had it before"; see Sears, 1988). Research on symbolic racism has been criticized on several grounds, the most common of which have been disputes about its exact content (Bobo, 1983, 1988; McLendon, 1985; Pettigrew, 1985; Schuman, Steeh, & Bobo, 1985; Sniderman & Tetlock, 1986a; Weigel & Howes, 1985). That dispute is irrelevant to the present point, which is simply that measures of racism (however they are characterized) have more political impact than do those of realistic racial threat, and are themselves not influenced by threat.

TABLE II

Effects of Symbolic Racism and Racial Threats on Preferences for White
Los Angeles Mayoralty Candidate[a]

	1969 (n = 178)	1973 (n = 220)
Symbolic racism		
Expressive racism	.31**	.30**
Opposition to busing	.26**	.11
Racial threats		
Neighborhood desegregation and interracial social contact		
Oppose neighborhood desegration	−.07	.08
Dislike social contact with blacks	.06	−.04
Likelihood of neighborhood desegregation	NA[b]	−.03
Economic competition		
Economic resentment of blacks	−.02	.11
Likelihood of black supervisor	NA	−.06
Likelihood of being affected by affirmative action	NA	−.11
Racial busing		
Children not in parochial school	.14*	NA
Children in public elementary school	NA	−.08
Children in public high school	NA	−.05
Likelihood of busing blacks in	NA	.01
Likelihood of busing whites out	NA	−.02
Black violence		
Closeness to Pacoima	.08	−.04
Fear of black violence	.16*	.11
Variance contributed by		
Symbolic racism	.223	.153
Racial threat	.096	.055
Both	.253	.144
Unique variance contributed by		
Symbolic racism	.157	.089
Racial threat	.030	−.009

[a]Entry is the standardized regression coefficient (β) for each predictor variable. Variables are coded so that a positive β reflects a positive effect of either racism or threat. R^2 is adjusted for number of variables in the analysis. (*Source*: Adapted from Kinder and Sears, 1981, p. 422.)

[b]NA, Not available.

*$p < .05$.

**$p < .01$.

opposition to it. The first study, using the 1972 National Election Studies (NES) sample, revealed no support for this hypothesis. The regression coefficients averaged .01, and only one was significant, as shown in Table III (Sears *et al.*, 1979). Nor did the self-interest variables show any additive or interactive effects; in combination (e.g., having children in districts with busing) they proved just as impotent as they did in isolation, as shown in the right-hand columns of Table III. Rather, racial intolerance dominated in all cases, yielding highly significant regression coefficients ranging from +.49 to +.36. A later replication using the 1976 NES survey obtained almost identical results (Sears *et al.*, 1980; see Studies 2 and 3 in Table I).

At about that time, the Los Angeles Unified School District introduced a plan with some mandatory busing. A local survey conducted in 1976 found some evidence that self-interest increased white opposition to the plan; parents of

TABLE III
DETERMINANTS OF THE OPPOSITION OF WHITES TO BUSING[a,b]

	All respondents (1)	Classified by busing in area		
		Happening (2)	Heard of (3)	Neither (4)
Symbolic attitudes				
Racial intolerance (cubed)	.39**	.36**	.49**	.36**
Conservatism	.19**	.03	.16	.26**
Conservatism squared	.10*	.01	.00	.13**
Self-interest				
Busing happening/heard of	−.01	—	—	—
Child in public school	.05	.08	−.06	.04
White neighborhood schools	−.02	−.07	.15	−.02
Demographic factors				
Education	−.05	−.01	−.33**	−.04
Age	.06*	.16*	−.14	.04
Southern residence	.05	.09	−.14	.04
Multiple *r*	.540	.480	.699	.574
R^2	29.1%	23.1%	48.8%	33.0%
N	853	153	82	537

[a]Computed from data collected in the 1972 National Election Studies survey (Sears, Hensler, and Speer, 1979).

[b]Entries are standardized regression coefficients, where each column is a separate regression equation.

*$p < .05$.

**$p < .001$.

children in the district were among the most opposed (Allen & Sears, 1979). To follow up this possible exception, we reviewed the results of eight surveys conducted at different stages of busing controversies (Sears & Allen, 1984). This (study 4 in Table I) permitted 52 separate tests of the self-interest hypothesis. Again, on average the effects were weak, with a mean regression coefficient of +.03; in contrast, a single-item index of symbolic racism yielded an average coefficient of +.26, again highly significant. This study did yield one apparently reliable self-interest effect, however; self-interest did prove to be a significant determinant of opposition to busing in the stage between announcement of a court order mandating some desegregation, and announcement of a specific plan implementing that order. We will return to this exception later on.

Others who have tested the self-interest hypothesis concerning busing have obtained much the same result. Numerous other cross-sectional studies have been done, typically using such measures of racial threat as having children in the public schools, having children being bused, and the distance of the bus ride. They have usually found no greater opposition to busing or integration among whites personally affected by it (e.g., Bobo, 1983, using national data; Gatlin, Giles, & Cataldo, 1978, in Florida; and McConahay, 1982, in Louisville, Kentucky). In a particularly interesting study, Jacobson (1978) compared surveys done before and after a desegregation ruling in Milwaukee, Wisconsin. Before the ruling, people with children in the public schools were trivially less opposed than others to integration and busing (by an average of 3% over four items). After the ruling, those with children in the public schools actually became somewhat more *pro*-busing than others (by an average of 5%).

The only apparent exception is that McClendon (1985) and McClendon and Pestello (1983), using Akron, Ohio data, found that having a child in the public schools (or perceiving busing as especially costly) did increase opposition to it. However, the two variables did not interact as they should according to the self-interest hypothesis: perceived costs were no more influential among parents than among nonparents. Moreover, those perceptions of the costs of busing themselves proved to be based in anti-black attitudes, and so the effects of being a parent washed out with perceived costs controlled (consistent with the notion that antibusing attitudes are most strongly rooted in racial prejudices). In short, the opposition of whites to busing has rarely been shown to have a self-interested basis.

3. Affirmative Action

Whites' opposition to affirmative action has also often been thought to be rooted in self-interest, such as in perceived personal competition with blacks for jobs. The landmark Bakke decision, after all, was stimulated by a white applicant who alleged that affirmative action quotas had deprived him of a position in medical school. However, a number of studies have found whites' attitudes toward affirmative action to be unaffected by self-interest. For example, Jessor (1988, p. 111) reports that a measure of racial self-interest (termed "outgroup interdependence"), based on whites' fears that they or a family member might not get a job, promotion, or admission to school because of preferential treatment for blacks, correlated with opposition to pro-black racial policies (in terms of federal spending, jobs, schools, etc.), but had no remaining significant effect once symbolic predispositions were controlled. "Ingroup interdependence" (the feeling that one's own opportunities would improve if those of whites did) had no effect at all. Similarly, Kluegel and Smith (1983) tested the effects of 4 dimensions of whites' self-interest on their attitudes toward affirmative action for blacks, and found 2 of the 16 coefficients were significant in the predicted direction, and 1 in the opposite direction. Jacobson's (1985) report of a small, statistically significant effect is compromised by use of measures of self-interest irrelevant to affirmative action (e.g., perceived probability of neighborhood and local school integration). And in all three cases, racial intolerance explained opposition to affirmative action far better than any measure of self-interest. Interestingly, Jacobson (1983) also found no evidence that self-interest influenced support for affirmative action among blacks.

4. Bilingual Education

Opposition to bilingual education among non-Hispanics might also be thought to be motivated by self-interest. Anglo parents might oppose it as a means of protecting their own children from what is perceived as inferior education, especially if their children are in public schools with many Hispanic children. Anglos with no language proficiency aside from English might be especially threatened by a bilingual society, and Anglos living in areas with many Hispanics might also be especially threatened by it. Yet a 1983 national survey revealed that opposition again proved to be governed more by racial attitudes than by self-interest or direct personal experience with it (Study 5 in Table I). The data are shown in detail in Table IV. There was no effect of threats to Anglo parents or of personal language proficiency. Indeed those with children in such programs were the most supportive of it (Huddy & Sears, 1989).

These studies, then, have uniformly yielded strong effects of racial intolerance on these attitudes toward racial policies or minority candidates. They have almost equally uniformly yielded no support for the self-interest hypothesis that racial or ethnic threats to the private lives of whites affect such attitudes.

B. ECONOMIC POLICIES

It might be argued that racial conflicts have a complex, profoundly emotional quality that masks or at least complicates the effects of self-interest. Economic

TABLE IV

THE OPPOSITION OF NON-HISPANICS TO BILINGUAL EDUCATION: BIVARIATE
CORRELATIONS AND REGRESSION ANALYSES[a,b]

	Full sample		Parents only	
	r (1)	β (2)	r (3)	β (4)
Racial attitudes				
Symbolic racism	.39	.30[**]	.36	.29[**]
Nationalism	.22	.08[*]	.15	.02
Anti-Hispanic affect	.18	.08[*]	.15	.00
Self-interest and personal experience				
Parental role				
Children				
Under 18 years	−.03	.01	.01	—
In public school	—	—	.06	.06
Hispanics in school	—	—	.04	.00
Learning Spanish	—	—	.03	.05
In bilingual program	—	—	−.08	−.12[*]
Bilingual experience				
Family bilingual	.04	.02	.06	.04
Current proficiency	−.01	.00	−.04	−.06
Hispanic context				
Objective	.14	—	.16	—
Subjective	.13	—	.07	—
Composite	.15	.15[**]	.14	.16[*]
Group conflict				
Educational conflict	.24	.12[**]	.25	.13
Economic threat	.14	.05[*]	.04	−.01
Pro-majority evaluations	−.06	.01	−.11	−.09
Social class				
Education	−.01	−.05	.05	−.01
Household income	.07	.03	.12	.04
Variance explained				
Self-interest and personal experience		2.4%		4.6%
Racial attitudes		16.8		13.3
Group conflict		7.3		6.8
Social class		0.7		1.5
All predictors		21.2		19.8

[a]The 1983 National Bilingual Education Survey (Huddy & Sears, 1989).

[b]The entries in columns (1) and (3) are Pearson correlations of predictors with opposition to bilingual education; in columns (2) and (4), standardized regression coefficients from equations including all predictors listed. The estimates of variance explained are based on regression equations including only the variables specified.

  [*]$p < .05$.

  [**]$p < .0001$.

issues, the presumptive "home turf" for theories of self-interest, might therefore be regarded as more appropriate venues for its impact on attitudes. If so, support for particular economic policies should be strongest among those most likely to benefit from them personally.

1. Employment

Our research on economic self-interest began with attitudes toward government-guaranteed full employment and national health insurance. The self-interest hypotheses were that support for the former would be greatest among the unemployed, laid off, or those hurt by a recent recession, and for the latter, would be greatest among those with inadequate or excessively costly personal health insurance (Sears et al., 1980). Half of these self-interest indicators did yield significant regression coefficients in the 1976 NES survey, but at a rather low level: they averaged +.05. Another national study (Sears & Lau, 1983), focusing on unemployment, inflation, and presidential economic performance, yielded an average correlation of +.02 with self-interest (over 18 tests; see Studies 6, 8, and 10 in Table I).

Others have obtained similarly weak findings. Green (1988) also reports weak self-interest effects on guaranteed employment and national health insurance from NES surveys. In an excellent in-depth national study of the effects of unemployment in the mid-1970s, Schlozman and Verba (1979) failed to find the unemployed to be unusually sympathetic to such radical proposals as assigning jobs, ending capitalism, taxing the rich to redistribute the wealth, or capping personal income. Nor did the length of unemployment or the jobless workers' appraisals of their chances of finding work have any effect on these attitudes. The few exceptions were some modest self-interest effects upon attitudes toward such moderate government policies as ending unemployment, being the employer of last resort, and providing for those in need. And job insecurity (e.g., perceptions of likelihood of job loss in the near future, short time on current job, and a history of unemployment) did prove to have significant effects on policy preferences, particularly on radical solutions.

2. Taxes and Spending

Our most comprehensive study (Sears & Citrin, 1985) took advantage of three California ballot propositions that proposed, respectively, a massive property tax reduction (Proposition 13 in 1978), a cap on state spending (Proposition 4 in 1979), and a 50% reduction in state income taxes (Proposition 9 in 1980). This represented a unique opportunity to study self-interest since two of the propositions promised large and concrete economic benefits to individual taxpayers, and all three threatened public services and public employment. It should have provided an optimal situation for the exercise of self-interest since these large potential consequences for personal well-being were placed before the voters with the intense and focused attention of hotly contested campaigns.

The dependent variables included support for the three ballot measures, attitudes toward smaller government and reduced spending on public services, and perceptions of waste and excessive wages for public employees. Four groups of self-interested respondents were identified. The "taxpayers" (those who were homeowners, felt burdened by heavy property and/or income taxes, expected large tax reductions from the propositions, and/or had high income) stood to profit handsomely from tax reductions. The generally economically discontented (those with declining family finances and/or feeling most hurt by inflation) presumably also should have had a stake in the personal economic benefits provided by reduced taxes. On the other hand, public employees and the recipients of various government services (public assistance, public schools, public health services, unemployment compensation, and so on) should have favored maintaining current levels of taxation, spending, and public employment. These four groups of self-interested respondents were partially overlapping, of course, so most of the analyses simply incorporated self-interest as variables in regression equations.

The "taxpayers" held quite self-interested political preferences. Both homeownership and feeling subjectively burdened by taxes were related to support for the ballot propositions (as summarized in a "tax rebel" index) and for smaller government and reduced spending on specific public services (such as schools and public health), as well as to perceptions of waste in government and beliefs that government workers were overpaid, as shown in Table V (see also Study 18 in Table I). Similar effects of homeownership on support for Proposition 13 were reported by Neiman and Riposa (1987). We will return to these findings.

General economic discontent, however, yielded only trivial regression coefficients, averaging $+.02$, as shown in Table V (see also Study 7 in Table I). Nor was there any evidence of interactions between the two types of economic discontent that might reflect the effects of "stagflation": those whose personal financial situation was slipping *and* who felt especially badly hurt by inflation showed no special support for the tax revolt (Sears & Citrin, 1985, pp. 137–139).

On the anti-tax-revolt side, the public employees did show some self-interest: relative to others, they were significantly more opposed to the tax revolt propositions ($\beta = .18$) and more likely to reject the claim that government workers were overpaid ($\beta = .20$; see Table I, Study 20). However, the recipients of government services did not show the expected defense of the public sector. The regression coefficients for service recipients averaged $+.03$, and none exceeded .06 (see Table V and Study 14 in Table I). To be sure, in some areas (public schools, welfare, and public health), service recipients did show significantly

TABLE V
EFFECTS OF SELF-INTEREST ON ATTITUDES TOWARD TAXING AND SPENDING[a,b]

	Tax revolt schema					Attention	
	Tax rebel index	Size of government	Service spending	Waste	Overpaid government workers	Issue salience	Opinion-ation
Pro-revolt interests							
Taxpayers							
Homeownership	.17**	.15**	.17**	.06*	.03	.07	.07*
Subjective tax burden	.20**	.15**	.18**	.21**	.14**	.18**	.06*
Economic discontent							
Declining finances	.02	.03	.04	.03	.01	-.03	.02
Inflation impact	.03	-.01	.03	.01	.01	.01	.02
Anti-revolt interests							
Public employees	.18**	.02	.01	.06*	.20**	.02	.03
Service recipients							
Government assistance	.01	.04	.07*	.04	.02	.04	-.01
Employment status	.05*	.04	.02	.04	.01	.02	-.07
Work problems	.06*	.06*	.06*	.02	.05	-.06*	.06*
Child in public school	.02	.01	.01	.04	.04	-.01	-.02
R^2	.113	.067	.079	.068	.065	.045	.020

[a]The 1979 California Tax Revolt Survey (Sears & Citrin, 1985, p. 114).

[b]Entries are standardized regression coefficients from equations including all interest variables. A positive entry indicates position is associated with the specified self-interest in the hypothesized direction.

*$p < .01$.
**$p < .001$.

greater support for increased spending on the services from which they specifically benefited than did other respondents, but the effects were quite weak ($\beta <$ .10, as shown in Table V). In toto, then, this study presented an interesting blend of success and failure for the self-interest hypothesis to which we will return.

A similar study was done in Massachusetts before and after the vote on its major property tax-cutting measure, Proposition $2\frac{1}{2}$, with quite similar results in virtually all these respects (Lau, Coulam, & Sears, 1983). The taxpayers showed some significant special support for tax cuts (Study 19 in Table I), and public employees showed significant opposition (Study 21), but service recipients again showed no special opposition (Study 15). Other studies of voting on ballot measures on taxes or attitudes toward tax legislation report similar results, if not always as dramatic. One dealing with two Michigan tax-cutting propositions found consistent (though modest) effects of property tax burden (Courant et al., 1980). A local rapid transit referendum in Atlanta, Georgia, was opposed most by those who both thought it would cause property tax increases and who did not expect to use it (Schroeder & Sjoquist, 1983). Income level and tax bracket significantly predicted support for the tax cuts, and use of capital gains and home mortgage deductions predicted support for those deductions, in the 1978 federal Tax Revenue Act (Hawthorne & Jackson, 1987). And respondents' own perceived federal tax burdens predicted their support for the Kemp–Roth tax cuts proposed in 1979, later implemented as part of President Reagan's budget plan in 1981 (Sears & Lau, 1983). In almost all these cases, then, taxpayers' self-interest in real ballot or legislative propositions have significantly influenced their support for them.

A number of other studies have focused on tax attitudes in the abstract or in hypothetical situations, and they have less consistently yielded self-interest effects. To be sure, Coughlin (1989) reports that higher income individuals in a General Social Survey (GSS) opposed income redistribution substantially more than did lower income individuals, at least among whites. But other studies are not always so confirmatory. In Norway, acceptance of tax cheating was found to be only slightly greater ($\beta = .10$) among higher income individuals and among those personally dissatisfied with their own financial situation, although it was not significantly related to homeownership or personal financial expectations (see Listhaug & Miller, 1985). Studies with Florida and national samples obtained almost no evidence for self-interested attitudes on the part of taxpayers (Beck & Dye, 1982; Lowery & Sigelman, 1981). A similar portrait emerges from a major study of taxes and spending in Sweden in 1981 (Hadenius, 1986). The principal dependent variables were again discontent about taxes and preferences about public spending. There were only scattered effects of vulnerability to taxes; e.g., higher income individuals were not more discontented with taxes, although they were more opposed to welfare spending. Those feeling especially economically pinched were especially discontented with taxes, as were employers (especially about corporate taxes; pp. 31–35). But little else mattered. And Rasinski and Rosenbaum (1987) found no effects of homeownership on opposition to local property tax increases for the schools.

These null findings are joined with a few studies suggesting that the economically disadvantaged, rather than the advantaged, most oppose new taxes. For example, Banfield and Wilson (1964) found that lower income individuals most opposed higher taxes to pay for local services. Beck, Rainey, and Traut (1990) found that economic disadvantage (slipping past or future personal finances, low income, and those perceiving taxes and utility charges as increasing) generated more complaints about taxes being too high. Nevertheless, the most common finding in these studies is that taxpayer self-interest does have a consistently significant effect.

Fairly sharp and distinctive opposition among public employees to other tax revolts has also turned up in studies of Proposition $2\frac{1}{2}$ (Ladd & Wilson, 1982) and of two tax-cutting propositions in Michigan (Courant, Gramlich, & Rubinfeld, 1980). However, there are exceptions: surveys in Florida, Sweden, and Norway, with no tax cut measure on the ballot, found few differences between public employees and others (Beck & Dye, 1982; Hadenius, 1986; Listhaug & Miller, 1985).

The lack of effects of being a service recipient on support for the public sector in general, with weak but significant effects on support for the particular service in question, obtained in our two tax-revolt studies have generally been duplicated in other studies as well. A few stronger effects have been reported: the low income and unemployed supported welfare spending more than did others in a national sample (Coughlin, 1989), and parents with children in the public schools supported increased school taxation in a local survey (though other factors proved considerably stronger among registered voters; see Rasinski & Rosenbaum, 1987). Similarly, Cleveland, Ohio, parents of children in the public schools voted more strongly than others for school bonds (Cataldo & Holm, 1983), but this special support eroded to nonsignificance when other variables were considered. Other studies of service recipients have generally found that they do not support service spending at unusual levels. In Hadenius' intensive study (1986) in Sweden, actual or potential service recipients did not have distinctive attitudes (see pp. 35, 37, and 100). Those whose economic situations were most fragile or deteriorated showed only slightly greater support for welfare spending than others did ($R^2 = 1.4\%$; see p. 99), and those on pensions were more favorable than others to spending on welfare, but his more detailed pursuit of special demand for public expenditures among specific client groups (such as parents of children at home, or those receiving sickness or unemployment benefits) proved fruitless (p. 104). Hadenius concludes that "political symbolic beliefs" (especially left–right placement and discontent with the distribution of power), not interests, best explain the views of citizens about taxation and public welfare (p. 121). And, finally, in two studies in Florida, self-interest did not influence service recipients' attitudes at all in one case (Beck & Dye, 1982), while economic disadvantage contributed to more dissatisfaction with local services in the other, but only indirectly, as mediated through more general disaffection from the community (Beck *et al.*, 1990).

In short, we find moderately consistent evidence in these studies for self-interest effects among taxpayers and public employees, to which we will return. But we find very little for service recipients or the generally economically discontented.

3. Women's Issues

The women's movement has raised numerous issues involving women's self-interest, such as job discrimination, pay equity, sexual harrassment, abortion, and child care. One hypothesis is that self-interest would generate special support among women in general for policies that benefit women more than men. However, few gender differences have been identified on these issues (Franklin & Kosaki, 1989; Mansbridge, 1985; Shapiro & Mahajan, 1986). A second set of hypotheses is that policies benefiting women should be most strongly supported among subsets of women who benefit most from them; working women and/or single mothers might be especially likely to support government-supported child care. However, our study using the 1984 NES national sample showed that for the most part symbolic predispositions rather than self-interest explained women's attitudes on these issues. The same held for their attitudes toward gender equality and feminism, and toward candidates favorable to women (such as Mondale and Ferraro in 1984). Feminism and abortion policy in particular proved to be almost purely symbolic issues, with attitudes toward the latter strongly influenced by political ideology and religiosity. The only real exceptions were that single mothers were especially supportive of government aid to women, and working women, of gender equality (Studies 11 and 16 in Table I; Sears & Huddy, 1990a). These findings parallel those obtained by Coughlin (1989) from GSS data; income had a weak but positive relationship to support for funding abortions for the poor, contrary to a self-interest hypothesis, and in any case its effects were overwhelmed by those of religious affiliation and attendance.

A particularly careful study of women's self-interest in the equal rights amendment (ERA), the women's liberation movement, and the human life amendment (HLA, an antiabortion measure) sprang from two local surveys by Del Boca (1982). In both cases, women's objective self-interest (working, desiring further education, and/or being divorced or separated) did not influence attitudes toward the human life amendment. In one case it did significantly increase support for the ERA and for women's liberation in general, but only at a modest level ($R^2 =$

4%). In contrast, such symbolic predispositions as prejudice against women and traditional American values had much stronger effects. The effects of subjective self-interest (concerning the potential impact of ERA on opposite-sex relationships and personal life goals, and perceived discrimination against the self and friends) on support for the ERA were also tested, as were perceived effects of the HLA on the self. In most cases the associations were positive and significant. However, as the author indicates, the causal inference in this case is suspect; the perceived effects of the policy measure on the self may be better interpreted as a cognitive component of that policy attitude than as an antecedent motive for adopting a particular preference.

It might be noted in passing that the effects of objective self-interest in the Del Boca study disappear with socioeconomic status and age controlled. In general, the young and the better-educated support abortion much more than do older or less-educated individuals (Sears & Huddy, 1990a), as they do spending on the environment (Coughlin, 1989). Trying to interpret these findings illustrates the dangers of interpreting demographic variables solely as indicators of self-interest. Younger individuals both are generally more personally affected by abortion policy than older people and have more of a stake in the future of the environment. Yet both abortion and environmental policy are emerging issues, the kind usually embraced by such vanguard segments of the population as the young and better educated, compromising a simple self-interest interpretation (Coughlin, 1989).

4. Social Security and Medicare

Two studies have examined political self-interest among the elderly. The self-interest hypotheses were that older people should support Social Security and Medicare more than young people do, especially lower income older people (because they are more dependent on such benefits), and be more opposed than the young to greater spending on education (since that typically benefits younger people and their children most). Huddy's (1989) literature review found no greater support for Social Security or Medicare spending among the elderly than among younger people, and Ponza, Duncan, Corcoran, and Groskind (1988) actually found less support among them (along with less support for spending on education). The latter also find no greater age differences in support for transfer payments either to low-income older people or to (presumably younger) low-income families with children. On the other hand, in both studies, support for greater benefits to the elderly was linked more closely to economic self-interest among older than younger people. In Huddy's (1989) study, low income and personal finances were associated considerably more strongly with support for Social Security and Medicare among the elderly (explaining 12.6% of the variance) than among younger age groups (4.7%).

5. Energy

A survey of Los Angeles County residents found that the personal impact of the 1973–1974 energy crisis in terms of perceived increase in difficulty of daily life, effects on employment, and residence in areas with restrictions on electricity use had no effect whatever on relevant policy attitudes, such as support for reduced consumption or increased resource development (Sears et al., 1978).

Economic policy preferences have not been shown to be closely tied to the individual's self-interest, then. Attitudes toward unemployment policy, national health insurance, women's issues, Social Security and Medicare, and energy consumption all have proved only weakly related to self-interest. Recipients of government services do not evidence any very general support for the public sector. The exceptions are scattered, but seem to cluster around discontent with taxes, public employees, and some tendency for service recipients to support the specific services from which they benefit.

C. POCKETBOOK VOTING

A related literature tests the "pocketbook voting" hypothesis that voters' own financial situations are major influences over their voting preferences in presidential and congressional elections. In this case economic self-interest is thought to dictate candidate choice through its impact on evaluations of the incumbent's performance rather than on policy preferences. As indicated above, Kramer (1971) showed that the electoral fortunes of congressmen of the incumbent president's party were influenced by the strength of the economy prior to the election. This was generally interpreted as reflecting self-interest; presumably voters whose own personal finances were improving had responded by rewarding the incumbent's party, while those whose finances had deteriorated had responded by punishing it.

This interpretation was challenged by Kinder and Kiewiet (1979, 1981), based on individual-level correlations between self-interest and voting preferences in the NES surveys. They used two measures of self-interest, both of which have become conventional indicators in this literature: perceived personal finances (e.g., "would you say you and your family living here are better off or worse off financially than you were a year ago?") and recent household unemployment experiences. They found that self-interest had little effect on voting behavior, while "sociotropic" judgments about the collective economic well-being of the nation had strong effects. They concluded that the fluctuations in aggregate vote observed by Kramer (1971) were due to sociotropic rather than to pocketbook (or self-interest) motives among individual voters.

1. Declining Personal Finances

These findings have led to considerable subsequent research. The most common hypothesis has been that perceptions of declining personal finances generates votes against the incumbent president's party in presidential, congressional, senatorial, and gubernatorial elections. The most supportive evidence comes from the presidential vote. Kiewiet (1983, Table 4.1) conducted probit analyses of seven NES surveys from 1956 to 1980. All personal finances terms were in the predicted direction (although it would appear that only 29% of the terms are statistically significant if the customary two-tailed, $p < .05$, criterion is used). According to our own calculations, the mean associations of perceived personal finances with presidential vote over that 1956–1980 period were of modest absolute magnitude, although statistically significant (raw correlations averaging slightly over .10, and regression coefficients, slightly under it; Lau, Sears, & Jessor, 1990). The data are shown in Table VI.

Most tests of the role of personal finances in other kinds of electoral contests yield null results. Kiewiet (1983) repeated the same analysis on congressional vote, and found that only 7% of the terms were significant, close to the chance level. In our analyses of the same data, shown in Table VI, the mean correlation over the full NES series has been .07, and the mean regression coefficient, .02. Lewis-Beck's (1988) thorough analysis of economic voting in Western Europe (Britain, France, West Germany, Italy, and Spain), using Euro-Barometer Surveys from 1983 and 1984, found that perceived personal finances had only small effects on the vote, on approval or disapproval of government economic policy, or, by and large, on expectations that government policies would improve the economy. In these studies, perceptions of collective economic well-being and symbolic predispositions again had much stronger effects than did self-interest. For example, Kiewiet (1983) found that the effects of party identification exceeded statistical significance in every single case, unlike self-interest, which did so less than a quarter of the time.

Scattered studies of senatorial and gubernatorial voting in the United States yield similar conclusions (Kiewiet & Rivers, 1984; although see Kuklinski & West, 1981, for an exception). An extensive study of gubernatorial and senatorial exit polls in 16 states in the recession year of 1982 reports strong effects of holding the President responsible for the state's economic problems on voting against Republican candidates as well as significant effects of declining personal finances, interpreted as pocketbook voting against Ronald Reagan, the Republican incumbent president (Stein, 1990). It can be argued, however, that brief exit polls taken immediately after voters leave the voting booth place unusual pressure upon them to rationalize their votes in terms of the explanatory items provided on the survey, and thus artifactually exaggerate such correlations (Sears & Lau, 1983).

TABLE VI

ASSOCIATION OF PERCEIVED PERSONAL FINANCES WITH VOTES AGAINST
INCUMBENT PRESIDENT'S PARTY[a,b]

Year	Presidential vote				Reported congressional vote	
	Vote intention		Reported vote		Reported vote	
	r	β	r	β	r	β
1956	.23	.15	.19	.11	.17	.07
1958					.16	.08
1960	.14	.05	.13	.05	.14	.07
1962					.03	.05
1964	.02	.07	.01	.06	−.03	.01
1966					−.02	−.04
1968	.11	.10	.11	.13	.07	.06
1970					.06	−.01
1972	.13	.09	.12	.07	.07	.00
1974					.00	.00
1976	.16	.06	.13	.06	.15	.08
1978					.00	.00
1980	.08	.08	.05	.07	.03	.00
1982					.12	.03
1984	.36	.18	.33	.18	.22	.11
1986					.08	.01
1988	.19	.07	.20	.10	.10	−.01
Mean, excluding 1984	.12	.08	.12	.08	.07	.02

[a]The 1956–1986 National Election Studies (Lau, Sears, & Jessor, 1990).

[b]The entries are associations between perceptions of improved personal finances over the past year and support for candidates of the incumbent president's party. In columns 1, 3, and 5 they are Pearson r values; in columns 2, 4, and 6, standardized regression coefficients from equations including income, education, political interest, and party identification.

Be that as it may, the major question seems to us to focus on the strength of the link of perceived personal finances to American presidential vote: Kiewiet and Rivers (1984, p. 377) feel it is a consistent association, while Feldman (1984, p. 248) concludes that "the accumulated evidence very strongly suggests that vote choice and presidential evaluations are at best modestly influenced by *personal* economic considerations." Our own perspective is that personal finances have consistently affected the presidential vote in the expected direction considering the full series of elections with available data, but the individual effects are small and usually unreliable.

2. Other Economic Indicators

Another version of the pocketbook voting hypothesis is that personal or family unemployment should be associated with voting for the party of the Left. The best study on this point is Kiewiet's (1983), using the same probit analyses cited above. Kiewiet finds that in most (30 of 36) presidential and congressional elections, unemployment has been associated with greater support for Democratic candidates, although only 20% of the comparisons were statistically significant. In a separate analysis, individuals who said that unemployment is their most serious personal problem voted more Democratic than did other respondents, but not significantly so. Schlozman and Verba's (1979) in-depth examination of the effects of unemployment in the mid-1970s also found only a slight tilt (of 4%) to the Democrats among the unemployed. Some other studies have failed to find significant effects of unemployment (or the personal impact of recessions) on voting or presidential job approval (Feldman, 1984; Kinder & Mebane, 1983). These findings are consistent with Kiewiet's view that personal unemployment usually yields a slight but usually statistically unreliable shove toward the Democratic side.

Most macroeconomic theories suggest that inflation most hurts the middle class, just as unemployment most hurts the working class. Historically parties of the middle class (e.g., the Republicans in the United States) have fought inflation more vigorously than they have unemployment. So perceptions of being especially hurt by inflation should be correlated with increased Republican voting. However, the personal impact of inflation quite consistently has had no influence on voters' political choices. Kiewiet (1983, Ch. 5) examined those who said inflation was their most serious personal problem, and found them to vote significantly more Republican in but one of five surveys. In other studies, feeling hurt by inflation had no significant effect on presidential job approval or on retrospective or prospective judgments of the severity of inflation in the nation as a whole (Conover, Feldman, & Knight, 1986, 1987), and very weak effects on presidential vote (Lewis-Beck, 1988, p. 122).

Finally, one might think that those most affected by such Reagan Administration policies as cutting direct economic benefits and federal taxes would have manifested self-interested attitudes toward Reagan and the Democratic Congress. However, Feldman's (1984) analysis of the 1982 NES survey showed that personal tax cuts affected neither approval of Reagan nor of Congress, and that feeling one's own benefits had been cut contributed only to disapproval of Reagan.

D. VIOLENCE

We have also considered the effects of violence. "Law and order" issues, such as the death penalty, gun control, permissive judges, and rights of the accused, have been major political issues since the 1960s. Attitudes on them might well have a self-interested basis: those who have been victimized by crime in the past or who feel vulnerable to future crime victimization might have self-interested reasons for supporting law and order policies. However, our analysis of the 1976 NES survey found that such self-interest variables explained only 0.4% of the variance, compared to 17.1% for the usual three symbolic predispositions (see Study 22 in Table I; Sears *et al.*, 1980). Other studies of support for law and order have generally also shown only weak self-interest effects. Past victimization by crime or fear of crime has not significantly affected support for the death penalty or opposition to gun control (Tyler & Weber, 1982; Tyler & Lavrakis, 1983). However, there was greater support for gun control in the 1984 GSS survey among those who had been threatened by a gun (Lotwis, 1989). A further exception would seem to be the special opposition to gun control displayed by gun owners and hunters in most surveys (e.g., *Gallup Report, 1985;* Lotwis, 1989). But in all these cases symbolic predispositions have had considerably stronger effects than has self-interest. Crime would seem to be more a symbolic than a personal issue in politics.

One might think war and other issues of national defense would also be compelling matters of self-interest, since they too can involve life and death. A major source of self-interest in war is vulnerability to combat. However, people with friends and relatives serving in Vietnam were not unusually opposed to the war there (Lau, Brown, & Sears, 1978; Mueller, 1973).

But what about the fear of war? Among a representative sample of UCLA undergraduates, in a study conducted during the 1979 confrontations with the Soviet Union over Afghanistan, personal vulnerability to the draft did not produce increased opposition to registration, draft, or military action toward the Soviet Union (Sears *et al.*, 1983). While one possible measure of self-interest, the perceived likelihood of war, was associated with antiwar and antidraft preferences, controls for symbolic predispositions completely eliminated any trace of a self-interest effect. Apparently in that context partisan cleavages arose between those opposed to confrontation and afraid of an outbreak of war, on the one hand, and those feeling confrontations did not risk war, on the other.

Studies of citizens' fears of nuclear war yield yet another puzzling failure of self-interest to generate seemingly appropriate policy preferences. Although throughout the postwar period many Americans perceived nuclear war as rather likely (e.g., in 1983, 40% as either "very" or "fairly" likely, and 28% as only "fairly unlikely"), and as horrific in consequences (about 70% feeling that chances of personal survival of it were poor), most people did not think about it much, worry about it much, or act politically in any way to try to minimize the risk of one (see Fiske, 1987; Kramer, Kalick, & Milburn, 1983). In short, even as personally devastating as war is, it apparently does not usually elicit passionately self-interested policy preferences (which may partly explain why there are so many wars).

E. ISSUE PUBLICS

Self-interest might be thought to attract attention to an issue or to political events even if it does not often affect preferences. In Converse's (1975) language, self-interest might breed "issue publics" for "doorstep issues" that affect the individual personally (also, see Krosnick, 1990). In three studies we have indeed found that self-interest in a political issue significantly (if not always enormously by absolute standards) increased public attention to it. The personal impact of the 1973–1974 energy crisis was strongly related to paying more attention to the crisis (Sears et al., 1978). Having family members, relatives, or close friends serving in the military in Vietnam generated more attention to the Vietnam issue (Lau et al., 1978). And in the California tax revolt, taxpayers were more likely than others to think that taxes and spending were one of California's most important problems, and to have opinions on all features of the tax revolt (see the right-hand columns of Table V; Sears & Citrin, 1985).

As usual, there are some contrary examples. In the tax revolt study, service recipients and the economically disadvantaged did not see taxation and spending as unusually important problems, nor were they any more likely to hold opinions about the tax revolt than other Californians. More surprisingly, the same held true for public employees (see Table V). But there does seem to be something of a tendency for self-interest to generate greater public attention, concern, and knowledge, and thus to be one factor in helping to create "issue publics" for a particular policy area.

F. SUMMARY

Clearly, averaging the effects of these quite heterogeneous studies cannot be meaningful in any rigorous sense, but a summary statement can perhaps convey a crude approximation of the overall pattern. We have found in our own work that self-interest correlates only weakly with policy or candidate preferences (an average bivariate correlation of $+.07$, and regression coefficient of $+.04$, as shown in Table I). These reflect only a minor explanatory contribution in terms of variance accounted for. Moreover, only about 20 to 25% of the self-interest terms meet the conventional standard of statistical significance at the .05 level, which is a minimal standard indeed, given the rather large samples used in this research.

Similarly, in most cases, simple measures of pocketbook motivation do not relate significantly to pro- or anti-incumbent voting. It should be said that the general style of the work on pocketbook voting following Kinder and Kiewiet (1979) has been rather inductive, often presenting a large number of regression equations and interpreting the occasional statistically significant self-interest term as a reliable effect. This runs some risk of using chance differences to reject the null hypothesis. Nonetheless, self-interest has generally had quite modest effects.

Moreover, in most of this research symbolic predispositions have had considerably greater power over policy and candidate preferences than has self-interest. In our initial studies of mayoral voting, racial attitudes explained 15.7 and 8.9% of the variance, while racial threat explained only 3.0% and 0.1% (see Table II); in the 1976 NES study the standard three symbolic predispositions explained an average of 14.0% in policy preferences regarding jobs, health insurance, busing, and crime, as against 1.7% for self-interest (Sears *et al.*, 1980); and even in the California tax revolt, with unusually strong self-interest effects, symbolic predispositions explained more variance (12.6 to 11.3%; see Table V).

In short, this research has investigated self-interest as a determinant of a wide variety of policy and candidate preferences. It has usually been of only minor importance in explaining the attitudes of ordinary citizens, usually far outstripped by symbolic predispositions. These conclusions parallel those arrived at in other major reviews of this literature (Citrin & Green, 1990; Feldman, 1984; Kiewiet & Rivers, 1984). They also parallel the conclusions obtained in the most extensive monograph-length studies of self-interest and political attitudes (Green, 1988), of pocketbook voting (by Kiewiet, 1983), and of unemployment (Schlozman & Verba, 1979). As Lewis-Beck (1988, p. 155) says on the basis of a careful study of pocketbook voting in five Western European countries, ''Does economics operate on these citizens through the pocketbook? Only a little.'' We would conclude, therefore, that personal self-interest generally has not been of major importance in explaining the general public's social and political attitudes.

G. FACT AND ARTIFACT

Moreover, it is possible that even this dismal portrait may exaggerate the role of self-interest somewhat. Some of the significant findings, especially in the pocketbook voting literature, may have resulted from two kinds of item–order artifacts. Placing a battery of items about the respondent's own economic situation immediately before the relevant attitude items might tend to *personalize* the latter, and induce artificially high levels of consistency between the two. A person whose finances have declined and who then is given a chance to blame the president may take that opportunity. Alternatively, respondents may be asked to estimate their economic well-being immediately after being asked for whom they had voted (as in exit polls on Election Day), which might provide an inducement to bias descriptions of their personal finances to rationalize their vote choice, thereby *politicizing* personal well-being.

We have tested for the potential impact of such artifacts in three ways. First, we conducted an experiment within a national survey that varied how closely personal items preceded the political attitude dependent variables in four economic areas (general personal finances, taxes, inflation, and unemployment). In the first three areas, self-interest and political attitudes were significantly correlated among the experimentally proximate respondents, but not among those in the so-called neutral condition (Sears & Lau, 1983).

This raised the possibility that item–order artifacts were responsible for the occasional reports of significant correlations between declining personal finances and presidential vote (or presidential approval) cited above. To test this, we reviewed the entire series of the National Election Studies to determine whether the strongest self-interest effects appeared when item proximity might have produced personalizing or politicizing biases. Ten of 11 cases yielding significant self-interest effects came from such interview schedules, while only 4 of the 13 cases with nonsignificant self-interest effects did so (Sears & Lau, 1983). Lewis-Beck (1985) reanalyzed these data, however, and concluded that item proximity had not been associated with stronger effects of personal finances on vote intention and actual vote. In a subsequent paper, Lau *et al.* (1990) criticized some of the procedures Lewis-Beck had used, especially the assessment of potentially contaminating item orders. They report that the effects of personal finances on a wider variety of political attitudes were almost twice as great in contaminated contexts as in neutral contexts, and were not statistically significant in the latter contexts. It is not possible to ascertain in any rigorous manner the exact magnitude of item–order contamination in such surveys, but some of the stronger reported effects of personal finances in the NES series do appear to be suspect.

Finally, we compared the association of personal finances with the vote in brief exit polls (which are framed explicitly to ask respondents to explain their votes) with longer and more complex surveys. Pocketbook voting was much stronger in the exit polls (Sears & Lau, 1983). As indicated earlier, Stein (1990) similarly reports fairly consistent pocketbook voting in exit polls concerning gubernatorial and senatorial elections, which, as indicated above, do not always yield such strong effects in other surveys.

VI. In Further Pursuit of the Effects of Self-Interest

Although the overall picture indicates a relatively small role for self-interest, it is clear that there are exceptions. These can point us to the more circumscribed conditions under which self-interest can be effective, and thereby to a more refined theoretical understanding of its role in attitude formation and change.

A. SOME EXCEPTIONS

We can identify five cases in which virtually every indicator of self-interest had a statistically significant effect on virtually every relevant dependent variable.

1. Taxpayers and Tax Cuts

The strongest and most consistent self-interest effects have been associated with paying taxes. In the California tax revolt, homeownership (which indexes property tax burden) and subjective perceptions of being especially personally burdened by state and local taxes affected both the vote personally and a variety of attitudes toward government services and public employees. These self-interest effects were consistent, statistically significant, and of substantial magnitude, as both Tables I and V show. In other analyses, the exact dollar return of proposed property or income tax reductions to the individual also proved to have very substantial effects. For example, Proposition 13 received 84% of the vote from homeowners who expected their property taxes would otherwise have increased greatly (over $1000/year), 67% of the vote from those who had expected modest increases (up to $200), and 52% from those who expected no increase (Sears & Citrin, 1985). Other studies conducted during referendum campaigns have also found significant effects of taxpayers' self-interest. Subjective tax burden and homeownership were both related to support for Proposition $2\frac{1}{2}$ in Massachusetts (although the latter only marginally so; see Lau et al., 1983).

As already noted, taxpayer self-interest is not always so powerful when assessed in the absence of active political campaigns that focus attention on taxes. Still, a number of studies have found fairly robust and consistent effects of taxpayer self-interest on political preferences, especially those done in the midst of tax-cut campaigns.

2. The Reagan Revolution: Politicizing Self-Interest

A second case also suggests that political events can sometimes politicize personal financial incentives, and thus induce strong self-interest effects. Ronald

Reagan appears to have succeeded in politicizing economic self-interest over the course of his presidency. As already indicated, perceived personal finances rarely has had much impact on voting behavior in the postwar period in the National Election Studies series, yielding mean correlations of $+.12$ and mean regression coefficients of $+.08$ with presidential vote intention and actual vote, as shown in Table VI (Lau *et al.*, 1990). Even when candidate Reagan quite explicitly asked Americans to vote in 1980 on the basis of self-interest ("ask yourself . . . , are you better off today than you were four years ago?"), perceived personal finances were only weakly associated with presidential vote (β = .07), and the new support he attracted toward the end of the campaign did not come disproportionately from those whose personal finances had been declining (Sears & Lau, 1983). Apparently this explicit appeal to self-interest became salient too late in the campaign to evoke widespread self-interested voting.

By 1984, the same plea for a self-interested vote was the centerpiece of his presidency and campaign for reelection. The association of personal finances with presidential preference showed a startling increase: the raw correlations jumped to $+.36$ and $+.33$, respectively, and the regression coefficients, to $+.18$ each, as shown in Table VI (with no case to be made for any item–order artifact in this survey). This reflects an increase in the strength of self-interest over his first 4-year term of some considerable magnitude. (And there is Stein's, 1990, evidence, reviewed earlier, that the 1982 senatorial and gubernatorial elections yielded unusually strong pocketbook voting effects, although these findings were based on exit polls which may exaggerate such effects.) Nevertheless, the fact that self-interest so rarely has a strong and systematic effect suggests that events and political campaigns are not often successful in mobilizing it, even when they try.

3. Public Employees Defending Their Jobs

Public employees were particularly opposed to the tax revolts in both California and Massachusetts, as indicated above. For example, averaging across 11 different comparisons, they opposed the California referenda by an impressive 24% more than other respondents (Sears & Citrin, 1985). In both states the effects held up with all other variables controlled (Lau *et al.*, 1983). Studies of the tax revolt in Michigan found similar results.

In the tax revolt cases, public employees' opposition seems to have been based on their desire to prevent job and pay cuts; their opposition to the California spending cap referendum was correlated with their perceptions that it would cut the number of public employees or their wages ($r = .24$), which was not the case for other citizens ($r = .02$; see Sears & Citrin, 1985). Similarly, Green (1988, p. 237) reports that public employees' particular opposition to the income tax-cutting proposition was greater among those who believed layoffs were "likely" than among those who believed they were "not likely."

This fear of lost jobs may have some more general effect on political attitudes. Schlozman and Verba (1979, p. 213), surveying the general population, found that fear of losing one's job had considerably more impact on attitudes about government aid to the needy or income redistribution than did even current or prior long-term unemployment. But it does not seem to be driven solely by a fear of economic losses in the future. Lewis-Beck (1988) systematically compared prospective and retrospective estimates of personal financial situation and found that prospective fears of declining personal finances did not have much effect in either the United States or in Western Europe (pp. 14 and 82). The fear of future personal economic disaster may have induced self-interest in the case of public employees, then, but it seems not to do so consistently in the general public as a whole.

4. Busing: On the Eve of the Unknown

Self-interest has not generally been very powerful in busing controversies, as indicated earlier. But it does seem to have been stimulated in one particular phase of them. Surveys in Los Angeles, California, done after a general court order had mandated school desegregation, but before announcement of any concrete plan for implementing it, found a substantial self-interest basis for whites' opposition to busing (all 10 regression coefficients were significant, averaging +.13). In contrast, surveys done prior to any court order or indeed much publicity about busing in the community, or done after implementation of the court order, yielded the usual crop of generally nonsignificant self-interest effects (only 17% of the regression coefficients were significant, averaging +.03: see Sears & Allen, 1984; other smaller sample studies done prior to the court order also obtained nonsignificant results: see Caditz, 1976, and Kinder & Sears, 1981). In short, whites' opposition to busing was motivated by self-interest only when busing seemed certain to occur in their own child's school district, yet the nature of the busing plan was as yet unknown.

5. Restrictions on Smokers

Another case of a strong and consistent self-interest effect is that smokers are considerably more unfavorable than nonsmokers to almost any anti-smoking policies, such as restrictions on smoking in public places, increases in cigarette taxes, or bans on cigarette advertising. In one survey, heavy smokers opposed banning smoking in public places more than did moderate smokers, who in turn were more opposed than light smokers, and they in turn more than nonsmokers. Sensitivity to smoke similarly was closely related to support for the ban. In a second survey, smokers were more opposed than nonsmokers to an increase in the cigarette tax. Moreover, as would be expected, there were both price and income effects only among smokers: larger proposed taxes and/or lower income produced more opposition to the tax among smokers but not among nonsmokers (Green & Gerken, 1989). These findings, based on two surveys, a variety of dependent variables, and conceptual replications of the self-interest finding, make a persuasive case that antismoking policies do evoke strongly self-interested preferences.

We would suggest, then, that self-interest has had a consistent and significant effect in five well-documented cases: when tax referenda or the Reagan presidency politicized positive financial incentives, and when public employees, white parents, and cigarette smokers were presented with severe and rather ambiguous personal threats. However, these represent exceptions to the general rule.

B. THE COGNITIVE NARROWNESS OF THE EFFECTS OF SELF-INTEREST

Self-interest only occasionally is an important determinant of policy and candidate preferences, then. But does it help to organize more general and abstract belief systems, as Marx and other economic determinists have contended? There is considerable debate in the public opinion literature about the prevalence of coherent, consistent, and far-ranging belief systems in the general public. Some feel that ordinary citizens have, at best, rather narrow and inconsistent belief systems (Converse, 1964), while others find broader belief systems organized by ideological preferences or basic values (e.g., Feldman, 1988; Sears *et al.*, 1980; for the general debate, see Kinder & Sears, 1985). Nevertheless, it turns out that the effects of self-interest are cognitively quite narrow. Even when it has significant effects, it usually influences only those attitudes that are specific to the narrow interests in question. And it does not play a major role in determining more basic and general predispositions, such as individuals' general political ideologies.

1. When Effective, Self-Interest Is Specific to Narrow Interests

We have identified five cases in which self-interest has had significant and consistent effects. But these effects prove to be quite narrow cognitively. Three cases should illustrate this point. First, public employees did manifest self-interested opposition to the tax revolt propositions in both California and Massachusetts, as indicated above. But beyond this, public employees' self-interest extended no further than a narrow defense of their own jobs and salaries. We looked at whether it also strengthened support for the public sector and for the moderate political Left. These were indexed with 11 questions ranging from the quite general (political ideology and party identification) to more concrete policies (desired size of government, levels of spending on public services, or imposition of tuition at public universities). As shown in Table VII, public employees did deny more than others that government workers were overpaid. They also expressed greater opposition than other respondents to the three ballot propositions, phrased in terms of their actual and probable effects. But otherwise they demonstrated no more support for the public sector than did other respondents, in terms of support for spending on government services, for liberals or the Democratic party, or in denying waste in the public sector. Their opposition to the tax revolt did not extend to any special support for the public sector or the political Left.

Second, in several studies service recipients have displayed some self-interested defense of the specific programs from which they personally benefited. For example, in the California tax revolt, people with children in the public schools showed some modest special support for spending on the schools, those on public assistance supported welfare spending more, and those on Medicare or Medicaid supported public health spending most, all shown in Table VIII. To be sure, these effects were not very strong in absolute terms, ranging only from $+.06$ to $+.09$ (β) and in any case being far outstripped by the effects of symbolic predispositions. And we have given a number of other examples in which service recipients have not had distinctive attitudes.

But again, even when service recipients have displayed significant self-interest effects, they prove to be cognitively quite specific to the individual's own narrow interest. In California, they did not show any special support for government spending other than on the domestic programs they directly benefited from, as shown in Table VIII. Parents were no more supportive than others of welfare or public health, and those on public assistance or Medicaid were no more supportive of the schools. Similarly, in Sweden, receiving sickness or unemployment benefits did not relate to support for welfare spending, nor did having a child at home relate to support for spending on education (Hadenius, 1986, p. 100). Finally, service recipients did not show any special opposition to more general policies affecting the public sector, such as general tax and spending cuts, or the drive for "smaller government" (see Tables V and VIII).

Third, as indicated earlier, our study of college students' attitudes toward resumption of military registration and the draft showed little evidence of self-interested attitudes (Sears et al., 1983). However, more fine-grained analyses did turn up two rather narrow and limited self-interest effects. One proposal had been that the draft would apply only to just one age cohort (e.g., 19 year olds), as it had in the waning days of the Vietnam war. In our study, students 21 and older self-interestedly favored restricting the draft to 18 to 20 year olds (30% supported the restriction) more than did those under 21 (16% supported it). Similarly, student deferments were supported more broadly by freshmen males, who pre-

TABLE VII

THE NARROWNESS OF PUBLIC EMPLOYEES' SELF-INTEREST IN THE CALIFORNIA TAX REVOLT[a,b]

	Public employee in family			
	Self (%)	Family member (%)	None (%)	Difference (%)
Support own pocketbook				
Government workers are not overpaid	85	66	58	+27*
Oppose Proposition 13 (property tax cut)				
Government spending cut too much since Proposition 13	32	21	22	+10
Proposition 13 had bad effect on education	50	51	34	+16*
Gann Amendment (spending cap)				
Would Gann cut public employment?	65	64	61	+4
Would Gann limit public-sector pay?	70	64	62	+8
Oppose Proposition 8 (state income tax cut)				
Would produce very serious service cuts	50	41	60	+20*
State surplus would cover little of revenue shortfall	51	50	36	+15*
Very likely to cut public employment	44	36	29	+15*
This is a very serious effect	51	38	24	+27*
Not likely to improve economy	50	50	40	+10
Not likely to slow inflation	68	62	61	+7
Very likely to hurt school quality	52	43	32	+20*
This is a very serious effect	56	63	53	+3
Will restrict access of poor to college	45	33	24	+21*
General support of public sector				
Democratic	45	46	48	−3
Liberal	40	40	37	+3
Government can cut at most 10%	24	27	25	−1
Want larger government in general	32	28	30	+2
Want increase in service spending (1978)	37	31	37	0
Want increase in service spending (1979)	77	70	72	+5
Support state bailout	80	71	71	+9
Losing local control over schools to the state is very bad	31	37	31	0
School can cut no more than 10%	50	49	42	+8
Should not impose tuition at public universities	68	75	61	+7

[a]California Poll 7807, Tax Revolt Survey, California Poll 8001, California Poll 8002.

[b]Adapted from Sears and Citrin (1985, p. 156).

*$p < .05$.

TABLE VIII

JOINT EFFECTS OF SYMBOLIC PREDISPOSITIONS AND SELF-INTEREST ON SERVICE SPENDING
PREFERENCES AND PREFERRED SIZE OF GOVERNMENT IN CALIFORNIA TAX REVOLT[a,b]

	Spending				Size of government
	Public schools	Welfare	Public health	All services	
Symbolic predispositions					
Ideology	.16**	.11**	.15**	.19**	.07*
Party identification	.09**	.09**	.15**	.13**	.16**
Symbolic racism	.16**	.26**	.14**	.22**	.19**
Self-interest					
Parent of school child	.09*	−.02	−.04	−.02	−.04
Service recipience					
On public assistance	.02	.07*	.04	.05	.08*
On medicare/medicaid	.01	.12*	.06*	.09**	.02
On unemployment compensation	.00	.01	.00	−.01	.01
Employment problems					
Work worry	.03	.08*	.05*	.04	.08**
Work problems	.06*	.00	.03	.05	.01
Variance accounted for (R^2)					
Symbolic predispositions only	9.6%	12.9%	0.9%	16.2%	9.9%
Self-interest only	2.5	5.4	2.6	3.6	3.6
Both combined	11.1	16.5	13.3	18.1	12.0

[a]Tax Revolt Survey. From Sears and Citrin (1985, p. 173).

[b]Each column is a separate regression equation. Entries are β values.

*$p < .05$.

**$p < .001$.

sumably could benefit from them, than by senior males (79 to 53%). Both self-interest effects are strongly statistically significant.

But once we moved to policy questions that were not explicitly age related, these age differences disappeared. The younger and older students did not differ significantly on either of the questions having to do with reinstituting registration and draft. Nor did they differ on questions concerning military responses to Soviet aggression. Their age-based self-interested attitudes did not generalize beyond issues specific to their age.

The taxpayers in the tax revolt study again provide one partial exception to this cognitive narrowness of self-interest. They displayed evidence of quite specific self-interested attitudes, as indicated earlier, but of some generality of them, as well. As well as opposing the tax revolt propositions, the heavily tax burdened were markedly more anti-public sector than were the less burdened in a wide variety of other respects, such as opposing service spending, favoring small government, and perceiving large amounts of waste in government, as shown in Table V. Also, being burdened by one kind of tax did transfer to support for cuts in other kinds of taxes; e.g., homeowners, especially those whose property taxes had been significantly cut by Proposition 13, continued to give more support than renters to the income tax cuts proposed by Proposition 9 (even with income controlled; see Sears & Citrin, 1985, pp. 125 and 131).

But aside from the taxpayers, the rather small self-interest effects uncovered in other areas turn out not only to be rather weak in absolute terms, or unreliable, but when present, to be quite specific to a particular narrow interest. They extend neither to issues affecting other groups with similar interests who normally are in political alliance with them, nor to more broadly applicable formulations of the policy in question.

2. Little Influence on Symbolic Predispositions

The cognitive generality or narrowness of self-interest can be tested in another way. Materialist theorists often propose that ideology, party preferences, and racial prejudice are themselves mere creatures of real economic interests (e.g., Bobo, 1988; LeVine & Campbell, 1972; Lipset, 1981). Even before consulting the data, though, it does not seem very likely that self-interest would strongly shape such symbolic predispositions. The affective preferences we have described as symbolic predispositions tend to crystallize and stabilize by the end of early adulthood (although they are not wholly invariant), and so should not be strongly responsive to the vagaries of adult material interests (Converse & Markus, 1979; Sears, 1989). Nevertheless, it is worth considering the possibility, given the popularity of the theory.

In fact, self-interest proves to be almost wholly uncorrelated with these symbolic predispositions. Three examples will perhaps make the general point. Our study of the origins of policy attitudes toward unemployment, health insurance, busing, and crime (Sears et al., 1980) generated 29 correlations between self-interest indices and these 3 symbolic predispositions. The largest was +.11, and the median, a nonsignificant +.05. In our study of the California tax revolt (which had yielded several significant self-interest effects) we regressed the same three symbolic predispositions on our seven basic self-interest indicators. Only 4 of the 21 self-interest terms were statistically significant (Sears & Citrin, 1985, pp. 169–170). Finally, our study of women's self-interest (Sears & Huddy, 1990a) generated 20 such correlations, but only 4 exceeded +.10, and the median was a nonsignificant +.05.

Moreover, if self-interest controlled symbolic predispositions, placing both in the same regression equation should reduce or even remove the effects of the latter on policy and candidate preferences. In our own research, this has virtually never occurred. Rather, the effects of symbolic predispositions remain undiminished in virtually all cases (e.g., Kinder & Sears, 1981; Sears & Citrin, 1985; Sears *et al.*, 1980). The same holds in Hadenius's (1986) extensive research on the determinants of attitudes toward taxation and spending (see summary regressions on pp. 58, 82, 118, and 125; also see Green, 1988; Sudit, 1988; Tyler & Lavrakis, 1983). These findings seem to reflect a pattern of chance relationships. They are typical of the results we have obtained in other studies, and indeed in studies done by others.

3. Can Cognitively Broad Self-Interest Effects Be Induced?

If self-interest effects can be created by politicizing personal experience (as in the Reagan presidency) or by personalizing political issues (as in our item-order experiment), can they also be made cognitively more encompassing? The limited evidence available to date would suggest that it is difficult to do so.

Our item-proximity experiment did induce several apparent self-interest effects, but they too prove to be cognitively quite specific (Sears & Lau, 1983). Placing questions about personal financial situations immediately before questions on presidential performance induced stronger correlations between them, but only when the time frame (past vs future) and arena (economic vs overall) exactly matched. For example, item proximity did induce consistency between perceptions of one's *past finances* and evaluations of *past* presidential *economic* performance. But it did not induce greater consistency between *past* personal finances and projections of the nation's *future* economic health, or (to a lesser extent) between past personal *finances* and *general* national performance ("how things are going in the country" with no reference to the economy). Similarly, item proximity increased the correlation of attitudes toward *federal* tax policy with perceived *federal* tax burden but not with perceived *state or local* tax burden.

These self-interest effects induced by item proximity are cognitively narrow in another way. They tend to occur only when the items are presented immediately after one another; even highly relevant items are unaffected if more distant. An experimental prime affected, at most, the first subsequent item in two experiments by Green (1988, pp. 189–193). And item proximity in the NES series of election surveys seems to have affected the correlation of perceived personal finances with political attitudes only when the items were in very close proximity (Lau *et al.*, 1990). This rapid dissipation parallels that occurring in laboratory priming studies (Bargh *et al.*, 1988).

In short, it would appear that not only are self-interest effects rare, but when they do appear, they are cognitively quite specific to narrow interests. Nor does self-interest influence more general symbolic predispositions. And attempts to induce self-interest effects may be successful only within a cognitively quite narrow and specific arena, and may quickly dissipate over time. So self-interest appears not to form a foundation for broader thinking about politics, or broader ideologizing.

VII. Possible Facilitating Conditions

Most of the time, then, self-interest has relatively little effect on social and political attitudes. But we have identified a few exceptions. What general principles can we extract from these successes, and the far more numerous failures, about the necessary conditions for self-interest effects?

A. LARGE STAKES

Most economic or cost–benefit models would assume that larger stakes would engage stronger self-interest motives. Perhaps in most of these studies the stakes have simply been too small. Indeed the strongest self-interest effects do seem to have emerged when unusually high stakes were offered. In the California tax revolt, the dollar benefits to the individual were substantial in absolute terms (e.g., the average southern California homeowner was likely to receive an annual savings of almost $2000 from the successful Proposition 13; Sears & Citrin, 1985). And support for that tax cut was quite specifically linked to indicators of such benefits. Similarly, support for the later proposed income tax cuts was closely related to the expected dollar return from them, rising to a considerable height (65%) among those expecting to save over $1000.

Another test of the role of large stakes is to experimentally vary them, as done in several studies by Green (1988). Greater proposed personal tax increases described as the likely cost of a particular policy proposal ($5 vs $50 annually) significantly diminished Californians' support for providing shelter for the homeless (from 86 to 75%) and for building a subway in Los Angeles (from 51 to 29%). Similarly positive findings emerged from experiments on cleaning up California's waterways and on a proposed increase in cigarette taxes (although not in experiments on support for bilingual education or an environmental bond issue; Green, 1988, p. 176).

Similarly, self-interest should have more powerful effects on policy preferences on issues that the individual regards as most important. Young, Borgida, Sullivan, & Aldrich (1987) found that respondents who said economic issues were highly important for both the country and themselves showed strong correlations of self-interest (personal and friends' employment problems, and government benefits received) with Reagan–Mondale voting in 1984 ($r = .36$, vs $+.11$ for the respondents to whom such issues had low importance).

So it appears that variations in the size of the stakes often tend to have a significant effect, at least when personal tax increases or reductions are direct, clear, and highly salient. And self-interest may emerge as a significant force only when the stakes are unusually high in an absolute sense.

B. INFORMATION ABOUT COSTS AND BENEFITS

Most rational choice theories assume that rationality depends on having adequate information. People with more information about the potential costs and benefits of a policy presumably can calculate and act on their interests better than the poorly informed. But three versions of this hypothesis should be distinguished (see Green & Gerken, 1989).

The *clarity* of costs and benefits may be a crucial factor. Green (1988) investigated attitudes toward a ballot proposition in California limiting rent control that was written in such confusing (and perhaps even deceptive) fashion that many mistakenly cast votes contrary to their real preferences. In this case, renters (the interested parties) were more likely to vote their own interests if correctly informed.

The *certainty* of costs and benefits may also be an important variable. In the California tax revolt case, the political remedy was certain. The dollar return to the individual was in effect written into the legislation, a constitutional amendment that would lock in a reduction in property assessments and a cap on tax rates. However, the personal costs and benefits of many other governmental policies are inherently ambiguous and uncertain; e.g., the likelihood of any affirmative action programs actually affecting one's own life, or that of a family member, is often quite uncertain.

Even if the stakes are objectively clear and certain, their *salience* may vary. The real stakes may not be salient because the individual may not be thinking about them when asked about his or her political preference. As a result, self-interest, like other personal constructs, should have more substantial effects on one's attitudes when it is chronically accessible and/or primed. In a study done by Young et al. (in press), self-interest was primed through hearing two men discussing money taken out of their paycheck for taxes. This produced a closer correlation between the listener's economic self-interest and policy preferences on another issue.

Political campaigns can, of course, make the personal stakes clearer, more certain, and more salient. Some of our cases of significant self-interest effects fit this pattern. In the California tax revolt, local newspapers ran preelection tables displaying the exact (and large) property or income tax reductions individual voters would be guaranteed to get. And, as already indicated, support for the propositions was directly related to the size of the anticipated reduction (Sears &

Citrin, 1985). Similarly, President Reagan's 1984 campaign to focus attention on the question of ''are you better off today than you were four years ago'' may have been partially responsible for the surge of self-interested voting for him.

Information about the stakes may often be greater in narrow interest groups. Businessmen's attitudes toward trade policy were influenced by self-interest in the study by Bauer *et al.* (1964). Similarly, Sudit (1988) found significant effects of all four of her measures of objective self-interest on medical students' attitudes toward national health insurance.

While all of this might seem to be consistent with rational choice theory, one should be somewhat cautious. In several cases self-interest had significant effects despite great uncertainty. The strongest self-interest effect on the busing issue occurred in Los Angeles when no specific busing plan had been agreed upon. Public employees opposed the tax revolt despite widely varying predictions about post-Proposition 13 layoffs. And no unreformed smoker really knows what total smoking deprivation is like. These issues allowed for the most threatening sorts of fantasies about one's own possible fate, helped along by the far-ranging rumors that gain circulation in a time of uncertainty and ignorance. In the busing case, for example, there was little real contact with and reality testing among most whites about blacks, and many lurid fantasies lurking just below the surface. The uncertainties and terrors of cigarette deprivation may seem less cosmic to readers who have never smoked, but perhaps not to those who are now or have in the past been heavy smokers. So we suspect respondents' estimates of the probability of very bad outcomes were exaggerated in these cases. Perhaps the devil we know does not motivate self-interest as much as the devil we imagine.

C. GENERAL POLITICAL INFORMATION

General political information is likely to contribute to developing more rational beliefs, and so another possible implication of rational choice models is that better informed individuals should be more influenced by self-interest. However, this hypothesis has failed in three studies. Sears *et al.* (1980) found that those above the median in general political information actually had *less* self-interested policy preferences in three of four issue areas, but, on average, the differences were trivial. Similarly, in our study of college students' attitudes about the novel, complex, and fast-changing set of government proposals about the draft, greater personal vulnerability to the draft actually was slightly more closely associated with *support* for the draft among the better informed (the variance accounted for was 11%, compared to 8% for the less informed; see Sears *et al.*, 1983). In our study of busing (Sears *et al.*, 1979), self-interest had no greater effect among the well educated than among the poorly educated.

It should also be noted that the contrary hypothesis has its supporters: one could argue that the poorly informed should be the more self-interested because they cannot look beyond the narrow confines of the family (Conover *et al.*, 1986, 1987; Weatherford, 1983). But these studies have found no more central a role for information. Personal finances, personal employment, and income change had only slightly (but nonsignificantly) greater impact on evaluations of government performance among the less informed in one case (Weatherford, 1983). Conover *et al.* (1986, 1987) found but one of eight such comparisons to be significant with respect to retrospective and prospective evaluations of national economic conditions.

D. FEAR VERSUS GREED

In several of the positive effects of self-interest cited earlier, feared negative outcomes appeared to be more salient than desired positive outcomes. Public employees fearing the loss of their jobs particularly opposed the tax revolts; self-interest sparked opposition to busing particularly when future busing plans were unclear but possibly massive; and threats of anti-smoking legislation were particularly likely to motivate opposition. To those might be added Bauer, Pool, and Dexter's (1964) findings that firms' interests in trade policy were more powerfully associated with their executives' policy attitudes and attempts to influence Congress when the firm's interest lay in protectionism and high tariffs (fear of foreign competition) than when it lay in free trade and low tariffs (desire for foreign exports).

These asymmetrical effects may reflect similar dynamics. In each case, high-stakes threats to personal well-being were present, combined with sufficient uncertainty about the exact nature of the threat to allow them to become exaggerated and distorted. While some readers might not feel that smoking deprivation is a major threat compared to public employees' possible loss of jobs, or white parents' fantasies about the fate of their children to be bused, they would perhaps be well advised not to make that observation to smokers (or even ex-smokers).

This parallels the now substantial laboratory evidence for asymmetrical responses to positive and negative events. Negative events seem to elicit stronger physiological responses, more strongly influence mood, focus attention more, influence judgment more powerfully, elicit more attributional activity, and lead to more social mobilization than do positive events (Taylor, 1991). So, too, the effort to avoid costs may motivate sociopolitical preferences more strongly than does the effort to accumulate gain. Of course in these cases there was no direct test of this contrast. And thorough testing of it in the case of taxpayer response to the tax revolt came to the opposite conclusion: those who stood to profit most (e.g., high-income homeowners) supported it more than those most vulnerable to loss (e.g., elderly low-income homeowners; see Sears & Citrin, 1985). So this hypothesis must remain speculative at this juncture.

E. ATTRIBUTIONS OF RESPONSIBILITY

The pocketbook voting hypothesis proposes that voters' support for incumbent candidates is based on how well they have fared during the period of that incumbency. But it requires another crucial assumption, that the incumbent be perceived as somehow responsible for those outcomes. A voter who has just been fired for drunkenness on the job cannot claim that as a rational basis for a vote against the incumbent president. So a common assumption is that self-interest will affect political preferences primarily when individuals attribute responsibility for their well-being to the government or to society at large, rather than to themselves.

At the aggregate level, congressional election outcomes are more closely correlated with changed economic conditions when one candidate is an incumbent (especially a long-term incumbent), as would be expected if voters were only punishing or rewarding those possibly responsible for the economic situation (Fiorina, 1983; Hibbing & Alford, 1981). On the other hand, Stein (1990) finds that pocketbook voting supported the incumbent-to-blame thesis for neither senators nor governors in 1982. Political issues also vary in whether or not their personal costs and benefits can unequivocally be attributed to government. Some can: successful tax-cutting propositions ensure that the government will cut taxes, and governments are clearly the cause of busing children to racially mixed schools. However, while tax cuts often do evoke strong self-interest effects, busing usually does not, as indicated earlier. And various other events usually attributed to government have not produced positive self-interest effects, such as inflation, the Reagan budget and tax cuts, or the 1982 recession (Conover *et al.*, 1986, 1987; Feldman, 1984; Kiewiet, 1983; Sears & Citrin, 1985; Sears & Lau, 1983).

But more appropriate tests of the attributional hypothesis again rely on individual-level data. Presidential approval has been shown to correlate with perceptions of presidential responsibility for economic conditions; e.g., President Reagan's performance ratings did not suffer particularly from the 1982 recession among those who blamed it on the predecessor Carter administration (Peffley & Williams, 1985).

Does self-interest indeed primarily affect political preferences in that subset of individuals who perceive government or society at large as responsible for their personal problems? Feldman (1982) found that perceived family finances affected political attitudes only among those who attributed trends in their own finances to societal, as opposed to personal, causes. Stein (1990) found that gubernatorial voting was influenced by perceived presidential responsibility for the state economy, while perceived gubernatorial responsibility for state economic problems had relatively little power over gubernatorial votes, consistent with his finding that governors are not generally held responsible for the state of the local economy. Other studies have variously supported the hypothesis

(Abramowitz, Lanoue, & Ramesh, 1988) or found nonsignificant differences in the predicted direction (Kinder & Mebane, 1983; Lau & Sears, 1981) or null findings (Sears *et al.*, 1980). The evidence seems mixed but mildly supportive on this point, then.

F. OTHER PERCEPTIONS AND VALUES

We might briefly mention four other plausible moderating variables that have so far turned out to be dry holes. Presumably, self-interest should influence those sociopolitical attitudes that are perceived as instrumental to the individual's own outcomes. Thus, its effects should be greatest when people believe their attitudes will influence government actions and thereby their own outcomes. However, we found that those above the medians on perceived government responsiveness and/or personal political efficacy did not exhibit stronger self-interest effects than did those below the medians (Sears *et al.*, 1980).

Some people value personal material gain more than others do, and so perhaps should exhibit stronger self-interest effects than others. Over several tests, materialistic values have sometimes generated more self-interested attitudes, but, just as often, less (see Green, 1988; Sears *et al.*, 1980). On the other hand, holding public-regarding values (valuing the outcomes of the collectivity more than the outcomes of the self) should generate less self-interested political preferences (Wilson & Banfield, 1964). One direct test of this hypothesis (Sears *et al.*, 1980) yielded no such differences, but should not be regarded as definitive. Other tests have been indirect, indexing public-regarding values with demographic variables such as social class and ethnicity; e.g., upper middle class Anglo-Saxon Protestants are assumed to be more public regarding, and working class ethnic Catholics, more private regarding (Wilson & Banfield, 1964; see also Bowman, Ippolito, & Levin, 1972; Lupsha, 1975). This seems to us an excessively crude test, since values, like self-interest, are quite imprecisely indexed by demographic variables.

G. SUMMARY

This brief excursion has dealt with several situational and dispositional conditions that have been thought to facilitate the self-interest motive. Self-interest is most potent when the issue provides large, clear, certain, and salient costs or benefits. At one point we semifacetiously pegged the price of a Californian's vote at around the value of a color television set, since support for state income tax cuts tipped over the 50% mark among those who would save $500 annually or more (Sears & Citrin, 1985). On the other hand, individual differences in general political information seem to have little effect one way or the other. That information about the specific interests at stake can help, while more general political information does not, is consistent with our general view that the occasional effects of self-interest occur under unusually facilitating conditions that are quite narrowly specific to the issue at hand.

There is some dispute about the role of attributions of responsibility for personal outcomes. The attributional hypothesis has taken on the status of an "almost ubiquitous" assumption in the literature on self-interest (Kiewiet & Rivers, 1984, p. 381). Yet the attribution of government responsibility sometimes fosters self-interest effects, and sometimes does not. In any case, these variables would seem at best necessary, but insufficient, conditions for the operation of self-interest.

Other values and dispositions have largely proved unsuccessful as moderators of self-interest effects. Perceived government responsiveness, political efficacy, materialistic values, and private-regarding values all have generally failed, even though they surface from quite plausible hypotheses. The very difficulties that self-interest faces in motivating important social and political attitudes, then, are indicated by the general failure to uncover powerful moderating variables specifying conditions for its emergence. Even the most plausibly facilitating conditions usually are inadequate to give it a major role.

VIII. Critiques of the Research

Challenging a hypothesis that is so often taken for granted inevitably generates some criticism. The most common critiques have concerned our conceptual definition of self-interest, especially regarding the role of group (as opposed to self-) interest, and our operationalization of it (see especially Bobo, 1983; Pettigrew, 1985; Sniderman & Tetlock, 1986a, 1986b).

A. CONCEPTUAL DEFINITION OF SELF-INTEREST

Perhaps the most common critique is that our definition of self-interest is too narrow, in three ways. First, it excludes nonmaterial interests. As indicated above, our definition was deliberately selected to align it with common usage. Excluding nonmaterial values does so, we believe. Ordinary people do not call each other "selfish" when they defend their own moral principles; e.g., a Shiite fundamentalist is not called "selfish" for opposing Western secular dress for women in his country.

Second, we exclude long-term self-interest. The view of such nineteenth century theorists as de Tocqueville was that political preferences are influenced by the individual's longer term sense of self-interest rather than merely by short-term self-interest. For example, a young woman's attitude toward social security taxes may be dictated by her anticipated needs for social security benefits in retirement as well as by concern about her current tax burden. Even symbolic predispositions could conceivably reflect long-term self-interest. A young business student may conclude that in the long run his interests will best be served by the Republican party, even though no partisan issues now affect his own well-being directly. Similarly, apparently disinterested sociotropic judgments could be based in long-term self-interest. People who perceive the Republicans as having presided over a period of great national prosperity may support Republican candidates because they think that a party that is good for the national economy will ultimately benefit them as well, whether or not they themselves have especially benefited from that prosperity.

We have excluded long-term self-interest for two reasons. In defining self-interest, we desired to generate a testable, falsifiable hypothesis. From a purely technical point of view, it is not obvious how one could obtain rigorous empirical tests of long-term self-interest, since it is extremely difficult to assess uncontaminated by other variables, given the rather projective quality of predicting into the distant mists of the future. But even if such methodological problems could be surmounted, we would still expect short-term self-interest to have a stronger political impact, since it is more proximal, emotionally evocative, and easier for the individual to calculate. In the one effort that we are aware of to make a direct empirical comparison between short-term and long-term self-interest, Lewis-Beck (1988, p. 121) found that voters' expectations about their financial prospects in the next year had a marginally significant effect on their 1984 presidential vote, whereas their expectations for 5 years hence had literally no effect. So there is currently no hard evidence that voters are more influenced by their long-term self-interest than by their short-term self-interest.

B. GROUP INTEREST

A third critique is that by focusing on egoistic concerns, and ignoring outcomes that affect the individual's group, we exclude the most potent forms of interest-maximizing behavior in public life. Politics is thought by many to revolve around group interests (see Conover, 1985; 1987). And even self-interest may be more potent if linked to one's group's interests. For example, individual whites' opposition to busing or affirmative action may be based more in their fears about threats to their group's racial hegemony than in racial threats to their personal well-being (Bobo, 1983, 1988; Pettigrew, 1985; Schuman, Steeh, & Bobo, 1985; Sniderman & Tetlock, 1986a).

1. Three Distinctions

To us, the issue is somewhat more complicated than that. Three key distinctions must be made to understand the relationship of group interest to self-interest
(also see Sears & Kinder, 1985). One is whether or not the relevant political
costs and benefits to the group also affect the self; that is, whether the self is
interdependent with the group. Voters may support the political positions of their
groups because they perceive their personal interests will be met if the group's
interests are (Campbell *et al.*, 1960). We might describe this as "self-oriented
group interest," because it intermixes group and self-interest. On the other hand,
an individual may support a policy because it benefits the group as a whole
irrespective of its impact on his or her own well-being. A successful black doctor
might support job training for unskilled workers because it would benefit blacks
as a whole, even though it would not affect her own well-being. Such "pure
group interest" is involved when individuals are motivated by the policy's impact on the group as a whole irrespective of its impact on their own well-being;
i.e., when self and group are not interdependent. This distinction, incidentally,
parallels that made by Sen (1977) about actions on behalf of others: they may be
motivated by egoistic costs and benefits, which he describes as "sympathy," or
by nonegoistic concerns, which he describes as "commitment," often motivated
by a sense of morality.

Second, group interest can be subdivided between "realistic group interest,"
involving real short-term material costs and benefits to the group, and "symbolic
group interest," which does not. The black doctor's support for job training may
be based in her expectation that it would provide material gains to young blacks.
On the other hand, postrevolutionary changes in national flags, such as in Eastern Europe in 1989 and 1990, tend to be more symbolic, and to draw support
because of affective responses to the relevant groups rather than from expectations of tangible, material gains for those groups.

Third, the interests of a particular group may or may not be in conflict with
those of another group. Most work on group interest has grown out of the
realistic group conflict hypothesis that people's own interests are mobilized when
their group is in competition with another group for scarce resources. A good
example is Bobo's (1983, 1988) theory that whites' opposition to racial policies
is based in their feeling that white hegemony (including their own personally
privileged position) is threatened by blacks' gains. In our terms, this adds the
further element of "perceived group conflict"; i.e., perceptions that the realistic
interests of blacks and whites are negatively interdependent, perhaps being in a
zero-sum game.

"Group interest," then, can take several forms which differ in consequential
ways: it may or may not involve outcomes to the self as well as to the group; it
may or may not involve realistic, material gains to the group; and it may or may
not involve competition with the interests of another group.

2. Self-Oriented Group Interest

Of these, self-oriented group interest is the most relevant to the self-interest hypothesis, since it involves outcomes to the self as well as to the group. The hypothesis would be that there is some added political clout to self-interest if it is mixed with group interest. But two still further variants of self-oriented group interest might be distinguished.

The self may be perceived as positively interdependent with the ingroup. For example, a racial majority's opposition to policies favoring minorities might be influenced by perceptions of material interdependence between the self and the majority ingroup. In one study, whites' perceived material interdependence with the ingroup (other whites) did contribute to their opposition to bilingual education (Huddy & Sears, 1989). However, in a second it proved irrelevant to their attitudes toward racial policies and Jesse Jackson (Jessor, 1988).

Second, the self may be perceived as negatively interdependent with a competitive outgroup. This was also tested in Jessor's (1988) two surveys of whites' attitudes. In this case, outgroup interdependence (the perception that one's own outcomes might be harmed by blacks' successes as a group in areas such as affirmative action) did correlate with opposition to racial policies and to Jesse Jackson. But when included in regressions with symbolic racism and affect toward blacks, it was uniformly nonsignificant. This suggests that perceived interdependence was symbolic rather than based in self-interest. These tests of self-oriented group interest have therefore yielded only limited support for it. However, in both cases there was strong evidence for the role of antiminority attitudes and other symbolic predispositions, consistent with the symbolic politics view.

There have also been some studies of what might appear to be "realistic group interest." The pocketbook politics hypothesis, testing whether voters reward and punish incumbents according to their own personal finances, has a group-level analog, in which their votes are influenced by perceptions of their own group's economic progress or decline. The findings have not been encouraging. Kinder, Adams, and Gronke (1989) found that such perceptions (by a number of groups) had no effects on the 1984 presidential vote, and Sears and Huddy (1990a) found that women's political attitudes were no more influenced than men's by perceptions that women's finances were declining. On the other hand, in Jessor's (1988) surveys, perceived intergroup conflict between whites and blacks did significantly increase whites' opposition to racial policies. However, none of these effects are relevant to "self-oriented group interest," and so do not really bear on the question of self-interest.

3. Fraternal Deprivation

A parallel contrast between self- and group-based motivations has been made with respect to relative deprivation (Runciman, 1966). Egoistic deprivation, the analog to self-interest, involves comparisons between one's own well-being and that of others. Fraternal deprivation, the analog to group interest, involves comparisons between the well-being of one's ingroup and that of other groups in society.

A considerable number of studies have found that fraternal deprivation has considerably more impact on sociopolitical attitudes than does egoistic deprivation. Pettigrew (1972; Vanneman & Pettigrew, 1972) found that fraternal deprivation (defined in either class or racial terms) had a considerable effect on anti-black racial attitudes, and on voting for the "white backlash" candidacies of George Wallace and white mayoral candidates. However, egoistic deprivation had little effect. Similarly, Guimond and Dubé-Simard (1983) found that fraternal, but not egoistic, deprivation contributed to Quebec nationalism. Crosby (1982, 1984) found that working women felt fraternal deprivation more acutely than they did egoistic deprivation: they felt that women in general were unfairly paid relative to men, but were just as satisfied with their own jobs as men (also see Taylor & Dubé, 1986). Gays' perceptions of discrimination against gays in general motivated militancy more than did their perceptions of being personally discriminated against (Birt & Dion, 1987). And fraternal deprivation significantly predicted protest orientation among unemployed workers in Australia, whereas egoistic deprivation did not (Walker & Mann, 1987).

The available research, then, suggests that "self-oriented" group interest is not especially more potent that ordinary self-interest. Perceived interdependence of the self with either the ingroup or the outgroup in racial conflicts does not generally influence racial attitudes. The evidence is more mixed on the role of pure group interest, dissociated from considerations of the self. The group analog of pocketbook politics has not so far been shown to have strong effects, but perceptions of intergroup conflict may. A number of studies have found that egoistic deprivation, like self-interest, has relatively little political clout. But concerns about the group's well-being—fraternal deprivation—may have a stronger influence on sociopolitical attitudes. Self-oriented or egoistic motives seem to be relatively weak, then, while group-oriented motives do have some greater strength. But it is not obvious that their strength depends on a linkage to the self.

C. OPERATIONALIZING SELF-INTEREST

There have also been three general critiques of our operational definitions of self-interest. One is that they are in some cases too broad, diluting self-interest by combining people with little interest along with the few genuinely interested parties. Clearly *not* having children in public schools would seem to exclude that source of self-interest in the busing issue, but merely having a child in public school would not by itself insure self-interest. The truly self-interested parents would need to have children directly vulnerable to the impact of busing. We have protected ourselves in most of these studies by examining both refining combinations of self-interest variables and interaction effects; e.g., whites who *both* have children in the public schools *and* live in a district with busing also fail to show unusually high levels of opposition to it (Sears *et al.*, 1979). Such refinements have rarely improved the case for self-interest.

A second critique is that our work has relied too heavily on objective measures of self-interest, and that subjectively perceived interests would give more predictive power (e.g., Bobo, 1983; Pettigrew, 1985). For example, subjective feelings of being threatened by the desegregation of one's neighborhood school may be more important than its objective desegregation. This is a quite reasonable point: subjective perceptions of objective conditions are indeed more proximal to the dependent variables in our causal models, and so should have more effect.

To be sure, over our entire research program, about two-thirds of the self-interest measures have been objective. But this reflects a deliberate methodological choice. Our concern has been about the reactivity of subjective self-interest measures, and the resulting threat to unequivocal causal interpretations. One danger comes from reverse-causality effects in which the dependent variable affects the index of self-interest. A concrete example comes from a study of medical students' self-interest in the national health insurance issue (Sudit, 1988). Opposition to national health insurance could easily influence such subjective self-interest measures as perceptions of whether it would affect the earnings of doctors. The dependent variable would seem less likely to influence such objective indicators of self-interest as the medical student's actual indebtedness at graduation. And indeed, subjective self-interest was correlated with opposition to national health insurance, while objective self-interest was not. A second danger is that subjective indicators of self-interest may be influenced by symbolic predispositions. For example, subjective perceptions of self-interest in the busing issue may be influenced by racial prejudice (McClendon, 1985).

However, in our research we have usually taken the precaution of using both objective and subjective measures of self-interest. And in fact the two have had very similar effects whenever parallel measures have been available. The objective fact of having children in the public schools in districts with busing did not increase whites' opposition to busing, but neither did the subjective probability of busing children in or out of the respondent's neighborhood schools (see Tables II and III). The objective proportion of Hispanics in one's county increased non-Hispanics' opposition to bilingual education as much as did subjective estimates of the proportion of Hispanics in the neighborhood (see Table IV). Objective personal tax obligations (homeownership) had about the same effect on support for the California tax revolt as did subjective feelings of tax burden (see Table V). Kiewiet (1983) actually found stronger effects of objective than of subjective measures of unemployment, contrary to expectation.

Part of the reason that their effects have been so similar in our research is that we have tried to make the subjective measures as unreactive as possible. Most important, we have tried to ensure that the subjective measures of self-interest have not simply been slightly altered versions of the dependent variable (e.g., not using items such as "do you think Proposition 13 will help or hurt your personal financial situation?"). We would suggest, then, that objective measures of self-interest are the more trustworthy, but that when nonreactive subjective measures are used, they prove to have about the same impact as do objective measures.[4]

A third criticism concerns our eschewing demographic variables, especially social class, as indicators of self-interest. Our view, to reiterate, is that they are generally too distal to measure self-interest precisely, being even more distal than the objective measures of personal impact just discussed. Beyond that, it might be noted, social class simply does not consistently have the effects predicted by a self-interest theory. Presumably high-income people should strongly support tax cuts. Yet in Sweden, income explained just over 1% of the variance in discontent with corporate and income taxes and none in general discontent with taxes. And social class had no residual effect with symbolic predispositions considered (Hadenius, 1986, pp. 31 and 118). Among American whites, social status has no overall relationship with support for government services and aid to the disadvantaged (jobs, health, and educational services). Nor does social class usually relate closely to attitudes on issues such as abortion, aid to minorities, or defense spending (Himmelstein & McRae, 1988). Indeed, the most marked aspect of upper stratum white Americans is not their self-serving economic conservatism but their partisan polarization (Shingles, 1989). In short, our abstention from the use of demographic variables as indicators of self-interest seems unlikely to have resulted in our ignoring strong self-interest effects.

D. GOVERNMENTALLY INDUCED VARIANCE

Finally, in critiquing the negative findings of pocketbook voting research, Kramer (1983) has contended that self-interest effects are relatively rare in cross-sectional survey studies precisely because government is in fact responsible for relatively little of the variance in individuals' material well-being, and such

---

[4]Where should the more proximal, reactive perceptions of subjective self-interest fit into our model, then? Del Boca (1982) suggests that quite reactive forms of subjective self-interest in the ERA, such as the perceived personal effects of a policy, could be treated as a cognitive component of the policy attitude itself rather than as self-interest. This resolution is methodologically conservative, but it may underestimate self-interest effects since it does not allow for the possibility that such perceived effects of a policy on the self do genuinely motivate preferences about it. However, we know of no sound way to extract a causal inference from such correlations.

studies are poorly equipped to distinguish governmentally induced changes from all others. The relatively small boost (or dampening) that government-induced macroeconomic changes give to individuals' personal finances may be swamped, in a cross-sectional study, by all the other sources of variance in them, and therefore not be revealed for the small but electorally decisive influence they truly represent.

Our response might be anticipated. First, some personal economic changes are unequivocally induced by government, such as the tax cuts in California's Proposition 13 or in Reagan tax and spending cuts; sometimes the political response is self-interested, but more often it is not. Second, we earlier reviewed research on attributions of responsibility for changes in personal well-being to government; they sometimes contribute to self-interest effects, but often do not help much. Third, people's perceptions of government-induced changes in their well-being have themselves been used as self-interest indicators. To test their effects, Lewis-Beck (1988, pp. 56 and 90) used a modification of the basic personal finances item that read, have "the government's policies" had a good or bad effect "with regard to the financial situation of your household?" This item turned out to have a slightly greater impact than did the apolitical version of personal finances, but was still generally nonsignificant. This critique, therefore, seems less to challenge the research than help to explain its outcomes: the assertion that individuals' well-being is not much influenced by government (and not all economists would agree) might help to explain why their attitudes are so rarely motivated very much by self-interest.

IX. Why Doesn't Self-Interest Usually Work?

If we accept the general finding that self-interest usually does not have a significant effect on Americans' social and political attitudes, why doesn't it? We offer four main explanations.

A. THE STAKES: USUALLY NOT LARGE, CLEAR, OR CERTAIN

One is that the personal stakes in most social and political issues are not usually large, clear, or certain to very many people. Ordinary people do not very often perceive government policy issues or candidate choices as having important personal costs and benefits. For example, the personal costs of unemployment may be intense, but they are concentrated in relatively small groups of people; only 3 or 4% cite unemployment as their most serious personal problem, according to Kiewiet (1983). Similarly, in the midst of a hotly contested campaign over the equal rights amendment, few women felt that it would much affect their own lives, and few (6 and 11% in two samples) explained their attitudes toward it in terms of those possible effects (Del Boca, 1982). At a time when affirmative action programs provoked great controversy, only 1% reported that they or someone in their family had been aided, and 7% had lost out in jobs or school admissions, because of affirmative action (CBS News/*New York Times*, 1977). In 1985, despite a much-publicized war on drugs, they were described as having created trouble in one's own family by only 9% (ABC News/*Washington Post*, 1985).

Frequently people do not perceive as serious problems issues that objectively should stimulate widespread self-interested revolt. An example is the curious phenomenon of public apathy about nuclear weapons. One might think humans would be united in vehement opposition to weapons that could eradicate all human civilization and indeed life on this planet. Yet researchers have consistently found very little public concern about them. For example, Schuman, Ludwig, and Krosnick (1986) found that in the early 1980s an average of only 6% cited nuclear war, or war in general, as the most important problem facing the nation (also see Fiske, 1987; Kramer *et al.,* 1983). The reason apparently was that most people saw it as impossible, or too far in the future to worry about.

The personal consequences of apparently horrendous macroeconomic changes are often unpredictable and even mixed. The personal costs of inflation, which officeholders treat as if it were the bubonic plague, are particularly difficult to establish. Prices go up, but for many, wages and/or the value of their real property go up much more, so short-term losses may be overshadowed by longer term gains.

The California tax revolt was a clear exception. As indicated earlier, the stakes were generally quite large; the property tax savings were likely to average almost $2000/year to southern California homeowners and about two-thirds of the adult population in California owned their own homes (Sears & Citrin, 1985, p. 118). Media coverage of these personal gains was extensive and concrete, making these gains quite salient. Implementation was assured if the voters supported Proposition 13 because it was a constitutional amendment with quite specific language about tax rate caps and assessment rollbacks. But these large, clear, and certain stakes were the exceptional case.

B. THE BIAS TOWARD INTERNAL ATTRIBUTIONS

External attributions (to government or society at large) for one's personal well-being seem on occasion to be crucial preconditions for self-interest effects. That represents yet another difficult hurdle for self-interest. Several researchers have observed a general genuine bias toward making internal attributions for one's own outcomes, whether described as "the illusion of control" (Langer, 1975), "the ethic of self-reliance" (Sniderman & Brody, 1977), or a "belief in a just world" in which people get the outcomes they deserve (Lerner, 1965). Moreover, Americans value this sense of internal control. Experimental subjects like people who believe human behavior is caused by internal causes better than those who believe it is caused by external causes; they themselves claim to believe in internal control more than the "average person" does; and when trying to ingratiate themselves with others, they bias their own self-presentation in the direction of claiming a belief in internal control (Jellison & Green, 1981).

This pervasive bias toward internal control should work against attributing one's own outcomes to broader collectivities. Indeed, empirically, people do seem only rarely to see society or government as responsible for either their present personal financial well-being or its future prospects (Feldman, 1982; Kinder & Mebane, 1983). The unemployed tend to perceive their unemployment as caused by individual, proximal circumstances, rather than seeing government or the society at large as responsible (Schlozman & Verba, 1979). This bias toward internality is, not surprisingly, stronger for positive than for negative outcomes; for example, in a national survey, only 1% of those whose economic situation had improved gave a societal attribution, whereas almost half did of those whose situation had worsened (Feldman, 1982; also see Ross & Sicoly, 1979). But even among those in worse positions, a majority did not blame society or government. Nor do people often feel that government should help them solve their personal economic problems (Brody & Sniderman, 1977).

This bias toward a sense of internal control might well be highly adaptive in some areas of life, especially in coping with illness, accidents, and traumas such as rape, as Taylor and Brown (1988) have argued. For example, it is probably useful for personal mental health that people display unrealistic optimism and exaggerated perceptions of mastery with respect to crime, accidents, and illness (Perloff & Fetzer, 1986; Weinstein, 1989). It may even have some societal advantage by lessening individuals' absorption with their own particularistic needs at the expense of the community. On the other hand, obstacles to the operation of self-interest in the political thinking of the general public can lead to problems of pluralistic ignorance and false consciousness, and therefore exploitation.

C. REFLEXIVE AFFECTIVE RESPONSES
TO POLITICAL SYMBOLS

At a number of points we have indicated that symbolic predispositions usually have considerably greater strength than does self-interest in determining policy and candidate preferences. This has held despite the use of rather conservative tests of their effects, generally using only party identification, political ideology, and/or racial intolerance as symbolic predispositions, often measured with but a single item. In one case, we did make a strenuous effort to milk these symbolic predispositions for every last jot of predictability, and we believe it represents a good example of what could be done more generally with more thorough measurement: Sears *et al.* (1979) report that an equation combining two symbolic predispositions (racial intolerance and ideology, both strongly significant) with self-interest and demographics (all with weak effects) accounted for a healthy 29.1% of the variance in whites' opposition to busing. Moreover, individuals with more information, who should therefore have more "rational" preferences, are even more influenced by symbolic predispositions than by self-interest. In most studies, symbolic predispositions have had far stronger effects among the well informed and/or well educated than among the poorly informed and/or poorly educated, while the effects of self-interest have not been enhanced by greater information (e.g., Sears *et al.*, 1979, 1980, 1983).

Why do symbolic predispositions have such strong effects? According to a symbolic politics theory, political attitudes reflect the affects previously conditioned to the specific symbols included in the attitude object. In its simplest form, it suggests that affects are tied quite closely to the manifest symbolic content of a particular attitude object, without detailed consideration of underlying or latent meanings (see Sears & Huddy, 1990b; Sears, Huddy, & Schaffer, 1986).

This then places a premium on cognitively simple symbols that are affectively evocative. And the external informational environment promotes this process of simplification, as indicated earlier. Politicians and journalists constantly condense the complexity of the political world into simplified symbolic terms. In contrast, individuals' personal experiences are perhaps too close at hand, complex, and individuated, to lend themselves to easy generalization; they are "morselized" and difficult to trigger by political symbols. In other words, the world of public affairs is coded to trigger symbolic predispositions, while the world of private life is not.

If political dialogue is coded into abstract, symbolic terms, while personal experience is morselized, attitudes toward the two should tend to be cognitively compartmentalized. And there is substantial evidence that judgments about one's personal well-being usually are quite independent of those made about group or national well-being even when they concern the same general domain of life. For example, perceived personal finances correlate only weakly with perceived trends in national business conditions (Kinder & Kiewiet, 1979), and studies of the unemployed (Schlozman & Verba, 1979) and of working women (Crosby, 1984) show that they compartmentalize personal and group well-being. This even held for men's attitudes about working women: "men . . . kept their sociopolitical attitudes separate from their personal lives. . . . dissociation of personal and public lives was not limited only to people who are, themselves, victims'' (Crosby & Herek, 1986, p. 64).

Attitudes about these two cognitive domains, personal experience and the public arena, can be accessed separately by appropriate framing of political issues, as Iyengar (1987, 1990) has shown in several experiments. Framing an issue in terms of societal conditions or national problems tends to produce attributions that place responsibility (for either problem or solution) on government or society at large, while framing it in terms of individual cases yields internal attributions. The same point is made by correlational data: personal experience with crime influenced judgments of personal vulnerability to it but not base-rate judgments of the general crime rate, which tend to be influenced more by mass media information on crime (Tyler, 1980). Similarly, Tyler and Cook (1984) found that exposure to base-rate information on risk of death due to firearms or drunk driving influenced perceptions of these problems' societal seriousness but did not change judgments of personal risk.

These findings lend support to the notion that people are slow to draw societal-level implications from personal-level information, and vice versa; the two seem to be cognitively compartmentalized. Our considerable discussion of the narrowness of even significant self-interest effects, other than those of taxpayers, makes the same point. Insofar as people do connect private interests to public life, it is done in a highly specific, morselized way; no general belief systems connect the two, and personal experience rarely gets related to more general societal or political symbols.

In short, the dominance of symbolic predispositions may come about because of a general tendency toward reflexive affective responses to political symbols. Political symbols may come semantically coded in ways that make them easy to link to symbolic predispositions, but difficult to connect to the blooming and buzzing confusion that is our daily personal experience. The two realms tend to be cognitively compartmentalized.

D. PUBLIC REGARDINGNESS

One possible reason for this compartmentalization is that most people may be politically socialized to respond to public issues in a principled and public-regarding manner. Even proponents of the rational choice perspective acknowledge this possibility: ''In reality, men are not always selfish, even in politics. They frequently do what appears to be individually irrational because they believe it is socially rational—i.e., it benefits others even though it harms them personally'' (Downs, 1957, p. 27). People may have been taught to weigh most heavily the collective good when they don their ''political hats,'' and to weigh their private good most heavily only when dealing with their personal affairs (Sears *et al.*, 1980). Indeed, some have taken public regardingness as the major alternative to self-interest. If "a vote . . . [that is] . . . incompatible with a certain voter's self-interest narrowly conceived . . . was not in some sense irrational or accidental, then it must be presumed that his action was based on some conception of 'the public interest' " (Wilson & Banfield, 1964, p. 876). If so, symbolic or sociotropic attitudes might express the adult's sense of the public good, and would be quite deliberately and self-consciously given more weight than private considerations in judgments about public policy.

This does not necessarily imply that the public-regarding view in question is a particularly noble one. One may support genocide in order to prevent the "mongrelization of the race," or oppose welfare because it simply rewards sloth. Nor would it necessarily rule out all forms of self-interest; e.g., de Tocqueville felt that personal and national interests converged in "enlightened self-interest." In any event, too little is known at the present time about the ordinary individuals' values in this respect; e.g., the extent to which they feel that self-interest is a legitimate basis for forming attitudes about social and political issues, and if so, under what conditions.[5]

X. Conclusions

To summarize, we have reviewed a large number of studies examining the effects of ordinary citizens' short-term material self-interest on their sociopolitical attitudes. We have examined attitudes toward racial policies and black candidates, economic policy issues, pocketbook voting, and attitudes toward political violence. The conclusion is quite clear: self-interest ordinarily does not have much effect upon the ordinary citizen's sociopolitical attitudes. There are only occasional exceptions, as when there are quite substantial and clear stakes (especially regarding personal tax burdens) or ambiguous and dangerous threats. Moreover, self-interest effects generally turn out not only to be rather small in absolute terms, or unreliable, but also, when present, to be quite specific to the policies most narrowly linked to the self-interest dimension in question. The effects of self-interest usually extend neither to other related policy issues nor to more general policy or ideological questions. The general public seems to think about most political issues, most of the time, in a disinterested frame of mind.

[5]One positive finding has been reported by Del Boca (1982, p. 63) concerning women and the ERA. Del Boca asked them if they regarded personal self-interest as a legitimate political motive. Among those who did, objective self-interest had a strong effect ($r = .38$), but it did not among those who did not ($r = .17$).

We have offered four main explanations for these weak effects: the individual's personal stakes in matters of public policy are rarely large, clear, and certain; they usually make internal attributions for their own personal outcomes; the world of personal experience is not cognitively coded in terms that relate easily to the abstractions and generalities of public life; and citizens may be socialized to a norm of public regardingness about policy issues affecting the broader community.

These conclusions complement other recent challenges to the assumptions of neoclassical economics about human nature (e.g., Etzioni, 1988; Hogarth & Reder, 1987; Lynn & Oldenquist, 1986; Mansbridge, 1990; Simon, 1985). The present article extends the challenge to a central element in society's mechanisms for resolving conflicts of interest, the ordinary individual's preferences about societal allocation of resources. Its primary focus, then, is on some of the phenomena about which that assumptive framework has some of its most provocative and consequential things to say.

If the data are as conclusive as we have suggested, why is the belief in the central political role of self-interest so pervasive? Our primary answer is that it persists because it is congruent with the dominant theories of human behavior, values, and social and economic structures of Western society. The focus upon the individual as self-oriented maximizer begun by Thomas Hobbes, and promoted further by Adam Smith and the utilitarians, continues to be a central theory in Western intellectual history. And it is consistent with reinforcement theory, perhaps the dominant psychological theory of this century; people are thought to pursue goals that they have basic and material incentives for pursuing.

The self-interest hypothesis is also congruent with the most fundamental of American values—individualism. Americans' belief that a political and economic system in which each individual pursues his own interests assures both freedom and equal opportunity. Privileging the collective interest of the community, rather than the individual's interest, is an ideal common in conservative political movements in Europe and in the cultural teaching of the Catholic Church. But that is not the dominant value in America, a fact much lamented in the wake of the "Reagan Revolution," decried as selfishly oriented (see Bellah, Madsen, Sullivan, Swidler, & Tipton, 1985; Etzioni, 1988; Mansbridge, 1990; Reich, 1988; Sandel, 1982).

Self-interest is central to the structure of the American economic and political systems as well. The economic system is founded on an Adam Smith version of the self-interest hypothesis: that the individual and the collectivity both prosper most if each individual pursues his or her own interest. And the Federalists argued that the fundamental basis for the American constitutional system—the "checks and balances" of tripartite government—were required to prevent any one of the many competing interests from prevailing. Indeed, it is likely that the political thinking of the ordinary person is not very salient in intellectuals' assessment of political motivation. More visible, doubtless, are the self-interested attempts of interest groups such as labor unions or manufacturers' associations to influence public policy.

Finally, perhaps, a belief in the ubiquity of the self-interest motive is especially appealing to certain kinds of people. Some people pride themselves on a cynical, selfish account of human behavior, whereas others are drawn to a generous, altruistic portrait. The hard-bitten, tough-minded, individual does not want to be taken advantage of, believes that everyone is trying to, and that it is a jungle out there. Aficionados of the political scene, such as journalists and political scientists, may often be drawn to such professions because of the allure of this cynical realism. At the other extreme, people drawn to the clergy or to clinical psychology may be more likely to believe in the inherent goodness and generosity of others, and may manifest a tender-minded and naive idealism. But accounts of political behavior tend to be written by journalists and political scientists, not the clergy or clinical psychologists.

If the public is in reality not driven strongly by self-interest, why are politicians apparently so afraid of it? We do not doubt for a minute that they are. A good example is their timidity today about the ''T word.'' We have two general observations here. One is that interest groups no doubt do respond quite intensely to the interests of their organizations. Threatened cuts in social security cost of living adjustment (COLA) payments arouse the wrath of the American Association of Retired Persons (AARP), and threats of gun control measures arouse the ire of the National Rifle Association (NRA). They may also arouse the passions of the ordinary citizens who are members of these groups, such as retirees who depend on social security or gun owners. But much more obscure policies may stimulate intense interest from such groups as medical associations or tobacco growers or shoe manufacturers without making much of a splash in the ordinary public.

Even if the citizenry is largely oblivious to these debates, their potential political costs and benefits to officeholders can be considerable. Interest groups control most campaign contributions. And their reactions to candidates' policy positions may have important indirect impacts on the ordinary voter's opinions. Perhaps incumbents prefer not to offend interest groups not so much for fear of antagonizing a self-interested general public as simply to let sleeping dogs lie. Opposing an interest group may make it squeal bloody murder, and that protest may in turn reach the voters in a more diffuse but quite damaging form, as some nasty mess associated with the incumbent. That can swing votes even without touching on the voters' sense of their own self-interests.

In closing, we should not be taken to claim that self-interest is never important in politics and society. We have five particular cautions in this regard. First, the personal stakes for the ordinary citizen are not always as minor, unclear, and uncertain as they are in most national and even statewide controversies. For example, as Converse (1975) and Green (1988) have suggested, self-interest may well operate more strongly on local "doorstep" issues, such as the "NIMBY" (not in my back yard) resistance to threatening local projects, such as prison "live-out" programs or public housing projects (Rothbart, 1973). Unfortunately, exploration of such issues is not as glamorous as matters of war and peace, presidential elections, or the control of Congress, and so research on them, to the extent that it is done at all, tends to be relegated to the less prestigeful academic venues and outlets.

Elites' interests may motivate their attitudes more than do the ordinary person's. Our focus has been on mass sociopolitical attitudes, but elites' goals may be more affected by social and political policy. For example, Bauer, Pool, and Dexter (1964) found businessmen's attitudes toward trade policy significantly influenced by their firms' "objective" (according to a panel of economists' ratings) interests (though not very much by their own subjective perceptions of their firms' interests).

Egoistically-based group interest (interdependence between self and group outcomes, in Jessor's 1988, terms, or "sympathy," in Sen's, 1977) may be more potent than pure self-interest. This is not the place to add to the earlier discussion of this point. But the caution offered by Bauer *et al.* (1964) regarding businessmen's alleged hard-headed self-interestedness is useful: is it really *self*-interest to advocate a trade policy favorable to one's firm? Whose interests are really at stake: the individual executive himself? Probably not very greatly. Management as a team? The firm's bottom line? The stockholder? The entire entity? It would seem most likely that the executive's primary goal is the well-being of the firm, with a secondary spillover onto his own financial well-being (though perhaps much more on his reputation and self-esteem). This would cast it more as a problem of group interest and of nonmaterial interests than of pure material self-interest.

Attention and *behavior* may conceivably be more readily influenced by self-interest than are attitudes themselves. We have discussed the formation of issue-publics around self-interest. And there is evidence of greater influence over political behavior; e.g., Green and Cowden (1990) find strong self-interest effects on Bostonians' participation in antibusing organizations, and Bauer *et al.* (1964), in businessmen's communicating with Congress about trade policy, both contrasting with relatively weak effects of self-interest on attitudes toward those same issues.

But a final caution is in order here. The idea of self-interest as a central motivator of human behavior has been at the core of Western thought for over three centuries (Hirschmann, 1977; Mansbridge, 1990a). It is an idea taken so for granted by so many that data seem almost irrelevant, or, if nonconfirmatory, wrong. The empirical evidence is now extensive on its quite modest role in forming sociopolitical attitudes in mass publics, but only fragmentary on these latter claims of more extensive effect. One should perhaps be cautious in too quickly accepting its "obvious" importance in these other contacts.

Acknowledgments

Earlier versions of this argument were presented at the 1981 annual meeting of the American Psychological Association in Montreal, Canada (Sears, 1980), and in brief summary form elsewhere (Sears & Funk, 1990a, 1990b). This chapter was prepared while David O. Sears was a John Simon Guggenheim Fellow and a fellow at the Center for Advanced Study in the Behavioral Sciences, Stanford, California. Both authors wish to express their profound appreciation to the staff at the center for their generous help with this project, and are grateful for financial support provided by National Science Foundation grant number BNS87-00864. We wish to express our thanks to Jane Mansbridge and the University of Chicago Press for their permission to use some of the same material here.

References

ABC News/*Washington Post* (1985). *Drugs, alcohol trouble millions of families. Reagan Survives Bitburg.* New York: ABC News Polling Unit.

Abelson, R. P. (1988). Conviction. *American Psychologist, 43,* 267–275.

Aberbach, J. D. (1990). Relations between organizations: Institutions, self-interest, and congressional oversight behavior in the United States. In J. J. Jackson (Ed.), *Institutions in American society* (pp. 135–161). Ann Arbor, MI: University of Michigan Press.

Abramowitz, A. I., Lanoue, D. J., & Ramesh, S. (1988). Economic conditions, causal attributions, and political evaluations in the 1984 presidential elections. *Journal of Politics, 50,* 848–863.

Abramowitz, A. I., & Segal, J. A. (1986). Determinants of the outcomes of U.S. Senate elections. *Journal of Politics, 48,* 433–439.

Ajzen, I., & Fishbein, M. (1980). *Understanding attitudes and predicting behavior.* Englewood Cliffs, NJ: Prentice-Hall.

Alford, R. R. (1963). *Party and society: The Anglo-American democracies.* Chicago: Rand McNally.

Allen, H. M., Jr., & Sears, D. O. (1979). Against them or for me: Community impact evaluations. In L. Datta & R. Perloff (Eds.), *Improving evaluations* (pp. 171–175). Beverly Hills, CA: Sage.

Alwin, D. F., & Krosnick, J. A. (1988). *Aging, cohorts, and change in political orientation: Exploring the aging–attitude stability relationship.* Paper presented at the annual meeting of the International Society of Political Psychology, Secaucus, NJ.

Apsler, R., & Sears, D. O. (1968). Warning, personal involvement, and attitude change. *Journal of Personality and Social Psychology, 9,* 162–166.

Bargh, J. A. (1982). Attention and automaticity in the processing of self-relevant information. *Journal of Personality and Social Psychology, 43,* 425–436.

Bargh, J. A. (1988). Automatic information processing: Implications for communication and affect. In L. Donohew, H. E. Sypher, & E. T. Higgins (Eds.), *Communication, social cognition, and affect* (pp. 9–32). Hillsdale, NJ: Erlbaum.

Bargh, J. A. (1989). Conditional automaticity: Varieties of automatic influence in social perception and cognition. In J. S. Uleman & J. A. Bargh (Eds.), *Unintended thought* (pp. 3–51). New York: Guilford.

Bargh, J. A., Lombardi, W. J., & Higgins, E. T. (1988). Automaticity of chronically accessible constructs in person × situation effects on person perception: It's just a matter of time. *Journal of Personality and Social Psychology, 55,* 599–605.

Barnes, S. H., Farah, B. G., & Heunks, F. (1979). Personal dissatisfaction. In S. H. Barnes & M. Kaase (Eds.), *Political action: Mass participation in five Western democracies* (pp. 381–407). Beverly Hills, CA: Sage.

Barry, B. (1965). *Political argument.* New York: Humanities Press.

Bauer, R. A., de Sola Pool, I., & Dexter, L. A. (1963). *American business and public policy.* New York: Atherton.

Beck, P. A., & Dye, T. R. (1982). Sources of public opinion on taxes: The Florida case. *Journal of Politics, 44,* 172–182.

Beck, P. A., Rainey, H. G., & Traut, C. (1990). Disadvantage, disaffection, and race as divergent bases for citizen fiscal policy preferences. *Journal of Politics, 52,* 71–93.

Beer, F. A., Healy, A. F., Sinclair, G. P., & Bourne, L. E., Jr. (1987). War cues and foreign policy acts. *American Political Science Review, 81,* 701–715.

Bellah, R. N., Madsen, R., Sullivan, W. M., Swidler, A., & Tipton, S. M. (1985). *Habits of the heart.* Berkeley, CA: University of California Press.

Bem, D. J., & McConnell, H. K. (1970). Testing the self-perception explanation of dissonance phenomena: On the salience of premanipulation attitudes. *Journal of Personality and Social Psychology, 14,* 23–31.

Berelson, B. R., Lazarsfeld, P. F., & McPhee, W. N. (1954). *Voting: A study of opinion formation in a presidential campaign.* Chicago: University of Chicago Press.

Berscheid, E., Graziano, W., Monson, T., & Dermer, M. (1976). Outcome dependency: Attention, attribution, and attraction. *Journal of Personality and Social Psychology, 34,* 978–989.

Birt, C. M., & Dion, K. L. (1987). Relative deprivation theory and responses to discrimination in a gay male and lesbian sample. *British Journal of Social Psychology, 26,* 139–145.

Bobo, L. (1983). Whites' opposition to busing: Symbolic racism or realistic group conflict? *Journal of Personality and Social Psychology, 45,* 1196–1210.

Bobo, L. (1988). Group conflict, prejudice, and the paradox of contemporary racial attitudes. In P. Katz & D. Taylor (Eds.), *Eliminating racism: Profiles in controversy.* New York: Plenum.

Borgida, E., & Howard-Pitney, B. (1983). Personal involvement and the robustness of perceptual salience effects. *Journal of Personality and Social Psychology, 45,* 560–570.

Bowman, L., Ippolito, D. S., & Levin, M. L. (1972). Self-interest and referendum support: The case of a rapid transit vote in Atlanta. In H. Hahn (Ed.), *Urban affairs annual review* (pp. 119–136). Beverly Hills, CA: Sage.

Brody, R. A., & Sniderman, P. M. (1977). From life space to polling place: The relevance of personal concerns for voting behavior. *British Journal of Political Science, 7,* 337–360.

Caditz, J. (1976). *White liberals in transition.* New York: Spectrum.

Caldeira, G. A., & Wright, J. R. (1988). Organized interests and agenda setting in the U.S. Supreme Court. *American Political Science Review, 82*; 1109–1127.

Campbell, A., Converse, P. E., Miller, W. E., & Stokes, D. E. (1960). *The American voter.* New York: Wiley.

Campbell, D. T. (1975). On the conflicts between biological and social evolution and between psychology and moral tradition. *American Psychologist, 30,* 1103–1126.

Cataldo, E. F., & Holm, J. D. (1983). Voting on school finances: A test of competing theories. *Western Political Quarterly, 36,* 619–631.

CBS News/*New York Times* (1977, October). Poll press release.

Cheng, P. W., & Novick, L. R. (1990). A probabilistic contrast model of causal induction. *Journal of Personality and Social Psychology, 58,* 545–567.

Chubb, J. E. (1988). Institutions, the economy, and the dynamics of state elections. *American Political Science Review, 82,* 133–154.

Citrin, J., & Green, D. P. (1990). The self-interest motive in American public opinion. In S. Long (Ed.), *Research in micropolitics* (Vol. 3, pp. 1–28). Greenwich, CT: JAI Press.

Collins, R. L., Taylor, S. E., Wood, J. V., & Thompson, S. C. (1988). The vividness effect: Elusive or illusory? *Journal of Experimental Social Psychology,* **24,** 1–18.

Conover, P. J. (1985). The impact of group economic interests on political evaluations. *American Politics Quarterly,* **13,** 139–166.

Conover, P. J. (1987). *Approaches to the political study of social groups: Measures of group identification and group affect.* Paper prepared for the National Election Studies Conference on Groups and American Politics, Stanford, CA.

Conover, P. J., Feldman, S., & Knight, K. (1986). Judging inflation and unemployment: The origins of retrospective evaluations. *Journal of Politics,* **48,** 565–588.

Conover, P. J., Feldman, S., & Knight, K. (1987). The personal and political underpinnings of economic forecasts. *American Journal of Political Science,* **31,** 559–583.

Converse, P. E. (1964). The nature of belief systems in mass publics. In D. E. Apter (Ed.), *Ideology and discontent* (pp. 206–261). New York: Free Press of Glencoe.

Converse, P. E. (1975). Public opinion and voting behavior. In F. I. Greenstein & N. W. Polsby (Eds.), *Handbook of political science* (Vol. 4, pp. 75–170). Reading, MA: Addison-Wesley.

Converse, P. E., & Markus, G. B. (1979). Plus ça change· . . .: The new CPS election study panel. *American Political Science Review,* **73,** 32–49.

Coughlin, R. M. (1986). Understanding (and misunderstanding) social security: A behavioral perspective on public policy. In S. Kaish and B. Gilad (Eds.), *Handbook of Behavioral Economics, Vol. B.* Greenwich, CT: JAI Press.

Coughlin, R. M. (1989). Spheres of self-interest: Economic man in sociological context. Paper presented at the Conference on Socioeconomics, Harvard University, Cambridge, MA.

Courant, P., Gramlich, E., & Rubinfeld, D. (1980). Why voters support tax limitation amendments: The Michigan case. *National Tax Journal,* **33,** 1–22.

Crosby, F. J. (1982). *Relative deprivation and working women.* New York: Cambridge University Press.

Crosby, F. J. (1984). The denial of personal discrimination. *American Behavioral Scientist,* **27,** 371–386.

Crosby, F. J., & Herek, G. M. (1986). Male sympathy with the situation of women: Does personal experience make a difference? *Journal of Social Issues,* **42,** 55–66.

Dawes, R. (1988). *Rational choice in an uncertain world.* San Diego, CA: Harcourt Brace Jovanovich.

Del Boca, F. (1982). *A test of three explanations of attitudes toward public policy concerning sexual equality: Self-interest, prejudice against women, and symbolic sexism.* Unpublished doctoral dissertation, Rutgers University, New Brunswick, NJ.

Downs, A. (1957). *An economic theory of democracy.* New York: Harper & Row.

Easton, D., & Dennis, J. (1969). *Children in the political system: Origins of political legitimacy.* New York: McGraw-Hill.

Edwards, W. (1954). The theory of decision-making. *Psychological Bulletin,* **51,** 380–417.

Erber, R., & Fiske, S. T. (1984). Outcome dependency and attention to inconsistent information. *Journal of Personality and Social Psychology,* **47,** 709–726.

Erikson, R. S. (1990). Economic conditions and the congressional vote: A review of the macrolevel evidence. *American Journal of Political Science,* **34,** 373–399.

Etzioni, A. (1988). *The moral dimension: Toward a new economics.* New York: Free Press.

Fazio, R. H. (1989). On the power and functionality of attitudes: The role of attitude accessibility. In A. R. Pratkanis, S. J. Breckler, & A. G. Greenwald (Eds.), *Attitude structure and function* (pp. 153–179). Hillsdale, NJ: Erlbaum.

Fazio, R. H., & Zanna, M. P. (1981). Direct experience and attitude–behavior consistency. In L.

Berkowitz (Ed.), *Advances in experimental social psychology* (Vol. 14). New York: Academic Press.

Feather, N. T. (Ed.). (1982). *Expectations and actions: Expectancy–value models in psychology.* Hillsdale, NJ: Erlbaum.

Feldman, S. (1982). Economic self-interest and political behavior. *American Journal of Political Science,* **26,** 446–466.

Feldman, S. (1984). Economic self-interest and the vote: Evidence and meaning. *Political Behavior,* **6,** 229–252.

Feldman, S. (1988). Structure and consistency in public opinion: The role of core beliefs and values. *American Journal of Political Science,* **32,** 416–440.

Fiorina, M. P. (1983). Who is held responsible? Further evidence on the Hibbing–Alford thesis. *American Journal of Political Science,* **27,** 158–164.

Fischhoff, B. (1975). Hindsight is not equal to foresight: The effects of outcome knowledge on judgment under uncertainty. *Journal of Experimental Psychology: Human Perception and Performance,* **1,** 288–299.

Fiske, S. T. (1987). People's reactions to nuclear war: Implications for psychologists. *American Psychologist,* **42,** 207–217.

Frank, R. H. (1988). *Passions within reason: The strategic role of the emotions.* New York: W. W. Norton.

Franklin, C. H., & Kosaki, L. C. (1989). Republican schoolmaster: The U.S. Supreme Court, public opinion, and abortion. *American Political Science Review,* **83,** 751–771.

Frohlich, N. (1974). Self-interest or altruism, what difference? *Journal of Conflict Resolution,* **18,** 55–73.

Gallup Report (1985, June). *Large majority favors handgun registration* (pp. 15–19).

Gatlin, D. S., Giles, M., & Cataldo, E. F. (1978). Policy support within a target group: The case of school desegregation. *American Political Science Review,* **72,** 985–995.

Giles, M. W., & Gatlin, D. S. (1980). Mass-level compliance with public policy: The case of school desegregation. *Journal of Politics,* **42,** 722–746.

Goethals, G. R., & Reckman, R. F. (1973). The perception of consistency in attitudes. *Journal of Experimental Social Psychology,* **9,** 491–501.

Green, D. P. (1988). *Self-interest, public opinion, and mass political behavior.* Unpublished doctoral dissertation, Department of Political Science, University of California, Berkeley.

Green, D. P., & Cowden, J. A. (1990). *Who protests: Self-interest and white opposition to busing.* Unpublished manuscript, Yale University, New Haven, CT.

Green, D. P., & Gerken, A. E. (1989). Self-interest and public opinion toward smoking restrictions and cigarette taxes. *Public Opinion Quarterly,* **53,** 1–16.

Greenwald, A. G. (1980). The totalitarian ego: Fabrication and revision of personal history. *American Psychologist,* **35,** 603–618.

Greenwald, A. G. (1982). Ego task analysis: An integration of research on ego-involvement and self-awareness. In A. Hastorf & A. M. Isen (Eds.), *Cognitive social psychology* (pp. 109–147). New York: Elsevier/North-Holland.

Guimond, S., & Dubé-Simard, L. (1983). Relative deprivation theory and the Quebec nationalist movement: The cognition–emotion distinction and the personal-group deprivation issue. *Journal of Personality and Social Psychology,* **44,** 526–535.

Gusfield, J. R. (1963). *Symbolic crusade.* Urbana, IL: University of Illinois Press.

Hadenius, A. (1986). *A crisis of the welfare state?: Opinions about taxes and public expenditure in Sweden.* Stockholm, Sweden: Almqvist & Wiksell.

Hamilton, R. F. (1972). *Class and politics in the United States.* New York: Wiley.

Harkness, A. R., DeBono, K. G., & Borgida, E. (1985). Personal involvement and strategies for making contingency judgments: A stake in the dating game makes a difference. *Journal of Personality and Social Psychology,* **49,** 22–32.

Hawthorne, M. R., & Jackson, J. E. (1987). The individual political economy of federal tax policy. *American Political Science Review*, **81**, 757–774.

Herek, G. M. (1986). The instrumentality of attitudes: Toward a neofunctional theory. *Journal of Social Issues*, **42**, 99–114.

Hewstone, M., & Brown, R. (1986). Contact is not enough: An intergroup perspective on the 'contact hypothesis.' In M. Hewstone & R. Brown (Eds.), *Contact and conflict in intergroup encounters* (pp. 1–44). Oxford, England: Blackwell.

Hibbing, J. R., & Alford, J. R. (1981). The electoral impact of economic conditions: Who is held responsible? *American Journal of Political Science*, **25**, 423–439.

Higgins, E. T., & Bargh, J. A. (1987). Social cognition and social perception. *Annual Review of Psychology*, **38**, 369–425.

Higgins, E. T., & King, G. (1981). Accessibility of social constructs: Information-processing consequences of individual and contextual variability. In N. Cantor & J. R. Kihlstrom (Eds.), *Personality, cognition, and social interaction* (pp. 69–122). Hillsdale, NJ: Erlbaum.

Himmelstein, J. L., & McRae, J. A., Jr. (1988). Social issues and socioeconomic status. *Public Opinion Quarterly*, **52**, 492–512.

Hirschman, A. O. (1977). *The passions and the interests: Political arguments for capitalism before its triumph.* Princeton, NJ: Princeton University Press.

Hirschman, A. O. (1985). Against parsimony. *Economics and Philosophy*, **1**, 7–21.

Hogarth, R. M., & Reder, M. W. (Eds.). (1987). *Rational choice: The contrast between economics and psychology.* Chicago: University of Chicago Press.

Homans, G. C. (1961). *Social behavior: Its elementary forms.* New York: Harcourt, Brace & World.

Howard-Pitney, B., Borgida, E., & Omoto, A. M. (1986). Personal involvement: An examination of processing differences. *Social Cognition*, **4**, 39–57.

Howell, S. E., & Vanderleeuw, J. M. (1990). Economic effects on state governors. *American Politics Quarterly*, **18**, 158–168.

Huddy, L. (1989). *Generational agreement on old-age policies: Explanations based on realistic interests, symbolic political attitudes, and age identities.* Unpublished doctoral dissertation, Psychology Department, University of California, Los Angeles.

Huddy, L., & Sears, D. O. (1989). *Opposition to bilingual education: Symbolic racism or realistic group conflict?* Unpublished manuscript, University of California, Los Angeles.

Iyengar, S. (1987). Television news and citizens' explanations of national affairs. *American Political Science Review*, **81**, 815–831.

Iyengar, S. (1989). How citizens think about national issues: A matter of responsibility. *American Journal of Political Science*, **33**, 878–900.

Iyengar, S. (1990). Framing responsibility for political issues: The case of poverty. *Political Behavior*, **12**, 19–40.

Iyengar, S., & Kinder, D. R. (1985). Psychological accounts of agenda-setting. In S. A. Kraus & R. M. Perloff (Eds.), *Mass media and political thought: An information-processing approach* (pp. 117–140). Beverly Hills, CA: Sage.

Jacobson, C. K. (1978). Desegregation rulings and public attitude changes: White resistance or resignation? *American Journal of Sociology*, **84**, 698–705.

Jacobson, C. K. (1983). Black support for affirmative action programs. *Phylon*, **44**, 299–311.

Jacobson, C. K. (1985). Resistance to affirmative action: Self-interest or racism? *Journal of Conflict Resolution*, **29**, 306–329.

Janis, I. L. (1967). Effects of fear arousal on attitude change: Recent developments in theory and experimental research. In L. Berkowitz (Ed.), *Advances in experimental social psychology* (Vol. 3, pp. 166–224). New York: Academic Press.

Jellison, J. M., & Green, J. (1981). A self-presentation approach to the fundamental attribution error: The norm of internality. *Journal of Personality and Social Psychology*, **40**, 643–649.

Jennings, M. K., & Niemi, R. G. (1981). *Generations and politics.* Princeton, NJ: Princeton University Press.

Jervis, R. (1976). *Perception and misperception in international politics.* Princeton, NJ: Princeton University Press.

Jessor, T. (1988). *Personal interest, group conflict, and symbolic group affect: Explanations for whites' opposition to racial equality.* Unpublished doctoral dissertation, Department of Psychology, University of California, Los Angeles.

Kahneman, D., Slovic, P., & Tversky, A. (Eds.). (1982). *Judgment under uncertainty: Heuristics and biases.* New York: Cambridge University Press.

Kahneman, D., & Tversky, A. (1984). Choices, values, and frames. *American Psychologist,* **39,** 341–350.

Katz, D. (1960). The functional approach to the study of attitudes. *Public Opinion Quarterly,* **24,** 163–204.

Key, V. O., Jr. (1949). *Southern politics in state and nation.* New York: Vintage.

Kiewiet, D. R. (1983). *Macroeconomics and micropolitics: The electoral effects of economic issues.* Chicago: University of Chicago Press.

Kiewiet, D. R., & Rivers, D. (1984). A retrospective on retrospective voting. *Political Behavior,* **6,** 369–393.

Kihlstrom, J. F., Cantor, N., Albright, J. S., Chew, B. R., Klein, S. B., & Niedenthal, P. M. (1988). Information processing and the study of the self. In L. Berkowitz (Ed.), *Advances in experimental social psychology* (Vol. 21, pp. 145–178). San Diego, CA: Academic Press.

Kinder, D. R., Adams, G. S., & Gronke, P. W. (1989). Economics and politics in the 1984 American presidential election. *American Journal of Political Science,* **33,** 491–515.

Kinder, D. R., & Kiewiet, D. R. (1979). Economic discontent and political behavior: The role of personal grievances and collective economic judgments in congressional voting. *American Journal of Political Science,* **23,** 495–527.

Kinder, D. R., & Kiewiet, D. R. (1981). Sociotropic politics. *British Journal of Political Science,* **11,** 129–161.

Kinder, D. R., & Mebane, W. R., Jr. (1983). Politics and economics in everyday life. In K. R. Monroe (Ed.), *The political process and economic change.* New York: Agathon.

Kinder, D. R., & Sears, D. O. (1981). Prejudice and politics: Symbolic racism versus racial threats to the good life. *Journal of Personality and Social Psychology,* **40,** 414–431.

Kinder, D. R., & Sears, D. O. (1985). Public opinion and political action. In G. Lindzey & E. Aronson (Eds.), *Handbook of social psychology* (3rd ed., Vol. 2, pp. 659–741). New York: Random House.

Klein, S. B., & Loftus, J. (1988). The nature of self-referent encoding: The contributions of elaborative and organizational processes. *Journal of Personality and Social Psychology,* **55,** 5–11.

Kluegel, J. R., & Smith, E. R. (1983). Affirmative action attitudes: Effects of self-interest, racial affect, and stratification beliefs on whites' views. *Social Forces,* **61,** 797–824.

Kramer, B. M., Kalick, S. M., & Milburn, M. A. (1983). Attitudes toward nuclear weapons and nuclear war. *Journal of Social Issues,* **39,** 7–24.

Kramer, G. H. (1971). Short-term fluctuations in U.S. voting behavior, 1896–1964. *American Political Science Review,* **65,** 131–143.

Kramer, G. H. (1983). The ecological fallacy revisited: Aggregate- versus individual-level findings on economics and elections and sociotropic voting. *American Political Science Review,* **77,** 92–111.

Krosnick, J. A. (1988a). Attitude importance and attitude change. *Journal of Experimental Social Psychology,* **24,** 240–255.

Krosnick, J. A. (1988b). The role of attitude importance in social evaluation: A study of policy preferences, presidential candidate evaluations, and voting behavior. *Journal of Personality and Social Psychology,* **55,** 196–210.

Krosnick, J. A. (1990). Government policy and citizen passion: A study of issue publics in contemporary America. *Political Behavior,* **12,** 59–92.

Kuklinski, J. H., & West, D. M. (1981). Economic expectations and voting behavior in United States House and Senate elections. *American Political Science Review,* **75,** 436–447.

Kunda, Z. (1987). Motivated inference: Self-serving generation and evaluation of causal theories. *Journal of Personality and Social Psychology,* **53,** 636–647.

Ladd, H. F., & Wilson, J. B. (1982). Why voters support tax limitations: Evidence from Massachusetts' Proposition 2½. *National Tax Journal,* **35,** 121–148.

Lane, R. E. (1962). *Political ideology: Why the American common man believes what he does.* Glencoe, IL: Free Press.

Langer, E. J. (1975). The illusion of control. *Journal of Personality and Social Psychology,* **32,** 311–328.

Lau, R. R., Brown, T. A., & Sears, D. O. (1978). Self-interest and civilians' attitudes toward the Vietnam war. *Public Opinion Quarterly,* **42,** 464–483.

Lau, R. R., Coulam, R. F., & Sears, D. O. (1983). *Proposition 2½ in Massachusetts: Self-interest, anti-government attitudes, and political schemas.* Paper presented at the annual meeting of the Midwest Political Science Association, Chicago, IL.

Lau, R. R., & Sears, D. O. (1981). Cognitive links between economic grievances and political responses. *Political Behavior,* **3,** 279–302.

Lau, R. R., & Sears, D. O. (Eds.). (1986). *Political cognition: The 19th Annual Carnegie Symposium on Cognition.* Hillsdale, NJ: Erlbaum.

Lau, R. R., Sears, D. O., & Jessor, T. (1990). Fact or artifact revisited: Survey instrument effects and pocketbook politics. *Political Behavior,* **12,** 217–242.

Lazarsfeld, P. F., Berelson, B., & Gaudet, H. (1948). *The people's choice* (2nd ed.). New York: Columbia University Press.

Lerner, M. J. (1965). The effect of responsibility and choice on a partner's attractiveness following failure. *Journal of Personality and Social Psychology,* **33,** 178–187.

Leventhal, H. (1970). Findings and theory in the study of fear communications. In L. Berkowitz (Ed.), *Advances in experimental social psychology* (Vol. 5, pp. 120–186). New York: Academic Press.

LeVine, R. A., & Campbell, D. T. (1972). *Ethnocentrism: Theories of conflict, ethnic attitudes, and group behavior.* New York: Wiley.

Lewis-Beck, M. S. (1985). Pocketbook voting in U.S. national election studies: Fact or artifact? *American Journal of Political Science,* **29,** 348–356.

Lewis-Beck, M. S. (1986). Comparative economic voting: Britain, France, Germany, Italy. *American Journal of Political Science,* **30,** 315–346.

Lewis-Beck, M. S. (1988). *Economics and elections: The major Western democracies.* Ann Arbor, MI: University of Michigan Press.

Lipset, S. M. (1981). *Political man.* Baltimore: Johns Hopkins University Press.

Listhaug, D., & Miller, A. H. (1985). Public support for tax evasion: Self-interest or symbolic politics? *European Journal of Political Research,* **13,** 265–282.

Lorge, I. (1936). Prestige, suggestion, and attitudes. *Journal of Social Psychology,* **7,** 386–402.

Lotwis, M. A. (1989). *The gun toter and the gun controller: Self-interest and ideology in political attitudes about gun control.* Paper presented at the annual meeting of the Midwest Political Science Association, Chicago, IL.

Lowery, D., & Sigelman, L. (1981). Understanding the tax revolt: Eight explanations. *American Political Science Review,* **75,** 963–974.

Lupsha, P. A. (1975). Social position and public regardingness: A new test of an old hypothesis. *Western Political Quarterly,* **28,** 618–634.

Lynn, M., & Oldenquist, A. (1986). Egoistic and nonegoistic motives in social dilemmas. *American Psychologist,* **41,** 529–534.

Mansbridge, J. J. (1985). Myth and reality: The ERA and the gender gap in the 1980 election. *Public Opinion Quarterly,* **49,** 164–178.

Mansbridge, J. J. (1990a). The rise and fall of self-interest in the explanation of political life. In J. J. Mansbridge (Ed.), *Beyond Self-Interest.* Chicago: University of Chicago Press.

Mansbridge, J. J. (Ed.). (1990b). *Beyond self-interest.* Chicago: University of Chicago Press.

Mansbridge, J. J. (1990c). Self-interest in political life. *Political Theory,* **18,** 132–153.

Markus, G. B. (1986). Stability and change in political attitudes: Observed, recalled and explained. *Political Behavior,* **8,** 21–44.

Markus, H., & Wurf, E. (1987). The dynamic self-concept: A social psychological perspective. *Annual Review of Psychology,* **38,** 299–337.

McClendon, M. J. (1985). Racism, rational choice, and white opposition to racial change: A case study of busing. *Public Opinion Quarterly,* **49,** 214–233.

McClendon, M. J., & Pestello, F. P. (1983). Self-interest and public policy attitude formation: Busing for school desegregation. *Sociological Focus,* **16,** 1–12.

McConahay, J. B. (1982). Self-interest versus racial attitudes as correlates of anti-busing attitudes in Louisville: Is it the buses or the blacks? *Journal of Politics,* **44,** 692–720.

McGuire, W. J. (1969). The nature of attitudes and attitude change. In G. Lindzey & E. Aronson (Eds.), *Handbook of social psychology* (2nd ed., Vol. 3, pp. 136–314). Reading, MA: Addison-Wesley.

McGuire, W. J. (1985). Attitudes and attitude change. In G. Lindzey & E. Aronson (Eds.), *Handbook of social psychology* (3rd ed., Vol. 2, pp. 223–346). New York: Random House.

Miller, N., & Brewer, M. B. (Eds.). (1984). *Groups in contact: The psychology of desegregation.* Orlando, FL: Academic Press.

Monroe, K. R. (1979). Econometric analyses of electoral behavior: A critical review. *Political Behavior,* **1,** 137–173.

Mueller, D. C. (1979). *Public Choice.* New York: Cambridge University Press.

Mueller, J. E. (1973). *War, presidents, and public opinion.* New York: Wiley.

Murray, H. A. (1938). *Explorations in personality.* New York: Oxford University Press.

Myers, M. L. (1983). *The soul of modern economic man: Ideas of self-interest: Thomas Hobbes to Adam Smith.* Chicago: University of Chicago Press.

Neiman, M., & Riposa, G. (1986). Tax rebels and tax rebellion. *Western Political Quarterly,* **39,** 435–445.

Neuberg, S. L., & Fiske, S. T. (1987). Motivational influences on impression formation: Outcome dependency, accuracy-driven attention, and individuating processes. *Journal of Personality and Social Psychology,* **53,** 431–444.

Niemi, R. G., Katz, R. S., & Newman, D. (1980). Reconstructing past partisanship: The failure of the party identification recall questions. *American Journal of Political Science,* **24,** 633–651.

Nisbett, R., & Ross, L. (1980). *Human inference: Strategies and shortcomings of social judgment.* Englewood Cliffs, NJ: Prentice-Hall.

Nuttin, J. M., Jr. (1985). Narcissism beyond Gestalt and awareness: The name–letter effect. *European Journal of Social Psychology,* **15,** 353–361.

Omoto, A. M., & Borgida, E. (1988). Guess who might be coming to dinner?: Personal involvement and racial stereotyping. *Journal of Experimental Social Psychology,* **24,** 571–593.

Osgood, C. E., & Tannenbaum, P. (1955). The principle of congruity and the prediction of attitude change. *Psychological Review,* **62,** 42–55.

Owens, J. R. (1984). Economic influences on elections to the U.S. Congress. *Legislative Studies Quarterly*, **9**, 123–150.

Owens, J. R., & Olson, E. C. (1980). Economic fluctuations and congressional elections. *American Journal of Political Science*, **24**, 469–493.

Peffley, M., & Williams, J. T. (1985). Attributing presidential responsibility for national economic problems. *American Politics Quarterly*, **13**, 393–425.

Perloff, L., & Fetzer, B. K. (1986). Self-other judgments and perceived vulnerability to victimization. *Journal of Personality and Social Psychology*, **50**, 502–510.

Pettigrew, T. F. (1972). When a black candidate runs for mayor: Race and voting behavior. In H. Hahn (Ed.), *Urban affairs annual review, 1972* (pp. 95–117). Beverly Hills, CA: Sage.

Pettigrew, T. F. (1985). New black–white patterns: How best to conceptualize them? *Annual Review of Sociology*, **11**, 329–346.

Pettigrew, T. F., & Campbell, E. Q. (1960). Faubus and segregation: An analysis of Arkansas voting. *Public Opinion Quarterly*, **24**, 436–447.

Petty, R. E., & Cacioppo, J. T. (1986). *Communication and persuasion: Central and peripheral routes to attitude change*. New York: Springer-Verlag.

Ponza, M., Duncan, G. J., Corcoran, M., & Groskind, F. (1988). The guns of autumn? Age differences in support for income transfers to the young and old. *Public Opinion Quarterly*, **52**, 441–466.

Pratkanis, A. R., Breckler, S. J., & Greenwald, A. G. (Eds.). (1989). *Attitude structure and function*. Hillsdale, NJ: Erlbaum.

Prentice, D. A. (1987). Psychological correspondence of possessions, attitudes, and values. *Journal of Personality and Social Psychology*, **87**, 993–1003.

Quattrone, G. A., & Tversky, A. (1988). Contrasting rational and psychological analyses of political choice. *American Political Science Review*, **82**, 719–736.

Rasinski, K., & Rosenbaum, S. M. (1987). Predicting citizen support of tax increases for education: A comparison of two social psychological perspectives. *Journal of Applied Social Psychology*, **17**, 990–1006.

Reich, R. R. (Ed.). (1988). *The power of public ideas*. Cambridge, MA: Ballinger.

Reiter, H. L. (1980). The perils of partisan recall. *Public Opinion Quarterly*, **44**, 385–388.

Rogers, T. B., Kuiper, N. A., & Kirker, W. S. (1977). Self-reference and the encoding of personal information. *Journal of Personality and Social Psychology*, **35**, 677–688.

Ross, L., Greene, D., & House, P. (1977). The "false consensus effect": An egocentric bias in social perception and attribution processes. *Journal of Experimental Social Psychology*, **13**, 279–301.

Ross, M. (1989). Relation of implicit theories to the construction of personal histories. *Psychological Review*, **96**, 341–357.

Ross, M., & Sicoly, F. (1979). Egocentric biases in availability and attribution. *Journal of Personality and Social Psychology*, **37**, 322–336.

Rothbart, M. (1973). Perceiving social injustice: Observations on the relationship between liberal attitudes and proximity to social problems. *Journal of Applied Social Psychology*, **3**, 291–302.

Runciman, W. G. (1966). *Relative deprivation and social justice*. London: Routledge & Kegan Paul.

Sandel, M. J. (1982). *Liberalism and the limits of justice*. Cambridge, England: Cambridge University Press.

Schlozman, K. L., & Tierney, J. T. (1986). *Organized interests and American democracy*. New York: Harper & Row.

Schlozman, K. L., & Verba, S. (1979). *Injury to insult: Unemployment, class, and political response*. Cambridge, MA: Harvard University Press.

Schroeder, L. D., & Sjoquist, D. L. (1983). The rational voter: An analysis of two Atlanta referenda on rapid transit. *Public Choice*, **33**, 27–44.

Schuman, H., Ludwig, J., & Krosnick, J. A. (1986). The perceived threat of nuclear war, salience, and open questions. *Public Opinion Quarterly,* **50,** 519–536.

Schuman, H., Steeh, C., & Bobo, L. (1985). *Racial trends in America: Trends and interpretations.* Cambridge, MA: Harvard University Press.

Sears, D. O. (1975). Political socialization. In F. I. Greenstein & N. W. Polsby (Eds.), *Handbook of political science* (Vol. 2, pp. 93–153). Reading, MA: Addison-Wesley.

Sears, D. O. (1980). *Public opinion and the personal impact of policy issues.* Paper presented at the annual meeting of the American Psychological Association, Montreal, Canada.

Sears, D. O. (1983). The persistence of early political predispositions: The roles of attitude object and life stage. In L. Wheeler & P. Shaver (Eds.), *Review of personality and social psychology* (Vol. 4, pp. 79–116). Beverly Hills, CA: Sage.

Sears, D. O. (1986). College sophomores in the laboratory: Influences of a narrow database on social psychology's view of human nature. *Journal of Personality and Social Psychology,* **51,** 515–530.

Sears, D. O. (1989). Whither political socialization research? The question of persistence. In O. Ichilov (Ed.), *Political socialization, citizenship education, and democracy* (pp. 69–97). New York: Teachers College Press.

Sears, D. O., & Allen, H. M., Jr. (1984). The trajectory of local desegregation controversies and whites' opposition to busing. In N. Miller & M. B. Brewer (Eds.), *Groups in contact: The psychology of desegregation* (pp. 123–151). Orlando, FL: Academic Press.

Sears, D. O., & Citrin, J. (1985). *Tax revolt: Something for nothing in California* (enlarged ed.). Cambridge, MA: Harvard University Press.

Sears, D. O., & Funk, C. L. (1990a). Self-interest in Americans' political opinions. In J. J. Mansbridge (Ed.), *Beyond self-interest* (pp. 147–170). Chicago: University of Chicago Press.

Sears, D. O., & Funk, C. L. (1990b). The limited effect of economic self-interest on the political attitudes of the mass public. *Journal of Behavioral Economics.*

Sears, D. O., Hensler, C. P., & Speer, L. K. (1979). Whites' opposition to "busing": Self-interest or symbolic politics? *American Political Science Review,* **73,** 369–384.

Sears, D. O., & Huddy, L. (1990a). On the origins of political disunity among women. In L. A. Tilly & P. Gurin (Eds.), *Women, politics, and change* (pp. 249–277). New York: Russell Sage Foundation.

Sears, D. O., & Huddy, L. (1990b). *Language conflict as symbolic politics: The role of symbolic meaning.* Paper presented at the Symposium on Group Dynamics: Conflict with and among Groups, Texas A&M University, College Station, TX.

Sears, D. O., Huddy, L., & Schaffer, L. (1986). A schematic variant of symbolic politics theory, as applied to racial and gender equality. In R. R. Lau & D. O. Sears (Eds.), *Political cognition: The 19th Annual Carnegie Symposium on Cognition* (pp. 159–202). Hillsdale, NJ: Erlbaum.

Sears, D. O., & Kinder, D. R. (1971). Racial tensions and voting in Los Angeles. In W. Z. Hirsch (Ed.) *Los Angeles: Viability and prospects for metropolitan leadership.* New York: Praeger.

Sears, D. O., & Kinder, D. R. (1985). Whites' opposition to busing: On conceptualizing and operationalizing group conflict. *Journal of Personality and Social Psychology,* **48,** 1141–1147.

Sears, D. O., & Lau, R. R. (1983). Inducing apparently self-interested political preferences. *American Journal of Political Science,* **27,** 223–252.

Sears, D. O., Lau, R. R., Tyler, T. R., & Allen, H. M., Jr. (1980). Self-interest vs. symbolic politics in policy attitudes and presidential voting. *American Political Science Review,* **74,** 670–684.

Sears, D. O., & McConahay, J. B. (1973). *The politics of violence: The new urban blacks and the Watts riot.* Boston: Houghton Mifflin. (Reprinted by University Press of America, 1981)

Sears, D. O., Steck, L., Lau, R. R., & Gahart, M. T. (1983). *Attitudes of the post-Vietnam generation toward the draft and American military policy.* Paper presented at the annual meeting of the International Society of Political Psychology, Oxford, England.

Sears, D. O., Tyler, T. R., Citrin, J., & Kinder, D. R. (1978). Political system support and public response to the 1974 energy crisis. *American Journal of Political Science, 22,* 56–82.

Shapiro, R. Y., & Mahajan, H. (1986). Gender differences in policy preferences: A summary of trends from the 1960s to the 1980s. *Public Opinion Quarterly,* 50, 42–61.

Shavitt, S. (1989). Operationalizing functional theories of attitude. In A. R. Pratkanis, S. J. Breckler, & A. G. Greenwald (Eds.), *Attitude structure and function* (pp. 311–337). Hillsdale, NJ: Erlbaum.

Sherif, M., & Cantril, H. (1947). *The psychology of ego-involvements.* New York: Wiley.

Sherman, S. J., Judd, C. M., & Park, B. (1989). Social cognition. *Annual Review of Psychology,* **40,** 258–271.

Shingles, R. D. (1989). Class, status, and support for government aid to disadvantaged groups. *Journal of Politics,* **51,** 933–962.

Sicoly, F., & Ross, M. (1977). Facilitation of ego-based attributions by means of self-serving observer feedback. *Journal of Personality and Social Psychology,* **35,** 734–741.

Simon, H. A. (1985). Human nature in politics: The dialogue of psychology with political science. *American Political Science Review,* **79,** 293–304.

Smith, M. B., Bruner, J. S., & White, R. W. (1956). *Opinions and personality.* New York: Wiley.

Smith, T. W. (1987). That which we call welfare by any other name would smell sweeter: An analysis of the impact of question wording on response patterns. *Public Opinion Quarterly,* **51,** 75–83.

Sniderman, P. M., & Brody, R. A. (1977). Coping: The ethic of self-reliance. *American Journal of Political Science,* **21,** 501–521.

Sniderman, P. M., & Tetlock, P. E. (1986a). Symbolic racism: Problems of motive attribution in political analysis. *Journal of Social Issues,* **42,** 129–150.

Sniderman, P. M., & Tetlock, P. E. (1986b). Reflections on American racism. *Journal of Social Issues,* **42,** 173–187.

Stein, R. M. (1990). Economic voting for governor and U.S. Senator: The electoral consequences of federalism. *Journal of Politics,* **52,** 29–53.

Sudit, M. (1988). Ideology or self-interest? Medical students' attitudes toward national health insurance. *Journal of Health and Social Behavior,* **29,** 376–384.

Sullivan, J. L., Piereson, J., & Marcus, G. E. (1982). *Political tolerance and American democracy.* Chicago: University of Chicago Press.

Taylor, D. M., & Dubé, L. (1986). Two faces of identity: The "I" and the "we." *Journal of Social Issues,* **42,** 81–98.

Taylor, S. E. (1975). On inferring one's attitudes from one's behavior: Some delimiting conditions. *Journal of Personality and Social Psychology,* **31,** 126–131.

Taylor, S. E. (in press). Asymmetrical effects of positive and negative events: The mobilization-minimization hypothesis. *Psychological Bulletin.*

Taylor, S. E., & Brown, J. D. (1988). Illusion and well-being: A sociopsychological perspective on mental health. *Psychological Bulletin,* **103,** 193–210.

Taylor, S. E., & Thompson, S. C. (1982). Stalking the elusive "vividness" effect. *Psychological Review,* **89,** 155–181.

Thibaut, J. W., & Kelley, H. H. (1959). *The social psychology of groups.* New York: Wiley.

Tufte, E. R. (1978). *Political control of the economy.* Princeton, NJ: Princeton University Press.

Tulving, E. (1983). *Elements of episodic memory.* New York: Oxford University Press.

Tyler, T. R. (1980). The impact of directly and indirectly experienced events: The origin of crime-related judgments and behaviors. *Journal of Personality and Social Psychology,* **39,** 13–28.

Tyler, T. R., & Cook, F. L. (1984). The mass media and judgments of risk: Distinguishing impact on personal and societal level judgments. *Journal of Personality and Social Psychology,* **47,** 693–708.

Tyler, T. R., & Lavrakas, P. J. (1983). Support for gun control: The influence of personal, sociotropic, and ideological concerns. *Journal of Applied Social Psychology, 13*, 392–405.

Tyler, T. R., & Weber, R. (1982). Support for the death penalty: Instrumental response to crime, or symbolic attitude? *Law & Society Review, 17*, 21–45.

Vanneman, R. D., & Pettigrew, T. F. (1972). Race and relative deprivation in the urban United States. *Race, 13*, 461–486.

Walker, I., & Mann, L. (1987). Unemployment, relative deprivation, and social protest. *Personality and Social Psychology Bulletin, 13*, 275–283.

Walker, J. L. (1983). The origins and maintenance of interest groups in America. *American Political Science Review, 77*, 390–406.

Wallach, M. A., & Wallach, L. (1983). *Psychology's sanction for selfishness: The error of egoism in theory and therapy.* San Francisco, CA: Freeman.

Weatherford, M. S. (1983). Economic voting and the "symbolic politics" argument: A reinterpretation and synthesis. *American Political Science Review, 77*, 158–174.

Weigel, R. H., & Howes, P. W. (1985). Conceptions of racial prejudice: Symbolic racism reconsidered. *Journal of Social Issues, 41*, 117–138.

Weinstein, N. D. (1989). Effects of personal experience on self-protective behavior. *Psychological Bulletin, 105*, 31–50.

Wilson, J. Q., & Banfield, E. C. (1964). Public-regardingness as a value premise in voting behavior. *American Political Science Review, 53*, 876–887.

Wu, C., & Shaffer, D. R. (1987). Susceptibility to persuasive appeals as a function of source credibility and prior experience with the attitude object. *Journal of Personality and Social Psychology, 52*, 677–688.

Young, J., Borgida, E., Sullivan, J., & Aldrich, J. (1987). Personal agendas and the relationship between self-interest and voting behavior. *Social Psychology Quarterly, 50*, 64–71.

Young, J., Thomsen, C. J., Borgida, E., Sullivan, J. L., & Aldrich, J. H. (in press). When self-interest makes a difference: The role of construct accessibility in political reasoning. *Journal of Experimental Social Psychology, 26.*

A TERROR MANAGEMENT THEORY OF SOCIAL BEHAVIOR: THE PSYCHOLOGICAL FUNCTIONS OF SELF-ESTEEM AND CULTURAL WORLDVIEWS

Sheldon Solomon

Jeff Greenberg

Tom Pyszczynski

I. Introduction

Contemporary social psychological discourse does not presently contain a general theoretical conception of human social behavior that can adequately account for the behavior of human beings in a cultural and historical context, organize and integrate existing empirical work in experimental social psychology, guide future research endeavors, and provide useful prescriptions for constructive individual and social changes. In an effort to work toward such a conception, we have recently proposed a *terror management* theory of social behavior (Greenberg, Pyszczynski, & Solomon, 1986; Solomon, Greenberg, & Pyszczynski, 1991). In this article we present an expanded version of the theory, review evidence relevant to the theory, and discuss the empirical, theoretical, epistemological, and practical implications of the theory.

WHY BROAD THEORIES?

Social psychology is currently dominated by a plethora of "minitheories," each of which addresses a relatively narrow and circumscribed component of social behavior. The mission of much of this work has been to explain in as much detail as possible the processes and mechanisms underlying particular discrete phenomena. Thus, the focus of the discipline has been on how, rather than why,

93

ADVANCES IN EXPERIMENTAL
SOCIAL PSYCHOLOGY, VOL. 24

particular behaviors occur. Although we believe that a detailed explication of the mechanisms through which social phenomena are produced should indeed be an important agenda for students of social behavior, we also believe that such analyses are ultimately unable to account for truly important human social phenomena unless they are embedded in a framework that considers the underlying functions that such mechanisms serve, and the cultural context in which the behaviors occur.

We therefore maintain that such frameworks are essential for scientific progress (cf. Greenberg, Solomon, Pyszczynski, & Steinberg, 1988; MacKay, 1988). Indeed, most other scientific disciplines operate within the context of a basic paradigm or central organizing principle (e.g., evolution in biology, quantum mechanics in physics) that serves to organize existing knowledge and focus attention on important issues for future inquiry.

In addition, broad theories have the potential to account for a wide range of behaviors and, consequently, to illuminate relationships among seemingly diverse phenomena. The question often arises, however, of whether one inevitably loses precision and detail by constructing broad theories. Although this can indeed happen, it need not be a problem if there is sufficient interplay between theories at varying levels of analysis. Just as the utility of minilevel theories for explaining real-world phenomena is enhanced by consideration of broad theoretical conceptions, the ability of broad theories to generate specific predictions is enhanced by a consideration of microlevel processes. The point here is simply that theories at any level of breadth and depth need to be informed by other conceptualizations at different levels. A thorough analysis of human behavior must therefore include an overarching general conception of the determinants of social behavior as well as fine-grained analyses of discrete phenomena.

In attempting to develop such a theory, we draw heavily on the work of Ernest Becker, who has written extensively on the role of self-esteem and culture in providing a sense of meaning, value, and security in a threatening, indeterminant universe. Becker argued persuasively in books such as *The Birth and Death of Meaning* (1962, 1971) and *The Denial of Death* (1973) that the work of many social scientists converges on certain basic insights about the human animal. Becker attempted to synthesize these ideas into a coherent explanation of human behavior. By drawing on Becker's insights, along with those of Peter Berger and Thomas Luckmann (1967), Norman Brown (1959), M.D. Faber (1981), Sigmund Freud (1975, 1976, 1984), Erving Goffman (1955, 1959), Robert Jay Lifton (1968, 1983, 1986), Otto Rank (1961, 1945, 1958, 1959), Harry Stack Sullivan (1953), and Gregory Zilboorg (1943), we have developed a relatively simple conceptual framework for understanding human social behavior. We believe that the resulting theory is useful because it explains a wide range of existing data on human social behavior, raises important questions and issues not currently addressed by other theoretical frameworks, and can be used to derive a wide variety of novel hypotheses.[1]

II. The Unique Needs of the Cultural Animal

In order to understand what guides social behavior, we must first understand how humans are both similar to and different from all other living creatures. At the most basic level, human beings are animals with basic biological needs. As Darwin, Freud, and many others have argued, all organisms are instinctively driven toward self-preservation and continued experience.[2]

Although humans share this basic evolutionary heritage with all other creatures, we are distinguished from other animals by our highly sophisticated intellectual abilities. Three cognitive abilities seem particularly important because they provide us with the incredible flexibility and adaptability that are characteristic of our species: the ability to conceptualize reality in terms of causality, the ability to conceive of future events, and the ability to reflect upon ourselves. Applying causal structure to the world and anticipating future events provide us with a basis for predicting and controlling future outcomes. In addition, the ability to reflect inward on the self as an object of attention is central to the self-regulation of behavior (cf. Carver & Scheier, 1981) and adds flexibility to our responses to environmental events.

However, the same cognitive abilities that enhance our ability to survive also unfortunately cause us to recognize problems concerning aspects of existence that we simply cannot control. Especially important is our awareness that we will inevitably die, that death can often occur prematurely and unexpectedly, and that we are unwillingly born into, and most certain to die out of, an uncontrollable and indeterminant universe.[3]

---

[1]It is perhaps worth noting that many of the ideas upon which this theory is based have previously been considered untestable and thus beyond the bounds of legitimate scientific inquiry. We suggest that this judgment is based on an erroneous conception of the nature of scientific inquiry (see our discussion of this issue in Section XV), and that methodologies within experimental social psychology have now developed to a point where many ideas that were previously viewed as "untestable" can now be employed to guide empirical endeavors.

[2]Some have argued (e.g., Dawkins, 1976) that the need for self-preservation at the individual level is ultimately in the service of preserving our genes rather than ourselves per se. We have no quarrel with this assertion, and accepting it would not significantly alter our conceptual analysis.

[3]Although our reasoning seems to imply that an absurdist, atheistic depiction of the world is an accurate perspective, our argument is not based on the notion that such a conception is absolutely true, but rather on the notion that as we develop cognitively we necessarily entertain this horrific possibility, and can never unequivocally disconfirm it.

For the human animal, the capacity to imagine possible futures, especially painful and tragic events, is a perpetual source of potential anxiety. Knowing that aversive events can and do occur creates a need for assurance that one can be spared such outcomes. Without such assurance, we would experience paralyzing terror. After all, a brain tumor could be waiting just beyond the next sunrise; but of course, if we're lucky, we live long enough to decay before we die. Given such awareness, humans could not function with equanimity if they believed that they were not inherently more significant and enduring than apes, lizards, or lima beans.

Becker hypothesized that humans confronted the physical problem of death and tragedy symbolically, through the creation of culture: humanly created symbolic perceptual constructions shared by groups of people to minimize the anxiety associated with the awareness of death.[4] Humans thus live within a shared symbolic conception of the universe that is culturally created and maintained, and yet is believed to be an absolute representation of reality by individual members of the culture. These cultural worldviews imbue the world with meaning, order, stability and permanence, and by so doing, buffer the anxiety that results from living in a terrifying and largely uncontrollable universe in which death is the only certainty. In essence, from birth on the culturally guided construction of reality embeds us in a symbolic world of meaning that elevates us above mere animal existence, which Becker (1975) aptly describes as:

> a gory spectacle, a science-fiction nightmare in which digestive tracts fitted with teeth at one end are tearing away at whatever flesh they can reach, and at the other end are piling up the fuming waste excrement as they move along in search of more flesh. (p. 1)

Thus, what distinguishes us from other animals is not that we are social animals (bees and ants are also social creatures), but rather that we are cultural animals.

From this perspective, any particular cultural worldview is a symbolic social construction that provides a meaningful context in which relatively anxiety-free action is possible. Berger and Luckmann (1967) came to quite similar conclusions regarding the nature and functions of culture, despite deriving them from a radically different theoretical orientation (i.e., Berger and Luckmann insisted that their position is antithetical to a psychological and/or psychoanalytic perspective). Berger and Luckmann observed that

---

[4]Whenever we refer to the terror of death, we do not mean the intense fear of death per se, but rather of death as *absolute annihilation*. Additionally, although we are focusing on what we believe is an essential function of culture (to assuage the terror associated with the uncontrollable and inevitable horrors of existence), we do not wish to claim that this is the only function that culture serves. Finally, whereas we are focusing on how culture helps us cope with uncontrollable horrors, culture also helps us actually forestall death in a variety of ways (e.g., medicine, consumer safety, "national security").

A strategic legitimating function of symbolic universes for individual biography is the "location" of death . . . . the most terrifying threat to the taken-for-granted realities of everyday life. The integration of death within the paramount reality of social existence is, therefore, of the greatest importance for any institutional order. This legitimation of death is, consequently, one of the most important fruits of symbolic universes. All legitimations of death must carry out the same essential task—they must enable the individual to go on living in society after the death of significant others and to anticipate his own death with, at the very least, terror sufficiently mitigated so as not to paralyze the continued performance of the routines of everyday life. . . . It is in the legitimation of death that the transcending potency of symbolic universes manifests itself most clearly, and the fundamental terror assuaging character of the ultimate legitimations of the paramount reality of everyday life is revealed. (p. 101)

III. The Dual-Component Cultural Anxiety Buffer: Worldview and Self-Esteem

To assuage the terror resulting from our awareness of vulnerability and death, it is necessary, but not sufficient, to adopt a particular cultural worldview. Cultural worldviews are constructed so that security can be maintained only through the belief that one is a valuable member of a meaningful universe. Accordingly, cultural representations of reality provide (1) standards by which the individual can be judged to be of value, and (2) an enduring place in the culture and, ultimately, immortality to those who live up to the standards of value. Consistent with this analysis of the function of cultural worldviews, Becker (1962) notes that although cultural worldviews vary greatly, they all offer a description of how the world was created, a prescription for what people should do to live "good" and "valuable" lives, and some promise of immortality to those who fulfill the prescription of value.

Self-esteem therefore consists of viewing oneself as a valuable participant in a meaningful cultural drama. Acquiring this sense of value requires that one both accept the standards of value as absolutely valid and view oneself as living up to those standards. To avoid the terror that would otherwise result from awareness of vulnerability and mortality, individuals' lives are therefore focused on maintaining self-esteem, which requires both faith in some internalized worldview, and satisfaction of culturally prescribed standards of value. By meeting these standards, people can sustain a sense of their own immortality.

But how does the cultural worldview provide a sense of immortality to those who live up to the cultural requirements of value? It does so in a number of ways, both literal and symbolic. First and most directly, for those who live up to the cultural standards, it promises literal immortality via religious and spiritual rituals and beliefs concerning a soul, an afterlife, and/or oneness with the universe. Second, it provides individuals with the sense that they are valued parts of something absolutely meaningful (i.e., the culture) that thrives and endures beyond individual death. Third, it provides individuals with ways to feel that they are making a permanent mark on the world by way of the things that they produce or receive, such as awards, monuments, buildings, books, group memberships, etc. Finally, it does so by conceptualizing and treating children as extensions of oneself into the future (cf. Rank, 1931).

IV. The Development and Functioning of the Cultural Anxiety Buffer for the Individual

It would be beyond the scope of this article (and the scope of our current understanding) to present a detailed developmental account of how the profoundly helpless and often distressed (i.e., whenever basic needs are not met) newborn becomes a person who is fully embedded in a cultural worldview and whose security is based on maintaining the cultural anxiety buffer. We do believe, however, that we can provide an overview of some of these processes.

Following a great deal of psychoanalytic, symbolic interactionist, attachment, and object relations theory (see, e.g., Faber, 1981), we propose that all knowledge and understanding of the world is guided by the need for self-preservation and the consequent affective concerns of the organism. The symbolic cultural worldview that develops from infancy on is thus conceptualized as an evolving metaschema guided by the organism's desire to minimize distress and anxiety. Security is sought through development of both active control of one's environment and cognitive control of one's conscious awareness and understanding of reality. Whereas the former effort pushes the organism toward an "accurate" knowledge of things (perhaps the driving force is control motivation manifested as curiosity), the latter effort requires the mastery of a relatively benign conception of reality that allows equanimity to be maintained.

Although both routes to equanimity are obviously critical, we would in fact argue that the latter effort predominates; first, because a profoundly physically immature creature cannot exert much actual control, and second, because, if riddled with distress, the creature would not be able to effectively develop its capacity for actual control. This analysis suggests that the most basic structural differentiation of the metaschema is threatening–neutral–comforting. As the control aspects develop, so does the capacity for self-reflection; thus, the second critical distinction is formulated to advance efforts to control: self and not self. Thus, the metaschema becomes further differentiated as self-knowledge and knowledge of the world.

Although the self–not self distinction is probably motivated by an effort to understand the boundaries between what one can and cannot control, once this distinction develops the foremost concern must be with establishing a secure positioning of the self as an object of primary value (and permanence) within the external world. The essential understanding of the self must therefore be of a valuable worthy participant in the internalized symbolic universe. The theory views the metaschema and this self-schema as the ultimate and penultimate bases of security for they provide the only available solution to the uncontrollable terrors of existence, including the paramount and perpetual threat to the organism, death. As they become established and function to provide equanimity, these security schemata guide the search for, assimilation of, and accommodation to perceived experiences in the world in such a way that the child's efforts to make sense of the world conform as much as possible to the parameters of satisfying the need for security.

This analysis focuses exclusively on the internal world of children; however, the security schemata are forged in the context of social relations. From birth onward, the parents provide for the needs of the helpless infant; in fact, they offer the only real solutions to the distress infants feel whenever threats to their continued existence arise. Of course, infants cannot conceptualize the nature of these threats; they simply experience negative affect whenever their basic needs are not met. As the capacities for self-awareness and imagining future events emerge, and the child becomes capable of imagining future pain and unfulfillment, the capacity for anxiety emerges.

Soon children learn that by being "good boys" or "good girls" they obtain good outcomes and are protected from bad outcomes by their apparently omnipotent parents; conversely, they learn that when they are "bad boys" or "bad girls," they are especially vulnerable to aversive experiences and even annihilation because they risk losing the ultimate protection provided by their parents or guardians. All one needs to do, then, to shield oneself from terror is to internalize parental perspectives and fulfill their requirements for being good (cf. Becker, 1962, 1973; Mead, 1934; Sullivan, 1953). Consistent with this reasoning, Rochlin (1965) has observed that as the child develops, the dread of object loss and abandonment seems to become transformed into a dread of being worthless.

This analysis suggests that children's sense of worth depends on the nature of the standards of goodness and how they are articulated by the parents, the children's abilities to meet those standards, and the parental feedback regarding the extent to which standards are being met. Thus, if standards of goodness are never clearly or consistently established, are too difficult to satisfy, or if children's value is not regularly acknowledged, their emerging sense of self-worth will be tenuous at best.

Clearly underlying the need for self-esteem is the implicit understanding that there is a contingency between the quality of one's behavior and personal attributes and one's consequent outcomes. Similarly, Lerner (1980) has proposed that individuals have a need to believe that the world is a fair and just place in which people get what they deserve and deserve what they get. This belief in a just world is transmitted both through direct experience with the contingency between one's own behavior and outcomes and through explicit cultural teachings of both a religious and secular nature that reinforce the notion that good behavior will be rewarded and bad behavior will be punished (see Lerner, Miller, & Holmes, 1976, for a discussion of the development of just world beliefs). Such a conception of the world provides people with a means of avoiding the aversive events that they fear, since if the world is truly fair, their good behavior will be rewarded.

Of course, at a conscious level, many of us do not believe that the world is just. Nevertheless, the positive affect and the sense of security that, over the course of childhood, became associated with perceiving oneself to be good, as well as the complementary intense anxiety associated with perceiving oneself to be bad, continues to exist, regardless of one's conscious beliefs.[5] From the perspective of terror management theory, it is this unconscious linkage between valued behavior and safety that imbues self-esteem with its anxiety-buffering properties.

The foregoing analysis doesn't tell the whole story, however, because from as early as age three, children begin to express interest in and concerns about death (see, e.g., Anthony, 1971; Rochlin, 1967; Yalom, 1980). Furthermore, as children's cognitive abilities develop, sooner or later they come to the realization that their own deaths are inevitable, that death will be the end of life, and that death may be an absolute end of existence. Although parental approval offers much protection, it alone cannot solve this terrifying problem. Consequently, children must shift their ultimate bases of security from parents to something greater, something that can transcend death.

For most people, deities and associated religious and spiritual concepts play a central role in this broader security base, but, as explained earlier, it really consists of the entire cultural worldview. The transition from parents to the culture as the basis for security is a relatively simple transition for most children, because parents convey their own anxiety-buffering versions of the cultural worldview throughout the socialization process. Value from the perspective of the death-transcending culture rather than simply the parents thus becomes imperative for security. Perhaps this explains the structure of the cultural anxiety buffer: it simply parallels the parental approval–security/disapproval–anxiety contingency on a grander scale.[6]

---

[5]Lerner (1980) has discussed a variety of ways in which people maintain the largely unconscious assumption that the world is just in spite of much concrete evidence of injustice (cf. Janoff-Bulman & Timko, 1987).

[6]Although there is very little evidence bearing directly on this analysis, research investigating social influences on self-esteem (see, e.g., Felson, 1989; Shrauger & Schoeneman, 1979) and a growing attachment literature guided largely by Bowlby's (1969, 1973, 1980) attachment theory and

V. The Architecture of Terror Management: The Relationship between the Fear of Death and Other Sources of Anxiety

Terror management theory views all anxiety as ultimately derived from the fear of the *absolute annihilation* that might result from death.[7] From this perspective, fear of death is simply the emotional manifestation of the basic self-preservation instinct:

> Such constant expenditure of psychological energy on the business of preserving life would be impossible if the fear of death were not as constant. The very term 'self-preservation' implies an effort against some force of disintegration; the affective aspect of this is fear, fear of death. (Zilboorg, 1943, p. 467)

Because of the need for self-preservation, anything that threatens one's continued existence becomes a source of intense anxiety. This anxiety is generally adaptive because it signals the need for behavior to remove oneself from threatening situations. The distinctly human problem is that our capacity to imagine future threatening events and to recognize that death will inevitably conquer our efforts at self-preservation would leave us continually anxious unless some mechanism existed to buffer these feelings.

According to terror management theory, a dual-component cultural anxiety buffer has evolved to fulfill this function. Thus, we posit that all anxiety-provoking events either remind us of our vulnerability and mortality or threaten the cultural anxiety buffer that protects us from this awareness. By maintaining the cultural anxiety buffer, the individual is able to keep the terror associated with awareness of his/her ultimate mortality out of consciousness. In essence, the

---

Ainsworth's (Ainsworth, Blehar, Waters, & Wall, 1978) conceptualization of attachment style are consistent with our theoretical perspective. Two recent findings concerning attachment style are particularly germane to our developmental account. Feeney and Noller (1990) have found that individuals who are secure in their relationships with others (i.e., have a secure attachment style) report especially positive perceptions of their early family relationships, and especially high self-esteem. Furthermore, Mikulincer, Florian, and Tolmacz (1990) found that securely attached individuals were especially low in concerns about death. These results conform to predictions derived from Bowlby's (1973) attachment theory. However, they also fit our terror management analysis in that individuals with positive early family relationships have high self-esteem and fewer conscious concerns about death.

[7]It should be noted that there is considerable empirical literature about attitudes toward death that we have virtually ignored in this article. Beyond establishing that death has a significant psychological impact on peoples' lives, we do not believe that this research is particularly informative for the present analysis. We are especially skeptical about the validity of available measures of fear of death, a skepticism also expressed by Feifel (1990) in a recent overview of the psychological literature on death (which we highly recommend to readers interested in that literature).

cultural anxiety buffer facilitates the repression of anxiety concerning one's vulnerability and mortality.

Although conclusive empirical evidence for the existence of repression has been notoriously difficult to produce (cf. Holmes, 1974), Erdelyi and Goldberg (1979) presented compelling arguments for the existence of this phenomenon. They suggested that what is currently known about the cognitive processes involved in memory is quite compatible with the existence of repression. Furthermore, they cited a broad range of clinical evidence that can be explained only through the operation of a process of active suppression of painful memories. In addition, recent research by Davis (1987), Davis and Schwartz (1987), and Hansen and Hansen (1988) all support the existence of repression. Following its psychoanalytic precursors, terror management theory posits that repression is an active process, accomplished, at least in part, by absorbing oneself in the cultural drama.

This analysis raises the question of precisely *how* the fear of death is related to the various sources of concern that ordinarily find their way into consciousness. Although we believe that most people do consciously consider the problem of mortality from time to time, most of their waking hours are filled with worries about rather circumscribed problems of living, such as whether they will get the job that they desire, whether their romantic relationships will work out, and so on. We suggest that it is precisely this preoccupation with the cultural drama that makes it possible to keep our deeper fears out of consciousness. When the cultural anxiety buffer is threatened, some of this repressed anxiety enters consciousness.

Although initially developed for a different purpose, we find that Carver and Scheier's (1981) *hierarchy of standards for self-regulation* (based on Powers, 1978) provides a useful model for conceptualizing the relationship between the fear of death and the goals and standards toward which our behavior is consciously regulated. Carver and Scheier suggest that behavioral standards are hierarchically organized, from the very concrete to the very abstract. As one moves up the hierarchy to increasingly abstract levels, achievement of a standard at any given level becomes one criterion for the next higher level standard. Thus the goal of doing well on a psychology exam, toward which a student's studying behavior is oriented, is a criterion behavior through which he or she can achieve the next highest level standard of getting a good grade in his/her psychology course. Getting a good grade in the psychology course is a criterion behavior through which he/she can meet the next highest standard of maintaining a high grade point average, and so on up the hierarchy.

As Carver and Scheier (1981) have noted, near the top of this hierarchy is the superordinate goal of maintaining a positive self-image. As one moves to the higher levels of the hierarchy there are a greater variety of pathways through which a goal can be met. Thus, subordinate to the superordinate goal of maintaining a positive self-image are the many specific roles and identities through which a positive self-image can be achieved and maintained. Subordinate to one's role and identity commitments are the even greater number of increasingly concrete means through which these goals are achieved.

From the perspective of our theory, the goal of self-preservation and continued experience is superordinate to all other goals in the hierarchy. This most basic of all human needs is the ultimate source of the terror of death and is served by a wide variety of more specific motives that can be roughly categorized as direct or symbolic means of self-preservation. Direct means of self-preservation include our basic biological needs for things such as food, water, temperature regulation, and so on, and are beyond the scope of this article. Symbolic means of self-preservation are ways of reducing the anxiety that result from our awareness of the ultimate futility of our desire for continued existence. The two components of the cultural anxiety buffer (worldview and self-esteem) are thus represented immediately subordinate to the self-preservation instinct on the symbolic side of the hierarchy. These symbolic means of self-preservation are, of course, the focus of this article. By maintaining faith in the cultural worldview and living up to its standards, the individual is able to avoid confrontation with the existential terror that results from awareness of the ultimate impossibility of meeting his or her most basic desire.

It seems clear that people are not always aware of the superordinate goals toward which their behavior is oriented. Although few people would argue with the contention that the need for self-esteem helps motivate achievement-related behavior, it is probably relatively rare for people to be aware of the superordinate goal of self-esteem maintenance when they are engaged in their academic or career pursuits. In a similar manner, we are suggesting that the superordinate goal of minimizing existential terror motivates behavior regardless of the fact that people are generally unaware of the operation of this motive. Although one's conscious attention may be focused on a specific goal at a relatively low level of abstraction, this goal is subservient to the meeting of deeper needs that lie outside of one's awareness. Conceptualizing different sources of anxiety at varying levels of a self-regulatory hierarchy illuminates the relationship between these various sources and explains how deep sources of anxiety may motivate behavior oriented toward more circumscribed ones. [For a more thorough discussion of these issues, see Pyszczynski, Greenberg, Solomon, and Hamilton (1990).]

VI. The Implications of Conceptualizing Self-Esteem as a Cultural Construction

An important component of our analysis is the notion that self-esteem is a cultural creation. People simply cannot have a sense of value without meeting the standards of the cultural worldview to which they subscribe; such prescriptions consist of both general standards and more specific role expectations (for both occupational and social positions). The general standards require certain competencies and moral attributes and corresponding behaviors from all members of a given culture. Other requirements for self-esteem vary depending on the individual's ascribed and chosen roles within the culture. Wicklund and Gollwitzer (1982) have proposed and empirically supported the related notion that individuals vary in their self-definitional needs (i.e., requirements for symbolic self-completion) as a function of their self-defining goals (e.g., to be a scientist). From our perspective, these self-definitional needs derive from the requirements of the particular roles from which an individual derives self-esteem.

By conceptualizing self-esteem as the individual's perception of the extent to which he or she is meeting cultural standards of value, terror management theory implies that the effect that a given behavior will have on an individual's self-esteem is largely dependent on how that behavior is viewed within a particular cultural context. Given the great diversity of cultural values revealed by anthropological research, this analysis suggests that the standards through which people acquire and maintain self-esteem are not intrinsically tied to goodness or value. These standards have meaning only because they are derived from a particular cultural worldview. Although specific cultural standards for acquiring value can probably be traced to some extent to historical events and pragmatic concerns, the theory posits that these standards acquire their power because they are legitimized by the cultural worldview rather than because of any adaptive or utilitarian function that they might serve (cf. Berger & Luckmann, 1967).

Accordingly, the same behavior which confers immense esteem in one cultural context might have a completely opposite effect in a different social milieu. For example, in corporate America, a ruggedly individualistic and competitive person who tries to succeed at the expense of others is held in high regard. However, the same type of person would be utterly ostracized in many Native American communities, where cooperative behavior is stressed and where success at the expense of another is viewed as immoral and indecent.[8]

Whereas anthropological work has made it clear that cultural standards of value are ultimately arbitrary, sociological analyses such as those of Goffman

[8]To highlight the arbitrary nature of the standards through which people acquire self-esteem, consider the American businessmen who wear dark three-piece suits on Wall Street in August (a rather maladaptive custom in the middle of the summer, at least from the perspective of thermodynamic regulation); presumably they do so because their attire contributes to their being viewed as important and influential. But if social standards changed such that important and influential men wore athletic supporters and tie-dyed shirts while crab-walking backward with basketballs in their mouths, we would expect the same businessmen to discard their three-piece suits and don the new status-conferring wardrobe and associated affectations.

(1959) and Berger and Luckmann (1967) have revealed another consequence of the cultural constitution of social reality: because the cultural anxiety buffer is by its very nature a fragile social construction, it requires continual maintenance and defense against threats. This is especially true because the vast array of competing beliefs to which we are exposed makes salient the possibility that one's worldview may not be valid. Similarly, the competitive nature of the social world, along with the wide variety of standards against which our value is measured, leads to uncertainty about the extent to which we, as individuals, are measuring up to the standards of value inherent in our worldviews. These problems, coupled with the frequent reminders of our vulnerability and mortality that we encounter as we go about our daily affairs, give rise to a need for ongoing confirmation of the validity of our worldview and our value as individuals (cf. Berger & Luckmann, 1967; Festinger, 1954; Goffman, 1959; Wicklund & Gollwitzer, 1982).

This validation of the cultural anxiety buffer is accomplished largely through interactions with others. The agreement and approval we receive from others provides consensual validation (cf. Kelley, 1967; Sullivan, 1953) of our worldviews and positive self-evaluations, thus increasing the stability and effectiveness of our anxiety buffer. Conversely, disagreement and disapproval from others threatens to undermine faith in our worldview and desired self-concept, and consequently reduces the effectiveness of the anxiety buffer. Thus from a terror management perspective, much self-presentational behavior is viewed as an attempt to elicit consensual validation of a desired worldview and self-image from others. When others agree with us or view us in a favorable light, it validates the worldview and positive self-image that we are motivated to maintain.

VII. Summary Statement of Terror Management Theory

We have argued that the human capacity for causal, symbolic, temporal, and self-reflective thinking gives rise to some uniquely human problems. Specifically, the abilities to ponder questions about why we exist, to conceive of our ultimate insignificance and vulnerability, and to anticipate future negative events, particularly death, provide the potential for paralyzing terror. Cultural reality, by elevating us above the rest of the living world and imbuing the world with order, predictability, meaning, and permanence, provides the possibility of minimizing our terror by denying our essential creatureliness (i.e., our ultimate vulnerability, helplessness, insignificance, and mortality). This shared cultural construction enables us to lead relatively anxiety-free lives and retain a sense of immortality to the extent that we can perceive ourselves to be living up to cultural standards of individual value.[9]

From this perspective, self-esteem can be viewed as a sense of personal value (or heroism, as Becker refers to it) that consists of two components: (1) faith in a cultural worldview and acceptance of the standards of value inherent in that worldview, and (2) the perception that one is meeting those standards of value and therefore has a significant role in the cultural conception of reality. The cultural anxiety buffer thus assuages the terror of absolute annihilation because it provides a sense that we are valuable parts of a meaningful, important, and enduring existence.

VIII. A Terror Management Analysis of Social Behavior

In the following sections we hope to show that by addressing deeper level "why" questions that explore basic motives, terror management theory can organize existing knowledge regarding a wide variety of social phenomena, shed new insights into the processes that produce these phenomena, and guide fruitful research endeavors. In correspondence with these goals, we will demonstrate the utility of the theory in three ways: first, by showing in some detail how it can account for the diverse research findings concerning self-esteem; second, by showing how it can be used as a general framework for organizing and understanding a wide array of trends in social behavior that have not previously been explicated within a single conceptual analysis; and third, by describing our recent research guided by hypotheses derived from the theory. Whereas separate sections will be devoted to each of the two former objectives, the descriptions of our research will be integrated throughout the article.

EMPIRICAL RESEARCH ON SELF-ESTEEM: A TALE OF TWO LITERATURES

Psychologists have long recognized the vitally important role that self-esteem plays in general psychological health and the guidance and direction of behavior. The notion that people have a strong and pervasive need to maintain positive

[9]Within a given culture, each individual's cultural drama shares basic values and conceptions of reality but obviously differs in specific characters, roles, and scenarios. This is largely a function of differences in the standards conveyed by those with whom one has had the most contact, and differences in perceived capacities to fulfill particular roles.

evaluations of themselves has been central to the work of a wide variety of theorists and researchers throughout the history of psychology (e.g., Adler, 1930; Allport, 1961; Becker, 1962, 1973; Coopersmith, 1967; Feuerbach, 1955; Freud, 1981; Horney, 1937; James, 1890; Kohut, 1977; Maslow, 1970; Rank, 1959; Rochlin, 1965; Rogers, 1959; Sullivan, 1953), and is presently receiving extensive attention from contemporary psychologists (e.g., Bowerman, 1978; Kaplan, 1982; Steele, 1988; Tesser, 1988). Furthermore, the self-esteem motive has been invoked to explain such diverse forms of behavior as attitude formation, altruism, aggression, delinquency, group cohesiveness, intergroup conflict, conformity, interpersonal attraction, romantic love, psychopathology, and loneliness (e.g., Becker, 1964; Jacobs, 1983; Turner, 1981; Wylie, 1979). Indeed, it is difficult to conceive of an area of behavior that has not been linked in some way to a need for self-esteem.

Although there is currently renewed interest in self-esteem and self-related issues, there is not yet a comprehensive theory that can account for the wide variety of social psychological phenomena that are believed to be related to, or mediated by, self-esteem. In addition, the very basic question of *why* people need self-esteem has been all but ignored. Scheff (1990) came to similar conclusions when observing that despite the existence of over 10,000 empirical studies investigating the relationship between self-esteem and various behaviors, there is not yet an adequate conceptual definition of what self-esteem is. Scheff argued that little progress can be made in the self-esteem area until a theory of self-esteem is developed:

> One obvious failing shared by all of the . . . studies was that they were all descriptive; that is, they did not test a hypothesis derived from a general theory. . . . Instead of balance between theory and method, in each of these studies, considerations involving METHOD prevailed over those involving theory. Although the methodology was sophisticated, utilizing experimental designs and reliable measurements, virtually no theoretical framework was provided. These studies, like most undertaken in the human sciences, were atheoretical. (p. 8)

Perhaps this can explain why, despite the vast empirical literature, most social psychology texts spend barely a page discussing the role of self-esteem in social behavior.

There are really two large bodies of research concerning self-esteem, neither of which has shown much recognition of the existence of the other. One is a substantial experimental social psychological literature that has assessed reactions to acute threats to self-esteem. The other is a massive literature from sociology, and social, personality, and clinical psychology, concerning the correlates of dispositional levels of self-esteem. A thorough review of either of these voluminous literatures would go beyond the scope of this article (for more thorough reviews, see Greenberg *et al.*, 1986; Solomon *et al.*, 1991). In the following sections, we use terror management theory to explain the major findings from each one.

IX. The Experimental Literature on Self-Esteem Maintenance: Consequences of Acute Threats to the Cultural Anxiety Buffer

A number of basic hypotheses concerning reactions to acute threats to self-esteem follow directly from terror management theory. First, such threats should cause anxiety. Second, such threats should motivate attempts to protect self-esteem. Third, when self-esteem is defended, anxiety should be reduced. Research on experimentally induced threats to self-esteem has yielded a wide array of findings that are highly consistent with all three of these hypotheses.

A. ANXIETY AND DEFENSE IN RESPONSE TO SELF-ESTEEM THREAT

Experiments, using a variety of control conditions, and assessing both physiological and self-report measures of anxiety, have shown that self-esteem-threatening situations produce anxiety (e.g., Bennett & Holmes, 1975; Burish & Houston, 1979; Leary, Barnes, & Griebel, 1986). Furthermore, it is now abundantly clear that threats to self-esteem instigate defensive reactions to either defuse the impact of the specific threat or restore one's more general sense of self-worth (see Greenberg et al., 1986, for a more detailed review of this evidence). The most thoroughly documented of these defensive maneuvers is the self-serving attributional bias, the tendency to attribute success to internal factors and failure to external factors (see Pyszczynski & Greenberg, 1987, for a review). In addition, after failure, subjects often deny the relevance of the threatened dimension for self-esteem (e.g., Greenberg & Pyszczynski, 1985; Greenberg, Pyszczysnki, & Solomon, 1982; Tesser & Campbell, 1980; Tesser & Paulhus, 1983), selectively seek information that supports a self-serving interpretation (e.g., Holton & Pyszczynski, 1989; Pyszczynski, Greenberg, & LaPrelle, 1985), evaluate evidence concerning the validity of the test in a self-serving manner (e.g., Pyszczynski, Greenberg, & Holt, 1985), and simply derogate the test (e.g., Frey, 1978; Greenberg et al., 1982). It also seems clear that subjects often either create or claim handicaps to their own success when such factors could serve as plausible self-esteem-protecting attributions for a feared failure (e.g., Berglas & Jones, 1978; Frankel & Snyder, 1978; Greenberg, Pyszczynski, & Paisley, 1984; Smith,

Snyder, & Handelsman, 1982). The fact that people create handicaps to their performance to protect self-esteem demonstrates that, at least in some instances, the implications of an outcome for the anxiety buffer are more important than the outcome itself.

Another common response to threats to self-esteem is to inflate the positivity of one's self-descriptions on the threatened dimension; this is especially likely when the dimension is a central aspect of one's identity (e.g., Gollwitzer & Wicklund, 1985; Gollwitzer, Wicklund, & Hilton, 1982; Wicklund & Gollwitzer, 1982). When not given an opportunity to defuse the specific threat, people often respond in a compensatory manner by inflating their self-evaluations on unrelated or general dimensions (e.g., Greenberg & Pyszczynski, 1985).

Research has also shown that social perceptions and affiliations are guided by self-esteem concerns. The fairly large literature on downward comparison tendencies shows that people prefer comparisons with others that enable them to view themselves in a superior light (for reviews, see Wills, 1981, 1987). In a related vein, Cialdini et al. (1976) demonstrated that individuals attempt to associate themselves with successful groups and dissociate themselves from unsuccessful groups.

Furthermore, Tesser and colleagues (e.g., Pleban & Tesser, 1981; Tesser, 1980; Tesser & Campbell, 1980) have found that when outperformed by another on a dimension important to self, individuals tend to minimize perceived similarity to that person, thus minimizing the appropriateness of an ego-threatening social comparison. In contrast, when the dimension is not important to self, individuals tend to maximize perceived similarity to the superior other, presumably in order to gain self-esteem by association (see Tesser, 1988, for a recent review of this work). Finally, it has also been shown that when self-esteem is threatened, individuals attempt to create a positive status differential between groups to which they belong and those to which they do not belong (e.g., Cialdini & Richardson, 1980; Meindl & Lerner, 1985).

B. THE ROLE OF ANXIETY IN SELF-ESTEEM DEFENSE

From a terror management perspective, all of these defensive maneuvers occur because of the vital anxiety-buffering function that self-esteem serves. It is perhaps worth noting that theoretical explanations for why individuals experience anxiety when self-esteem is threatened have rarely, if ever, been offered, despite both the empirical evidence and the clear and pervasive manifestations of this phenomenon in everyday life. Terror management theory explains that self-esteem functions as a cultural anxiety buffer; when this buffer is threatened, some of the anxiety that the buffer serves to minimize is released. This anxiety should generally motivate the individual to engage in defense of the buffer.

Consistent with this analysis, studies have shown that encouraging subjects who have received negative feedback to attribute arousal to a neutral source reduces their tendency to make defensive attributions (Stephan & Gollwitzer, 1981) and to derogate the test (Fries & Frey, 1980). In addition, following failure, increasing subjects' perceptions of arousal or their actual arousal increases their tendencies to attribute the failure to external factors (Gollwitzer, Earle, & Stephan, 1982; Stephan & Gollwitzer, 1981). To the extent that negatively labeled arousal is perceived as anxiety, these studies suggest that defensive maneuvers are mediated by the perception of anxiety.

Also consistent with our analysis is evidence that defensive beliefs reduce the anxiety and negative affect that threats to self-esteem otherwise create. McFarland and Ross (1982) found that self-serving attributions for failure minimize the negative effects of failure on both self-esteem and affect. Bennett and Holmes (1975) found that encouraging failure subjects to believe that there was high consensus for their failure (i.e., that their friends would have done poorly on the test too) reduces their anxiety on both self-report and physiological measures (cf. Burish & Houston, 1979).

Studies have also shown that downward comparison following failure is associated with a decrease in self-reported distress, anxiety, and depressive mood (Crocker & Gallo, 1985; Hakmiller, 1966). Arkin and Baumgardner (1985, cited in Baumgardner & Arkin, 1987) and Leary (1986) found that the availability of plausible excuses for feared future failure leads to less anxiety while later performing the threatening task. Finally, Mehlman and Snyder (1985) showed that merely making it easier for failure subjects to express self-esteem-defensive beliefs (by providing a questionnaire that enables them to minimize the implications of the failure) can reduce their anxiety. According to terror management theory, defensive beliefs reduce anxiety by restoring the integrity of one's anxiety-buffering self-concept.

Whereas threats to self-esteem should engender anxiety, it also follows from the theory that if self-esteem is an anxiety buffer, then anxiety-provoking stimuli should motivate individuals to bolster self-esteem to reduce that anxiety. Although this hypothesis has not yet been tested directly, Paulhus and Levitt (1987) have reported results consistent with it. In their study, subjects judged whether each of a series of trait adjectives was characteristic of themselves while being exposed to death-related (e.g., blood, coffin, death, torture) or innocuous (e.g., lake, cloud, station, outside) distractor words. They found that endorsements of positive traits and denials of negative traits were increased by the death-related words. Paulhus and Levitt proposed a Hullian arousal-based enhancement of dominant responses as an explanation for these results. However, terror management can also explain these findings; exposing subjects to anxiety-provoking death-related words made them especially prone to bolster their anxiety buffers by claiming positive traits and denying negative traits.

C. DIRECT TESTS OF THE SELF-ESTEEM AS ANXIETY-BUFFER HYPOTHESIS

Although the extant literature on self-esteem-maintenance processes is consistent with our proposition that self-esteem functions to buffer anxiety, it does not provide directly assess this hypothesis. We have recently conducted three experiments to do so. If self-esteem does function to buffer anxiety, then enhancing self-esteem should reduce susceptibility to anxiety among individuals exposed to anxiety-provoking stimuli. In one study (Greenberg, Solomon, Burling, Rosenblatt, Pyszczynski, Simon, & Lyon, 1991, Study 1), subjects were given either positive or neutral personality feedback and then were exposed to either a gory death-related videotape or innocuous material. As expected, the positive personality feedback increased the favorability of subjects' self-reports on the Rosenberg (1965) Self-Esteem Inventory. More importantly, and consistent with the anxiety-buffer hypothesis, the death scenes led to an elevation in self-reported anxiety on the Spielberger State Anxiety Inventory (Spielberger, Gorsuch, & Lushene, 1970) in the neutral personality feedback condition but not in the positive personality feedback condition. Increasing subjects' self-esteem completely eliminated the anxiety-provoking effect of the death scenes.

A second study (Greenberg, Solomon, et al., 1991, Study 2) provided a conceptual replication of this anxiety-buffering effect of enhanced self-esteem. Subjects were given success or no feedback on an ego-relevant test and then were led to expect either random shocks or no shocks. Galvanic skin responses indicated that, although the threat of shock led to significantly elevated arousal among all subjects, those who had previously received successful feedback show less of an elevation than those who had previously received no feedback. This physiological effect in the threat of shock paradigm has also been replicated (Greenberg, Solomon, et al., 1991, Study 3) using false personality feedback to manipulate self-esteem.[10] We are currently conducting further research on this hypothesis in an effort to tease apart self-esteem, mood, and distraction explanations for this effect. Pending the outcome of this research, the available evidence is consistent with the proposition that self-esteem provides a buffer against

[10]In Studies 2 and 3, self-reports of anxiety, although in the predicted directions, did not yield the significant interactions found on GSR. We would speculate that the threat of shock places a high demand on subjects to report anxiety, whether felt or not; however, further research will be needed to determine the precise causes of this discrepancy between self-report and physiological measures of anxiety.

anxiety. Increasing subjects' self-esteem makes them less reactive to anxiety-provoking stimuli.

D. PUBLIC AND PRIVATE ASPECTS OF SELF

Over the last decade or so, there has been a controversy regarding the roles of public and private self-image concerns in motivating defensive behavior. In 1978, Bradley argued that all of the evidence for the self-serving attributional bias could be interpreted as resulting from a motivation to protect public image rather than private self-image. Terror management theory, in contrast, most definitely posits a motivation to maintain a positive private self-image. In support of a private need for self-esteem, research has provided evidence of a self-serving attributional bias under conditions of both private threat and private attribution assessment (e.g., Greenberg et al., 1982; House, 1980) and under bogus pipeline conditions, which should encourage honest private attributions (Riess, Rosenfeld, Melburg, & Tedeschi, 1981). There is also evidence that other self-esteem-maintenance strategies function to protect private self-esteem (e.g., Greenberg & Pyszczynski, 1985; Greenberg et al., 1984; Tesser & Paulhus, 1983).

Tetlock and Manstead (1985) have argued that there can be no ultimate resolution to the apparent conflict between impression management and intrapsychic theories of social behavior, and that the most productive approach to this problem is the development of an overarching conceptual framework capable of integrating both perspectives. We suggest that terror management theory can provide such an integration. Although the terror management analysis clearly posits a private need for self-esteem, it also views self-esteem as a social construction based on a shared cultural conception of reality that requires continual validation from others. Thus, whereas a private failure known to no one but the self can threaten self-esteem to the extent that it signals a shortcoming on some culturally valued dimension, a failure on such a dimension known to others should be even more threatening because we rely on others for validation of our self-worth.

This analysis can help make sense of the existing literature concerning responses to public and private threats. The theory proposes that because others are the ultimate validators of our self-worth, our self-esteem is threatened whenever others believe we have a shortcoming. Consistent with this reasoning, research has shown that public evaluation settings create more anxiety than private evaluation settings (Leary et al., 1986), that failure is a greater threat to private self-esteem if it is publicly known than if it is not (e.g., Frey, 1978; Greenberg & Pyszczynski, 1985), and that a public perception that one has failed threatens self-esteem even when the person knows that they actually succeeded and that the public perception is based on erroneous information (e.g., Tesser & Paulhus, 1983).

Research has also shown that public awareness of a failure increases the tendency to defend self-esteem in whatever manner is available to the individual. Perceived public awareness of failure can lead to image bolstering for the failure-perceiving audience (e.g., Baumeister & Jones, 1978), image bolstering in the presence of a new audience (Apsler, 1975; Gollwitzer & Wicklund, 1985), or private minimization of the failure (Frey, 1978; Greenberg & Pyszczynski, 1985; Tesser & Paulhus, 1983). The fact that even the perception that others erroneously believe one has failed leads to private defense underscores the great extent to which our precious self-worth depends on the public affirmation of our value.

E. COGNITIVE DISSONANCE AND SELF-AWARENESS PROCESSES

There are two areas not generally linked to self-esteem that also can be interpreted as documenting self-esteem maintenance. Over the years, a number of theorists have argued that in virtually all of the research on cognitive dissonance, the attitude change that occurred could be interpreted as rationalizations motivated by a desire to deny that one has done something that is either unintelligent or immoral (e.g., Aronson, 1968; Bowerman, 1978). The fact that such attitude change occurs only when one has freely chosen to engage in behavior that produces foreseeable negative consequences is highly consistent with this perspective. From our perspective, the arousal of cognitive dissonance is a particular instance of the more general release of anxiety that occurs when the cultural anxiety buffer is threatened. In a series of studies, Steele and colleagues (see Steele, 1988, for a review) have shown that an opportunity for self-affirmation on a dimension unrelated to the original dissonant act eliminates the attitude change that would otherwise occur; these findings demonstrate the general nature of the threat posed by dissonant behavior. In fact, Scher and Cooper (1989) have recently found that "dissonance" reduction is motivated entirely by the perception of personal responsibility for negative consequences regardless of whether or not the behavior was counterattitudinal. In other words, people alter their attitudes to deny that they have done something bad or stupid. Clearly, self-esteem needs rather than consistency needs initiate dissonance-reducing behavior.

Terror management theory also provides a rather unique perspective from which to view the literature on self-awareness processes (for a review, see Carver & Scheier, 1981). As we argued at the outset, the evolutionary development of the capacity for self-awareness created the potential for existential terror and necessitated the creation of a cultural anxiety buffer (cf. Becker, 1971; Rank, 1961). It is when we are self-aware that our individual creatureliness and vulnerability are likely to be salient. Thus it would be consistent with our position if self-awareness motivated efforts to maintain self-esteem.

Interestingly, one of the strongest findings in the self-awareness literature is that heightened self-awareness motivates individuals to behave in accord with both external and internalized cultural standards. These effects can be easily interpreted as suggesting that self-awareness increases subjects' concerns for living up to cultural standards of value. There is also evidence that self-awareness increases the use of self-serving attributions (Federoff & Harvey, 1976; Hull & Levy, 1979) and self-handicapping strategies (Kernis, Zuckerman, Cohen, & Sparafora, 1982). Thus, it appears that one of the most important consequences of self-awareness is that of encouraging self-esteem-maintaining behavior.

This analysis may also help explain why self-awareness leads to comparisons with standards and subsequent behavior oriented toward matching the standards that have been accessed. Although these two effects are the cornerstones of both the Duval and Wicklund (1972) and Carver and Scheier (1981) theories of self-awareness processes, neither theory explains why they occur; rather, these effects are taken as unexplained postulates. If, as terror management theory posits, meeting cultural standards provides immunity from the anxiety that results in part from self-awareness, then self-awareness would be expected to instigate processes aimed at ensuring that these standards are met. Comparison of one's current state with salient standards of value and then engaging in behavior to bring one's current state in line with that standard would be an effective way of bolstering the anxiety buffer when confronted with a source of anxiety. Thus from our perspective, self-awareness leads to comparisons with standards and behavior oriented toward reducing any discrepancies that are detected because such behavior circumvents the anxiety that self-awareness would otherwise create (for a more thorough discussion of the relationship between terror management and self-awareness processes, see Pyszczynski, Miller, & Greenberg, 1990).

X. The Correlational Literature on Self-Esteem: Consequences of Long-Term Deficiencies in the Cultural Anxiety Buffer

Terror management theory proposes that low self-esteem results when people are unable to sustain a sense that they are valuable members of a meaningful universe. As the developmental analysis presented earlier suggested, self-esteem is derived from the quality of the relationship between children and their primary caretakers; however, this does not preclude the possibility that subsequent events over the course of a lifetime also significantly influence self-esteem.

Low self-esteem could reflect a failure to maintain one or both components of the cultural anxiety buffer. In some instances, individuals may accept the world-view provided by their culture, but simply be unable to perceive themselves as valuable within that context (e.g., a person who believes that all Americans who try hard enough can be financially successful, but who earns minimum wage and therefore sees him/herself as a failure).

Similarly, there may be circumstances where maintaining a meaningful conception of the world is difficult or impossible (in which case there can be no sense of value). Available worldviews may simply be inadequate for acquiring meaning given specific individual circumstances; or, alternatively, some people may simply be constitutionally or experientially unable to sustain meaning entirely. Becker (1973) has suggested that this may be the case for schizophrenics.

Given the evidence of the stability of self-esteem over time (e.g., Coopersmith, 1967), many of these difficulties may stem from conceptions of the world and the self developed in childhood. However, the prevalence of anxiety and depression through the life span suggests that level of self-esteem in childhood is not inevitably maintained throughout one's life (cf. Rosenberg, 1986). Meaning and value may be easier to sustain in youth, before the inevitable onset of disillusioning experiences (e.g., death, disease, divorce, knowledge of corruption in cherished institutions and heroes) and while one has many potential talents and avenues to establish value (ofttimes potential is never realized and life choices are narrowed to none). It may also be the case that some peoples' chosen bases of self-worth in youth erode over time (e.g., physical attractiveness, athletic ability).

Our theory suggests that people who are unable to maintain a sense of value and meaning will either suffer chronically low self-esteem and its consequences (discussed below), or will find an alternative worldview that is more compelling (although the latter option may be problematic for schizophrenics). Regardless of the cause, the absence of self-esteem will engender anxiety, which results in maladaptive psychological and/or physical responses. Research suggests that this anxiety may directly contribute to psychological and physical problems (Yalom, 1980); in addition, the anxiety may contribute indirectly to such problems via its relation to stress. Our analysis and research (the self-esteem anxiety-buffer studies reported above) suggest that low self-esteem individuals will respond to stressful events with anxiety. This is likely to intensify the individual's level of stress in two ways. First, it is highly likely that anxiety is itself stressful (cf. Gray, 1982); thus, responding to stress with anxiety will add to the stress.

Second, anxiety is likely to interfere with the implementation of adaptive coping strategies to alleviate the stress, thereby prolonging and amplifying the individual's exposure to stress.

Because anxiety and ineffective coping with stress contribute to a variety of mental health problems, low self-esteem individuals should be particularly vulnerable to such problems. Additionally, there is now a large body of evidence that suggests that anxiety and stress cause a host of physical problems (ranging in severity from nausea to cancer) by undermining the integrity of the immune system (see, e.g., Jemott, 1985, and Tecoma & Huey, 1985, for reviews of current empirical work in psychoneuroimmunology). Thus, low self-esteem may result in physical as well as psychological problems.

Correlational research has yielded findings that are highly consistent with this analysis. Relationships between low self-esteem and ineffective responses to stress have been found for police officers (Lester, 1986), firemen (Petrie & Rotheram, 1982), recently widowed elderly people (Johnson, Lund, & Dimond, 1986), wives of soldiers sent to war (Hobfoll & London, 1986), women who have experienced difficult pregnancies (Hobfoll & Leiberman, 1987), recently unemployed individuals (Pearlin, Lieberman, Menaghan, & Mullan, 1981), medical students completing surgical internships (Linn & Zeppa, 1984), abused children (Zimrin, 1986), and new parents (Osofsky, 1985).

Additionally, with regard to physical problems, studies have shown a relationship between low self-esteem and poor physical health (Antonucci & Jackson, 1983), headaches (Khouri-Haddad, 1984), children's visits to school sick bays (Harper & Field, 1986), hypochondriasis (Barsky & Klerman, 1983), and nervous breakdowns (Ingham, Kreitman, Miller, & Sasidharan, 1986). Regarding psychological problems, low self-esteem is associated with anxiety in general (e.g., French, 1968; Lipsitt, 1958; Rosenberg & Simmons, 1972; Strauss, Frame, & Forehand, 1987), death anxiety in particular (Templer, 1971), aggressive behavior in male children (Lochman & Lampron, 1986), bulimic behavior in women (Crowther & Chernyk, 1986), smoking in adolescence (Penny & Robinson, 1986; Ahlgren, Norem, Hochhauser, & Garvin, 1982), male spouse abuse (Goldstein & Rosenbaum, 1985; Neidig, Friedman, & Collins, 1986), depression (e.g., Brown, Andrews, Harris, & Adler, 1986; Brown, Bifulco, Harris, & Bridge, 1986; Brown, Craig, & Harris, 1985; Mollon & Parry, 1984), anxiety disorders (Strauss *et al.*, 1987), and paranoid schizophrenia (Zigler & Glick, 1988).[11]

Whereas all of the research reported above is entirely consistent with our theoretical analysis, two points should be noted. First, a compelling case could also be made from the correlational literature that self-esteem is unrelated to a

---

[11]This is by no means a complete list of the correlational evidence linking self-esteem to a variety of psychological and physical problems.

variety of factors that our theory would suggest should be related to self-esteem. As Scheff (1990) contends, a careful consideration of the self-esteem literature would reveal massive inconsistencies in findings.

Second, and perhaps related to the first point, the study of dispositional self-esteem is very much hampered by conceptual and methodological ambiguities. Conceptually, there are legitimate concerns regarding the structure of self-esteem, e.g., the utility of global conceptions of self-worth versus conceptions of specific dimensions of self-worth (see, e.g., Marsh, 1986). Methodologically, the most pervasive problem is the likely influence of self-presentational concerns on self-reports of self-esteem (cf. Baumeister, Tice, & Hutton, 1989). Consequently, an individual who scores very high on a self-report self-esteem scale may in fact be massively insecure and profoundly devoid of self-regard, but may nevertheless defensively present him- or herself in a highly desirable fashion (as Horney, 1937, among others, has proposed). People who are designated as having high self-esteem on the basis of self-esteem inventories may thus actually have high self-esteem, or low self-esteem. These findings may account in part for the inconsistencies in the correlational literature. They also render much of the research on dispositional self-esteem problematic pending further conceptual and methodological advances.

A. SUMMARY OF THE TWO SELF-ESTEEM LITERATURES

The experimental evidence concerning threats to self-esteem shows that such threats create anxiety, that they are responded to with a variety of defensive strategies, and that the employment of those strategies reduces anxiety resulting from the threat. In addition, public threats are especially anxiety provoking and motivate especially strong defense of self-esteem. Evidence also suggests that experimentally raised self-esteem minimizes anxiety when individuals are exposed to threatening stimuli. Finally, correlational evidence indicates that high self-esteem is associated with low anxiety, superior physical and mental health, and effective coping with stress. Although our explanations of prior research are, of course, necessarily posthoc, terror management theory can account for the findings in both literatures. Additionally, it is worth noting that the theory was not induced from these research findings; rather it was developed independently based on a conceptual analysis of the work of Becker and others. In fact, the notion that self-esteem is an anxiety buffer and that public behavior serves private self-image can be found in Becker's (1962) first book (*The Birth and Death of Meaning*), which predates almost all of the research that we have reviewed.

Although other theories provide useful insights into various parts of these literatures, we know of no other theory capable of tying its diverse strands together into a coherent whole. Furthermore, although evidence that people are motivated to maintain self-esteem is strong, we know of no explanations for why this motive exists, except the one offered by terror management theory.

B. MAINTENANCE OF THE CULTURAL ANXIETY BUFFER

We propose that because of the important terror management functions served by the cultural worldview and self-esteem, a substantial portion of our social behavior is directed toward sustaining faith in a shared cultural worldview (which provides the basis for self-esteem) and maintaining a sense of value within that cultural context. We turn now to a demonstration of how this conceptualization can be used to help understand a wide variety of human social behaviors. To accomplish this, we will consider how individuals maintain a sense of personal value within the cultural worldview and how they maintain faith in the cultural worldview itself. Finally, we will consider the problem of inadequate terror management.

XI. Maintaining a Sense of Value within the Cultural Worldview

A. GENERAL MAINTENANCE

1. Conformity, Obedience, and Self-Presentation

Because self-esteem is a cultural construction, the simple notion that people need continual consensual validation of their value can help explain the tendencies toward uniformity, conformity, and obedience which are so pervasive in human behavior. We all want to be accepted as valued participants in some valid cultural drama, so we strive to do what others in the culture, particularly others highly representative of our view of the cultural drama, deem appropriate and admirable. The literatures on conformity, obedience, and specific ways in which we adjust our behavior to gain the approval of others are generally consistent with this idea (e.g., Asch, 1958; Gergen & Wishnov, 1965; Milgram, 1974). Indeed, as Insko (1985) has noted, the two primary motives for conformity seem to be the desire to be liked and the desire to be correct; the former motive serves the self-esteem component of terror management, and the latter serves the worldview component.

In addition, research has shown that these tendencies are heightened when the others involved are highly valued or representative of the culture (e.g., Milgram, 1974; Schlenker, 1980). Research has also shown that when others express disapproval of us, thereby threatening our value, we react negatively and often aggressively (e.g., Geen, 1968). Similarly, research on interpersonal attraction demonstrates the importance of being valued by others by documenting our positive responses to those who praise us and those who like us (e.g., Byrne, 1971; Jones, 1973; Shrauger, 1975).

A recent study by Pyszczynski *et al.* (1990) demonstrated that the tendency to like those who praise us and dislike those who criticize us depends on the implications of such feedback for self-esteem. Subjects were instructed to either be themselves or take the role of another person in a getting acquainted exercise, and were then given either positive or negative evaluations from their interaction partners. Praise led to more liking and criticism led to more disliking when subjects were behaving as themselves, but did not affect liking when they were taking the role of another person.

2. Friendship and Love as a Basis for Self-Esteem

Among the most potent interpersonal sources of self-esteem are friendships and romantic and familial relationships involving mutual love. These relationships validate our worth on a daily basis because our friends, lovers, and families acknowledge and affirm our worth virtually every time we interact with them. In such relationships, each individual imbues the other with great value; therefore, the greater the value that A attaches to B, the more effective B's esteem for A is in increasing A's sense of self-worth. The exclusive nature of many romantic love relationships further increases their potential to bolster self-esteem; a highly valued person forsaking all others for one special relationship provides a particularly dramatic affirmation of one's own value. This may help explain the intensity of familial and romantic love and the importance placed on long-term love relationships in many cultures. From this perspective, jealousy, the strong emotional reaction that often occurs when a romantic love relationship is threatened, can be viewed as anxiety resulting from the threat of loss of a potent source of self-esteem (cf. Fenichel, 1955; Freud, 1955; Mead, 1931). Consistent with this point, White (1981) has found that a propensity for jealousy is associated with low self-esteem and with high dependency on one's romantic partner for self-esteem.

In this regard, the parent–child relationship generally may be the most potent source of self-esteem. As many theorists have suggested, young childrens' sense of value is derived from the love shown by their caretakers. Equally important, but less commonly noted, is the fact that offspring typically provide parents with a tremendous sense of value (e.g., Miller, 1981). Parents can view themselves as responsible for the existence of these creations. Therefore, any value one's child has (from being cute to winning the Nobel Prize) imparts value to the parent(s). Furthermore, parents (or caretakers) know they are essential to the current and future well-being of their children and, at least up to a certain age, children are very demonstrative of their love for their parent(s). Finally, children may provide a sense of permanent value and immortality to the extent that they are viewed as physical and symbolic extensions of the parents who themselves can have children, *ad infinitum*. Thus, when adolescents rebel and reject the parents' cherished values, one important component of the parents' striving for immortality may be threatened. The stronger the parents' investment in that source of a sense of immortality, the stronger the parents' negative reaction will be.

3. Socially Valued Behaviors that Enhance Self-Esteem

More generally, individuals can feel valuable to the extent that they meet cultural standards of value. Providing help to those in need, especially those who are deemed particularly worthy of help within the culture, is one example of how meeting cultural standards of value provides individuals with a sense of personal value. The positive reactions that helpers often receive from others add to the private experience of meeting important cultural standards and thus play an important role in maintaining helping behavior. Consistent with this analysis are findings that social approval facilitates helping (e.g., Moss & Page, 1972; Satow, 1975), that helping increases when relevant social norms are made salient (e.g., Berkowitz, 1972; Macaulay, 1970), and that helping decreases when extrinsic causal attributions for helping are made salient (e.g., Paulhus, Shaffer, & Downing, 1977). Thus, a great deal of helping behavior may be seen as a way to establish or maintain self-esteem. In addition, Nadler and Fisher (1986) argued that the available research indicates that recipient reactions to help are largely determined by the extent to which the help threatens or bolsters the recipient's self-esteem.

Acts of aggression may also serve to maintain or enhance self-esteem. In many cultures, attributes such as strength, agility, courage, and boldness are highly valued; given that acts of aggression can imply these attributes, in many contexts, they may be used to build self-esteem. Indeed, the appeal of war and other violent situations, especially among children and in fantasy form (e.g., games and movies), may derive primarily from the grand displays of heroism such situations allow.

4. Material Possessions as a Basis of Self-Esteem

Of course, there are also more tangible symbols of value (i.e., status) in all cultures. In contemporary United States culture, for example, a wide variety of material objects from jewelry to automobiles may serve as evidence of value. Indeed, for many Americans it may be that, in their conception of the cultural drama, their worth is based on and symbolized by their level of material wealth. What may be so appealing about such a basis of self-esteem is its concrete nature; an individual's value is externalized and thus objectified. The near-unanimous agreement on the importance of material wealth also adds to its utility within the culture as a basis for self-worth. As Becker (1975) observed:

> By continually taking and piling and computing interest and leaving to one's heirs, man contrives the illusion that he is in complete control of his destiny. After all, accumulated things are a visible testimonial to power, to the fact that one is not limited or dependent. (p. 89)[12]

5. Vicarious Sources of Self-Esteem

Aside from establishing a sense of worth by fulfilling valued roles, eliciting the approval of others, becoming desired by others, and accumulating material possessions, individuals may also establish a sense of worth vicariously, through identification with real and mythical cultural heroes. By identifying with someone who seems special and important, particularly someone who has confronted life-threatening situations and survived, one may attain a feeling of being significant and immortal, even if for only a moment. Cialdini and Richardson (1980) have demonstrated such "basking in reflected glory," showing that, when self-esteem is threatened, people attempt to increase their association with others with positive qualities and decrease their association with others with negative qualities. From the present perspective, the appeal of much entertainment derives from the portrayal of heroism (cf. Bettleheim, 1977). Through identification with heroes in religion, literature, film, and sports, the individual can share the glory (e.g., by being a fan of a sports team); perhaps one of the clearest examples of this is the Spanish bullfight, in which the heroic matador, as the representative of the culture, defies death by vanquishing a terrifying animal. Such identification can also help individuals frame their own lives in heroic terms (e.g., in the United States, one might be the Richard Pryor of psychology teachers, the Michael Jordan of short-order cooks, the John Wayne of computer troubleshooters, or the Clint Eastwood of international politics).

Similarly, participatory forms of entertainment, such as gambling, video games, board games (Dungeons and Dragons may be an extreme example of this), theater groups, and participatory sports, allow individuals the possibility of attaining momentary heroism. By absorbing oneself in these activities one

---

[12]We do not endorse Becker's (1975) use of sexist language and we hope that readers are not overly offended by it. It should be noted, however, that Becker's use of the term man for humanity in this and subsequent quotes reflects the accepted, albeit sexist, literary convention of his time.

temporarily abandons the norms and standards that govern behavior in everyday life and moves into a realm where heroism is easier to achieve and the costs of failure are much less severe. This framework may therefore help explain the enormous amount of energy, money, and emotion spent on entertainment in many cultures: entertainment serves the important psychological function of bolstering individuals' cultural anxiety buffers.[13]

B. RESPONSES TO THREAT

1. Private Recognition of Shortcomings

Our theory suggests that there are two conditions under which one's value within a cultural context can be threatened and anxiety-reducing defenses are needed. The first is when individuals become aware that some aspect of themselves may undermine their efforts to fulfill a valued role, gain social approval, avoid disapproval, be desired by others, or accumulate symbols of worth. A particular activity will therefore be ego involving to the extent that it has the potential to provide information concerning attributes relevant to the individual's ability to be a valued participant in his or her own particular cultural drama.

Consistent with this first condition, social psychological research has shown that individuals employ a variety of self-esteem-maintenance strategies when they anticipate or experience an outcome that has unfavorable implications for present or future maintenance of a valued cultural role—even if no other person will have knowledge of that outcome (see the large body of research on self-esteem-maintenance strategies reviewed in the previous section).

2. Public Recognition of Shortcomings

Although many of the studies cited earlier have demonstrated efforts to defend self-esteem under conditions in which concerns about evaluations from others

---

[13]Given the great variety of ways in which people can enhance their self-esteem, it is important to consider to what extent, and for how long, particular modes of self-esteem enhancement satisfy the individual needs. Of course, answers to these questions will depend on a variety of factors concerning the individual and would require substantial refinements in both the conceptualization and measurement of self-esteem. It is clear, however, that the need for indications of our own value is rarely, if ever, satisfied for long. Consider, for example, a faculty member in a psychology department. A compliment from a student may provide a sense of value for a few hours, acceptance of a manuscript for publication may do so for a few days, and a Nobel Prize for a few months. Individuals always seem to adapt to the indicators of self-value sooner or later (cf. Brickman and Campbell, 1971). They then need new ones, or at least to be reminded of old ones they had not considered for a while. Perhaps dwelling on any given achievement long enough leads the individual to consider the limits and inadequacies of that achievement as an indicator of value.

were minimal, our theory posits that the opinions of others in the culture are of great relevance to self-esteem because they provide a link to the cultural context from which self-esteem is derived. Given the subjective and ambiguous nature of any evaluation, we require consensual validation of our positive self-images from others. Being a valuable person means living up to shared cultural standards for being valuable; if others within the culture do not agree that we have met those standards, our own beliefs that we have done so are threatened. Becker (1971) uses the following anecdote to illustrate the extent to which people are driven by a need for social validation of their value:

> Nietzsche said of Schopenhauer that he was a model for all men because he could work in isolation and care nothing for the plaudits of the human market place. The implication is that he had his sense of value securely embedded in himself and his own idea of what his work was worth. Yet this same Schopenhauer spent his lonely life scanning the footnotes of learned journals to see whether there was ever going to be recognition of his work. (p. 70)

Thus, the second condition of direct threat to self-worth is when individuals become aware that their value as perceived by others within the culture falls short of their own aspirations. The previously reviewed evidence that public threat leads to especially vigorous efforts to defend self-esteem provides support for this notion (e.g., Frey, 1978; Greenberg & Pyszczynski, 1985; Tesser & Paulhus, 1983).

This analysis suggests that self-esteem concerns are aroused not only in evaluative achievement settings but in most, if not all, social settings. In contrast to a number of theories of self-presentation (e.g., Jones & Pittman, 1982; Tedeschi, 1981), we argue that public self-presentational behavior is designed primarily not to garner specific rewards and avoid specific punishments from a particular present audience, but to maintain and bolster self-esteem. This position is quite consistent, however, with Goffman's (1955) discussion of the need, in all social encounters, to protect the "sacred self"; it also helps explain the intensity of people's concerns about their public images.

For example, when a teacher gets up in front of his/her first class, the intense anxiety about doing well is far greater than would be expected if only rewards and punishments from the particular student audience were at stake—clearly, a potential threat to self-esteem is involved. When a man alone in a bar very much wants female companionship but refuses to approach attractive women because he is "afraid of rejection," clearly what he is avoiding is not merely looking bad to the particular denizens of the bar, but the consequent threat to his self-esteem. When a woman who is physically abused by her husband is more concerned with hiding that fact from others than with seeking relief from the abuse, again we see that concerns about what other people think are far greater than consideration of tangible rewards and punishments from the particular audience would suggest.

In each of these examples, and innumerable others, we can see what a driving force the need for self-esteem is. Phenomenologically, what are people doing when they try to avoid "looking bad" before others? They are trying to minimize negative feelings that have been described as anxiety, embarrassment, guilt, humiliation, and shame (Scheff, 1988). Our theory suggests that these feelings are a leakage of the basic existential terror from which self-esteem protects us. Damage to public image threatens self-esteem and thereby disrupting equanimity in the face of ultimate vulnerability.

XII. Sustaining Faith in the Cultural Worldview

A. GENERAL MAINTENANCE

It would be far beyond the scope of this article to detail the many ways in which faith in a given culture is developed and maintained. Clearly, much of the socialization and education of children is geared toward instilling the values and worldview of the culture (see, e.g., Henry, 1963). Formal and informal historical and religious teachings seem to play particularly central roles in conveying a cultural conception of reality that provides meaning and the possibility of significance and immortality. Parents and other agents of the culture are highly motivated to pass their version of the cultural worldview on to their offspring because of their intense desire to believe that their conception is true, and their intense desire to ensure the perpetuation of their culture.

Throughout our lives, cultural symbols (e.g., in the United States, such things as churches, monuments, flags, currency, golden arches, and crosses) and cultural rituals (e.g., in the United States, activities such as singing the national anthem, going to church, visiting historical locations and theme parks, and following the news, fashion, entertainment, and sports) help us maintain a sense that the cultural drama is real, significant, and enduring, by objectifying it and demonstrating social consensus. This can be seen on a grand scale in a major soccer match in many countries or at an important football or basketball game in the United States. The intense concern and enthusiasm exhibited by the spectators reaffirms the significance of the event that is unfolding. Throughout the world, cultural rituals also help maintain the cultural anxiety buffer by affirming cultural values.

An aid to maintenance of faith in the worldview may be the false consensus effect. A variety of studies have shown that individuals tend to overestimate the extent to which their attitudes are shared by others within the culture (e.g., Nisbett & Kunda, 1985; Ross, Greene, & House, 1977; Sanders & Mullen, 1983). Consistent with terror management theory, a number of researchers have concluded from their findings that false consensus effects result in part from a self-serving desire to believe that one's beliefs or attitudes are valid (e.g., Campbell, 1986; Sherman, Presson, & Chassin, 1984; Sherman, Presson, Chassin, Corty, & Olshavsky, 1983). For example, Sherman *et al.* (1984) found a false consensus effect when a subject's self-esteem had been threatened but not when it had been bolstered. Similarly, Campbell (1986) found a false consensus for attitudes, but a false uniqueness effect for abilities. In both studies, consensus estimates seemed to be adjusted to suit the self-validation needs of the estimators.

B. RESPONSES TO THREAT

Terror management theory posits that we must have faith in the absolute validity of our worldview. Thus, the mere existence of others who do not share our central attitudes, beliefs, and values is threatening because, if others do not agree with us, it implies that we might be wrong. Consequently, different others motivate action to eradicate the threat and thereby defend the validity of the worldview. Social psychological findings, along with historical events and everyday experience, are replete with examples of how individuals respond to such threats to their cultural context. The present perspective has implications for understanding reactions to deviants, dissimilar others, outgroup members, and to information and ideas that run counter to the cultural worldview.

1. Reactions to Deviants, Moral Transgressors, Heroes, and Victims

In a previous section, we argued that a great deal of conforming behavior can be explained as an attempt to bolster the anxiety buffer provided by self-esteem by garnering the approval of other valued participants in the cultural drama. This, of course, is the process of normative social influence discussed by Festinger (1950), Kelley (1952), and others. In this section we consider why people generally react with hostility to those who deviate from social norms. Indeed, research has shown that encounters with deviant individuals lead to attempts to convert them to one's own point of view and, if that fails, to a tendency to reject them (e.g., Miller & Anderson, 1979; Schachter, 1951). From a terror management perspective, those who deviate from cultural norms make salient the lack of social consensus for our beliefs and thus threaten our confidence in the absolute validity of our own worldviews.

This tendency to reject those who are different emerges even when their nonconforming behavior seems to be harmless to others. One common example in this culture is the reaction to those who do not maintain an appearance in accord with cultural prescriptions for a particular role. If a male is to remain in the employ of an accounting firm, he must wear the right type of suit and it must be unwrinkled and in good condition. Likewise, if a professor wears a baseball cap to a faculty meeting or lecture, colleagues may be bothered by this behavior and may even request the removal of the offending chapeau.

Clearly, such deviant behavior poses no direct tangible threat to the well-being of the individuals who witness it. Such threats are symbolic in nature. Individuals' negative reactions to such seemingly trivial acts of nonconformity (and more extreme reactions to more serious deviant acts) result from the threat to the values underlying the cultural prescriptions that have been violated. If individuals derive a sense of self-worth by viewing their occupation as a highly valued cultural role, then someone with the same occupation who has the appearance of a "common laborer" or a graduate student poses a threat to that occupation as an anxiety buffer. Reactions to the deviant appearance of others can also be looked at from a more general perspective—someone who does not maintain an appropriate appearance threatens others because she/he is implicitly denying the importance of "looking good."[14]

Of course the more central the value that is being violated, the more severe the negative sanctions tend to be. Among the most important components of peoples' cultural worldviews are the principles and values that are used to assess their morality. For most people, the belief that one is an ethical and virtuous individual is a particularly important determinant of their sense of self-worth. In addition, for many people, moral principles are part of a system of religious beliefs and values that very explicitly provide hope of transcending death and insignificance. Individuals who deviate from these values are viewed with disdain because such deviance implies a rejection of the values through which we acquire our own sense of equanimity.

2. The Mortality Salience Paradigm

In a series of six experiments designed to test the hypothesis that negative reactions to moral transgressors result from terror management concerns, Rosenblatt, Greenberg, Solomon, Pyszczynski, and Lyon (1989) assessed the effects of reminding subjects of their mortality on reactions to such individuals. To the extent that the cultural worldview functions to protect the individual from the anxiety of awareness of mortality, it follows that stimuli that increase the salience of vulnerability and mortality should increase the need to protect and defend

---

[14]It is also interesting to note that in America over the years, looking good has consisted largely of moving further and further from looking like an animal (e.g., cutting and shaping hair, shaving faces and legs, wearing clothes that simulate ideal geometric contours, painting nails, using make-up to hide "imperfections," and perfumes to hide body odors). In a very similar vein, Goffman (1959) has noted that with "progress," cultural norms shift bathroom behavior more and more backstage.

one's cultural anxiety buffer. Osarchuk and Tatz (1973) provided initial support for this hypothesis by showing that exposing individuals who believe in life after death to death-related stimuli increases their faith in the existence of an afterlife. In our research, we have focused on how making mortality salient affects reactions to others who explicitly or implicitly validate or threaten the individual's cultural worldview.

The general procedure employed in the Rosenblatt *et al.* (1989) research is the model for a variety of studies to be discussed here. In all of the studies, subjects were told that we were interested in studying the relationship between personality traits and how people make judgments about specific situations and/or individuals (the particular judgment in question varied between studies and constituted our primary dependent measure for each study). Subjects then completed several filler questionnaires, which were actually standard personality assessments that served to sustain the cover story.

Afterward, experimental subjects were asked to fill out a brief questionnaire concerning their thoughts and feelings about their own death. The mortality salience manipulation was presented as a "Mortality Attitudes Personality Assessment Survey." The survey was described as a new projective personality assessment in which responses to questions about death would be analyzed to gain information about the subjects' personalities. Subjects then completed two open-ended questions: "Please briefly describe the emotions that the thought of your own death arouses in you," and "Jot down, as specifically as you can, what you think will happen to you as you physically die and once you are physically dead." Control subjects either filled out parallel questionnaires dealing with innocuous issues (food or television) or did not fill out a preliminary questionnaire of any kind (depending on the specific study).

In the Rosenblatt *et al.* (1989) studies, all subjects were then asked to read a case brief concerning a woman accused of prostitution and recommend a dollar amount at which bail should be set. It was hypothesized that mortality salience would lead to especially negative reactions to someone suspected of committing a moral transgression. In the first study, actual municipal court judges were especially punitive when mortality was made salient. This finding was replicated in a sample of college students in Study 2, but only among subjects with negative attitudes toward prostitution; this finding demonstrates that it is the individual's own unique version of the cultural worldview that must be protected. Study 3 replicated the effect of mortality salience on responses to a moral transgressor and also showed that mortality salience increases the positivity of responses to a target who heroically upholds cultural values. Specifically, when subjects were reminded of their mortality they recommended an especially large reward for a woman who risked her own safety by turning in a criminal. Study 4 replicated the basic finding and demonstrated that mortality salience does not simply amplify responses to any affectively valenced stimuli (ratings of descriptions of a series of pleasant and unpleasant events) and that a self-awareness manipulation (a mirror) does not produce similar effects.

Study 5 again replicated the basic finding and demonstrated that the mortality salience manipulation does not produce measurable increases in physiological arousal (as indicated by galvanic skin response, pulse rate, and blood pulse volume); thus it appears that the mortality salience-enhanced derogation of those who threaten the cultural worldview is not mediated by physiological arousal. Finally, in Study 6 the basic finding was replicated with a different mortality salience manipulation [in this study, subjects completed Boyar's (1964) Fear of Death Scale in place of our death questionnaire; the scale consists of 18 true or false questions about perceptions of death]. Across all six experiments, reminding subjects of their mortality consistently increased the negativity of reactions to those whose behavior deviated from cultural values and the positivity of reactions to those whose behavior upheld such values.

In all of the mortality salience studies that we have conducted, affect measures were obtained [Multiple Affect Adjective Check List (MAACL), Zuckerman & Lubin, 1965; and Positive and Negative Affect Scale (PANAS), Watson, Clark, & Tellegen, 1988]. Interestingly, self-reported affect was not influenced by the mortality salience manipulation and, based on within-cell correlations, did not appear to mediate the effects that we found on the evaluations of the moral transgressor and the hero. This suggests that reminders of mortality can activate terror management processes without the conscious experience of negative affect. These findings are highly consistent with our earlier contention that the terror of death is largely repressed, and with our analysis of how its wide-ranging influence on behavior occurs primarily outside of consciousness. They are also consistent with Greenwald's (1989) speculative hypothesis that defensive reactions often occur so quickly and effectively that they completely eliminate the subjective experience of anxiety.

3. Reactions to Ideas Discrepant
from the Cultural Worldview

The previous section considered reactions to those whose behavior deviates from cultural norms. More generally, terror management theory posits that any information that implies that the cultural worldview is wrong or that alternative, incompatible worldviews are equally valid should also engender anxiety and encourage efforts to bolster faith in the accepted worldview. Thus the theory predicts that attitude-discrepant communications should generate emotional arousal and attempts to refute the validity of the information conveyed. Research demonstrating the generation of counterarguments in response to counterattitudinal messages is generally consistent with this proposition (for a review, see Petty & Cacioppo, 1986); this research suggests active attempts to refute attitude-discrepant information. At a societal level, this notion can help explain the censorship of deviant but potentially persuasive ideas that occurs in a wide variety of cultures (e.g., the late Islamic leader Khomeini's death threats to Salman Rushdie, the author of *Satanic Verses,* a book critical of Mohammed).

A study by Batson (1975) illustrates such defensive responses when individuals are exposed to information inconsistent with their cultural worldviews. He presented Christian churchgoers with strong evidence that one of their central beliefs was fallacious; one common response of the subjects was to increase their commitment to their religion. In a related vein, before the 1980 United States presidential election, Cooper and Mackie (1983) induced members of a pro-Reagan group to write arguments supporting the reelection of Carter. These subjects subsequently became more negative in their attitudes toward members of a pro-Carter group. Cooper and Mackie argued that when the pro-Reagan subjects wrote the arguments that contradicted the primary belief of their groups, they experienced dissonance, a negative tension state, which was then misattributed to dislike of the opposing pro-Carter group. Terror management theory suggests a simpler explanation for their results: when people's values are threatened, they often try to reassert their faith in their own group by derogating members of other groups.

In a study designed to explicitly assess the terror management function of reactions to ideas supportive and threatening to the cultural worldview, Greenberg, Pyszczynski *et al.* (1990, Study 3) induced half of their subjects to fill out the death questionnaire and the other half to fill out a parallel questionnaire concerning food; we then exposed the subjects to an interview in which the interviewee expressed either positive, mixed, or highly negative opinions about the United States political system. The subjects then indicated their levels of agreement with the opinions and their liking for the interviewee. Mortality salience led to especially positive evaluations of the pro-American interview and interviewee and especially negative evaluations of the anti-American interview and interviewee. These findings indicate that reminders of mortality intensify attempts to bolster and defend the validity of one's cultural worldview.

4. Reactions to Similar and Dissimilar Others and Ingroup and Outgroup Members

The research reported above demonstrates the terror management function of reactions to behavior and ideas that directly threaten the cultural worldview. As noted at the outset of this section, the mere existence of those different from oneself implicitly threatens the cultural worldview. A large body of literature on interpersonal attraction has shown that the less similar others are to ourselves, the less we like them, the less likely we are to offer them help when it is needed, and the more likely we are to aggress against them (for reviews, see Byrne, 1971;

Rokeach, 1968). We suggest that such negative reactions occur because dissimilar others threaten one's own worldview by making salient a lack of social consensus.

Greenberg, Pyszczynski *et al.* (1990, Study 2) assessed the terror management function of such reactions by investigating the effects of mortality salience on liking for others with attitudes similar and dissimilar to one's own. As in previous research, subjects were first asked to fill out the death questionnaire or one about food. They were then given information indicating that a person they were about to meet agreed with them on either 75 or 25% of the issues on an attitude questionnaire they had previously filled out. When asked to fill out an Interpersonal Judgment Scale which assesses their impressions of their partners (Byrne, 1971), liking for the dissimilar partners was lower among mortality salient subjects than among control subjects; this finding was statistically significant, however, only among subjects scoring high on a measure of authoritarianism (Adorno, Frenkel-Brunswick, Levinson, & Sanford, 1950). This demonstrates that mortality salience can increase the tendency to reject those with dissimilar attitudes, but that individuals differ in their likelihood of responding to existential threat in any particular way.

Interestingly, high authoritarians were more rejecting of the dissimilar other than were low authoritarians only in the death salient condition. Thus it appears that mortality salience activated subjects' authoritarian tendencies. Adorno *et al.* (1950) conceptualized the authoritarian personality as an essentially defensive personality pattern characterized by rigid thought patterns, respect for authority, and a tendency to respond with hostility to those who are different. Thus it seems likely that such individuals would be particularly likely to respond to reminders of their mortality with disdain toward dissimilar others.

The present analysis also has implications for understanding prejudice, discrimination, and intergroup conflict. There is considerable evidence that negative reactions to outgroupers result largely from the perception that they do not have similar cultural values (e.g., Goldstein & Davison, 1972; Moe, Nacoste, & Insko, 1981; Rokeach, 1968). It is when confronted with others who view the world quite differently that negative reactions are most likely.

This reasoning suggests that when mortality is made salient, individuals should react especially positively to fellow ingroupers and especially negatively to outgroupers. Greenberg, Pyszczynski *et al.* (1990, Study 1) provided support for this hypothesis in a study in which Christian subjects were either given the death questionnaire or not, and were then asked to evaluate (in private cubicles) two other supposed subjects in the study based on a series of demographic and attitudinal questionnaires all subjects had filled out earlier. The real subjects actually saw two bogus sets of forms, one apparently filled out by an ingrouper (a Christian) and the other apparently filled out by an outgrouper (a Jew). They then evaluated the targets on Byrne's (1971) Interpersonal Judgment Scale and ratings of the applicability of a series of positive and negative traits.

Subjects in the mortality salient condition were more positive in their evaluations of the Christian and more negative in their evaluations of the Jew than were subjects in the control condition. In fact, preference for the Christian over the Jew emerged only in the mortality salient condition. In general, then, the evidence so far supports our contention that the existence of groups that are different from our own is aversive because it raises the possibility of alternative conceptions of the world, thereby threatening faith in the absolute validity of our own conception (cf. Wilder & Shapiro, 1984). When mortality is salient, faith in the worldview is most important; it is then that the threat of different others must be responded to most strongly.

From the present perspective, we would predict that such negative reactions to outgroupers would be increasingly likely the more incompatible and compelling the alternative conception of reality appears to be, and the more committed to this conception the outgroup members appear to be, and the more salient the alternative conception.

5. Historical Reactions to Deviant Individuals and Groups

Historically, people have responded to threats to their cultural worldviews in a number of ways. One way to minimize the threat to one's own worldview is to derogate alternative conceptions. For example, people who do not share a culture's mainstream religious views can be dismissed as ignorant savages; similarly, if a deistic approach to reality is not part of the conception held by a given culture or subculture, those who do hold such a conception can be viewed as insecure and superstitious. Likewise, those who disagree with current mainstream political positions in the United States can be labeled as unpatriotic or as communists. Derogating those who view the world differently undermines their credibility and thus defuses the threat posed by the alternative point of view.

If, however, these deviant individuals or groups persist in their views and further contact with or thoughts about them cannot be avoided, then more elaborate measures may be necessary to minimize the threat. Under such conditions the threat implied by the existence of alternative conceptions can often be eliminated by processes of assimilation and accommodation: either convincing others to drop their perspectives in favor of one's own, or actually incorporating small portions of the alternative view into one's own so that it is no longer threatening. Missionary activities are good examples of assimilation. Successful conversion supports the notion that we have a monopoly on truth and that it is thus our duty to "help" others understand the world the way that we do—it bolsters our own faith in the absolute validity of our perspective.

Rock music is an interesting contemporary example of accommodation. What started as a distinctly countercultural phenomenon in the 1960s has been incorporated into mainstream American culture as a money-making enterprise. Rock stars who formerly initiated anti-American activities now promote beer and fast food in American television commercials. Protest songs that would in general offend the average American are now enjoyed by all in shopping malls, doctor's offices, and elevators after they are divested of their original meaning when transformed into "easy listening" versions. Any threat that rock music may have posed as social criticism is thus easily nullified by its accommodation into the cultural mainstream. Similarly, blue jeans and granola bars were originally popularized as part of a movement toward simplicity, devaluing appearance, and eating more basic and healthy foods. Now we have designer jeans and chocolate-covered granola bars; any association with alternative cultural values has been completely severed.

A fourth way to respond to the threat engendered by those who do not share our own cultural illusion is to simply annihilate them, thus proving that our conception of the world must have been the "right" one after all. Of course, this extreme response is likely only when the other ways to minimize the threat are not sufficiently effective. Religious wars are an example of this phenomenon. The Crusades, the wars between the Sikhs and the Hindus, the Hindus and the Moslems, the Arabs and the Jews, and the Protestants and the Catholics are just a few examples of long-term armed conflicts where political and economic considerations seem to be secondary to ideological contentions, at least in the minds of most of the participants. Only by recognizing the terror-assuaging function of cultural illusions can we understand why peaceful coexistence is so difficult for those who do not share the same worldviews. Lifton (1983) makes a similar observation:

> wars and persecutions are, at bottom, expressions of rivalry between contending claims to immortality and ultimate spiritual power. Religious victimization is a one-sided version of that process with the specific psychological functions of finding a target for death anxiety, sweeping away cosmic doubt, and achieving (or maintaining) revitalization. (p. 315)

Such a conceptualization poses a challenge to those who believe that armed conflicts are entirely explicable and/or resolvable in purely economic and/or political terms, as it suggests that wars may be more appropriately understood as battles between competing terror-shielding illusions and are, therefore, fundamentally psychological in nature. From this perspective, the so-called cold war between the United States and the Soviet Union was a battle between promoters of two cultural realities, both trying to assimilate as many others cultures as possible to strengthen their respective terror shields. Although this is far from a novel idea, it is one that is often overlooked.

The key point is that, although political and economic considerations are certainly factors in many conflicts, major wars throughout recorded history have involved clashes of worldviews—it is the ideological threat, rather than the economic or pragmatic political concerns, that seems necessary to motivate masses of people into battle. For example, whereas historians have debated the causes of the Vietnam War by focusing on the political and economic motives of American power figures, the propaganda targeted for the masses focused almost entirely on persuading the people that the war was necessary to defend the American way of life (democracy and capitalism) from communism (see, e.g., Griffen & Marciano, 1979; Stone, 1966).

Ironically, this analysis explains how earnest, loyal, and courageous individuals, motivated to defend only what is good, and to destroy what is evil, can be responsible for more destruction than all of the psychotic mass murderers who have ever lived. People have to defend their worldview and assert their worth within the context of that worldview; additionally, they have to find controllable sources of evil (scapegoats) to substitute for the uncontrollable ones. As Becker (1975) puts it:

> The result is one of the great tragedies of human existence, what we might call the need to 'fetishize' evil, to locate the threat to life in some special places where it can be placated and controlled. It is tragic precisely because it is sometimes very arbitrary: men make fantasies about evil, see it in the wrong places, and destroy themselves and others by uselessly thrashing about. This is the great moral of Melville's *Moby Dick*, the specific tragedy of a man driven to confine all evil to the person of a white whale. . . . Men cause evil by wanting heroically to triumph over it, because man is a frightened animal who tries to triumph, an animal who will not admit his own insignificance, that he cannot perpetuate himself and his group forever, that no one is invulnerable no matter how much of the blood of others is spilled to try to demonstrate it. (pp. 148 and 151)

XIII. What Happens When the Cultural Anxiety Buffer Breaks Down?

There may be circumstances under which individuals simply cannot maintain the cultural anxiety buffer, either because they cannot maintain a sense of value within the cultural drama, or because they can no longer sustain faith in the cultural drama itself. One possibility for such people is to find an alternative shared cultural worldview that is more compelling and better enables them to obtain self-esteem. Dramatic examples of this are individuals who experience religious conversions, join "cults," or emigrate to other cultures. Consistent with this analysis, Ullman (1982) found that religious conversions are often preceded by acute stress and low self-esteem and Paloutzian (1981) found that following religious conversions, people report having a greater purpose in life and a diminished fear of death.

However, for some individuals, such options are not readily available. Lacking an anxiety buffer, such individuals are completely overwhelmed with terror (i.e., become psychotic), or attempt to cope with the terror in ways that the culture deems maladaptive and abnormal (e.g., neuroses, drug addictions). Consistent with the notion that psychological problems may stem from a breakdown in the cultural anxiety buffer, studies have found that anxious thoughts typically center on two themes: explicit thoughts of physical vulnerability and death, and thoughts about threats to self-esteem (e.g., Beck, Laude, & Bohnert, 1974; Kendall, 1978). From this perspective, mental illness can be viewed broadly as a failure in terror management that is ultimately shared by the individual and the culture.

This analysis has implications at both the individual and the cultural level. With regard to individuals, Becker (1971) gives this advice to psychotherapists: "If you . . . want to understand directly what is driving your patient, ask yourself simply how he thinks of himself as a hero, what constitutes the framework of reference for his heroic strivings—or better, for the clinical case, why he does *not* feel heroic in his life" (p. 77). Regarding cultures, this analysis suggests that they can be evaluated on the basis of how well they fulfill the responsibility of providing a compelling conception of reality that allows the greatest number of people to derive self-esteem with the least expense to others inside and outside of the culture (see Solomon *et al.,* 1991, for a more detailed discussion of the implications of terror management theory for both individual and social change).

There are historical instances in which cultures have failed to fulfill this responsibility on a grand scale (see Turnbull, 1972, for a particularly striking and well-documented instance). When a cultural drama becomes ineffective as an anxiety buffer for many of its members (because of historical events), an extreme shift in beliefs and values may occur. In fact, when cultures begin losing their credibility as worldviews and, thus, their utility as a basis for self-esteem, a new leader may emerge who espouses a "new order." Indeed, it is difficult to understand the extreme devotion to a Ghandi or a Hitler without viewing such phenomena as a massive shift by individuals having difficulty sustaining the cultural anxiety buffer to an alternative worldview from which they can derive self-esteem (cf. Becker, 1973; Lifton, 1968).

At such times people need a new hero, someone with a clear vision who can convince them of their own value. Unfortunately, in the 1920s and 1930s, it was Hitler telling the beleaguered German people they were superior—that it was the gypsies, the communists, and the Jews who were animals and who were responsible for their problems and the evil in their lives. In fact, Hitler portrayed himself as the individual chosen to fulfill the "divine will," by leading the great Aryan race to its ultimate destiny (cf. Burke, 1957; Duncan, 1962, 1968; Lifton, 1986).

This analysis can also help account for less dramatic political shifts. For example, in the United States in the 1980s, former Thespian Ronald Reagan spearheaded a popular conservative movement by portraying himself as a hero (to the extent of using lines from Clint Eastwood films), and by telling Americans that they are a special breed of human, and that simply being an American means that one is of value. Thus, the need for self-esteem can lead to submission to a wide variety of social systems. Becker (1973) critically, but, we believe incisively, assessed the consequence:

> just as there are useless self-sacrifices in unjust wars, so too is there an ignoble heroics of whole societies: it can be the viciously destructive heroics of Hitler's Germany or the plain debasing and silly heroics of the acquisition and display of consumer goods, the piling up of money and privileges that now characterizes whole ways of life, capitalist and Soviet. (p. 7)

Aside from cases in which isolated individuals have difficulty with the cultural anxiety buffer or most members of a culture have such difficulties, there are also cases in which subgroups within the culture may have such problems. Indeed, the problems of some minority groups (e.g., physical and mental health problems and "achievement" problems from the perspective of the standards of the dominant culture) may stem from an inability to establish or maintain a cultural anxiety buffer.

There are a number of reasons why this might happen. One is that, even if members of the group accept the dominant cultural worldview, they may not be allowed to attain sufficient social validation to maintain a durable sense of self-worth; alternatively, perhaps they don't strive sufficiently to do so, because they don't *believe* that they will be allowed to (because of perceived derogation and discrimination against their group). It may also be that members of certain minority groups are not able to accept the dominant worldview because of atrocities the dominant culture has perpetrated against their group in the past; such individuals may therefore be unable to embrace the dominant cultural worldview as a basis for self-esteem.

It should be noted that Crocker and Major (1989) recently reviewed the literature on minority group self-esteem and concluded that minority group members in this country do not typically report lower self-esteem than majority group members. As we explained earlier, we have serious reservations about the validity of standard measures of dispositional self-esteem; thus, we do not believe that firm conclusions can be drawn from this literature. We are especially skeptical because compensatory self-inflation has been shown to be one defensive response to the perception that one is viewed negatively by others (e.g., Greenberg & Pyszczynski, 1985); to the extent that minority group members believe that they are viewed negatively by others, this suggests that self-inflation may be a means of defense for such individuals. Beyond this issue, it may be that minority self-esteem is not particularly low, but, rather, is especially unstable (cf. Kernis,

Grannemann, & Barclay, 1989) and hard to sustain through the life span. With less social validation, and less material and career success, many minority group members may have to derive self-worth primarily from relatively tenuous sources that dissipate over time.

A partial solution to this problem may be to maintain a compelling alternative worldview or subculture that does provide a durable basis for self-esteem. Unfortunately, for many minority groups, such as blacks and American Indians in the United States, the traditional cultures may have been all but destroyed, or, to the extent that they still persist, prescribe standards that either seriously conflict with those of the ruling culture, or are incompatible with their current environment. In such groups, contemporary subcultures may develop that provide some basis of self-worth, but often these subcultures will be severely limited because, by rejecting the abhorrent dominant cultural values, over time they tend to lead to clashes with established social, economic, and legal forces. Subcultures of violence that have arisen in certain United States ghettos may be one distorted and extreme example of this phenomenon (Wolfgang & Ferracuti, 1967).

BRIEF CONCLUSION

In this section, we have attempted to use terror management theory to explain a variety of common social behaviors. Although the treatments of each specific phenomenon have necessarily been brief and cursory, we hope to have shown how a consideration of terror management concerns can enhance our understanding of both specific findings and general patterns of behavior across a diverse array of topics studied in psychology and other social science disciplines. A great deal of human behavior seems to be guided by the need to maintain and defend self-esteem and faith in one's worldview.

XIV. New Directions for Theory and Research on Terror Management

We have already found this theory to be a fertile source of research hypotheses. More importantly, we suspect (and certainly hope) that others will also find the theory to be a potent stimulus for new and creative research directions. Over the course of this chapter, we have discussed the results of 12 completed studies; we have recently completed 2 additional studies, to be described in the following paragraphs. However, this work only begins to scratch the surface of the many interesting and researchable questions that the theory leads one to consider.

In this section, we describe our most recent research and outline some questions for future research. Thus far, our research has been focused on demonstrating the terror management functions of self-esteem and the cultural worldview. Our strategy for demonstrating such a function has consisted of testing two general hypotheses. If both the cultural worldview and self-esteem are necessary for terror management, then (1) strengthening either component should make subjects less prone to anxiety in a threatening situation, and (2) reminding subjects of their mortality should increase their need for validation of either component and, consequently, should intensify their reactions to those who impinge upon it.

We have used the former strategy in our studies of the anxiety-buffering function of self-esteem and the latter in our studies of the effects of mortality salience on responses to those who impinge upon the cultural worldview. Ultimately, both hypotheses should be assessed for each component of the cultural anxiety buffer. Thus, if mortality concerns are activated, we would expect intensified concerns about self-esteem and, consequently, stronger striving for self-esteem. Similarly, increasing one's faith in the cultural worldview should make one less prone to experience anxiety in response to threats.

A. RESEARCH ON SELF-ESTEEM

We have frankly found our hypotheses concerning the self-esteem component of the theory to be particularly difficult to assess. Although the three studies discussed earlier have yielded supportive results, we have been slowed by inconsistencies between measures of anxiety and problems with both the manipulation and measurement of self-esteem. One of the difficulties has been manipulating self-esteem without also affecting mood; this problem cuts both ways in that it may also be difficult to manipulate mood without influencing self-esteem.

Along with pursuing solutions to these problems, we are assessing the responses to anxiety-provoking death-related stimuli by subjects who are dispositionally high or low in self-esteem. We are also examining the effects of manipulating self-esteem on defensive beliefs about death. Additionally, we are planning to investigate the effects of mortality salience on self-evaluation and self-esteem strivings. Finally, we hope to examine the notion that the prime organizing theme of the self-schema is the affectively anchored belief in one's valued position within the metaschema of reality (the internalized cultural worldview).

B. RESEARCH ON THE CULTURAL WORLDVIEW

One of the questions left unresolved by the mortality salience studies (Greenberg, Pyszczynski, *et al.,* 1990; Rosenblatt *et al.,* 1989) is whether reminders of unpleasant events other than death might also encourage bolstering and defense of the cultural worldview. To address this issue, a control condition is needed that makes salient a potentially anxiety-provoking event that is unrelated to death. Of course, our hierarchical analysis of sources of anxiety implies that all sources of anxiety are ultimately derived from the self-preservation instinct and the consequent fear of death. However, most of the things that people worry about are not linked to mortality in a conscious or direct way; rather they are derived from the need to maintain the cultural anxiety buffer. Whether such distal threats will intensify reactions to those who impinge on the anxiety buffer is thus an important question.

Obviously, as noted earlier, threats to the worldview component encourage bolstering of the worldview. On the other hand, threats to the self-esteem component should not necessarily do so; if one's self-worth is threatened, strengthening faith in the values by which one judges oneself will not necessarily reduce the threat. Thus, we would expect that making salient aversive events linked specifically to self-esteem would not result in bolstering of the worldview.

To investigate this issue, we (Greenberg, Simon, Solomon, Lyon, & Pyszczynski, 1991) recently replicated the mortality salience effect on bond for a prostitute and added a condition in which some subjects were asked to write about their next important test; an event that, like death, will happen to them in the future and is potentially anxiety provoking, but that should not motivate defense of the worldview. The means for this study are displayed in Table I. Mortality salience led to significantly higher bonds than both test salience and television salience (the control condition), with the latter two conditions not differing from each other. In addition, test salience led to significantly more negative affect (as measured by the PANAS; Watson *et al.*, 1988) than did either mortality salience or the control condition. Even though test salience created negative affect and mortality salience did not, only the latter condition motivated defense of the worldview. In conjunction with our other studies, these findings confirm that mortality salience activates defense without arousing any affect. Apparently, the buffer is so automatic that it does not require affective impetus to be operative.

TABLE I
MEAN BOND ASSESSMENT FOR ALLEGED PROSTITUTE[a]

	Mortality salient	Test salient	Control
Bond	$659[*]	$182[**]	$89[**]
Negative affect	15[**]	22[*]	13[**]

[a]A high mean indicates a large bond or a high degree of negative affect. For each measure, means that do not share the same superscript differ at $p < .05$, two-tailed.

C. THE PSYCHODYNAMICS
OF TERROR MANAGEMENT

Of course, these findings leave unanswered important questions about the intrapsychic processes underlying the mortality salience effects, for example, about the role of affect and the roles of conscious, nonconscious, and automatic processes. With regard to affect, it may be that as soon as the subjects in our mortality salience studies explained how they feel about death and what will happen to them when they die and once they are dead, the defenses are activated. If our typical mortality salience treatment does indeed allow and even encourage immediate defense of the worldview (via responses to the questions), it may be necessary to make mortality salient but inhibit the marshaling of defenses (e.g., with a cognitive distraction task) to detect affective responses to mortality salience. Perhaps then we would find affective mediation of defense of the worldview.

To further explore the processes by which mortality salience encourages defense of the worldview, it would be useful to contrast our current mortality salience manipulation with other more and less impactful inductions. A more impactful treatment that encouraged an affective reaction could be created, perhaps by adapting the confession technique developed by Pennebaker (e.g., Pennebaker, Colder, and Sharp, 1990). We suspect that such a treatment would not generate automatic defense in the way that the low-impact mortality salience treatment does. Rather, one might find a period of rumination followed by a shoring up of defenses.

It would also be useful to expose subjects to nonconscious death-related stimuli (see Hardaway, 1990, for a review of studies of nonconscious psychodynamic processes, and Baldwin, Carrell, & Lopez, 1990, for an interesting example of this work). One possibility is that such stimuli would generate negative affect because, without being consciously salient, they may not activate normal defenses—if such defenses are mediated by consciousness. If, however, defenses are activated by whatever monitors stimuli not consciously perceived, then we would expect defense of the worldview, similar to that produced by our usual mortality salience treatment. Obviously, the outcome of studies of this sort would add immensely to our understanding of the operation of the anxiety buffer.

D. INDIVIDUAL AND CROSS-CULTURAL
DIFFERENCES IN WORLDVIEWS

In addition to exploring the intrapsychic processes involved in the operation of the anxiety buffer, we have also begun to explore the effects of individual differences in worldviews on reactions to mortality salience. Worldviews may vary in their effectiveness in protecting one from anxiety and in the types of behavior that they encourage to ward off threat. For example, it may be the case that some worldviews are constructed in a way that makes it less likely that different others will be perceived as threatening. Indeed, Greenberg, Pyszczynski *et al.* (1990, Study 2) found that although high authoritarians derogated a dissimilar other, low authoritarians did not. This finding led us to hypothesize that because open-mindedness and tolerance tend to be part of the liberal worldview, rather than becoming more intolerant under mortality salient conditions, liberals might actually become more tolerant. For liberals, displaying tolerance and open-mindedness may be a more effective way to bolster their worldview than would derogating dissimilar others.

To test this hypothesis, we (Greenberg, Simon, Solomon, Chatel, & Pyszczynski, 1991) selected conservative and liberal subjects, exposed them to either the standard death questionnaire or a parallel television questionnaire, and then asked them to evaluate two other subjects, one with similar political beliefs and one with dissimilar political beliefs. The subjects indicated their evaluations on the Interpersonal Judgment Scale (Byrne, 1971) and on a set of positive and negative traits. The means for both measures are displayed in Table II. Significant three-way interactions on both measures conformed closely to predictions. For conservatives, mortality salience encouraged more favorable reactions to a similar target and more unfavorable reactions to a dissimilar target. In contrast,

TABLE II

CELL MEANS FOR THE THREE-WAY INTERACTION OF POLITICAL ORIENTATION, MORTALITY SALIENCE, AND TARGET SIMILARITY ON ATTRACTION AND TRAIT RATINGS[a]

	Mortality salient		Television salient	
	Similar target	Dissimilar target	Similar target	Dissimilar target
Interpersonal judgment scale ratings				
Conservative subjects	37.59*	15.65‡	33.11**	18.98†
Liberal subjects	28.95**	23.52***	31.37**	20.79†
Trait ratings				
Conservative subjects	7.58*	4.04‡	6.92**	4.88‡
Liberal subjects	6.12***	5.65†	6.41***	4.93‡

[a]Interpersonal Judgment Scale (IJS) ratings could vary from 6 (extremely negative evaluation) to 42 (extremely positive evaluation); trait ratings could vary from 1 (extremely unfavorable) to 9 (extremely favorable). Within each measure, means that do not share a subscript differ at $p < .05$, one-tailed.

for liberals, mortality salience led to no change in reactions to the similar target and less unfavorable reactions to the dissimilar target.

In support of our explanation of these results, the conservative subjects scored higher on an authoritarianism scale than did the liberal subjects and, in a separate sample, liberal subjects were stronger in their advocacy of tolerance of different others than were conservative subjects. Whereas all of our previous findings suggest that mortality salience leads to positive reactions to those who validate one's worldview and negative reactions to those who dispute it, this most recent study suggests that those with worldviews that encourage tolerance of differences may actually respond to such inductions with less negative reactions toward those who are different. This suggests the theoretical possibility of the development of worldviews that, even under mortality salient conditions, encourage more peaceful relationships among individuals and nations.

There are undoubtedly many other dimensions of one's worldview that also have implications for how one responds to threats. For example, beliefs about justice, control, and the value of human life may all exert important influences. Similarly, a wide range of other individual differences may also influence the operation of the anxiety buffer. For example, as noted earlier, Mikulincer *et al.* (1990) have recently presented evidence suggesting that individual differences in attachment style are associated with conscious concerns about death. Specifically, relative to those with a secure attachment style, those with both ambivalent and avoidant attachment styles seemed to exhibit high levels of concern about death in their responses to a thematic apperception test.

It is also important to consider the possibility of cross-cultural variation in the operation of the anxiety buffer. It has been argued that although self-esteem is a potent psychological concern in individualistic cultures, it may be a much less potent force in more collectively oriented societies (e.g., Weiss, Rothbaum, & Blackburn, 1984). Perhaps in collectivist societies, secure attachment to the group is sufficient to manage terror; of course in such cultures it could be argued that self-worth is obtained through humble submission to the larger group (Markus & Kitayama, 1991). Given our claim that the fear of death is biologically rooted and universal and that culture is the primary human mechanism for dealing with this fear, it is important to assess the extent to which terror management hypotheses can be supported in cultures different from our own. The theory suggests that although the content of the anxiety-buffering system will vary from culture to culture, the underlying dynamics of the system are universal.

The preceding discussion suggests a need for cross-cultural and developmental research on the genesis and vicissitudes of worldviews, anxiety (about death, the worldview, and one's self-worth), and the need for self-esteem across the life span. Research with clinical populations (e.g., terminally ill, depressives, paranoid schizophrenics, those with anxiety disorders) and in settings in which death is encountered on a daily basis (e.g., hospitals, nursing homes, war zones) is also sorely needed. Although we have only hinted at possible clinical implications of our analysis here, we have elaborated them somewhat in Solomon *et al.* (1991).

In summary, although the existing research is highly supportive, a great deal of additional evidence concerning the theory's propositions is needed. The current findings also raise a variety of intriguing questions that go beyond the domain of the existing conceptual framework. Frankly, we are not particularly qualified or suited to pursue some of these directions and we hope that these ideas are sufficiently stimulating to motivate colleagues with cognitive, cross-cultural, developmental, and clinical interests and expertise to do so.

XV. Metatheoretical Issues: Why Death, and Is This a Testable Theory?

There are two metatheoretical concerns that we have repeatedly encountered regarding terror management theory: first, the question of why our theory focuses on death anxiety rather than anxiety in general; and second, the question of whether or not terror management theory is testable, and hence "scientific."

A. WHY DEATH?

The assumption that all anxieties (and a great deal of behavior) are derived from the instinct for self-preservation and the consequent terror of death is obviously rather unorthodox, but we believe that it is defensible and useful for a number of reasons. First, it follows from an evolutionary perspective on humankind, and thus provides an essential link with the other biological sciences. Second, this assumption also seems to follow from our developmental analysis and our hierarchical analysis of motivation. Third, viewing death as a primary source of anxiety helps account for the content of cultural institutions and worldviews in terms of individual psychological needs and propensities.

Finally, and most importantly, viewing annihilation as the central source of anxiety affords the theory a great deal of parsimony and power by enabling it to explain such diverse phenomena as (1) obvious evidence of the fear of death, such as medicine, consumer safety efforts, the power of threats of violence in controlling behavior, and anxiety in response to doctors and hospitals, (2) the prevalence of death concerns and immortality beliefs and rituals in all known cultures [indeed, one of the very oldest known written documents, the 6000-year-old *Epic of Gilgamesh* (see, e.g., Hooke, 1963), concerns the search for immortality], (3) the frequency of posttraumatic stress disorders in individuals exposed to life-threatening situations (e.g., Vietnam Veterans; Fairbank & Nicholson, 1987), (4) the occurrence of conscious thoughts about death when individuals experience traumatic but not life-threatening events [e.g., depressed individuals who have lost a central source of self-worth may ruminate about death (Yalom, 1980)], (5) the strength of cultural affiliations, and (6) the many manifestations of the need for self-esteem. Even behaviors that superficially seem inconsistent with the primacy of the fear of death, such as ritual suicides to restore honor and giving up one's life for one's culture, are readily explicable. Individuals in dire situations may actually seek their own physical deaths in order to restore or enhance their own cultural value and thereby secure transcendence of ultimate annihilation (cf. Lifton, 1983).

B. HOW CAN THE THEORY BE EVALUATED?

The second metatheoretical issue is how a broad theory of this nature should be evaluated. Because it is derived from psychoanalytic and existential philosophical traditions, terror management theory contrasts sharply with most contemporary social psychological theorizing with regard to both its depth and its scope. Since the late 1950s, a number of well-known criticisms have been lodged against psychoanalytic approaches and other forms of grand theorizing, as well (e.g., Marx & Hillix, 1963). We believe, however, that there are strengths to such approaches and that it is time for contemporary academic psychology to recognize that they can be useful and complementary to more conventional work.

The most popular criticism of grand theories is that they are not testable. Historians and philosophers of science, statisticians and methodologists agree that, regardless of their breadth, theories can never be unequivocally confirmed (see, e.g., Popper, 1959). There is, however, a belief prevalent in psychology that a good theory should be disconfirmable. Unfortunately, unequivocal disconfirmation of a theory is also not possible for two reasons (see Laudan, 1977, 1984, for a detailed discussion of this issue).

First, disconfirmed predictions can always be attributed to countervailing mediating factors. For example, if one fails to find attitude change in a cognitive dissonance paradigm, would this imply disconfirmation? Although that would certainly be one possible interpretation, a myriad of other alternatives are also possible: choice, commitment, or foreseeability may not have been manipulated properly; the attitude may not have been sufficiently important; the wrong modes of dissonance reduction may have been assessed; or the measurements taken may have been insensitive to real changes that did, in fact, occur.

A second reason that theories cannot be unambiguously disconfirmed is that individual theories rarely consist exclusively of conceptual components that can be directly observed. Concrete predictions can therefore be made only by combining a number of theories, including theories about the function and operation of measuring instruments. For example, testing a theory which hypothesized that self-esteem serves to buffer anxiety would entail a host of theoretical concerns in addition to the theory that is presumably being tested. Because self-esteem and anxiety cannot be directly observed, testing a hypothesis that explores the relationship between them would involve theories about what self-esteem is and how it is measured, what anxiety is and how it is measured [e.g., what a physiograph machine does and the relationship between the information recorded (e.g., skin conductance) and the conceptual constructs that the measures presumably represent (i.e., theories about the relationship between skin conductance and anxiety)]. As Laudan (1977) observed, when a theoretical prediction is not obtained:

> we can never deduce with certainty which theoretical element(s) in the complex has been refuted or falsified by the recalcitrant observation. All we learn from experience . . . is that we have gone astray somewhere, but the logic of scientific inference is too imprecise to allow us with certainty to pin the blame on any particular component or components in the theoretical complex. It follows that we can never legitimately claim that any theory has ever been refuted. (p. 41)

The point here is that because theories cannot be unequivocally confirmed or disconfirmed, they must therefore be judged by other standards. Following Laudan (1984), Lewin (1951), and many others, we believe that theories ultimately must be evaluated in terms of their usefulness. This evaluation, of course, depends in turn on a consideration of the ways in which a theory might be useful. Laudan argued that the usefulness of theories depends on an ongoing non-hierarchical dialectical consideration of values (what questions are important to ask), theories (how do given theories provide answers to important questions), and empirical concerns (by what methods can a theory be evaluated and how do available data bear on existing theories and questions).

The relationship between values, theories, and empirical concerns is non-hierarchical in that the three factors are of equal importance; it is dialectical in the sense that each factor interacts with and consequently influences (transforms) the other factors (e.g., a consideration of specific data might change the theory which provided the original impetus to collect the data, which in turn might change the character of the questions that one chooses to ask).

At the most basic level, a theory is a tool that should facilitate our ability to generate functional conceptions of reality. The first step, then, is for the theory to direct one toward important questions. The quality and importance of the questions that the theory compels one to ask are thus as important to consider as are the analyses and data that are generated to answer them. And, as Laudan has argued, the value that a scientific discipline attaches to any particular question is determined by a wide range of social, historical, and political factors. Consequently, the very substance matter of all scientific disciplines evolves and changes over time.

In addition to the quality of the questions that a theory addresses there should be an evaluation of the extent to which a theory is coherent and internally consistent. Harris (1979) makes a similar observation:

> Although for the empiricist the evaluation of competing paradigms must ultimately rest on the productivity and comprehensiveness of testable theories, this does not mean that the logical structure of paradigms is any less important . . . . if we make one crucial assumption about the purpose of science, then the possibility arises that some paradigms and theories can be evaluated even prior to the examination of the substantive products. This one crucial assumption is that the overall aim of science is to discover the maximum amount of order inherent in the universe or in any field of inquiry. (p. 25)

Another basic function of theory is to explain and organize what is currently known about the conceptual domain of the theory. A good theory should be able to explain both existing empirical work and the events in the "real world" to which the theory ultimately pertains (it is too easy to forget that the raw data of social psychological inquiry is the everyday behavior of human beings in a cultural and historical context). The theory should explain how or why the phenomenon occurs and how it is related to other phenomena that fall within its conceptual domain.

A theory should also be evaluated in terms of its generative power. A good theory should generate new questions, new ways of understanding the world, and new directions for research. Put simply, the theory should lead one toward ideas that would not have been considered in the absence of the theory. The important role that theories play in generating research hypotheses is widely agreed upon. Less commonly noted, however, is the importance of theories in generating new ideas and questions that go beyond those that form the core of the original system. To the extent that a theory is a tool for thinking, it should provide new ways of understanding a broad range of phenomena. The more basic the issues with which the theory is concerned, the broader are its implications for other related areas of inquiry.

Finally, a theory should be evaluated in terms of the outcomes of research stimulated by it. As we have argued above, in the final analysis, theories can be neither confirmed nor disconfirmed by the outcome of empirical "hypothesis-testing" research. This should not be taken to imply, however, that the outcomes of empirical inquiries should be irrelevant to one's assessment of a theory. Even though absolute confirmation or disconfirmation is impossible, the outcome of empirical research certainly bears on the utility of the theory. Furthermore, a theory that is unsuccessful in generating supportive empirical findings is far less useful than one that is able to do so. Empirical research provides an important check on the ability of the theory to adequately account for the phenomena on which it is focused and provides an important source of information regarding the need for changes and refinements in the theory's conceptual structure.

In summary, theories serve a variety of equally important functions, all of which are oriented toward improving our ability to think about and understand the subject matter of our discipline. The enterprise of science is made up of a dialectical interplay in which these functions influence and are influenced by each other. Theories can be formulated at a variety of levels of breadth and depth. Whereas minitheories provide detailed explanations of the mechanisms underlying specific phenomena, broad theories provide general explanatory schemes that illuminate the relationships among superficially diverse phenomena and provide frameworks through which the workings of microlevel processes can be related to each other and to the phenomena of interest to the discipline. A well-functioning discipline is therefore likely to accord important roles to theories with both broad and narrow foci.

We feel that terror management theory is a useful theory when evaluated against the criteria described above. Specifically, we believe that the theory raises interesting questions, and that the theoretical construction is sound (i.e., logical and internally consistent). In addition, we think that the theory can account for a wide variety of empirical findings in social psychology, and a diverse array of historical events and social phenomena documented by other disciplines but rarely addressed by social psychology. Finally, we believe that the theory can be a fertile catalyst for generating novel ideas and hypotheses, and that empirical investigations of those hypotheses to date have yielded results quite consistent with the theory. We recognize however, that, as our own theory suggests, those who develop a theory are not in the best position to evaluate it, and that the ultimate value of a theory can be judged only by a retrospective assessment of its impact on progress in the discipline.

XVI. Conclusion: Toward an Applied Theoretical Social Psychology

Terror management theory attempts to contribute to the understanding of social behavior by focusing on the essential being and circumstance of the human animal. The theory posits that all human motives are ultimately derived from a biologically based instinct for self-preservation. It then builds on this basic assumption to explore the effect of our sophisticated intellectual abilities on the way this biological propensity is manifested in the symbolic universe that we create. This led to our proposal that human behavior is guided largely by the need to minimize the terror resulting from the uniquely human awareness of vulnerability and death. Relative equanimity in the face of these existential realities is made possible through the creation and maintenance of culture, which serves

...nize the terror by providing a shared symbolic context that imbues the ...h order, meaning, stability, and permanence.

...worldview provides for the possibility of leading a good, endur-...which is accomplished by being a valued participant in the cultural ...ich one subscribes. The feeling that one is indeed such a valued ...which we call self-esteem, serves the essentially defensive anxiety-...function of imbedding the individual within a transcendent cultural ...Accordingly, much social behavior is directed toward preserving faith in ...ural worldview and the belief that one is a valuable contributor to that cu... ..

We believe that terror management theory may prove useful for several reasons. First, the theory is a comprehensive one that can provide plausible explanations for a wide range of distinctly human behaviors, and interesting conceptions of a number of human problems. Second, this theory may also be useful because it provides an essential theoretical link between the function and dynamics of cultural organizations and individual psychological processes. Social scientists outside of psychology have often studied the effects of cultural institutions (e.g., various religious, political, and economic organizations) on individual behavior, but without adequately explaining either the development and functions of those cultural institutions, or the psychological bases of their influence. Unfortunately, social psychology has not adequately explained these phenomena either. This is most likely because social psychology has traditionally been an ahistorical and acultural discipline (cf. Gergen, 1973; McGuire, 1973; Sampson, 1978). Therefore, many issues concerning past and ongoing human events have been ignored or dismissed as beyond the bounds of legitimate psychological discourse, and thus have been left to historians, sociologists, anthropologists, political scientists, and economists.

As Marcuse (1955) has suggested, however, any adequate explanation of human social behavior must account for the development and function of cultural institutions in terms of individual psychological propensities. Accordingly, we have proposed that cultural institutions are shaped by the individual need for absolute value engendered by the anxiety associated with the awareness of vulnerability and mortality. Cultural institutions, in turn, provide a shared symbolic context from which self-esteem can be derived. By focusing on the relationship between individual and culture, terror management theory takes a step toward explaining historical, cultural, and economic behavior in terms of the psychological needs of the individual. In doing so, we hope that this theory will play some role, however small, in encouraging greater communication and integration among the social science disciplines.

Third, terror management theory may provide a useful framework for organizing current knowledge of social behavior. A substantial proportion of existing empirical work in experimental social psychology is consistent with terror management theory. The theory can therefore provide a theoretical link between superficially unrelated substantive areas. For example, although other psychological theories have posited that people are motivated to maintain a positive self-image, they have not attempted to explain why this might be the case, nor have they attempted to explicate the relationship between the self-esteem motive and other aspects of the individual's conception of reality. By addressing these questions, terror management theory illuminates commonalities among important areas of social psychological inquiry not previously considered within a unified conception of social behavior. Furthermore, addressing these questions provides new and useful insights into the processes involved in both the operation of the self-esteem motive itself and the social behavior engaged in to fulfill this need.

Of course, many of the specific phenomena which we claim to be explicable in terms of terror management theory can also be explained in other ways (usually in terms of the specific theories which generated the work itself). We are claiming that the terror management explanations for these findings are equally plausible, and that no single theoretical conception of which we are aware has as much explanatory power or conceptual parsimony as does terror management theory. By accounting for a diverse array of phenomena within a single conceptual framework, terror management theory demonstrates the essential relatedness of a wide range of social psychological processes.

In many cases, the terror management explanation of a given phenomenon is in fact complementary rather than antithetical to other explanations. Rather than ruling out the operation of other processes, terror management theory adds to existing conceptualizations by providing explanations for processes posited as explanations by the existing theories. For example, Byrne (1971) has suggested that one important reason why people are attracted to similar others is that such others provide consensual validation of their attitudes and beliefs. Terror management theory can help explain why people need such consensual validation. Similarly, impression management theories (e.g., Baumeister, 1982; Schlenker, 1980) posit that a great deal of social behavior is oriented toward controlling the impressions that others form of us. Terror management theory addresses the question of why we are so concerned with how others view us. Likewise, self-esteem-maintenance theories (e.g., Steele, 1988; Tesser, 1988) suggest that a great deal of social thought and action is motivated by a desire to maintain a positive self-image. Terror management theory can help explain why people need self-esteem. Indeed, throughout this article we have attempted to show how the theory can contribute to a deeper understanding of both these and a variety of other well-established phenomena.

Fourth, in addition to its explanatory and integrative utility, we believe that terror management theory can be useful for generating interesting and useful hypotheses that can be subjected to empirical scrutiny. In this article, we have described experiments designed to assess hypotheses derived from the theory concerning self-esteem, anxiety, prejudice, the similarity–attraction relationship, political attitudes, reactions to moral transgressors and heroes, and reactions to praise and criticism of the accepted culture. Although additional research on all of these applications is clearly needed, the 14 studies completed thus far have provided consistent support for terror management hypotheses. Still, this is a broad theory that can generate a wide variety of novel hypotheses that have yet to be investigated. Thus, ultimate assessment of the utility of the theory and refinements of the theory will necessarily depend on an accumulation of further empirical work.

In closing, it is important to acknowledge that this theory focuses on one particular motive (surely there are pleasure-seeking nondefensive motives as well), and that, although it may be the motive that makes us distinctly human and, unfortunately, distinctly destructive (see, especially, Becker, 1975), many other factors, both historical and psychological, need to be considered to fully understand the determinants of any particular human behavior. Our present hope is simply that this work contributes to a basic understanding of both documented historical events and what people are doing in their individual lives.

Whether or not this goal is achieved depends on the ideas themselves, our ongoing research, and how others react to this work. At this point, we are more confident that the questions that the theory raises are important and useful than that the answers it provides are ultimately correct. However, we feel strongly that an existential psychodynamic perspective on human behavior is extremely important and should no longer be ignored by contemporary academic psychology:

> whatever man does on this planet has to be done in the lived truth of the terror of creation, of the grotesque, of the rumble of panic underneath everything. Otherwise it is false. . . .
> (Becker, 1973, pp. 284–285)

Acknowledgments

Responsibility for this article is shared equally among the authors. Thanks to Jack Brehm, John Burling, Keith James, Donna Morganstern, Abram Rosenblatt, Catherine Wylie, Challenger Vought, and several anonymous reviewers for their contributions to this work. Versions of this theory were presented at the Society for Experimental Social Psychology meeting in October, 1984, the Rocky Mountain Psychological Association meeting in April, 1985, and the Second Annual Nags Head Conference on the Self in May, 1985. This work was partially supported by a Skidmore College Faculty Development Grant and a National Science Foundation Grant (BNS-8910876). Correspondence concerning this chapter should be addressed to Sheldon Solomon, Department of Psychology, Skidmore College, Saratoga Springs, New York 12866, or Jeff Greenberg, Department of Psychology, University of Arizona, 85721, or Tom Pyszczynski, Department of Psychology, University of Colorado, Colorado Springs, Colorado 80933–7150.

References

Adler, A. (1930). *Understanding human nature.* New York: Greenberg.

Adorno, T., Frenkel-Brunswick, E., Levinson, D., & Sanford, R. N. (1950). *The authoritarian personality.* New York: Harper.

Ahlgren, A., Norem, A., Hochhauser, M., & Garvin, J. (1982). Antecedents of smoking among pre-adolescents. *Journal of Drug Education,* **12,** 325–340.

Ainsworth, M. D. S., Blehar, M. C., Waters, E., & Wall, S. (1978). *Patterns of attachment: A psychological study of the strange situation.* Hillsdale, NJ: Erlbaum.

Allport, G. W. (1961). *Pattern and growth in personality.* New York: Holt, Rinehart & Winston. (Original work published 1937)

Anthony, S. (1971). *The discovery of death in childhood and after.* Harmondsworth, England: Penguin Education.

Antonucci, T., & Jackson, J. (1983). Physical health and self-esteem. *Family and Community Health,* **6,** 1–9.

Apsler, R. (1975). Effects of embarrassment on behavior towards others. *Journal of Personality and Social Psychology,* **32,** 145–153.

Aronson, E. (1968). Dissonance theory: Progress and problems. In R. P. Abelson, E. Aronson, W. J. McGuire, T. M. Newcomb, M. J. Rosenberg, & P. H. Tannenbaum (Eds.), *Theories of cognitive consistency: A source-book.* Chicago: Rand McNally.

Asch, S. E. (1958). Effects of group pressure upon modification and distortion of judgments. In E. E. Maccoby, T. M. Newcomb, & E. L. Hartley (Eds.), *Readings in social psychology* (3rd ed.). New York: Holt, Rinehart & Winston.

Baldwin, M. W., Carrell, S. E., & Lopez, D. F. (1990). Priming relationship schemas: My advisor and the Pope are watching me from the back of my mind. *Journal of Experimental Social Psychology,* **26,** 435–460.

Barsky, A., & Klerman, G. (1983). Overview: Hypochondriasis, bodily complaints, and somatic styles. *American Journal of Psychiatry,* **140,** 273–283.

Batson, C. D. (1975). Rational processing or rationalization? The effect of disconfirming information on a stated religious belief. *Journal of Personality and Social Psychology,* **32,** 176–184.

Baumeister, R. F. (1982). A self-presentational view of social phenomena. *Psychological Bulletin,* **91,** 3–26.

Baumeister, R. F., & Jones, E. E. (1978). When self-presentation is constrained by the target's knowledge: Consistency and compensation. *Journal of Personality and Social Psychology,* **36,** 608–618.

Baumeister, R. F., Tice, D. M., & Hutton, D. G. (1989). Self-presentational motivations and personality differences in self-esteem. *Journal of Personality,* **57,** 547–577.

Baumgardner, A. H., & Arkin, R. M. (1987). Coping with the prospect of disapproval: Strategies and sequelae. In C. R. Snyder & C. E. Ford (Eds.), *Coping with negative life events: Clinical and social psychological perspectives.* New York: Plenum.

Beck, A., Laude, R., & Bohnert, M. (1974). Ideational components of anxiety neurosis. *Archives of General Psychiatry,* **31,** 319–325.

Becker, E. (1962). *The birth and death of meaning.* New York: Free Press.

Becker, E. (1964). *The revolution in psychiatry: The new understanding of man.* London: Collier-Macmillan.

Becker, E. (1971). *The birth and death of meaning* (2nd ed.). New York: Free Press.

Becker, E. (1973). *The denial of death.* New York: Free Press.

Becker, E. (1975). *Escape from evil.* New York: Free Press.

Bennett, D. H., & Holmes, D. S. (1975). Influences of denial (situational redefinition) and projection on anxiety associated with threat to self-esteem. *Journal of Personality and Social Psychology, 32*, 915–921.

Berger, P. L., & Luckmann, T. (1967). *The social construction of reality: A treatise in the sociology of knowledge.* Garden City, NY: Anchor.

Berglas, S., & Jones, E. E. (1978). Drug choice as a self-handicapping strategy in response to a noncontingent success. *Journal of Personality and Social Psychology, 36*, 405–417.

Berkowitz, L. (1972). Social norms, feelings and other factors affecting helping and altruism. In L. Berkowitz (Ed.), *Advances in experimental social psychology* (Vol. 6). New York: Academic Press.

Bettleheim, B. (1976). *The uses of enchantment.* New York: Knopf.

Bowerman, W. (1978). Subjective competence: The structure, process, and function of self-referent causal attributions. *Journal for the Theory of Social Behavior, 8*, 45–75.

Bowlby, J. (1969). *Attachment and loss: Vol. 1. Attachment.* New York: Basic Books.

Bowlby, J. (1973). *Attachment and loss: Vol. 2. Separation: Anxiety and anger.* New York: Basic Books.

Bowlby, J. (1980). *Attachment and Loss: Vol. 3. Loss.* New York: Basic Books.

Boyar, J. I. (1964). The construction and partial validation of a scale for the measurement of the fear of death. *Dissertation Abstracts, 25*, 20–21.

Bradley, G. W. (1978). Self-serving biases in the attribution process: A reexamination of the fact or fiction question. *Journal of Personality and Social Psychology, 36*, 56–71.

Brickman, P., & Campbell, D. T. (1971). Hedonic relativism and planning the good society. In M. H. Appley (Ed.), *Adaptation-level theory.* New York: Academic Press.

Brown, G., Andrews, B., Harris, T., & Adler, Z. (1986). Social support, self-esteem and depression. *Psychological Medicine, 16*, 18–31.

Brown, G., Bifulco, A., Harris, T., & Bridge, L. (1986). Life stress, chronic subclinical symptoms and vulnerability to clinical depression. *Journal of Affective Disorders, 11*, 1–19.

Brown, G., Craig, T., & Harris, T. (1985). Depression: Distress or disease? Some epidemiological considerations. *British Journal of Psychiatry, 147*, 612–622.

Brown, N. O. (1959). *Life against death: The psychoanalytic meaning of history.* New York: Viking.

Burish, T. G., & Houston, B. K. (1979). Causal projection, similarity projection, and coping with threat to self-esteem. *Journal of Personality, 47*, 57–70.

Burke, K. (1957). *The philosophy of literary form.* New York: Vintage.

Byrne, D. (1971). *The attraction paradigm.* New York: Academic Press.

Campbell, J. D. (1986). Similarity and uniqueness: The effects of attribute type, relevance, and individual differences in self-esteem and depression. *Journal of Personality and Social Psychology, 59*, 281–294.

Carver, C. S., & Scheier, M. (1981). *Attention and self-regulation.* New York: Springer-Verlag.

Cialdini, R. B., Borden, R. J., Thorne, A., Walker, M. R., Freeman, S., & Sloan, L. R. (1976). Basking in reflected glory: Three (football) field studies. *Journal of Personality and Social Psychology, 34*, 366–375.

Cialdini, R. B., & Richardson, K. D. (1980). Two indirect tactics of image management: Basking and blasting. *Journal of Personality and Social Psychology, 39*, 406–415.

Cooper, J., & Mackie, D. (1983). Cognitive dissonance in an intergroup context. *Journal of Personality and Social Psychology, 44*, 536–544.

Coopersmith, S. (1967). *The antecedents of self-esteem.* San Francisco, CA: Freeman.

Crocker, J., & Gallo, L. (1985). Self-enhancing effects of downward comparison: An experimental test. In T. A. Wills (Chair), *Self-esteem maintenance: Theory and evidence.* Symposium presented at the meeting of the American Psychological Association, Los Angeles.

Crocker, J., & Major, B. (1989). Social stigma and self-esteem: The self-protective properties of stigma. *Psychological Review, 96*, 608–630.

Crowther, J., & Chernyk, B. (1986). Bulimia and binge eating in adolescent females: A comparison. *Addictive Behaviors,* **11,** 415–424.

Davis, P. J. (1987). Repression and the inaccessibility of affective memories. *Journal of Personality and Social Psychology,* **53,** 585–593.

Davis, P. J., & Schwartz, G. E. (1987). Repression and the inaccessibility of affective memories. *Journal of Personality and Social Psychology,* **52,** 155–162.

Dawkins, R. (1976). *The selfish gene.* New York: Oxford University Press.

Duncan, H. D. (1962). *Communication and social learning.* New York: Bedminster.

Duncan, H. D. (1968). *Symbols in society.* New York: Oxford University Press.

Duval, S., & Wicklund, R. A. (1972). *A theory of objective self-awareness.* New York: Academic Press.

Erdelyi, M. H., & Goldberg, B. (1979). Let's not sweep repression under the rug: Toward a cognitive psychology of repression. In J. Kihlstrom & F. Evans (Eds.), *Functional disorders of memory* (pp. 355–402). Hillsdale, NJ: Erlbaum.

Faber, M. D. (1981). *Culture and consciousness: The social meaning of altered awareness.* New York: Human Sciences Press.

Fairbank, J. D., & Nicholson, R. A. (1987). Theoretical and empirical issues in the treatment of posttraumatic stress disorder in Vietnam veterans. *Journal of Clinical Psychiatry,* **43,** 44–55.

Federoff, N. A., & Harvey, J. H. (1976). Focus of attention, self-esteem, and attribution of causality. *Journal of Research in Personality,* **37,** 437–455.

Feeney, J. A., & Noller, P. (1990). Attachment style as a predictor of adult romantic relationships. *Journal of Personality and Social Psychology,* **58,** 281–291.

Feifel, H. (1990). Psychology and death: Meaningful rediscovery. *American Psychologist,* **45,** 537–543.

Felson, R. B. (1989). Parents and the reflected appraisal process: A longitudinal analysis. *Journal of Personality and Social Psychology,* **56,** 965–971.

Fenichel, O. (1955). *The psychoanalytic theory of neurosis.* London: Routledge & Kegan Paul.

Festinger, L. (1950). Informal social communication. *Psychological Review,* **57,** 271–282.

Festinger, L. (1954). A theory of social comparison processes. *Human Relationships,* **1,** 117–140.

Feuerbach, L. A. (1955). *The essence of Christianity.* New York: Blanchard. (Original work published 1843)

Frankel, A., & Snyder, M. L. (1978). Poor performance following unsolvable problems: Learned helplessness or egotism? *Journal of Personality and Social Psychology,* **36,** 1415–1423.

French, J. R. P. (1968). The conceptualization and measurement of mental health in terms of self-identity theory. In S. B. Bells (Ed.), *The definition and measurement of mental health.* Washington, DC: U.S. Department of Health, Education, and Welfare.

Freud, A. (1981). The widening scope of psychanalytic child psychology: Normal and abnormal. In *The writings of Anna Freud* (Vol. 18). New York: International Universities Press. (Original work published 1972)

Freud, S. (1975). *Group psychology and the analysis of the ego.* New York: Norton. (Original work published 1921)

Freud, S. (1955). *Some neurotic mechanisms in jealousy, paranoia, and homosexuality* (Std. ed., Vol. 18). London: Hogarth. (Original work published 1922)

Freud, S. (1976). *The future of an illusion.* New York: Norton. (Original work published 1927)

Freud, S. (1984). *Civilization and its discontents.* New York: Norton. (Original work published 1929)

Frey, D. (1978). Reactions to success and failure in public and private conditions. *Journal of Experimental Social Psychology,* **14,** 172–179.

Fries, A., & Frey, D. (1980). Misattribution of arousal and the effects of self-threatening information. *Journal of Experimental Social Psychology,* **16,** 405–416.

Geen, R. G. (1968). Effects of frustration, attack and prior training in aggressiveness upon aggressive behavior. *Journal of Personality and Social Psychology*, **9**, 316–321.

Gergen, K. J. (1973). Social psychology as history. *Journal of Personality and Psychology*, **26**, 309–320.

Gergen, K. J., & Wishnov, B. (1965). Others' self-evaluation and interaction anticipation as determinants of self-presentation. *Journal of Personality and Social Psychology*, **2**, 348–358.

Goffman, E. (1955). On face-work: An analysis of ritual elements in social interaction. *Psychiatry*, **18**, 213–231.

Goffman, E. (1959). *The presentation of self in everyday life*. Garden City, NY: Doubleday.

Goldstein, M., & Davison, E. E. (1972). Race and beliefs: A further analysis of the social determinants of behavioral intentions. *Journal of Personality and Social Psychology*, **22**, 346–355.

Goldstein, D., & Rosenbaum, A. (1985). An evaluation of the self-esteem of maritally violent men. *Journal of Applied Family and Child Studies*, **34**, 425–428.

Gollwitzer, P. M., Earle, W. B., & Stephan, W. G. (1982). Affect as a determinant of egotism: Residual excitation and performance attributions. *Journal of Personality and Social Psychology*, **43**, 702–709.

Gollwitzer, P. M., & Wicklund, R. A. (1985). Self-symbolizing and the neglect of others' perspectives. *Journal of Personality and Social Psychology*, **43**, 702–715.

Gollwitzer, P. M., Wicklund, R. A., & Hilton, J. L. (1982). Admission of failure and symbolic self-completion: Extending Lewinian theory. *Journal of Personality and Social Psychology*, **43**, 358–371.

Gray, J. A. (1982). *The neuropsychology of anxiety*. London: Oxford University Press.

Greenberg, J., & Pyszczynski, T. (1985). Compensatory self-inflation: A response to the threat to self-regard of public failure. *Journal of Personality and Social Psychology*, **49**, 273–280.

Greenberg, J., Pyszczynski, T., & Paisley, C. (1984). The effect of extrinsic incentives on the use of test anxiety as an anticipatory attributional defense: Playing it cool when the stakes are high. *Journal of Personality and Social Psychology*, **47**, 1136–1145.

Greenberg, J., Pyszczynski, T., & Solomon, S. (1982). The self-serving attributional bias: Beyond self-presentation. *Journal of Experimental Social Psychology*, **18**, 56–67.

Greenberg, J., Pyszczynski, T., & Solomon, S. (1986). The causes and consequences of a need for self-esteem: A terror management theory. In R. F. Baumeister (Ed.), *Public self and private self*. New York: Springer-Verlag.

Greenberg, J., Pyszczynski, T., Solomon, S., Rosenblatt, A., Veeder, M., Kirkland, S., & Lyon, D. (1990). Evidence for terror management theory II: The effects of mortality salience reactions to those who implicitly or explicitly threat or support the cultural worldview. *Journal of Personality and Social Psychology*, **58**, 308–318.

Greenberg, J., Simon, L., Solomon, S., Chatel, D., & Pyszczynski, T. (1991). *Political ideology and terror management: The effects of mortality salience on liberals' and conservatives' reactions to similar and dissimilar others*. Unpublished manuscript, University of Arizona.

Greenberg, J., Simon, L., Solomon, S., Lyon, D., & Pyszczynski, T. (1991). *Investigating alternative explanations for terror management effects: Support for the role of mortality salience*. Unpublished manuscript, University of Arizona.

Greenberg, J., Solomon, S., Burling, J., Rosenblatt, A., Pyszczynski, T., Simon, L., & Lyon, D. (1991). *The effects of raising self-esteem on physiological and affective responses to subsequent threat*. Unpublished manuscript, University of Arizona.

Greenberg, J., Solomon, S., Pyszczynski, T., & Steinberg, L. (1988). A reaction to Greenwald, Pratkanis, Leippe, and Baumgardner (1986): Under what conditions does research obstruct theory progress? *Psychological Review*, **95**, 566–571.

Greenwald, A. G. (1989). Self-knowledge and self-deception. In J. S. Lockard & D. L. Paulhus (Eds.), *Self-deception: An adaptive mechanism?* New York: Prentice-Hall.

Griffen, W. L., & Marciano, J. (1979). *Teaching the Viet Nam war*. Montclair, NJ: Allanheld, Osmum.

Hakmiller, K. L. (1966). Threat as a determinant of downward comparison. *Journal of Experimental Social Psychology*, **2**, 32–39.

Hansen, R. D., & Hansen, C. H. (1988). Repression of emotionally tagged memories: The architecture of less complex emotions. *Journal of Personality and Social Psychology*, **55**, 811–818.

Hardaway, R. A. (1990). Subliminally activated symbiotic fantasies: Facts and artifacts. *Psychological Bulletin*, **107**, 177–195.

Harper, J., & Field, G. (1986). A preliminary study of children who visited a school sick bay. *Mental Health in Australia*, **1**, 8–11.

Harris, M. (1979). *Cultural materialism: The struggle for a science of culture*. New York: Random House.

Henry, J. (1963). *Man against culture*. New York: Random House.

Hobfoll, S., & Leiberman, J. (1987). Personality and social resources in immediate and continued stress resistance among women. *Journal of Personality and Social Psychology*, **52**, 18–26.

Hobfoll, S., & London, P. (1986). The relationship of self-concept and social support to emotional distress among women during war. *Journal of Social and Clinical Psychology*, **4**, 189–203.

Holmes, D. S. (1974). Investigation of repression: Differential recall of material experimentally or naturally associated with ego threat. *Psychological Bulletin*, **81**, 632–653.

Holton, B., & Pyszczynski, T. (1989). Biased information search in an interpersonal context. *Personality and Social Psychology Bulletin*, **15**, 42–51.

Hooke, S. H. (1963). *Middle Eastern mythology*. Middlesex, England: Penguin.

Horney, K. (1937). *The neurotic personality of our time*. New York: Norton.

House, W. C. (1980). Effects of knowledge that attributions will be observed by others. *Journal of Research in Personality*, **14**, 528–545.

Hull, J. G., & Levy, A. S. (1979). The organizational functioning of the self: An alternative to the Duval and Wicklund model of self-awareness. *Journal of Personality and Social Psychology*, **37**, 756–768.

Ingham, J., Kreitman, N., Miller, P., & Sasidharan, S. (1986). Self-esteem, vulnerability and psychiatric disorder in the community. *British Journal of Psychiatry*, **148**, 373–385.

Insko, C. A. (1985). Balance theory, the Jordan paradigm, and the Wiest tetrahedron. In L. Berkowitz (ed.), *Advances in experimental social psychology*, (Vol. 18). Orlando, FL: Academic Press.

Jacobs, D. H. (1983). Learning problems, self-esteem, and delinquency. In J. E. Mack & S. L. Albon (Eds.), *The development and sustenance of self-esteem in childhood*. New York: International Universities Press.

James, W. (1890). *The principles of psychology*. New York: Dover.

Janoff-Bulman, R., & Timko, C. (1987). Coping with traumatic events: The role of denial in light of people's assumptive worlds. In C. R. Snyder & C. E. Ford (Eds.), *Coping with negative life events: Clinical and social psychological perspectives*. New York: Plenum.

Jemott, J. B. (1985). Psychoneuroimmunology: The new frontier. *American Behavioral Scientist*, **28**, 497–509.

Johnson, R., Lund, D., & Dimond, M. (1986). Stress, self-esteem and coping during bereavement among the elderly. *Social Psychology Quarterly*, **49**, 273–279.

Jones, E. E., & Pittman, T. S. (1982). Toward a general theory of strategic self-presentation. In J. Suls (Ed.), *Psychological perspectives of the self*. Hillsdale, NJ: Erlbaum.

Jones, S. C. (1973). Self and interpersonal evaluations: Esteem theories versus consistency theories. *Psychological Bulletin*, **79**, 185–199.

Kaplan, H. B. (1982). Prevalence of the self-esteem motive. In M. Rosenberg & H. B. Kaplan (Eds.), *Social psychology of the self-concept*. Arlington Heights, IL: Davidson.

Kelley, H. H. (1952). Two functions of reference groups. In G. E. Swanson, T. M. Newcomb, & E. L. Hartley (Eds.), *Readings in social psychology* (2nd ed.). New York: Holt, Rinehart & Winston.

Kelley, H. H. (1967). Attribution theory in social psychology. In D. Levine (Ed.), *Nebraska Symposium on Motivation*. Lincoln, NE: University of Nebraska Press.

Kendall, P. C. (1978). Anxiety: States, traits—Situations? *Journal of Consulting and Clinical Psychology, 46*, 280–287.

Kernis, M. H., Grannemann, B. D., & Barclay, L. C. (1989). Stability and level of self-esteem as predictors of anger arousal and hostility. *Journal of Personality and Social Psychology, 56*, 1013–1022.

Kernis, M. H., Zuckerman, M., Cohen, A., & Sparafora, S. (1982). Persistence following failure: The interactive role of self-awareness and the attributional basis for negative expectancies. *Journal of Personality and Social Psychology, 43*, 1184–1191.

Khouri-Haddad, S. (1984). Psychiatric consultation in a headache unit. *Headache, 24*, 322–328.

Kohut, H. (1977). *The restoration of the self*. New York: International Universities Press.

Laudan, L. (1977). *Progress and its problems: Towards a theory of scientific growth*. Berkeley, CA: University of California Press.

Laudan, L. (1984). *Science and values: An essay on the aims of science and their role in scientific debate*. Berkeley, CA: University of California Press.

Leary, M. R. (1986). The impact of interactional impediments on social anxiety and self-presentation. *Journal of Experimental Social Psychology, 22*, 122–135.

Leary, M. R., Barnes, B. D., & Griebel, C. (1986). Cognitive, affective, and attributional effects of potential threats to self-esteem. *Journal of Social and Clinical Psychology, 4*, 461–474.

Lerner, M. J. (1980). *The belief in a just world: A fundamental delusion*. New York: Plenum.

Lerner, M. J., Miller, D. T., & Holmes, J. G. (1976). Deserving and the emergence of forms of justice. In L. Berkowitz and E. Walster (Eds.), *Advances in experimental social psychology* (Vol. 9). New York: Academic Press.

Lester, D. (1986). Subjective stress and self-esteem of police officers. *Perceptual and Motor Skills, 63*, 1334.

Lewin, K. (1951). Problems of research in social psychology. In D. Cartwright (Ed.), *Field theory in social science*. New York: McGraw-Hill.

Lifton, R. J. (1968). *Revolutionary immortality: Mao Tse-Tong and the Chinese cultural revolution*. New York: Vintage.

Lifton, R. J. (1983). *The broken connection: On death and the continuity of life*. New York: Basic Books.

Lifton, R. J. (1986). *The Nazi doctors: Medical killing and the psychology of genocide*. New York: Basic Books.

Linn, B., & Zeppa, R. (1984). Stress in junior medical students: Relationship to personality and performance. *Journal of Medical Education, 59*, 7–12.

Lipsitt, L. P. (1958). A self-concept scale for children and its relationship to the childrens' form of the Manifest Anxiety Scale. *Child Development, 29*, 463–472.

Lochman, J., & Lampron, L. (1986). Situational social problem-solving skills and self-esteem of aggressive and nonaggressive boys. *Journal of Abnormal Child Psychology, 14*, 605–617.

Macaulay, J. (1970). A skill for charity. In J. Macaulay & L. Berkowitz (Eds.), Altruism and helping behavior: Social psychological studies of some antecedents and consequences (pp. 43–59). New York: Academic Press.

MacKay, D. G. (1988). Under what conditions can theoretical psychology survive and prosper? Integrating the rational and empirical epistemologies. *Psychological Review, 95*, 559–565.

Marcuse, H. (1955). *Eros in civilization.* Boston: Beacon.

Markus, H., & Kitayama, S. (1991). Culture and the self: Implications for cognition, emotion, and motivation. *Psychological Review,* **98,** 224–253.

Marsh, H. W. (1986). Global self-esteem: Its relation to specific facets of self-concept and their importance. *Journal of Personality and Social Psychology,* **51,** 1224–1236.

Marx, M. H., & Hillix, W. A. (1963). *Systems and theories in psychology.* New York: McGraw-Hill.

Maslow, A. H. (1970). *Motivation and personality.* New York: Harper & Row.

McFarland, C., & Ross, M. (1982). Impact of causal attributions on affective reactions to success and failure. *Journal of Personality and Social Psychology,* **43,** 937–946.

McGuire, W. J. (1973). The yin and yang of progress in social psychology: Seven koan. *Journal of Personality and Social Psychology,* **26,** 446–456.

Mead, G. H. (1934). *Mind, self, and society.* Chicago: University of Chicago Press.

Mead, M. (1931). Jealousy: Primitive and civilized. In S. D. Schnalhausen & V. F. Calverton (Eds.), *Women's coming of age.* New York: Liveright.

Mehlman, R. C., & Snyder, C. R. (1985). Excuse theory: A test of the self-protective role of attributions. *Journal of Personality and Social Psychology,* **49,** 994–1001.

Meindl, J. R., & Lerner, M. J. (1985). Exacerbation of extreme responses to an out-group. *Journal of Personality and Social Psychology,* **47,** 71–84.

Mikulincer, M., Florian, V., & Tolmacz, R. (1990). Attachment styles and fear of personal death: A case study of affect regulation. *Journal of Personality and Social Psychology,* **58,** 273–280.

Milgram, S. (1974). *Obedience to authority.* New York: Harper & Row.

Miller, A. (1981). *Prisoner of childhood.* New York: Basic Books.

Miller, C. E., & Anderson, P. D. (1979). Group decision rules and the rejection of deviates. *Social Psychology Quarterly,* **42,** 354–363.

Moe, J. L., Nacoste, R. W., & Insko, C. A. (1981). Belief versus race as determinants of discrimination: A study of Southern adolescents in 1966 and 1979. *Journal of Personality and Social Psychology,* **41,** 1031–1050.

Mollon, P., & Parry, G. (1984). The fragile self: Narcissistic disturbance and the protective function of depression. *British Journal of Medical Psychology,* **57,** 137–145.

Moss, M. K., & Page, R. A. (1972). Reinforcement and helping behavior. *Journal of Applied Social Psychology,* **2,** 360–371.

Nadler, A., & Fisher, J. D. (1986). The role of threat to self-esteem and perceived control in recipient reactions to help: Theory development and empirical validation. In L. Berkowitz (Ed.), *Advances in experimental social psychology* (Vol. 19). Orlando, FL: Academic Press.

Neidig, P., Friedman, D., & Collins, B. (1986). Attitudinal characteristics of males who have engaged in spouse abuse. *Journal of Family Violence,* **1,** 223–233.

Nisbett, R. E., & Kunda, Z. (1985). Perception of social distributions. *Journal of Personality and Social Psychology,* **48,** 297–311.

Osarchuk, M., & Tatz, S. J. (1973). Effect of induced fear of death on belief in afterlife. *Journal of Personality and Social Psychology,* **27,** 256–260.

Osofsky, H. (1985). Transition to parenthood: Risk factors for parents and infants. *Journal of Psychosomatic Obstetrics and Gynecology,* **4,** 303–315.

Paloutzian, R. F. (1981). Purpose in life and value changes following conversion. *Journal of Personality and Social Psychology,* **41,** 1153–1160.

Paulhus, D. L., & Levitt, K. (1987). Desirable responding triggered by affect. *Journal of Personality and Social Psychology,* **52,** 245–259.

Paulhus, D. L., Shaffer, D. R., & Downing, L. L. (1977). Effects of making blood donor motives salient upon donor retention: A field experiment. *Personality and Social Psychology Bulletin,* **3,** 99–102.

Pearlin, L., Lieberman, M., Menaghan, E., & Mullan, J. (1981). The stress process. *Journal of Health and Social Behavior, 22,* 337–356.

Pennebaker, J. W., Colder, M., & Sharp, L. K. (1990). Accelerating the coping process. *Journal of Personality and Social Psychology, 58,* 528–537.

Penny, G., & Robinson, J. (1986). Psychological resources and cigarette smoking in adolescents. *British Journal of Psychology, 77,* 351–357.

Petrie, K., & Rotheram, M. (1982). Insulators against stress: Self-esteem and assertiveness. *Psychological Reports, 50,* 963–966.

Petty, R. E., & Cacioppo, J. T. (1986). The elaboration likelihood model of persuasion. In L. Berkowitz (Ed.), *Advances in experimental social psychology* (Vol. 19, pp. 123–205). Orlando, FL: Academic Press.

Pleban, R., & Tesser, A. (1981). The effects of relevance and quality of another's performance on interpersonal closeness. *Social Psychological Quarterly, 44,* 278–285.

Popper, K. (1959). *The logic of scientific discovery.* New York: Basic Books.

Powers, W. T. (1978). Quantitative analysis of purposive systems: Some spadework at the foundations of scientific psychology. *Psychological Review, 85,* 417–435.

Pyszczynski, T., & Greenberg, J. (1987). Toward an integration of cognitive and motivational perspectives on social inference: A biased hypothesis-testing model. In L. Berkowitz (Ed.), *Advances in experimental social psychology* (Vol. 20). Orlando, FL: Academic Press.

Pyszczynski, T., Greenberg, J., & Holt, K. (1985). Maintaining consistency between self-serving beliefs and available data: A bias in information evaluation following success and failure. *Personality and Social Psychology Bulletin, 11,* 179–190.

Pyszczynski, T., Greenberg, J., & LaPrelle, J. (1985). Social comparison after success and failure: Biased search for information consistent with a self-serving hypothesis. *Journal of Experimental Social Psychology, 21,* 195–211.

Pyszczynski, T., Greenberg, J., Solomon, S., & Hamilton, J. (1990). A terror management analysis of self-awareness and anxiety: The hierarchy of terror. *Anxiety Research, 2,* 177–195.

Pyszczynski, T., Miller, M., & Greenberg, J. (1990). *Interpersonal evaluations, self-esteem, and interpersonal attraction.* Unpublished manuscript, University of Colorado, Colorado Springs.

Rank, O. (1961). *Psychology and the soul.* New York: Perpetua. (Original work published 1931)

Rank, O. (1945). *Will therapy and truth and reality.* New York: Knopf. (Original work published 1936)

Rank, O. (1958). *Beyond psychology.* New York: Dover. (Original work published 1941)

Rank, O. (1959). *The myth of the birth of the hero, and other writings.* New York: Vintage.

Riess, M., Rosenfeld, P., Melburg, V., & Tedeschi, J. T. (1981). Self-serving attributions: Biased private perceptions and distorted public descriptions. *Journal of Personality and Social Psychology, 41,* 224–231.

Rochlin, G. (1965). *Griefs and discontents: The forces of change.* Boston: Little, Brown.

Rochlin, G. (1967). How younger children view death and themselves. In E. A. Grollman (Ed.), *Explaining death to children.* Boston: Beacon.

Rogers, C. R. (1959). A theory of therapy, personality, and interpersonal relationships, as developed in the client-centered framework. In S. Koch (Ed.), *Psychology: A study of a science* (Vol. 3). New York: McGraw-Hill.

Rokeach, M. (1968). *Beliefs, attitudes, and values.* San Francisco, CA: Jossey-Bass.

Rosenberg, M. (1965). *Society and the adolescent self image.* Princeton, NJ: Princeton University Press.

Rosenberg, M. (1986). Self-concept from middle childhood through adolescence. In J. Suls (Ed.), *Psychological perspectives on the self* (Vol. 3). Hillsdale, NJ: Erlbaum.

Rosenberg, M., & Simmons, R. G. (1972). *Black and white self-esteem: The urban school child.* Washington, DC: American Sociological Association.

Rosenblatt, A., Greenberg, J., Solomon, S., Pyszczynski, T., & Lyon, D. (1989). Evidence for terror management theory I: The effects of mortality salience or reactions to those who violate or uphold cultural values. *Journal of Personality and Social Psychology*, **57**, 681–690.

Ross, L., Greene, D., & House, P. (1977). The "false consensus effect": An egocentric bias in social perception and attribution processes. *Journal of Experimental Social Psychology*, **13**, 279–301.

Sampson, E. E. (1978). Scientific paradigms and social values: Wanted—A scientific revolution. *Journal of Personality and Social Psychology*, **36**, 1332–1343.

Sanders, G. S., & Mullen, B. (1983). Accuracy in perception of consensus: Differential tendencies of people with majority and minority positions. *European Journal of Social Psychology*, **13**, 57–70.

Satow, K. L. (1975). Social approval and helping. *Journal of Experimental Social Psychology*, **11**, 501–509.

Schachter, S. (1951). Deviation, rejection and communication. *Journal of Abnormal and Social Psychology*, **46**, 190–207.

Scheff, T. (1988). Shame and conformity: The deference–emotion system. *American Sociological Review*, **53**, 395–406.

Scheff, T. (1990). *Crisis in the academic system: Is the Emperor wearing clothes?* Unpublished manuscript, University of California, Santa Barbara.

Scher, S. J., & Cooper, J. (1989). Motivational basis of dissonance: The singular role of behavioral consequences. *Journal of Personality and Social Psychology*, **56**, 899–906.

Schlenker, B. R. (1980). *Impression management: The self-concept, social identity, and interpersonal relations*. Belmont, CA: Brooks/Cole.

Sherman, S. J., Presson, C. C., & Chassin, L. (1984). Mechanisms underlying the false consensus effect: The special role of threats to the self. *Personality and Social Psychology Bulletin*, **10**, 127–138.

Sherman, S. J., Presson, C. C., Chassin, L., Corty, E., & Olshavsky, R. (1983). The false consensus effect in estimates of smoking prevalence: Underlying mechanisms. *Personality and Social Psychology Bulletin*, **9**, 197–207.

Shrauger, J. S. (1975). Responses to evaluation as a function of initial self-perceptions. *Psychological Bulletin*, **82**, 581–596.

Shrauger, J. S., & Schoeneman, T. (1979). Symbolic interactionist view of the self-concept: Through the looking-glass darkly. *Psychological Bulletin*, **86**, 549–573.

Smith, T. W., Snyder, C. R., & Handelsman, M. M. (1982). On the self-serving function of an academic wooden leg: Test anxiety as a self-handicapping strategy. *Journal of Personality and Social Psychology*, **42**, 314–321.

Solomon, S., Greenberg, J., & Pyszczynski, T. (1991). Terror management theory of self-esteem. In C. R. Snyder and D. Forsyth (Eds.), *Handbook of social and clinical psychology: The Health Perspective* (pp. 21–40). New York: Pergamon.

Spielberger, C. D., Gorsuch, R. L., & Lushene, R. E. (1970). *Trait anxiety inventory (self-evaluation questionnaire)*. Palo Alto, CA: Consulting Psychologist Press.

Steele, C. M. (1988). The psychology of self-affirmation: Sustaining the integrity of the self. In L. Berkowitz (Ed.), *Advances in experimental social psychology* (Vol. 21, pp. 261–302). San Diego, CA: Academic Press.

Stephan, W. G., & Gollwitzer, P. M. (1981). Affect as a mediator of attributional egotism. *Journal of Experimental Social Psychology*, **17**, 443–458.

Stone, G. L. (1966). *War without honour*. Brisbane, Australia: Jacaranda.

Strauss, C., Frame, C., & Forehand, R. (1987). Psychosocial impairment associated with anxiety in children. *Journal of Clinical Child Psychology*, **16**, 235–239.

Sullivan, H. S. (1953). *The interpersonal theory of psychiatry*. New York: Norton.

Tecoma, E. S., & Huey, L. Y. (1985). Psychic distress and the immune response. *Life Sciences*, **36**, 1799–1812.

Tedeschi, J. T. (1981). *Impression management theory and social psychological research*. New York: Academic Press.

Templer, D. I. (1971). The relationship between verbalized and non-verbalized death anxiety. *Journal of Genetic Psychology*, **119**, 211–214.

Tesser, A. (1980). Self-esteem maintenance in family dynamics. *Journal of Personality and Social Psychology*, **39**, 77–91.

Tesser, A. (1988). Toward a self-evaluation maintenance model of social behavior. In L. Berkowitz (Ed.), *Advances in experimental social psychology* (Vol. 21, pp. 181–227). San Diego, CA: Academic Press.

Tesser, A., & Campbell, J. (1980). Self-definition and self-evaluation maintenance. In J. Suls & A. G. Greenwald (Eds.), *Psychological perspectives on the self* (Vol. II). Hillsdale, NJ: Erlbaum.

Tesser, A., & Paulhus, D. (1983). The definition of self: Private and public self-evaluation maintenance strategies. *Journal of Personality and Social Psychology*, **44**, 672–682.

Tetlock, P. E., & Manstead, A. S. (1985). Impression management versus intrapsychic explanations in social psychology: A useful dichotomy? *Psychological Review*, **92**, 59–77.

Turnbull, C. M. (1972). *The mountain people*. New York: Simon & Schuster.

Turner, J. (1981). The experimental social psychology of intergroup behavior. In J. Turner & A. Giles (Eds.), *Intergroup behavior*. Chicago: University of Chicago Press.

Ullman, C. (1982). Cognitive and emotional antecedents of religious concern. *Journal of Personality and Social Psychology*, **43**, 183–192.

Watson, D., Clark, L. A., & Tellegen, A. (1988). Development and validation of brief measures of positive and negative affect: The PANAS scales. *Journal of Personality and Social Psychology*, **54**, 1063–1070.

Weiss, J., Rothbaum, F., & Blackburn, T. (1984). Standing out and standing in: The psychology of control in America and Japan. *American Psychologist*, **39**, 955–969.

White, G. (1981). Some correlates of romantic jealousy. *Journal of Personality*, **49**, 129–147.

Wicklund, R. A., & Gollwitzer, P. M. (1982). *Symbolic self-completion*. Hillsdale, NJ: Erlbaum.

Wilder, D. A., & Shapiro, P. N. (1984). The role of outgroup cues in social identity. *Journal of Personality and Social Psychology*, **47**, 342–348.

Wills, T. (1981). Downward comparison principles in social psychology. *Psychological Bulletin*, **90**, 245–271.

Wills, T. (1987). Downward comparison as a coping mechanism. In C. R. Snyder & C. E. Ford (Eds.), *Coping with negative life events: Clinical and social psychological perspectives*. New York: Plenum.

Wolfgang, M. E., & Ferracuti, F. (1967). *The subculture of violence*. London: Tavistock.

Wylie, R. C. (1979). *The self-concept, Vol. 2: Theory and research on selected topics*. Lincoln, NE: University of Nebraska Press.

Yalom, I. (1980). *Existential psychotherapy*. New York: Basic Books.

Zigler, E., & Glick, M. (1988). Is paranoid schizophrenia really camouflaged depression? *American Psychologist*, **43**, 284–290.

Zillboorg, G. (1943). Fear of death. *Psychoanalytic Quarterly*, **12**, 465–475.

Zimrin, H. (1986). A profile of survival. *Child Abuse and Neglect*, **10**, 339–349.

Zuckerman, M., & Lubin, B. (1965). *Manual for the Multiple Affect Adjective Check List*. San Diego, CA: Educational and Industrial Testing Service.

MOOD AND PERSUASION: AFFECTIVE STATES INFLUENCE THE PROCESSING OF PERSUASIVE COMMUNICATIONS

Norbert Schwarz
Herbert Bless
Gerd Bohner

I. Introduction

Attempts to persuade another person are often accompanied by efforts to change this person's mood. From little kids who say nice things to Daddy before they ask him a favor, to professionals in the advertising business who create funny and entertaining television spots to persuade consumers, we are all familiar with persuasion strategies that include attempts to change the recipient's mood. The frequent use of this persuasion strategy, and practitioners' faith in it, suggests that it may actually be effective. However, the exact mechanisms by which recipients' affective states may mediate persuasion processes are not yet well understood. In the present article, we shall outline different mediating processes that are consistent with current theorizing on the interplay of emotion and cognition, and shall evaluate these assumptions in the light of the available evidence.

In line with current theorizing on persuasion, we shall present our arguments in the context of the "cognitive response" approach to persuasion and attitude change (Greenwald, 1968; Petty, Ostrom, & Brock, 1981). According to this approach, recipients of a persuasive communication may arrive at an attitude judgment by one of two ways. On the one hand, they may carefully consider the content of the message, paying close attention to the implications of the presented arguments. On the other hand, recipients may not engage in a thorough consideration of message content, but may rely on simple cues, such as the communicator's prestige or likableness. While the former, content-oriented, processing strategy is known as "systematic processing" (Chaiken, 1980, 1987), or

ADVANCES IN EXPERIMENTAL
SOCIAL PSYCHOLOGY, VOL. 24

the "central route to persuasion" (Petty and Cacioppo, 1986a, 1986b), the latter strategy is known as "heuristic processing," or the "peripheral route to persuasion."

If a central route of persuasion is traveled, or—in other terms—the message is processed systematically, the resulting attitude change is a function of the recipients' cognitive responses to the message: the more thoughts come to mind that support the position advocated in the message, the more pronounced the intended attitude change will be. Accordingly, messages that present strong arguments are more effective than messages that present weak or flawed arguments. The quality of the message affects attitude change less, however, if the peripheral route is traveled, or—in other terms—the message is processed heuristically. Accordingly, comparisons of the impact of strong and weak arguments are a key criterion in distinguishing between a central, or systematic, and a peripheral, or heuristic, route to persuasion, and we shall draw heavily on this criterion in the remainder of this article.

Which route to persuasion is more likely to be used depends on recipients' motivation and ability. If the recipient is sufficiently motivated and able to process the content of the message, the central route is likely to predominate. The peripheral route, on the other hand, is likely to be used if motivation and/or ability are low.

Current theorizing on the interplay of affect and cognition suggests at least five ways in which recipients' mood may influence persuasion processes within this general framework (see also Petty, Cacioppo, & Kasmer, 1988). Each of these possibilities has different implications for recipients' attitude change, their cognitive responses to the message, and their evaluation of the presented arguments, as will be outlined below. Moreover, the various assumptions differ in the processing stages at which they hypothesize affective states to have an impact. Some assumptions imply an impact of affective states on the encoding of the persuasive message, whereas others imply an impact of affective states at the judgment stage. In the former case, mood effects should be obtained only if the mood is present at the time of exposure to the message; in the latter case, they should be obtained only if the mood is present at the time of judgment. We shall first discuss these different process assumptions and then review data that bear on them.

II. Theoretical Approaches to Mood and Persuasion

A. MOOD AS A PERIPHERAL CUE HYPOTHESIS

Recipients' affective state may itself serve as a peripheral cue if it becomes associated with the attitude object or with the source. This prediction has a long tradition in learning theory approaches to attitude change (Berkowitz & Knurek, 1969; Razran, 1940; A. W. Staats & C. K. Staats, 1958; Staats, Staats, & Crawford, 1962; C. K. Staats & A. W. Staats, 1957; Zanna, Kiesler, & Pilkonis, 1970). Within the learning theory framework, a number of studies used a first order classical conditioning approach by repeatedly pairing word stimuli with pleasant or unpleasant experiences, such as the offset vs. onset of electric shock (Zanna *et al.*, 1970), music (e.g., Gorn, 1982), or food (e.g., Dabbs & Janis, 1965). In other studies, higher order conditioning procedures were employed, pairing concepts or nonsense syllables with words that have positive or negative evaluative meaning (e.g., Staats & Staats, 1958).

In both paradigms, it could be demonstrated that subjects expressed more positive (or negative, respectively) attitudes toward concepts that had repeatedly been paired with positive (negative) stimuli. Moreover, the induced attitudes generalized to semantically or categorically similar attitude objects (Berkowitz & Knurek, 1969; Zanna *et al.*, 1970). While some of the earlier studies (A. W. Staats & C. K. Staats, 1958; C. K. Staats & A. W. Staats, 1957) are open to criticism concerning demand characteristics inherent in the experimental procedures (cf. Page, 1969), this is not the case for the Berkowitz and Knurek (1969) and Zanna *et al.* (1970) studies, as these authors used elaborate cover stories and separated the conditioning procedure from the attitude assessment.

Thus, the available evidence suggests that attitudes toward verbal concepts can be formed while these concepts are paired with unpleasant or pleasant experiences. Within an information-processing framework, these effects can be reinterpreted as effects of affective states serving as a peripheral cue. However, it is yet unclear if cue effects of this kind do occur in a *persuasion* setting, when a complex message is presented while recipients are in a positive or negative affective state, or if they are restricted to situations in which little, if any, content information is available. Moreover, most of the support for the classical conditioning model of attitudes comes from studies in which previously *neutral* or new attitude objects were presented, whereas attitudes toward stimuli that were already positive or negative to begin with seem to be unaffected (e.g., Zanna *et al.*, 1970).

Similar predictions may be derived from the assumption that affective states may serve informative functions. According to this hypothesis (Schwarz, 1987, 1988, 1990; Schwarz & Clore, 1983, 1988), individuals may simplify complex judgmental tasks by using their affective reaction to the attitude object as an informational basis according to a "How do I feel about it?" heuristic. In doing so, however, it is difficult to distinguish between one's affective reaction to the object of judgment and one's preexisting mood state. Accordingly, individuals may mistake their preexisting feelings as a reaction to the message, which may result in more favorable evaluations under good than under bad mood.

Note, however, that individuals will rely on their affective state as a basis of judgment only if its diagnostic value for the judgment at hand has not been called into question. In line with this assumption, Schwarz and Clore (1983) observed that individuals evaluated their life more positively when interviewed on sunny rather than rainy days, reflecting their mood at the time of judgment. However, when their attention was drawn to the weather as a potential source of their current mood, its impact was eliminated. Specifically, respondents called on rainy days reported being as happy and satisfied with their life as respondents called on sunny days, when the interviewer, who pretended to call from out of town, opened the interview with a private aside, "How's the weather down there?" This manipulation presumably directed respondents' attention to the weather, suggesting that their current feelings may be due to this transitory influence, and may thus not provide a diagnostic basis of information for evaluating the overall quality of their life. Accordingly, a measure of current mood, assessed at the end of the interview, was correlated with judgments of life satisfaction only if respondents' attention was not drawn to the weather. This and related research (see Schwarz, 1990; Schwarz & Clore, 1988, for reviews) suggests that recipients of a persuasive communication may use their feelings at the time of judgment as a peripheral cue only if their informational value has not been called into question.

In summary, both the learning theory and the "mood-as-information" variant of the hypothesis, that moods may serve as peripheral cues, imply that mood effects on attitude change should be obtained primarily if a peripheral route to persuasion is traveled, but should be weak if a central route is traveled. Accordingly, they predict a main effect of mood on attitude change, which should be independent of the quality of the presented arguments. Moreover, both notions do not predict effects of mood on message-related cognitive responses or recall. Both notions differ, however, with regard to the processing stage at which the impact is supposed to occur. Whereas the mood-as-information hypothesis assumes that an impact of affective states reflects respondents' feelings at the time of judgment, independently of what evoked these feelings in the first place, this is not the case for the learning theory approaches. Specifically, the classical conditioning approach requires that the attitude object and affectively laden stimuli be paired at the encoding stage, whereas an instrumental conditioning approach requires that previous related attitude judgments be paired with affective consequences (e.g., Cialdini & Insko, 1969). All of these assumptions, however, have received most support in research on the formation of new attitudes, rather than in research on attitude change.

B. MOOD CONGRUENCY HYPOTHESIS

As a second hypothesis, one may assume that recipients' mood states may influence the associations generated during exposure to the message, due to the increased accessibility of mood congruent material stored in memory (Bower, 1981; Isen, Shalker, Clark, & Karp, 1978; see Blaney, 1986, for a review). This may result either in more positive elaborations of the content of the message, or in more positive reactions to peripheral cues, such as the appearance of the communicator, when recipients are in a good rather than bad mood. Accordingly, the mood congruent recall hypothesis predicts a main effect of mood on attitude measures, with greater persuasion under good than under bad moods. However, this main effect on attitude measures may or may not be paralleled by effects of mood on cognitive responses, depending on whether the mood congruent associations pertained to the content of the message or to peripheral cues. According to this model, the impact of mood states may occur at the encoding stage, that is, when the message is elaborated, or at the judgment stage, if the judgment is based on what can be recalled from a previously encoded message. In either case, the model holds that the impact of mood is independent of the source to which one's mood is attributed (cf. Schwarz & Clore, 1988).

C. CHANGE IN CRITERIA HYPOTHESIS

As a third possibility, subjects' affective state may influence the criteria that they use to evaluate the quality of the message. Specifically, it seems plausible to suppose that subjects in a bad mood may use harsher criteria to evaluate a persuasive message than subjects in a good mood. If so, subjects in a bad mood should evaluate the message less favorably and should show less attitude change than subjects in a good mood. This would imply a main effect of mood on both attitude change and the relative number of supportive and refutational cognitive responses that is independent of the quality of the presented arguments. An interaction prediction could only be derived if one assumed that mood affects recipients' threshold for the acceptability of an argument, and that all arguments above or below the threshold are treated equally, without further consideration of their absolute level of plausibility. In that case, individuals in a negative mood may be receptive of strong arguments and dismissive of weak arguments, whereas individuals in a positive mood may be equally receptive to strong and weak arguments, reflecting a lower threshold. In either case, the change-in-criteria hypothesis implies that mood effects should only be observed when the mood is present at the time of exposure to the message.

D. MOTIVATIONAL HYPOTHESES

Fourth, recipients' affective state may influence their motivation to elaborate on the content of the message. In this regard, it has been hypothesized that moods may affect individuals' preferred processing style, and that persons in a good mood are more likely to engage in simplified, heuristic processing strategies, whereas persons in a bad mood may spontaneously engage in more effortful and detail-oriented analytic processing strategies (Schwarz, 1990; see also Fiedler, 1988; Isen, 1987; Kuhl, 1983, for related hypotheses). This prediction is derived from the assumption that "emotions exist for the sake of signaling states of the world that have to be responded to, or that no longer need response and action" (Frijda, 1988, p. 354).

If so, negative feelings may inform individuals that their current situation is problematic. They may therefore trigger processing styles that are adequate for analyzing the problematic situation in order to determine adequate reactions. However, any mechanism that increases the accessibility of relevant procedural knowledge may also increase the likelihood that the respective procedures will be applied to other tasks to which they are applicable while the individual is in a negative affective state. Moreover, individuals in a negative state may be motivated to avoid erroneous decisions in a situation that is already characterized as problematic. Consistent with this assumption, a large body of literature indicates that individuals are more likely to use effortful, detail-oriented, analytical processing strategies spontaneously when they are put in a bad rather than in a good mood (see Schwarz, 1990, for a review).

Positive affective states, on the other hand, inform individuals that their current environment is a safe place. Accordingly, individuals in a good mood may be more likely to take risks and to use simple heuristics in information processing. Moreover, they may have better access to a variety of different procedural knowledge, given that no specific procedure is activated to cope with the current situation. In combination, this may facilitate the higher creativity that has been observed under elated mood, but may inhibit the spontaneous use of effortful analytic processing strategies, unless they are required by other active goals. Again, a considerable body of research supports this assumption (see Schwarz, 1990, for a review).

In a related vein, Isen and colleagues (Isen, 1984; Isen & Levin, 1972; Isen, Means, Patrick, & Nowicki, 1982) suggested that individuals in a good mood may avoid cognitive effort that could interfere with their ability to maintain their pleasant affective state. If so, persons in a good mood may be unlikely to elaborate the message for that reason. The prediction of a more analytic reasoning style under bad mood, on the other hand, is more controversial. Severely depressed states have also been found to accompany decreased motivation (e.g., Beck, 1967; Peterson & Seligman, 1984) and may thus decrease the likelihood of message elaboration. Moreover, negative events, which trigger negative moods, may attract a high degree of attention, thus limiting the cognitive capacity that individuals have available for working on other tasks, as will be discussed below. Note, however, that experimentally induced moods are usually not very severe, rendering a depression-like decrease in motivation unlikely.

In combination, these considerations suggest that analytic elaborations of the quality of persuasive arguments may be more likely when recipients are in a bad rather than a good mood at the time of exposure to the message. In contrast to the preceding hypotheses, this notion predicts an interaction effect of mood and argument quality, rather than a main effect of mood. Specifically, recipients of a persuasive message that presents *strong arguments* should be more persuaded when they are in a bad, rather than in a good mood. On the other hand, recipients of a message that presents *weak arguments* should be more persuaded when they are in a good, rather than in a bad mood. Moreover, this interaction of mood and message quality should be obtained on attitude change measures as well as on measures of recipients' cognitive responses, reflecting the impact of mood on message elaboration.

In addition, the motivational hypothesis results in different predictions for different processing stages, an issue to which we shall later return in more detail.

E. COGNITIVE CAPACITY HYPOTHESES

As a fifth hypothesis, affective states may influence recipients' ability to elaborate the message in various ways. Specifically, the presence of mood-related thoughts may decrease subjects' information-processing capacity and may thus interfere with their ability to elaborate the message. However, it is unclear whether good moods or bad moods are more likely to have this interference effect.

On the one hand, it has been suggested that positive mood increases the accessibility of positive material, which is assumed to be more extensive and more interrelated in memory (Isen *et al.*, 1982; Matlin & Stang, 1979). Thus positive mood could potentially elicit a great number of positive thoughts. Many of these thoughts may not be relevant for the processing of the persuasive communication and may thus reduce the capacity for the processing of this message.

On the other hand, negative events that elicit bad moods may be more likely to stimulate a search for explanations (e.g., Abele, 1985; Bohner, Bless, Schwarz, & Strack, 1988; Schwarz, 1987; Schwarz & Clore, 1983), and this may also interfere with the performance of other tasks. Note, however, that such an interference may be less likely in experiments than in natural situations, because the introduced negative event has limited implications and can usually not be changed, thus limiting the necessity and adaptive value of extensive event-related analyses. Similarly, Ellis and Ashbrook's (1988) resource allocation model holds that depressed states may decrease individuals' cognitive capacity, and this assumption is well supported by memory research (see Ellis & Ashbrook, 1988, for a review).

Finally, affective states may influence an individual's arousal level, which in turn has been shown to have curvilinear effects on cognitive capacity (Kahneman, 1970). Because this latter possibility pertains to the intensity rather than the valence of affective states, however, it will not be considered in detail.

In general, the cognitive capacity hypotheses predict an interaction of affective state and message quality, as do the motivational hypotheses. Specifically, individuals whose cognitive capacity is reduced by their current affective state should be less persuaded by strong arguments, and more persuaded by weak arguments, than individuals whose cognitive capacity is not affected. Moreover, this interaction should be obtained on measures of attitude change as well as on measures of recipients' cognitive responses, reflecting the impact of cognitive capacity on message elaboration. However, whether being in a good or a bad mood is more likely to reduce individuals' cognitive capacity remains an open issue. Finally, like the motivational hypotheses, the capacity hypotheses result in different predictions at different processing stages, as will be discussed later.

The fact that the capacity and motivational hypotheses generate potentially identical predictions raises the question of how the two may be distinguished. It seems that a mood-induced lack of motivation to engage in effortful analyses of the content of the message may be overridden by other attempts to motivate recipients to pay attention to the quality of the message presented to them. Such attempts should show little effect, however, if recipients do not have the required cognitive capacity at their disposal. Conversely, giving recipients sufficient time to process the content of a message despite restricted cognitive capacity may overcome the impact of limited capacity, but may show little effect if individuals are not motivated to engage in effortful processing strategies. We shall later return to this issue in more detail.

Let us now review experimental findings that bear on the impact of recipients' mood at the time of exposure to a persuasive communication.

III. Mood at Exposure and the Processing of Persuasive Messages

A. IS THERE AN INFLUENCE?

To begin with a real world illustration, suppose that you want to use a public telephone. But before you can place your call, you are approached by a person who asks you to let him make his own call first. Would you be more likely to comply with this request if you were in a good rather than in a bad mood? Probably yes, as a considerable number of studies on mood and helping behavior suggest (see Isen, 1984; Schaller & Cialdini, in press, for reviews). But more germane to the present issue is the following: Would the quality of this fellow's excuse make more of a difference when you are in a good mood or when you are in a bad mood?

To explore this issue, Bohner (1988) conducted a field experiment with 52 users of a public telephone in a German city. Half of the subjects happened to find a one-deutsche mark (DM) coin in the telephone booth, equivalent to half a United States dollar, while the others did not. Pretests demonstrated that finding a coin did improve subjects' current mood.

In the main experiment, subjects were approached by a confederate who asked them for permission to advance in line and to make her own call first. This was done after subjects had or had not found a coin, but before they could place their telephone call. For half of the subjects, the confederate provided a reasonable excuse, by informing the subject that she had to contact her boss, who would only be in his office for another 5 minutes. For the other half, the confederate's request was not accompanied by a plausible reason.

Overall, subjects' mood did not influence their compliance. While 63% of the good-mood subjects complied with the confederate's request, the same was true for 66% of the control group subjects. Thus, no main effect of mood was obtained. On the other hand, subjects were twice as likely to comply with the confederate's request when a plausible reason was given (85%) than when it was not (44.5%). This latter finding, however, depended on subjects' mood. Specifically, 39% of the control group subjects, who did *not* find a coin, complied with the request without receiving a plausible reason, whereas 92% complied when a reason was provided. Good-mood subjects, on the other hand, who *did* find a coin, were not significantly affected by the quality of the excuse. They complied with the request independently of whether it was accompanied by a plausible reason (75%) or not (50%). Although this pattern did not result in a significant interaction, the simple main effect of type of excuse was significant for subjects in a neutral mood, but insignificant for subjects in a positive mood. Thus the findings of this field experiment suggest that subjects in a good mood may be less likely to pay attention to the quality of a request than subjects in a nonmanipulated mood.

A related laboratory experiment (Bless, Bohner, Schwarz, & Strack, 1990) provides more systematic insight into the impact of *good* and *bad* moods on recipients' processing of persuasive counterattitudinal communications that present *strong* or *weak* arguments. Subjects were 87 female students at a German university. To induce a good or bad mood, subjects were first asked to provide a vivid report of a pleasant or an unpleasant life event, purportedly to help with the construction of a "Heidelberg Life-Event Inventory." They were encouraged to relive the event in their mind's eye, and to provide a vivid description of the event and the feelings that accompanied it. Subjects were given 15 minutes to complete their report. This procedure resulted in a reliable difference on a manipulation check ("How do you feel right now, at this very moment?," 1 = "very bad" and 9 = "very good"; $M = 7.0$ for the positive, and 6.1 for the negative event conditions, respectively).

As part of a purportedly independent second study, subjects were subsequently exposed to a tape-recorded communication that presented either strong or weak arguments in favor of an increase in student services fees. Some of the subjects were informed that this second study was concerned with language comprehension, whereas others were told that the study was concerned with the evaluation of persuasive arguments. To provide an attitude baseline, a nonfactorial control condition was included, in which subjects were neither exposed to a mood manipulation nor to a persuasive message, but only reported their attitude toward an increase in student services fees.

For the time being, we will restrict our discussion to the language comprehension conditions because these conditions are most relevant to the impact of mood states on subjects' *spontaneous* processing of persuasive messages. We shall later return to the impact of moods under conditions where subjects are explicitly instructed to pay attention to message quality. After listening to one of the taped messages, subjects' attitudes toward an increase in student services fees, their cognitive responses to the message, their memory for the message's content, and their evaluation of the message were assessed.

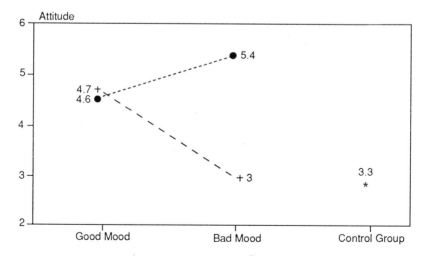

Fig. 1.   Attitude change as function of mood and message quality. (●·····●), Strong message quality; (+---+), weak message quality. Adapted from Bless, Bohner, Schwarz, and Strack (1990, Experiment 1).

As shown in Fig. 1, subjects in a bad mood reported more favorable attitudes toward an increase in student services fees when they were exposed to strong arguments than when they were exposed to weak arguments (see Table I, presented below, for the significance of comparisons between individual means). Subjects in a good mood, on the other hand, were equally persuaded by strong *and* by weak arguments, and showed moderately positive attitude change, irrespective of the quality of the arguments. This suggests that subjects in a good mood may have been less likely to elaborate the specific content of the message than subjects who were in a bad mood.

This conclusion is supported by an analysis of subjects' cognitive responses. Specifically, subjects in a bad mood reported a higher proportion of favorable thoughts in response to strong rather than weak arguments, as shown in the top panel of Fig. 2. Similarly, they reported a higher proportion of unfavorable thoughts in response to weak rather than strong arguments, as shown in the bottom panel of Fig. 2. Thus, the cognitive responses of subjects in a bad mood reflect systematic elaboration of message content. Not so, however, for subjects in a good mood. Neither the proportion of favorable, nor the proportion of unfavorable, thoughts reported by these subjects differed as a function of argument strength, indicating a low degree of systematic message elaboration.[1]

Nevertheless, when subjects were subsequently asked to rate the quality of the presented arguments, these ratings were unaffected by their affective state. Rather, subjects in a good as well as in a bad mood rated the weak arguments as less convincing ($M = 3.5$) than the strong arguments ($M = 6.0$, along a scale of $1 =$ not strong at all to $9 =$ very strong), with no indication of a mood effect whatsoever (all F values < 1). This suggests that subjects in a good mood did note the quality of the arguments, at least when explicitly asked, but did not spontaneously consider it in making their attitude judgments.

Conceptually equivalent findings were obtained in a number of other studies, which will be reviewed shortly, all indicating that the observed interaction of mood and argument strength on measures of attitude change and cognitive responses is a robust and reliably replicable finding (Bless *et al.*, 1990, Experiment 2; Bless, Mackie, & Schwarz, in press; Innes & Ahrens, in press; Mackie & Worth, 1989; Worth & Mackie, 1987). In combination, these results support the hypothesis that the impact of mood on persuasion is mediated by its impact on subjects' processing strategies. While subjects in a bad (Bless *et al.*, 1990, 1991) or in a nonmanipulated mood (Innes & Ahrens, in press, Experiment 2; Mackie & Worth, 1989; Worth & Mackie, 1987) spontaneously elaborated the content of the message according to a central route of persuasion, subjects in a good mood

---

[1]The absolute number of cognitive responses reported by subjects was not affected by the manipulations, and about one-third of the responses were coded as "neutral" or "irrelevant" thoughts (see Bless *et al.*, 1990, for details).

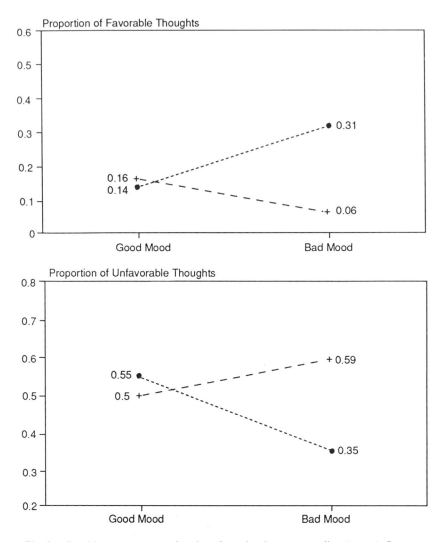

Fig. 2.   Cognitive responses as a function of mood and message quality. (●·····●), Strong message quality; (+———+), weak message quality.

did not do so. The interaction effects of mood and argument strength obtained in these studies are incompatible with the mood-as-peripheral-cue hypothesis and the mood-congruent-recall hypothesis. As noted before, these hypotheses predict main effects of mood rather than interaction effects of mood and message quality. Accordingly, they cannot account for the observed effects—which is not to say that they are generally invalid, an issue to which we shall return later.

Finally, the change-in-criteria hypothesis introduced above may in principle generate an interaction prediction, but cannot account for the present findings because subjects' ratings of argument quality were unaffected by their mood state.

B. HOW CRUCIAL ARE SUBJECTS' COGNITIVE RESPONSES?

While the parallel effects on measures of attitude change and recipients' cognitive responses suggest that the impact of mood on attitude change is mediated by its impact on recipients' cognitive elaboration of the message, a more direct test of this mediating assumption would be welcome. If this assumption is correct, the observed interaction of mood and message quality should be affected by other variables that are known to influence message elaboration. According to the elaboration likelihood and the heuristic/systematic model, the amount of message elaboration is determined by the recipient's motivation and ability to process the message, and variables like distraction, personal relevance, repetition, and prior knowledge can decrease or increase message elaboration (cf. Chaiken, 1987; Chaiken, Liberman, & Eagly, 1989; Petty & Cacioppo, 1986a, 1986b). Most importantly, distraction has been shown to interfere with the systematic processing of a message. Distracted subjects are less likely to generate favorable cognitive responses in reaction to strong arguments or negative cognitive responses in reaction to weak arguments. As a consequence, distraction reduces the differential impact of strong and weak messages (cf. Petty & Brock, 1981), as has been discussed in the context of the capacity hypothesis.

Accordingly, one can test the hypothesis that the impact of mood on persuasion is mediated by its impact on subjects' cognitive responses by introducing a distraction manipulation. If subjects in a bad mood are likely to elaborate the message, introducing a distraction manipulation should eliminate the advantage of strong over weak arguments. If subjects in a good mood are not motivated, or not able, to process the content of the message to begin with, introducing a distractor task should not affect their responses.

To test this hypothesis, 75 female subjects were put in a good or bad mood, and were exposed to strong or weak arguments (Bless et al., 1990, Experiment 2), replicating the procedures used in the study reported above. In addition, half of the subjects were distracted while they listened to the message. Specifically, these subjects had to solve simple computation tasks that were presented on slides while they listened to the tape. Again, the manipulation check, as described above, revealed a reliable mood difference of about one scale unit ($M =$ 6.4 and 5.5, for good and bad mood conditions, respectively).

As shown in Fig. 3, the data of the nondistracted subjects replicated the

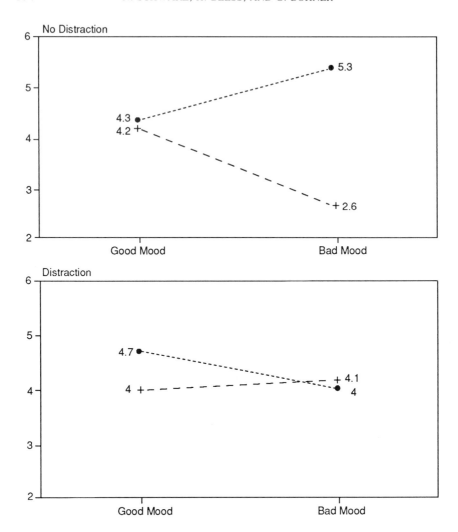

Fig. 3   Attitude change as a function of mood, message quality, and distraction. (●·····●), Strong message quality; (+———+), weak message quality. Adapted from Bless, Bohner, Schwarz, and Strack (1990, Experiment 2).

previous findings. Again, subjects in a bad mood were persuaded by strong but not by weak arguments, whereas subjects in a good mood were moderately persuaded by both messages. However, introducing a distractor task during exposure to the message eliminated the advantage of strong over weak arguments under bad mood conditions. Subjects in a good mood, on the other hand, were not affected by the distractor task, presumably because they did not elaborate the message to begin with.

This conclusion is again supported by an analysis of subjects' cognitive responses. Separate analyses under each distraction condition indicated that non-distracted subjects in a bad mood reported a higher proportion of favorable and a smaller proportion of unfavorable thoughts in response to the strong rather than the weak arguments. However, this pattern was significantly less pronounced when bad-mood subjects were distracted than when they were not. The cognitive responses reported by subjects in a good mood, on the other hand, were not affected by the distraction manipulation, again paralleling the attitude change data.

Although the quality of the arguments affected neither attitude judgments nor cognitive responses of distracted and/or good-mood recipients, it should be noted that when explicitly asked to evaluate the quality of the arguments, subjects in all mood and distraction conditions were able to differentiate between strong and weak arguments. This finding excludes the possibility that the distraction task may have been too involving and may have inhibited any meaningful processing of the message. Moreover, by replicating previous studies (Bless *et al.*, 1990, Experiment 1; Mackie and Worth, 1989), this finding supports the idea that the formation of an attitude judgment and the perception of the quality of the arguments should be considered as being at least partly independent of each other. It seems plausible to assume that the formation of an attitude judgment requires more and deeper processing than the mere evaluation of the quality of message content.

In summary, the obtained results indicate that the impact of moods on recipients' responses to persuasive messages is mediated by their impact on respondents' elaboration of the content of the presented arguments. They are consistent with the predictions generated by the motivational hypotheses as well as by the capacity hypotheses. We shall now turn to the limited data that bear on their relative merit.

C. DIFFERENTIAL MOTIVATION OR DIFFERENTIAL CAPACITY?

As mentioned previously, one may assume that a mood-induced lack of motivation to engage in effortful analyses of the content of the message may be overridden by other attempts to motivate recipients to pay attention to the quality of the message presented to them. Such attempts should show little effect, however, if recipients do not have the required cognitive capacity at their disposal. Conversely, giving recipients sufficient time to process the content of a message despite restricted cognitive capacity may overcome the impact of limited capacity, but may show little effect if individuals are not motivated to engage in effortful processing strategies. Three studies bear on these considerations.

In one study, part of which we already discussed (Bless *et al.*, 1990, Experiment 1), recipients' motivation to elaborate message content was independently manipulated. Half of the subjects were informed that the study was concerned with the evaluation of arguments, and they were explicitly instructed to pay attention to the arguments. The remaining subjects, on the other hand, were told that the study was concerned with language comprehension, to direct their attention to content-unrelated features of message presentation. As discussed above, and shown in Figs. 1 and 2, these latter subjects were more likely to *spontaneously* elaborate the message when they were in a bad rather than in a good mood. However, how does subjects' mood at the time of encoding influence message elaboration when subjects' are explicitly instructed to pay attention to the quality of the presented arguments? Most importantly, do subjects in a good mood engage in message elaboration under this condition? Table I shows the full

TABLE I

ATTITUDE CHANGE AS A FUNCTION OF MOOD, MESSAGE QUALITY, AND FOCUS OF ATTENTION[a]

	Focus of attention			
	On arguments		On language	
	Good mood	Bad mood	Good mood	Bad mood
Attitude change				
Approval				
Strong arguments	5.4*	7.3*	4.6*	5.4*
Weak arguments	3.0	3.0	4.7*	3.0
Recommended fee				
Strong arguments	53.98*	59.29*	51.11	54.00*
Weak arguments	47.78	45.63	56.43*	48.75
Control group: Approval: 3.3				
Recommended fee: 48.44				
Cognitive responses				
Favorable thoughts				
Strong arguments	.19	.37	.14	.31
Weak arguments	.19	.15	.16	.06
Unfavorable thoughts				
Strong arguments	.48	.33	.55	.35
Weak arguments	.54	.49	.50	.59

[a]Means with an asterisk differ significantly from the control group at $p < .05$. The recommended fee is given in deutschemärks; the possible range of values for approval is 1 ("strongly disapprove") to 9 ("strongly approve"). Adapted from Bless, Bohner, Schwarz, and Strack (1990, Experiment 1).

pattern of results. As comparisons with the nonfactorial control group indicate, subjects in a good mood were influenced by strong arguments but not by weak arguments when they were *explicitly instructed* to evaluate the quality of the arguments. Without this explicit instruction, however, good mood subjects were equally influenced by strong as well as by weak argument, as discussed earlier. Subjects in a bad mood, on the other hand, were influenced by strong but not by weak arguments, irrespective of whether they were instructed to pay attention to the quality of the arguments or not. Thus, being in a bad mood seems functionally equivalent to being instructed to focus on the quality of the presented arguments, and either of these manipulations resulted in a differential impact of strong and weak arguments.

These findings bear on the hypothesis that the impact of mood states on message elaboration may be mediated by motivational factors rather than by capacity constraints. If subjects in a good mood were severely restricted in their processing capacity, simply instructing them to pay attention to the quality of the arguments should be unlikely to overcome these constraints. Note, in this regard, that the persuasive messages were presented from a tape, at a fixed speed, thus eliminating the possibility that subjects could spend more time on processing the message when instructed to pay attention to the quality of the arguments. If they were not motivated to process the message in any detail, on the other hand, despite having the necessary capacity at their disposal, increasing their motivation to do so by explicit instructions should overcome the motivational deficits, much as the above findings indicate. Accordingly, we consider these findings to support the motivational, rather than the capacity, hypothesis.

In a related vein, Innes and Ahrens (in press, Experiment 2) observed that instructing subjects "to imagine themselves in the situation of having been requested to lead a round table discussion to introduce ideas on the issue" presented in the message, eliminated the impact of being in an elated rather than a neutral mood. Specifically, elated subjects given this instruction differentiated between strong and weak arguments, whereas elated subjects who were instructed "to read the message as if they had to present an appraisal of the contents to another group for class discussion" did not. Although it remains an open issue why the first instruction increased subjects' motivation to elaborate the content of the message, whereas the second did not, the data converge with the findings of Bless *et al.* (1990, Experiment 1) by indicating that processing instructions may override the impact of affective states. Accordingly, Innes and Ahrens (in press) concluded that the impact of mood states is mediated by motivational variables rather than by decreased cognitive capacity.

However, the available evidence is mixed. In an explicit test of the cognitive capacity hypothesis, Mackie and Worth (1989) manipulated the amount of time that subjects had available for processing the message. In two experiments, with different mood inductions and different topics, a persuasive message with strong or weak arguments was presented to subjects in a positive or a nonmanipulated mood. Half of the subjects were informed that the message would appear on a computer screen for a limited amount of time, ''just long enough . . . to read the message through once'' (p. 28). The other subjects were informed that they could proceed from reading the message to completing the dependent measures ''whenever they were ready. Thus, these subjects were aware that they could look at the speech for as long as they wanted'' (p. 29).

The authors found that offering subjects more time to process the message increased good-mood subjects' elaboration to a level that no longer differed from neutral-mood subjects' elaboration, as indicated by similar patterns of subjects' cognitive responses and attitude judgments, as well as correlations between the favorability of content-related cognitive responses and attitude change. They concluded from this pattern that good-mood subjects were apparently motivated to process the message, or else they would not have spent more time on it when they had the chance to do so. Accordingly, Mackie and Worth (1989) attributed elated subjects' limited message elaboration under restricted exposure time to limited processing capacity.

Note, however, that an alternative interpretation of these findings in terms of instructional differences is not implausible. Specifically, telling subjects that they may use as much time as they want to read the message, and may go over it again, may implicitly convey that the experimenter is interested in a carefully considered response to the message, quite in contrast to telling subjects that time is just sufficient to read the message once. If so, Mackie and Worth's (1989) unlimited exposure time condition may be similar to the explicit instruction of Bless *et al.* (1990) to pay attention to the quality of the arguments, whereas their limited exposure time condition may resemble the instruction by Bless *et al.* to focus on language comprehension. On the other hand, subjects who were in-structed to pay attention to the quality of the arguments in the Bless *et al.* study may have taken more time to think about the message before they reported their attitude judgment. Although the exposure time of the tape-recorded message itself was constant across conditions, it is possible that subjects took more or less time to form a judgment, and data on this possibility are not available. Similarly, subjects in Innes and Ahrens's (in press, Experiment 2) study may have spent more time reading the persuasive message under the processing instructions that were found to reduce the impact of being in an elated mood.

In summary, additional research is needed to distinguish between the moti-vational and cognitive capacity hypotheses. Most importantly, this research will need to manipulate processing capacity in ways that are not open to a moti-vational reinterpretation. For the time being, we conclude from the finding that subjects in an elated mood were able to process the content of the message if explicitly instructed to do so, that the hypothesized constraints on processing capacity that may be induced by elated moods are unlikely to be very severe.

IV. Mood at the Time of Judgment

The findings reported so far indicate that recipients' affective states influence the style in which they process persuasive communications. In all reported studies, however, mood was induced directly before the message was presented and attitude judgments were assessed immediately afterward. As the messages used were all rather short, subjects' mood was probably still pronounced when attitude judgments were made. Accordingly, the impact of mood state may have occurred at the encoding stage, i.e., when subjects received the message, as well as at the judgment stage, i.e., when subjects responded to the dependent variables. Recall, however, that different process assumptions make different predictions about the processing stage at which recipients' affective state is likely to affect the persuasive impact of the message, as discussed in the introduction. An evaluation of their relative merit does therefore require separate explorations of the impact of mood states at the encoding as well as the judgment stage.

To address this issue, Bless and Schwarz (Bless *et al.,* 1991, Experiment 1) conducted a study in which a positive or negative mood was induced either before encoding or after encoding but before judgment. The mood induction was identical to the one used in the Bless *et al.* (1990) studies described above, with significant differences of about two scale units on the manipulation check. Subjects were exposed to the strong or weak counterattitudinal messages used in the Bless *et al.* (1990) studies under instructions that were designed to prevent subjects from forming online judgments.[2] Attitude judgments were assessed after a delay of 15 minutes, so that positive or negative mood could be induced either before the message was presented or before attitude judgments were made. Moreover, this delay guaranteed that the mood that was induced before message presentation had dissipated by the time the attitude judgment was made.

When good or bad moods were induced before the message was presented, the results replicated the previously reported findings: As shown in Table II, differential effects of strong versus weak arguments were obtained for subjects in a bad mood, but not for subjects in a good mood. As the confound of mood and processing stage common to the previous studies was avoided, these results indicate that the impact of mood on recipients' encoding of the presented message is sufficient to obtain an interaction of mood and argument quality.

However, the impact of subjects' mood was not restricted to the encoding stage. Rather, mood effects on subjects' processing strategy could also be ob-

[2]Specifically, the cover story informed subjects that various texts were being pretested for a study on ''language comprehension,'' and a number of questions was presented that focused on various linguistic aspects of the message. These instructions were all intended to prevent subjects from making attitudinal judgments during encoding of the message by directing their attention to the form rather than the content of the communication.

TABLE II
ATTITUDE CHANGE AS A FUNCTION OF MOOD, TIMING OF MOOD
INDUCTION, AND ARGUMENT QUALITY[a]

| | Timing of mood induction | | | |
| | Before encoding | | Before judgment | |
	Positive mood	Negative mood	Positive mood	Negative mood
Approval				
Strong arguments	3.6	4.1	5.2	3.8
Weak arguments	3.4	1.9	1.6	2.3
Recommended fee				
Strong arguments	48.50	54.29	54.33	50.50
Weak arguments	50.56	49.38	46.50	48.30

[a]The possible range of values for approval is 1 ("strongly disapprove") to 9 ("strongly approve"). The recommended fee is given in deutsche marks. Adapted from Bless, Mackie, and Schwarz (1991, Experiment 1).

served at the judgment stage. If subjects were exposed to the message in a neutral mood, but positive or negative moods were induced before the attitude judgments were made, the interaction of mood and message quality showed a reversed pattern. Although all subjects were affected by the quality of the arguments, this effect was significantly more pronounced for subjects in a *good* mood, who reported more extreme judgments than subjects in a bad mood.

We assume that this pattern of results again indicates that subjects in a good mood simplified their processing task. Specifically, subjects who were in a good mood at the time of judgment may have been less likely to recall detailed representations of the presented arguments than subjects who were in a bad mood. Rather, they may have relied on a global evaluative representation, such as "These were pretty good arguments," in forming an attitude judgment. If subjects in a bad mood, on the other hand, tended to use detail-oriented processing strategies, they may have recalled more of the presented information, including arguments that were less convincing. If so, the present findings would parallel previous research, conducted in other content domains, that indicated that simplifications of judgmental processes, due to suboptimal information (Linville, 1982) or insufficient processing time (Strack, Erber, & Wicklund, 1982), may result in more extreme judgments. Most important, Linville & Jones (1980) observed that subjects provided more extreme judgments the less information about the target was available. Linville suggested that the likelihood of extreme judgments may decrease the more information is considered in making the judgment, reflecting that a wider range of information may draw attention to different implications. Similarly, Strack *et al.* (1982) observed greater reliance on a single piece of salient information under time pressure, again resulting in more extreme judgments. Thus, the extremity of judgments may decrease when individuals consider a wider range of detailed information with potentially different implications. If so, the above findings may reflect that recipients' mood state influenced the amount of information that they considered in making a judgment.

To provide a direct test of this hypothesis, Bless and Mackie (see Bless *et al.,* in press, Experiment 2) conducted a study in which subjects were induced to form either a global or a detailed representation of the persuasive message presented to them. As in the previous studies, subjects received a counterattitudinal communication that presented either strong or weak arguments, again under instructions designed to prevent online attitude judgments. Subsequently, half of the subjects were required to evaluate the perceived quality of the arguments, whereas the remaining subjects were asked to indicate the number of *different* arguments presented to them. Whereas the first task was designed to form a global evaluative representation, the second task was designed to form a more differentiated, detail-oriented representation. In fact, forming this more detailed representation took subjects almost twice as long as simply judging the perceived quality of the arguments.

Following this task, subjects were put in a good, neutral, or bad mood and were asked to report their attitudes on the issue. Specifically, subjects in whom positive mood was to be induced watched a 5-minute video clip taken from the television comedy show "Saturday Night Live," whereas subjects assigned to the neutral mood condition watched a 5-minute segment on wine corking. Subjects assigned to the negative mood condition saw a 5-minute video report on a summer camp for children with cancer. Manipulation checks revealed a significant impact of these manipulations on subjects' mood, with means of $M = 7.2$, 6.0, and 4.1, for the positive, neutral, and negative conditions, respectively, along a scale with endpoints labeled "sad" (1) and "happy" (9).

The results provide strong support for the hypothesis that subjects in good and bad moods rely on different representations of the message, as shown in Table III. If subjects had previously formed a global evaluative representation of the message, the differential impact of strong and weak arguments was *more* pronounced for subjects in a good or a neutral mood, than for subjects in a bad mood. This indicates that subjects in a positive or neutral mood were more likely to use global representations, which have been demonstrated to lead to more extreme judgments than more detailed representations (Judd & Lusk, 1984; Large & Vega, 1989; Linville & Jones, 1980). Subjects in a bad mood, on the other hand, were apparently less likely to rely on a global representation, even though it was easily accessible.

If no global representation of the content of the message had previously been

TABLE III
ATTITUDE CHANGE AS A FUNCTION OF MOOD, TYPE OF REPRESENTATION,
AND ARGUMENT QUALITY[a]

| | Type of representation | | | |
| | Summary | | Detail | |
	Strong argument quality	Weak argument quality	Strong argument quality	Weak argument quality
Agreement				
Positive mood	5.9	3.2	3.9	4.1
Neutral mood	6.0	3.8	4.3	3.2
Negative mood	4.5	3.5	4.1	3.1

[a]The possible range of values for agreement is 1 ("strongly disagree") to 9 ("strongly agree"). Adapted from Bless, Mackie, and Schwarz (1991, Experiment 2).

formed, however, the differential impact of strong and weak arguments was *less* pronounced for subjects in a good mood than for subjects in a neutral or in a bad mood. This indicates that subjects in a bad or a neutral mood were more likely to engage in careful processing of a more detailed representation than subjects in a good mood. Apparently, the latter subjects formed their judgment by using some other heuristic. One simple cue that they may have used is the number of different arguments presented (Petty & Cacioppo, 1984a), although the data do not allow us to evaluate this possibility.

In summary, subjects in a neutral mood used either a global or a detailed representation, depending on which was more accessible. Subjects in a good mood, however, preferred a global representation, and made less use of a more detailed one, even if easily available. Conversely, subjects in a bad mood preferred a more detailed representation, and made less use of a global one, even if easily available.

In combination, the reported findings demonstrate that the influence of affective states on the processing of persuasive communications is not restricted to a specific processing stage. Rather, elated moods foster the use of simplified processing strategies, and depressed moods the use of more effortful, detail-oriented processing strategies, both at the encoding stage and at the judgment stage. Depending on the processing stage at which mood has its impact, however, these strategies result in markedly different effects of strong and weak arguments. At the encoding stage, the advantage of strong over weak arguments is increased if recipients are in a bad mood, but decreased if they are in a good mood. Conversely, at the judgment stage, the advantage of strong over weak arguments is increased if recipients are in a good mood, but decreased if they are in a bad mood. Both of these diverging impacts, however, reflect the operation of the same general influence of affective states on individuals' preferred processing strategy.

V. Mood and the Impact of Peripheral Cues

The finding that subjects in a good mood relied more on a global representation of the message than did subjects in a bad mood (Bless *et al.,* in press, Experiment 2) is compatible with the general assumption that reliance on simple cues will increase as the systematic elaboration of message content decreases. This assumption follows from the elaboration likelihood model (ELM), which postulates a ''tradeoff between argument elaboration and the operation of peripheral cues'' (Petty & Cacioppo, 1986b, p. 21; see Petty & Cacioppo, 1984b, for a more detailed discussion). In the related ''heuristic–systematic model of persuasion'' (HSM) (Chaiken, 1987; Chaiken *et al.,* 1989), such a trade-off has been discussed as the ''attenuation hypothesis'' (Chaiken *et al.,* 1989, p. 220).

According to this model, however, systematic *and* heuristic processing may also occur simultaneously under certain conditions. Specifically, if motivation to process is high, the impact of heuristic (or ''peripheral'') cues is assumed to be enhanced when systematic (or ''central'') processing *alone* does not provide the person with sufficient information to assess the validity of the message. This may be due to either personal (e.g., high need for cognition) or situational factors (e.g., if the content is insufficient to form a judgment; see Chaiken *et al.,* 1989, p. 226). In either case, individuals may consider the content of the message *and* peripheral cues (such as the expertise of the communicator) in combination to assess the validity of the message.

If one assumes that being in a negative mood increases the motivation to use effortful, detail-oriented processing strategies, whereas being in a positive mood increases the likelihood of simplifying processing strategies, different predictions about the impact of mood states on the processing of noncontent cues may be derived, depending on several factors. Suppose that the content of the message is sufficient to evaluate its validity, but that reliance on peripheral cues allows a reduction in cognitive effort and that a relevant heuristic is easily accessible to make sense of the implications of the peripheral cues (Chaiken, 1987; Chaiken *et al.,* 1989). If so, we may expect that individuals in a positive mood will be likely to rely on peripheral cues, at the expense of message elaboration. In contrast, individuals in a negative mood should be likely to engage in message elaboration, and may pay little attention to peripheral cues, given that they can evaluate the message on the basis of its content.

Suppose, however, that the content of the message is *not* sufficient to evaluate its validity. If so, individuals in a *negative* mood may be particularly likely to turn to peripheral cues as an *additional* source of information in their attempt to evaluate the validity of the message. Thus, negative moods may in fact increase the processing of noncontent cues, as part of a detail-oriented and exhaustive processing strategy, if the content of the message seems insufficient to form a judgment. We shall now review the limited empirical evidence that bears on these hypotheses.

In two studies, Mackie and Worth (1989, Experiment 2; Worth & Mackie, 1987) explicitly manipulated source expertise independently of argument strength and subjects' mood. As predicted by the ELM, as well as the HSM's attenuation hypothesis, positive mood subjects tended to base their attitude judgments more on the expertise cue than did neutral mood subjects. However, the obtained impact of source expertise was small and only marginally significant. In our reading, there are two plausible reasons that may account for the failure to detect the clear-cut mood effects on cue reliance that the attenuation hypothesis would predict.

First, the salience of the expertise cue may have been low, relative to the salience of the presented arguments. Specifically, subjects received a short description of the source, pertaining to its expertise, before a message with eight (Mackie & Worth, 1989, Experiment 2) or nine (Worth & Mackie, 1987) arguments was presented. It is conceivable that the single piece of information on source expertise was not easily accessible after the presentation of the arguments. Consistent with this possibility, Mackie and Worth (1989, p. 34) reported that subjects' judgments of source expertise were more strongly influenced by argument strength than by the expertise manipulation.

Second, and more important, Chaiken and colleagues suggested that peripheral cues, such as source expertise, may not affect attitude judgments unless a relevant heuristic (e.g., "experts can be trusted") is easily accessible at the time of judgment (Chaiken, 1987; Chaiken *et al.*, 1989). If so, it may be important that the cues provided to recipients match the heuristic that is suggested by the purported rationale of the study. In retrospect, this may not have been the case in the studies by Mackie and Worth. Specifically, their subjects were instructed to pay attention to "how delegates represent the views of their constituents at conferences." It is conceivable that these instructions increased the accessibility of heuristics that pertained to presentation style rather than source expertise. If so, good-mood subjects may have used peripheral cues other than the one that was explicitly manipulated, resulting in the surprisingly low impact of the source expertise manipulation.

In contrast to this suggestive evidence for an increased impact of peripheral cues under *elated* moods, Bohner, Crow, Erb, and Schwarz (in press) observed an increased impact of peripheral cues under *depressed* moods, when a highly salient consensus cue was presented in combination with only one piece of content information. In their study, 64 subjects were run in individual sessions and received positive or negative feedback on a bogus "Vocational Aptitude Test," resulting in a reliable mood difference (M = 6.5 and 4.8, for good and bad mood conditions, respectively, along a scale from 1 = "very bad" to 9 = "very good"). Following this mood manipulation, each subject was left alone in the hall, waiting for another study, to begin a few minutes later. Shortly after the experimenter had left the subject alone, he or she was approached by a female confederate who was unaware of the subject's mood condition. The confederate wore a name tag that identified her as a member of a (fictitious) local organization supporting disabled students. She greeted the subject and asked him or her to donate some money to her organization, which would be used to increase the accessibility of university buildings through wheelchair ramps (high argument quality), or to establish a separate library for disabled students (low argument quality). Simultaneously, she showed the subject a sheet with the heading "List of Contributors," which contained 2 (weak consensus cue) or 19 names (strong consensus cue). Thus, the study provided orthogonal manipulations of subjects' mood, message quality, and strength of the peripheral cue.

The key dependent variables were subjects' willingness to donate and the amount of money donated. After the confederate left, subjects were informed that the collection of money constituted the second, independent experiment for which they had been waiting, and were asked to list their cognitive responses, to rate the usefulness of the alleged cause of the donation, and to list any details of the situation that they could remember.

Table IV shows the percentages of subjects who donated, along with the means of the amount donated.[3] When a weak consensus cue was presented, the willingness to donate was significantly influenced by message quality for subjects in a bad mood, but not for subjects in a good mood, resulting in a significant simple interaction of mood and message quality, which again replicates the previous findings. The amount of money donated showed a parallel, although nonsignificant, pattern. More important, however, presentation of a strong consensus cue influenced only subjects who were in a bad mood, but not subjects who were in a good mood. Specifically, subjects in a bad mood were more willing to donate, and gave more money, when a strong rather than a weak cue was presented. In contrast, no significant impact of cue strength emerged for subjects in a good mood.

Analyses of subjects' cognitive responses and their evaluation of the collection's usefulness revealed patterns that paralleled the behavioral data reported in

---

[3]Each subject had at least DM 5 available to donate, because this amount (approximately $3 at the exchange rate of the time), in small change, had been paid for participation at the beginning of the alleged first experiment.

TABLE IV
PERCENTAGE OF DONORS AND AMOUNT DONATED AS A FUNCTION OF
MOOD, STRENGTH OF CONSENSUS CUE, AND ARGUMENT QUALITY[a]

	Strong		Weak	
	Positive mood	Negative mood	Positive mood	Negative mood
Percentage of donors				
Strong arguments	88	88	100	88
Weak arguments	75	88	100	25
Amount donated				
Strong arguments	1.94	2.34	2.25	1.75
Weak arguments	2.16	2.67	2.30	0.50

[a]The amount donated is given in deutsche marks. Adapted from Bohner, Crow, Erb, and Schwarz (in press).

Table IV. In addition, the recall data suggested that subjects in a bad mood recalled more details of the persuasive situation than did subjects in a good mood, indicating more extensive processing of both content and noncontent information under negative mood.

In summary, subjects in a bad mood were affected by both message quality *and* the strength of a noncontent cue, and this influence was reflected in their cognitive responses and their overt behavior. In contrast, subjects in a good mood were neither influenced by variations in message quality nor by peripheral cues. Thus, the results of this study (Bohner *et al.,* in press) apparently contradict the findings reported by Mackie and Worth (1989, Experiment 2; Worth & Mackie, 1987), reviewed above. However, both sets of findings seem compatible if one takes the HSM's "sufficiency criterion" (Chaiken *et al.,* 1989) into account. According to that criterion, recipients may consider peripheral cues as an additional source of information if the content of the message is insufficient to evaluate its validity. If so, the impact of peripheral cues should reflect an interaction of message quality, bearing on the sufficiency criterion, and recipients' mood. Specifically, being in a bad mood may increase systematic processing of *all* potentially available information. If the content of the message alone is sufficient to form a judgment, the attitude judgments and behavioral decisions of individuals who are in a bad mood are likely to reflect their elaboration of message content. If the content of the message is insufficient, however—for example, because very few arguments are presented to begin with—recipients who are in a bad mood may use noncontent cues as an additional source of information to arrive at a judgment. Individuals in a good mood, on the other hand, may be willing to use simple decision rules based on heuristic cues. Moreover, they may be particularly likely to do so if the judgmental task seems complex, as is the case, for example, when numerous different arguments are presented. This raises the intriguing possibility that the impact of peripheral cues decreases with message complexity for recipients who are in a bad mood, but increases with message complexity for recipients who are in a good mood.

While the available data (Bohner *et al.*, in press; Mackie & Worth, 1989, Experiment 2; Worth & Mackie, 1987) are consistent with the hypotheses offered above, a more stringent test would be welcome. To provide this test, future studies should include orthogonal manipulations of the number of message arguments and the presentation of peripheral cues. If our reasoning is correct, the direction of the interaction between mood and peripheral cues should directly depend on the amount of content information presented in the message.

VI. Theoretical Implications

We began this article by introducing a number of different ways by which recipients' mood states may influence the impact of persuasive messages. We shall now turn to an evaluation of these possibilities and shall finally discuss the implications of the present findings for current models of affective influences on cognitive processes, broadly conceived.

A. MOOD AND PERSUASION

1. Evaluation of Hypotheses

The studies reviewed in the present article most clearly support the notion that recipients' affective states may influence the extent of argument processing. In line with previous suggestions about the impact of affective states on individuals' strategies of information processing (Schwarz, 1990), individuals in an elated mood were found to be less likely to engage in extensive processing of the presented arguments than individuals in a nonmanipulated or a mildly depressed mood. Accordingly, all studies showed significant interaction effects of recipients' mood states and the quality of the arguments presented to them. Moreover, these effects emerged under conditions that may be considered to reflect moderate elaboration, and were eliminated under conditions of decreased or increased elaboration. Thus, decreasing the amount of elaboration by a distractor task (Bless et al., 1990, Experiment 2), as well as increasing the amount of elaboration by instructing subjects to pay attention to the arguments (Bless et al., 1990, Experiment 1) or by providing additional time for processing (Mackie and Worth, 1989), eliminated the effects of mood on the amount of processing. However, neither under decreased nor under increased elaboration conditions did we observe evidence for mood effects that could *not* be attributed to mood's impact on message elaboration, contrary to some of the hypotheses we derived from the literature.

To begin with the *change-in-criteria* hypothesis, the presented findings did not support the notion that recipients in a bad mood may be more critical of any message presented to them than recipients in a good mood. While recipients in a bad mood did engage in a more critical examination of the presented arguments, they did appreciate the quality of strong arguments and were *more* influenced by them than were recipients in a good mood. Moreover, when recipients were explicitly asked to rate the quality of the presented arguments, their ratings did *not* differ as a function of their mood state (Bless et al., 1990, Experiment 1). Accordingly, we found no support for the folk wisdom that people in a bad mood are more likely to react negatively to just about anything, whereas people in a good mood may be generally uncritical. Rather, our findings suggest that individuals evaluate argument quality independently of their mood state, provided that their attention is drawn to the issue, contrary to what the change-in-criteria hypothesis would suggest. However, individuals in different mood states seem to differ in the extent to which they spontaneously elaborate the implications of the message and use these elaborations as a basis for their attitude judgments. As a result we find that individuals in a bad mood are not generally less likely to be influenced—they are only less likely to be influenced by poor arguments.

Similarly, we found no support for the *mood-congruent-recall* hypothesis, which holds that recipients' mood may influence the valence of the thoughts that they generate in response to the persuasive message or the communicator. Note, however, that mood congruent recall may be most likely for strongly valenced self-related material (cf. Blaney, 1986). If so, support for the hypothesis may be detected in content domains that are more clearly self-related, e.g., pertaining to the quality of recipients' marriage or to recipients' self-concept.

With regard to the *feelings-as-information* hypothesis, the findings are less conclusive. This hypothesis holds that individuals may use their perceived affective reaction to the attitude object, or to the communicator, in making a judgment according to a "How do I feel about it?" heuristic (Schwarz & Clore, 1988). In doing so, they may misread their preexisting mood state as a reaction to features of the persuasive situation, resulting in more favorable judgments when they are in a good rather than in a bad mood, unless the informational value of their current feelings is discredited (e.g., Schwarz & Clore, 1983). Although these predictions received considerable support in experiments that assessed complex judgments (see Schwarz, 1990; Schwarz & Clore, 1988, for reviews), the predicted main effect of mood did not emerge in the present persuasion experiments. Moreover, differences in recipients' attitude judgments were accompanied by parallel differences in their cognitive responses, contrary to the predictions made by the feelings-as-information assumption.

Note, however, that the quality of the presented arguments affected recipients' attitude judgments and cognitive responses only when they were in a bad mood, but not when they were in a good mood at the time of message exposure. This raises the question, on which basis, other than message quality, recipients in a good mood may have formed their attitude judgment? It is conceivable that these subjects did in fact consult their feelings in making an attitude judgment, resulting in similarly positive judgments irrespective of message quality. Obviously, additional experiments that manipulate the perceived informational value of recipients' mood by introducing misattribution manipulations are needed to provide an adequate test of this hypothesis. In general, however, this possibility is nicely compatible with the theoretical assumptions made. If individuals in a good mood attempt to simplify the judgmental process, reliance on the "How do I feel about it?" heuristic would provide an efficient way to do so. Moreover, they should be the more likely to use this heuristic the less other easily accessible information allows them to form a judgment without too much effort.

In line with this assumption, we observed that recipients did not differentiate between strong and weak messages when they were in a good mood at the time of encoding. However, their attitude judgments clearly reflected message quality when they had formed a simple evaluative representation of the message while in a neutral mood, but had to form an attitude judgment while in a good mood. We offer the conjecture that this pattern of findings reflects that elated subjects based their attitude judgment on the informational implications of their feelings, unless they had the even simpler opportunity to recall a previously formed global evaluation of the message.

In addition, the present findings suggest an alternative interpretation for a previous study that has been interpreted as supporting the operation of the "How do I feel about it?" heuristic in a persuasion context. Specifically, Schwarz, Servay, and Kumpf (1985) exposed heavy smokers to a fear-arousing movie that vividly portrayed the negative side effects of smoking. Relative to a control group that was not exposed to the movie, subjects who saw the movie reported a higher intention to cut down the number of cigarettes smoked. This intention was less pronounced, however, when subjects could misattribute their affective reactions to a placebo pill that was said to have arousing side effects. Subjects who were informed that the pill had tranquilizing side effects, on the other hand, reported a higher intention to reduce smoking than did subjects who had not expected side effects from the pill.

These discounting and augmentation effects (Kelley, 1972) were interpreted to indicate that subjects used their affective reactions to the movie as a basis for evaluating the described risk, resulting in the perception of the highest risk when they experienced arousal "despite" being tranquilized, and in the perception of the lowest risk when they could attribute their arousal to the pill. In light of the present theorizing, one may alternatively assume that recipients' feelings of fear prompted them to elaborate the strong arguments presented in the fear-arousing movie, but that the impact of their feelings on message elaboration was cut short when they misattributed their feelings to another source. Specifically, subjects who attributed their arousal to the side effects of the pill may have seen little reason to elaborate the message (and may instead have been thinking about the risks involved in taking pills). If so, the obtained results would reflect the use of one's affective state as a basis for making decisions about which information to attend to, rather than as a basis for evaluating the described risk per se.

In retrospect, the Schwarz et al. (1985) study nicely illustrates the shortcomings of studies that use only one level of message quality. Specifically, affective influences that are mediated by their impact on message elaboration can only be distinguished from other mediating processes if at least two levels of message quality are introduced. In the present case, the feelings-as-information hypotheses advanced by Schwarz et al. (1985) would predict effects of fear and its perceived cause that are independent of message quality, whereas the fear-induced-elaboration hypothesis considered here would predict an interaction of this factor with message quality. The same methodological point holds for the other hypotheses considered here. For example, had we constrained ourselves to the use of weak arguments in the studies reported in this article, the obtained results would have been equally compatible with the change-in-criteria or mood-congruent-recall hypotheses as with the mood-induced-elaboration assumption.

2. Music, Food, and Pleasant Circumstances

The same methodological issue renders it difficult to determine the applicability of the present analysis to the large body of research that explored the impact of music, food, or other pleasant situational influences on recipients' yielding to persuasive messages. For example, Janis, Kaye, and Kirshner (1965; see also Dabbs & Janis, 1965) observed more pronounced attitude change when recipients were eating while reading a persuasive communication than when they were not, whereas Galizio and Hendrick (1972) found a similar impact of pleasant music (see also Gorn, 1982; Milliman, 1982, 1986). In a related vein, Rosnow (1968; see also Corrozi & Rosnow, 1968) reported that exposure to rewarding or punishing events influenced the effectiveness of two-sided persuasive communications. Unfortunately, these and related studies were typically restricted to the use of a single level of message quality. Their findings may therefore be interpreted in a conditioning framework (which was preferred by most of these authors), or may be construed to reflect the impact of affective states on processing style. Specifically, if we assume that the presented arguments were not very strong, the observation that exposure to pleasant stimuli increased persuasion relative to control conditions would parallel the findings reviewed in the present article. In fact, Dabbs and Janis's (1965) suggestion that pleasant activities may create a momentary ''mood of compliance'' is nicely compatible with the more process-oriented account offered here.

Alternatively, however, we may construe the same findings as reflecting the use of the ''How do I feel about it?'' heuristic (Schwarz & Clore, 1988). In line with this latter hypothesis, Gorn, Goldberg, and Basu (1990) observed that exposure to pleasant or unpleasant music influenced subjects' evaluation of a consumer product only under conditions where their attention was *not* drawn to the nature of the music. When subjects were explicitly asked to evaluate the music before evaluating the consumer product, however, the latter judgments were unaffected by the type of music presented. As Gorn *et al.* (1990) note, this may reflect that drawing subjects' attention to the potential impact of the music may have discredited their current feelings as a basis of judgment, much as suggested by Schwarz and Clore (1983, 1988). In fact, differences in subjects' awareness of the source of their feelings may underlie the apparently conflicting results obtained in studies concerned with the impact of background music on consumer behavior (see Gorn, 1982; Kellaris & Cox, 1989; Milliman, 1982, 1986).

As this discussion indicates, it is impossible to determine the mechanism that underlies an observed impact of pleasant stimulation on attitude change in the absence of experimental conditions that include variations of message quality. Accordingly, the design of future research in this area will need to reflect the potential complexity of higher order interactions identified in this article.

3. Applied Implications

Turning to the applied implications of the reviewed research, we note that putting recipients in a good mood when we want to influence them may not always be a good idea. Specifically, when we have strong arguments to present in favor of our case, recipients' good mood may reduce their impact by interfering with recipients' systematic elaboration of the message. This interference is particularly undesirable because attitude change via a central route of persuasion has been found to be more stable than attitude change via a peripheral route (cf. Petty & Cacioppo, 1986b). Accordingly, strong arguments are likely to be more persuasive, and the induced attitude change is likely to be more resistant to change, when the arguments are delivered to an audience that is in a neutral or mildly depressed mood. Weak arguments, on the other hand, are more effective when recipients do not elaborate them. Therefore, if we have nothing compelling to say, putting the audience in a good mood may be a smart choice—much as many advertisers seem to have known for quite a while (cf. Stayman, Aaker, & Bruzzone's, 1989, content analysis of television spots).

B. AFFECT AND INFORMATION PROCESSING

1. Informational and Motivational Functions of Affective States

In a broader theoretical context, the present findings illustrate that individuals' affective states may have a strong impact on the strategies that they use to process information. As a growing body of literature indicates (see Fiedler, 1988; Schwarz, 1990; Schwarz & Bless, 1991, for reviews), individuals' cognitive performance on a wide variety of tasks may be profoundly influenced by the affective state they are in. These influences may be conceptualized by assuming that affective states may serve informative functions (see Schwarz, 1990; Schwarz & Bless, 1991, for a more detailed discussion). As many authors pointed out (e.g., Arnold, 1960; Frijda, 1988; Higgins, 1987; Ortony, Clore, & Collins, 1988), different affective states are closely linked to different psychological situations. In Frijda's (1988) words, "emotions arise in response to the meaning structures of given situations, [and] different emotions arise in response to different meaning structures." In general, "events that satisfy the individual's goals, or promise to do so, yield positive emotions; events that harm or threaten the individual's concerns lead to negative emotions" (p. 349).

For the purpose of the present argument, we assume that the relationship between emotions and the "meaning structures" that constitute a "psychological situation" (Higgins, 1987) is bidirectional: While different psychological situations result in different emotions, the presence of a certain emotion also informs the individual about the nature of its current psychological situation. At a general level, we may assume that a positive affective state informs the individual that the world is a safe place that does not threaten the person's current goals. That is, positive feelings tell us that our current situation is neither characterized by a lack of positive outcomes, nor by a threat of negative outcomes. Negative affective states, on the other hand, inform the individual that the current situation is problematic, and that it is characterized either by a lack of positive outcomes, or by a threat of negative outcomes. If so, one's affective state could serve as a simple but highly salient indicator of the nature of the situation one is in. Indeed, empirical evidence indicates that different emotions are associated with different states of "action readiness" that are evident in physiological changes (e.g., Lacey & Lacey, 1970; Obrist, 1981) and overt behavior (e.g., Ekman, 1982; Izard, 1977), as well as in introspective reports (e.g., Davitz, 1969; Frijda, 1986, 1988). Accordingly, many theories of emotion hold that "emotions exist for the sake of signaling states of the world that have to be responded to, or that no longer need response and action" (Frijda, 1988, p. 354).

These considerations suggest that individuals' processing strategies may be tuned to meet the requirements of the psychological situation that is reflected in their feelings. If negative affective states inform the individual about a lack of positive, or a threat of negative, outcomes, the individual may be motivated to change his or her current situation. Attempts to change the situation, however, initially require a careful assessment of the features of the current situation, an analysis of their causal links, and explorations of possible mechanisms of change and their potential outcomes (cf. Bohner et al., 1988). Accordingly, it would be highly adaptive if negative feelings increased the cognitive accessibility of procedural knowledge that is adequate for handling negative situations. Increased accessibility of this procedural knowledge, however, would also increase the likelihood that the respective procedures are applied to other tasks that one works on while in a bad mood, resulting in a generalized use of analytic reasoning procedures under bad mood when they are applicable (cf. Higgins, 1989). Moreover, individuals may be unlikely to take risks in a situation that is already considered problematic, and may therefore avoid simple heuristics as well as novel solutions. Accordingly, their thought processes may be characterized by what Fiedler (1988) called "tightening," a term borrowed from Kelly (1955).

If positive feelings inform the individual that his or her personal world is currently a safe place, on the other hand, the individual may see little need to engage in cognitive effort, *unless* this is required by other currently active goals. In pursuing these goals, the individual may also be willing to take some risk, given that the general situation is considered safe. Thus, simple heuristics may be preferred to more effortful, detail-oriented judgmental strategies; new procedures and possibilities may be explored; and unusual, creative associations may be elaborated. Moreover, a diverse body of procedural knowledge may be equally accessible, given that no specific procedure was activated to deal with a problematic situation, further increasing the potential for unusual solutions. Accordingly, the thought processes of individuals in a positive affective state may be characterized by what Fiedler (1988) has called "loosening."

2. Some Limiting Conditions

These conjectures predict numerous mood-induced differences in processing style, for which considerable support can be found in a diverse body of literature (see Schwarz, 1990, for a review and discussion). It is important, however, to consider a number of limiting conditions. First, the increase in analytic performance under the influence of a bad mood may be limited by the extent to which handling the negative situation itself binds a considerable degree of subjects' cognitive capacity, thus restricting the individual's capacity to work on an unrelated task. The underlying assumption that negative states may have a disruptive impact on information processing has a long tradition in psychological theorizing (see Easterbrook, 1959, for an early review). In the persuasion domain, it is reflected in findings that indicate a disruptive effect of pronounced temporary or chronic fear on the processing of persuasive messages (see Jepson & Chaiken, 1990). Moreover, any potential advantage of different processing styles cannot be observed if individuals are not motivated to work on a task to begin with, as is frequently the case under severe depression. Accordingly, the literature on depressive realism (see Ruehlman, West, & Pasahow, 1985, for a review) suggests that severe depression, in contrast to being in a "depressed mood," is *unlikely* to improve analytic performance. It is interesting to note, however, that phenomenological studies of the subjective experience of severe depression (see Tölle, 1982, for a review) indicate that the experience of "sadness" or of "being in a bad mood" is *not* part of the melancholic state that characterizes severe depression. Thus, the subjective experiences that accompany severe depression may be of a different nature than the "normal" negative affective states considered in the present article. Moreover, the experiences associated with severe depression are likely to endure over extended periods of time with limited variation, and may therefore lose whatever informational value they may have had at their onset.

Finally, other currently active goals (cf. Srull & Wyer, 1986) may override the impact of affective states, as has been demonstrated in the Bless *et al.* (1990, Experiment 1) study reviewed above. Note, however, that the present argument implies that it should be easier to induce individuals in a good mood to use an analytic processing style than to induce individuals in a bad mood to use a heuristic style. If positive feelings inform us that no action is needed, overriding this message due to other action requirements poses no problem. In contrast, if negative feelings inform us about current problems, ignoring this message would not be adaptive. Accordingly, one may expect that the impact of negative feelings on processing style is more immune to the influence of other variables than is the impact of positive feelings. Obviously, future research should address these plausible limitations.

For the time being, however, we note that the informative functions approach to the interplay of affect and cognition (Schwarz, 1990; Schwarz & Bless, 1991; Schwarz & Bohner, 1990) provides a heuristically fruitful framework for conceptualizing the impact of affective states on individuals' spontaneous use of processing strategies. Most important, the basic assumption that affective states may serve informative functions is clearly in line with a long tradition of theorizing about the nature of emotions (see Frijda, 1986, 1988, for reviews), and it invites an explicit consideration of what the specific information is that may be provided by different moods and emotions. One may expect that current explorations of the conditions that give rise to different emotions (e.g., Higgins, 1987; Oatley & Johnson-Laird, 1987; Ortony *et al.*, 1988; Weiner, 1985), as well as research on people's knowledge about their emotions (e.g., Stein & Levine, 1987), will result in a more precise understanding of their respective informational value. In principle, one may assume that affect-elicited cognitive tuning is the more functional for an organism, the more closely different types of emotions correspond to different situational requirements. If so, future insights into situational determinants of emotions are likely to allow more precise specifications of the processing requirements that are signaled by different affective states, providing a theoretical basis for more specific predictions about the impact of different moods and emotions on strategies of information processing.

Acknowledgments

The reported research was supported by grants from the Deutsche Forschungsgemeinschaft (Schw 278/2 and Str 264/2 to N. Schwarz and F. Strack, and Schw 278/5 to N. Schwarz, H. Bless, and G. Bohner) and a fellowship from the DAAD (German Academic Exchange Service) to H. Bless. Our thinking on these issues was greatly influenced by stimulating discussions with Shelly Chaiken, Bob Cialdini, Gerald Clore, Dave Hamilton, Tory Higgins, Diane Mackie, Tom Ostrom, Fritz Strack, and Bob Wyer, as well as the insightful comments of Mark Zanna and an anonymous reviewer on a previous draft. Correspondence should be addressed to Norbert Schwarz, ZUMA, P.O. Box 122 155, D-6800 Mannheim, Germany.

References

Abele, A. (1985). Thinking about thinking. Causal, evaluative and finalistic cognitions about social situations. *European Journal of Social Psychology*, **15**, 315–332.

Arnold, M. B. (1960). *Emotion and personality* (Vols. 1 and 2). New York: Columbia University Press.

Beck, A. T. (1967). *Depression. Clinical experimental, and theoretical aspects.* New York: Harper & Row.

Berkowitz, L., & Knurek, K. A. (1969). Label-mediated hostility generalization. *Journal of Personality and Social Psychology*, **13**, 200–206.

Blaney, P. H. (1986). Affect and memory: A review. *Psychological Bulletin*, **99**, 229–246.

Bless, H., Bohner, G., Schwarz, N., & Strack, F. (1990). Mood and persuasion: A cognitive response analysis. *Personality and Social Psychology Bulletin*, **16**, 331–345.

Bless, H., Mackie, D. M., & Schwarz, N. (1991). *Mood effects on encoding and judgmental processes in persuasion.*

Bohner, G. (1988, April). *"Würden Sie mich bitte vorlassen?" Stimmungsvermittelte Informationsverarbeitung in einer Alltagssituation* ["Would you please let me advance in line?" Affect-mediated information processing in an everyday situation]. 30th Tagung experimentell arbeitender Psychologen, Marburg, Germany.

Bohner, G., Bless, H., Schwarz, N., & Strack, F. (1988). What triggers causal attributions? The impact of valence and subjective probability. *European Journal of Social Psychology,* **18,** 335–345.

Bohner, G., Crow, K., Erb, H.-P., & Schwarz, N. (in press). Affect and persuasion: Mood effects on the processing of message content and context cues, and on subsequent behavior.

Bower, G. H. (1981). Mood and Memory. *American Psychologist,* **36,** 129–148.

Chaiken, S. (1980). Heuristic versus systematic information processing and the use of source versus message cues in persuasion. *Journal of Personality and Social Psychology,* **39,** 752–766.

Chaiken, S. (1987). The heuristic model of persuasion. In M. P. Zanna, J. M. Olson, & C. P. Herman (Eds.), *Social influence: The Ontario Symposium* (Vol. 5, pp. 3–39). Hillsdale, NJ: Erlbaum.

Chaiken, S., Liberman, A., & Eagly, A. H. (1989). Heuristic and systematic information processing within and beyond the persuasion context. In J. S. Uleman & J. A. Bargh (Eds.), *Unintended thought: Limits of awareness, intention, and control* (pp. 212–252). New York: Guilford.

Cialdini, R. B., & Insko, C. A. (1969). Attitudinal verbal reinforcement as a function of informational consistency: A further test of the two-factor-theory. *Journal of Personality and Social Psychology,* **12,** 342–350.

Corrozi, J. F., & Rosnow, R. L. (1968). Consonant and dissonant communications as positive and negative reinforcements in opinion change. *Journal of Personality and Social Psychology,* **1,** 27–30.

Dabbs, J. M., & Janis, I. L. (1965). Why does eating while reading facilitate opinion change? *Journal of Experimental Social Psychology,* **1,** 133–144.

Davitz, J. R. (1969). *The language of emotion.* New York: Academic Press.

Easterbrook, J. A. (1959). The effect of emotion on cue utilization and the organization of behavior. *Psychological Review,* **66,** 183–201.

Ekman, P. (1982). *Emotion in the human face.* New York: Cambridge University Press.

Ellis, H. C., & Ashbrook, P. W. (1988). Resource allocation model of the effects of depressed mood states on memory. In K. Fiedler & J. Forgas (Eds.), *Affect, cognition and social behavior* (pp. 25–43). Toronto: Hogrefe.

Fiedler, K. (1988). Emotional mood, cognitive style, and behavior regulation. In K. Fiedler & J. Forgas (Eds.), *Affect, cognition and social behavior* (pp. 100–119). Toronto: Hogrefe.

Frijda, N. H. (1986). *The emotions.* London: Cambridge University Press.

Frijda, N. H. (1988). The laws of emotion. *American Psychologist,* **43,** 349–358.

Galizio, M., & Hendick, C. (1972). Effect of musical accompaniment on attitude: The guitar as a prop for persuasion. *Journal of Applied Social Psychology,* **2,** 350–359.

Gorn, G. J. (1982). The effects of music in advertising on choice behavior: A classical conditioning approach. *Journal of Marketing,* **46,** 94–101.

Gorn, G. J., Goldberg, M. E., & Basu, K. (1990). *Music and product preferences: An empirical test using improved conditioning procedures.* Unpublished manuscript, University of British Columbia, Vancouver.

Greenwald, A. G. (1968). Cognitive learning, cognitive response to persuasion, and attitude change. In A. G. Greenwald, T. C. Brock, & T. M. Ostrom (Eds.), *Psychological foundations of attitudes* (pp. 148–170). New York: Academic Press.

Higgins, E. T. (1987). Self-discrepancy: A theory relating self and affect. *Psychological Review,* **94,** 319–340.

Higgins, E. T. (1989). Knowledge accessibility and activation. In J. S. Uleman & J. A. Bargh (Eds.), *Unintended thought* (pp. 75–123). New York: Guilford.

Innes, J. M., & Ahrens, C. R. (in press). Positive mood, processing goals, and the effects of information on evaluative judgment. In J. Forgas (Ed.), *Emotion and social judgment*. Oxford, England: Pergamon.

Isen, A. M. (1984). Toward understanding the role of affect in cognition. In R. S. Wyer, Jr., & T. K. Srull (Eds.), *Handbook of social cognition* (Vol. 3, pp. 179–236). Hillsdale, NJ: Erlbaum.

Isen, A. M. (1987). Positive affect, cognitive processes, and social behavior. In L. Berkowitz (Ed.), *Advances in experimental social psychology* (Vol. 20, pp. 203–253). San Diego, CA: Academic Press.

Isen, A. M., & Levin, P. F. (1972). The effect of feeling good on helping: Cookies and kindness. *Journal of Personality and Social Psychology, 21,* 384–388.

Isen, A. M., Means, B., Patrick, R., & Nowicki, G. (1982). Some factors influencing decision making strategy and risk-taking. In M. S. Clark & S. T. Fiske (Eds.), *Affect and cognition: The 17th Annual Carnegie Mellon Symposium on Cognition*. Hillsdale, NJ: Erlbaum.

Isen, A. M., Shalker, T. E., Clark, M. S., & Karp, L. (1978). Affect, accessibility of material in memory, and behavior: A cognitive loop? *Journal of Personality and Social Psychology, 36,* 1–12.

Izard, C. E. (1977). *Human emotions*. New York: Plenum.

Janis, I. L., Kaye, D., & Kirshner, P. (1965). Facilitating effects of eating while reading on responsiveness to persuasive communications. *Journal of Personality and Social Psychology, 1,* 181–186.

Jepson, C., & Chaiken, S. (1990). Chronic issue specific fear inhibits systematic processing of persuasive communications. *Journal of Social Behavior and Personality, 2,* 61–84.

Judd, C. M., & Lusk, C. M. (1984). Knowledge structures and evaluative judgments: Effects of structural variables on judgment extremity. *Journal of Personality and Social Psychology, 46,* 1193–1207.

Kahneman, D. (1970). Remarks on attention control. *Acta Psychologica, 33,* 118–131.

Kellaris, J. J., & Cox, A. D. (1989). The effects of background music in advertising: A reassessment. *Journal of Consumer Research, 16,* 113–118.

Kelley, H. H. (1972). *Causal schemata and the attribution process*. Morristown, NJ: General Learning Press.

Kelly, G. (1955). *The psychology of personal constructs*. New York: Norton.

Kuhl, J. (1983). Emotion, Kognition und Motivation, II. *Sprache und Kognition, 4,* 228–253.

Lacey, J. I., & Lacey, B. C. (1970). Some autonomic nervous system relationships. In P. Black (Ed.), *Physiological correlates of emotion* (pp. 205–227). New York: Academic Press.

Large, M. D., & Vega, L. A. (1989). *The effect of schema extensity on extremity of decision making*. Paper presented at the annual meeting of the Western Psychological Association, Reno, NV.

Linville, P. W. (1982). The complexity–extremity effect and age based stereotyping. *Journal of Personality and Social Psychology, 42,* 193–211.

Linville, P. W., & Jones, E. E. (1980). Polarized appraisals of outgroup members. *Journal of Personality and Social Psychology, 38,* 698–703.

Mackie, D., & Worth, L. T. (1989). Processing deficits and the mediation of positive affect in persuasion. *Journal of Personality and Social Psychology, 57,* 27–40.

Matlin, M., & Stang, D. (1979). *The Pollyanna principle*. Cambridge, MA: Schenkman.

Milliman, R. E. (1982). The effects of background music upon the shopping behavior of supermarket patrons. *Journal of Marketing, 46,* 86–91.

Milliman, R. E. (1986). The influence of background music on the behavior of restaurant patrons. *Journal of Consumer Research, 13,* 286–289.

Oatley, K., & Johnson-Laird, P. N. (1987). Towards a cognitive theory of emotions. *Cognition and Emotion*, **1**, 29–50.

Obrist, P. A. (1981). *Cardiovascular psychophysiology*. New York: Plenum.

Ortony, A., Clore, G. L., & Collins, A. (1988). *The cognitive structure of emotions*. Cambridge, England: Cambridge University Press.

Page, M. M. (1969). Social psychology of a classical conditioning of attitudes experiment. *Journal of Personality and Social Psychology*, **11**, 177–186.

Peterson, C., & Seligman, M. E. P. (1984). Causal explanations as a risk factor for depression: Theory and evidence. *Psychological Review*, **91**, 347–374.

Petty, R. E., & Brock, T. C. (1981). Thought disruption and persuasion: Assessing the validity of attitude change experiments. In R. E. Petty, T. M. Ostrom, & T. C. Brock (Eds.), *Cognitive responses in persuasion*. Hillsdale, NJ: Erlbaum.

Petty, R. E., & Cacioppo, J. T. (1984a). The effects of involvement on responses to argument quantity and quality: Central and peripheral routes to persuasion. *Journal of Personality and Social Psychology*, **46**, 68–81.

Petty, R. E., & Cacioppo, J. T. (1984b). Source factors and the elaboration likelihood model of persuasion. *Advances in Consumer Research*, **11**, 668–672.

Petty, R. E., & Cacioppo, J. T. (1986a). The elaboration likelihood model of persuasion. In L. Berkowitz (Ed.), *Advances in experimental social psychology* (Vol. 19, pp. 123–205). Orlando, FL: Academic Press.

Petty, R. E., & Cacioppo, J. T. (1986b). *Communication and persuasion*. New York: Springer-Verlag.

Petty, R. E., Cacioppo, J. T., & Kasmer, J. A. (1988). The role of affect in the elaboration likelihood model of persuasion. In L. Donohue, H. E. Sypher, & E. T. Higgins (Eds.), *Communication, social cognition, and affect* (pp. 117–146). Hillsdale, NJ: Erlbaum.

Petty, R. E., Ostrom, T. M., & Brock, T. C. (Eds.). (1981). *Cognitive responses in persuasion*. Hillsdale, NJ: Erlbaum.

Razran, G. H. S. (1940). Conditioned response changes in rating and appraising sociopolitical slogans. *Psychological Bulletin*, **37**, 481.

Rosnow, R. L. (1968). A spread of effect in attitude formation. In A. C. Greenwald, T. C. Brock, & T. M. Ostrom (Eds.), *Psychological foundations of attitudes* (pp. 89–107). New York: Academic Press.

Ruehlman, L. S., West, S. G., & Pasahow, R. J. (1985). Depression and evaluative schemata. *Journal of Personality*, **53**, 46–92.

Schaller, M., & Cialdini, R. B. (1990). Happiness, sadness, and helping: A motivational integration. In E. T. Higgins & R. M. Sorrentino (Eds.), *Handbook of motivation and cognition: Foundations of social behavior* (Vol. 2, pp. 265–296). New York: Guilford.

Schwarz, N. (1987). *Stimmung als Information: Untersuchungen zum Einfluß von Stimmungen auf die Bewertung des eigenen Lebens* [Mood as information]. Heidelberg, Germany: Springer-Verlag.

Schwarz, N. (1988). Stimmung als Information. (Mood as information). *Psychologische Rundschau*, **39**, 148–159.

Schwarz, N. (1990). Feelings as information: Informational and motivational functions of affective states. In E. T. Higgins & R. M. Sorrentino (Eds.), *Handbook of motivation and cognition: Foundations of social behavior* (Vol. 2, pp. 527–561). New York: Guilford.

Schwarz, N., & Bless, B. (1991). Happy and mindless, but sad and smart? The impact of affective states on analytic reasoning. In J. Forgas (Ed.), *Emotion and social judgment* (pp. 55–71). London: Pergamon.

Schwarz, N., & Bohner, G. (1990). Stimmungseinflüsse auf Denken und Entscheiden [The impact of mood states on thinking and decision making]. In P. Maas & J. Weibler (Eds.), *Börse und Psychologie* (pp. 162–189). Cologne, Germany: Deutscher Institutsverlag.

Schwarz, N., & Clore, G. L. (1983). Mood, misattribution, and judgments of well-being: Informative and directive functions of affective states. *Journal of Personality and Social Psychology,* **45,** 513–523.

Schwarz, N., & Clore, G. L. (1988). How do I feel about it? Informative functions of affective states. In K. Fiedler & J. Forgas (Eds.), *Affect, cognition, and social behavior* (pp. 44–62). Toronto: Hogrefe.

Schwarz, N., Servay, W., & Kumpf, M. (1985). Attribution of arousal as a mediator of the effectiveness of fear-arousing communications. *Journal of Applied Social Psychology,* **15,** 74–84.

Srull, T. K., & Wyer, R. S. (1986). The role of chronic and temporary goals in social information processing. In R. M. Sorrentino & E. T. Higgins (Eds.), *Handbook of motivation and cognition: Foundations of social behavior* (Vol. 1, pp. 503–549). New York: Guilford.

Staats, A. W., & Staats, C. K. (1958). Attitudes established by classical conditioning. *Journal of Abnormal and Social Psychology,* **57,** 37–40.

Staats, A. W., Staats, C. K., & Crawford, H. L. (1962). First-order conditioning of meaning and the parallel conditioning of a GSR. *Journal of General Psychology,* **67,** 159–167.

Staats, C. K., & Staats, A. W. (1957). Meaning established by classical conditioning. *Journal of Experimental Psychology,* **54,** 74–80.

Stayman, D. M., Aaker, D. A., & Bruzzone, D. E. (1989). The incidence of commercial types broadcast in prime time: 1976–1986. *Journal of Advertising Research,* **29,** 26–33.

Stein, N. L., & Levine, L. J. (1987). Thinking about feelings: The development and organization of emotional knowledge. In R. E. Snow & M. J. Farr (Eds.), *Aptitude, learning, and instruction: Conative and affective processes* (Vol. 3, pp. 165–197). Hillsdale, NJ: Erlbaum.

Strack, F., Erber, R., & Wicklund, R. A. (1982). Effects of salience and time pressure on ratings of social causality. *Journal of Experimental Social Psychology,* **18,** 581–594.

Tölle, R. (1982). *Psychiatrie* (6th ed.). Heidelberg, Germany: Springer-Verlag.

Weiner, B. (1985). ''Spontaneous'' causal thinking. *Psychological Bulletin,* **97,** 74–84.

Worth, L. T., & Mackie, D. M. (1987). Cognitive mediation of positive affect in persuasion. *Social Cognition,* **5,** 76–94.

Zanna, M. P., Kiesler, C. A., & Pilkonis, P. A. (1970). Positive and negative attitudinal affect established by classical conditioning. *Journal of Personality and Social Psychology,* **14,** 321–328.

A FOCUS THEORY OF NORMATIVE CONDUCT: A THEORETICAL REFINEMENT AND REEVALUATION OF THE ROLE OF NORMS IN HUMAN BEHAVIOR

Robert B. Cialdini

Carl A. Kallgren

Raymond R. Reno

During the past two decades, the state of the natural environment has become an increasingly important concern in our society. Consequently, public and private groups at the local, state, and national levels have undertaken a wide variety of programs designed to discourage behaviors that damage or despoil the environment. One of the most visible such programs can be seen in the consistent efforts of the Keep America Beautiful, Inc. organization to reduce the amount of litter that occurs in public places. Although the organization has attacked this problem effectively in numerous ways, it has perhaps made its greatest impression on the public consciousness through its sponsorship of a series of televised public service announcements (PSAs) against littering.

Easily the most famous of these PSAs is one that is renowned within the Keep America Beautiful, Inc. organization as the single most powerful and memorable message that has ever been sent to the American people against litter. It begins with a shot of a stately, buckskin-clad American Indian paddling his canoe up a river that carries the scum and trash of various forms of industrial and individual pollution. After coming ashore near the littered side of a highway, the Indian watches as a bag of garbage is thrown, splattering and spreading along the road, from the window of a passing car. From the refuse at his feet, the camera pans up slowly to the Indian's face, where a tear is shown tracking down his cheek, and the slogan appears: "People Start Pollution, People Can Stop It."

By now, millions of us have seen and been affected by this touching piece of public service advertising—called the "Iron Eyes Cody spot" after the Native American actor who starred in its several versions. However, despite the fame and recognition value of the advertisement, our research suggests that it contains

ADVANCES IN EXPERIMENTAL
SOCIAL PSYCHOLOGY, VOL. 24

features that may be less than optimal, and perhaps even negative, in their impact on the littering actions of those who see it. That is, certain unintended and untoward effects may be produced in the audience that are contrary to the purposes of the advertisement and its sponsor. To understand fully the nature of those potentially problematic features, it is necessary to consider the basic nature and current status of a long-standing and controversial concept in social science.

I. The Concept of Social Norms

Despite a history of long and extensive use within the discipline, there is no current consensus within social psychology about the explanatory and predictive value of social norms. On the one hand are those who see the concept as crucial to a full understanding of human social behavior (e.g., Berkowitz, 1972; Fishbein & Ajzen, 1975; McKirnan, 1980; Pepitone, 1976; Sherif, 1936; Staub, 1972; Triandis, 1977). On the other hand are those who view the concept as vague and overly general, often contradictory, and ill-suited to empirical test (e.g., Darley & Latané, 1970; Krebs, 1970; Krebs & Miller, 1985; Marini, 1984). A parallel controversy has developed in academic sociology where ethnomethodological and constructionist critics have faulted the dominant normative paradigm of that discipline (Garfinkel, 1967; Mehan & Wood, 1975). What are we to make of such a state of affairs? What are we to believe about the concept of social norms when one set of respected voices assigns it undeniable, and in some instances predominant, influence over much of human social conduct while a set of equally respected voices calls its demonstrated influence weak at best?

Informed by the results of the research program described in this article, our own answer to the puzzle has been to recognize the concurrent validity of both positions. That is, it is our view that both camps are correct: Norms do have a strong and regular impact on behavior, but the force and form of that impact can only be soundly established through theoretical refinements that have not been traditionally or rigorously applied. The first such refinement is definitional.

A. DESCRIPTIVE AND INJUNCTIVE NORMS

Part of the ambiguity attendant to the role of norms in accounting for human action can be traced to confusion in the meaning of the term. As is true in everyday language, "norm" has more than one meaning in academic usage (Schaffer, 1983). It can refer either to what is commonly done—that is, what is normal—or to what is commonly approved—that is, what is socially sanctioned.

It is important to recognize that, despite the shared label, evidence as to what others commonly do and evidence as to what others commonly approve represent separate sources of human motivation [cf. Deutsch and Gerard's (1955) classic distinction between informational social influence and normative social influence]. Thus, with reference to a given social group, we will refer to norms that characterize the perception of what most people do as *descriptive norms* (or the norms of "is") and we will refer to norms that characterize the perception of what most people approve or disapprove as *injunctive norms* (or the norms of "ought").[1]

There is little controversy surrounding the impact of descriptive norms on behavior. From the early days of experimental social psychology, researchers regularly have been able to document the magnetic pull of the typical response, even in matters wholly lacking an "ought" component (e.g., Asch, 1956; Crutchfield, 1955; Sherif, 1936). For instance, by progressively enlarging the size of a group of confederates looking up from a street corner at an empty spot in the sky, Milgram, Bickman, and Berkowitz (1969) were able to increase dramatically (to 84%) the number of passers-by who followed suit.

Descriptive norms motivate by providing evidence as to what will likely be effective and adaptive action: "If everyone is doing or thinking or believing it, it must be a sensible thing to do or think or believe." Cialdini (1988) has argued that such a presumption offers an information-processing advantage and a decisional shortcut when one is choosing how to behave in a given situation. By simply registering what most others are doing there and imitating their actions, one can usually choose efficiently and well. No doubt this is one reason that advertisers frequently load their television commercials with scenes of crowds moving toward their stores or of many hands depleting shelves of their products; and no doubt it is the same reason that they claim their products to be the "fastest growing" or "largest selling." In this fashion, they need not convince us directly that their product is good; they need only convince us that many others think so, which, among consumers, is often proof enough (Venkatesan, 1966).

In contrast to descriptive norms, which specify what is done, injunctive norms specify what ought to be done. They constitute the moral rules of the group. Such norms motivate action by promising social rewards and punishments (informal sanctions) for it. Whereas descriptive norms inform behavior, injunctive norms

---

[1]Descriptive norms as we mean them have sometimes been called *popular* norms; and injunctive norms as we mean them have sometimes been called *prescriptive* norms. Foregoing the opportunities for creating rhyming or alliterative terms for the two norm types (e.g., "descriptive and prescriptive" or "popular and prescriptive"), we opted against such mnemonics in favor of conceptual clarity. That is, in the instance of the first kind of norm, a common definition of popular implies a necessary sense of approval—something we think important to reserve for the second kind of norm. As regards the second kind of norm, prescriptive is too restrictive a term for our preferred meaning, which includes proscriptions as well as prescriptions.

enjoin it. Thus, it could be argued that one reason people may be helpful in our society is to act in accord with the societal norm for helpfulness, which is positively sanctioned (Berkowitz, 1972). Similarly, one reason people may repay the gifts, favors, and services they have received is to conform to the norm for reciprocity, thereby garnering social approval and avoiding social disapproval (Gouldner, 1960).

Much of the controversy surrounding the concept of social norms swirls around the contention that widely held injunctive norms account for much of human behavior. Writers such as Darley and Latané (1970), Krebs (1970), Krebs and Miller (1985), and Marini (1984) have despaired at the ability of this concept to predict or explain a significant amount of the variance in social behavior. They have pointed out, for example, that frequently within the same societal group mutually incompatible norms exist simultaneously (e.g., the norm for getting involved and the norm for minding one's own business). Consequently, no matter which type of behavior were to occur, it could be attributed to the action of norms; of course, when a concept can explain any behavior pattern after the fact, one suspects that it is too vague or circular to explain anything. These authors argue further that the majority of human responding is only sometimes in keeping with the dominant social norms; if the same norms are in place when behavior is norm inconsistent as when it is norm consistent, why should we believe that norms mediated any of it?

Criticisms of these sorts have been helpful to us in identifying the second major theoretical refinement that must be rigorously applied before the utility of normative explanations can be confidently established: Whether a particular norm will influence responding is dependent on the degree to which the respondent's attention is focused on that norm.

B. THE IMPORTANCE OF NORMATIVE FOCUS

There is substantial evidence that shifting an individual's attention to a specific source of information or motivation will change the individual's responses in ways that are congruent with the features of the now more prominent source (Agostinelli, Sherman, Fazio, & Hearst, 1986; Kallgren & Wood, 1986; Millar & Tesser, 1989; Storms, 1973). In keeping with this evidence, Deaux and Major (1987) concluded that the occurrence of gender-consistent behavior is frequently determined by situational factors that shift attention to the construct of gender, thereby making it more salient. A similar relationship appears to obtain in the normative arena. That is, norms motivate and direct action primarily when they are activated (i.e., made salient or otherwise focused upon); thus, persons who are dispositionally or temporarily focused on normative considerations are decidedly more likely to act in norm-consistent ways (Berkowitz, 1972; Berkowitz &

Daniels, 1964; Gruder, Romer, & Korth, 1978; Miller & Grush, 1986; Rutkowski, Gruder, & Romer, 1983; Schwartz & Fleishman, 1978).

An analysis of this sort allows us to retain a belief in the usefulness of normative explanations in the face of the insightful criticisms discussed earlier. That is, it becomes wholly understandable why the dominant norms of a society—that are presumably always in place—may only sometimes predict behavior: They should activate behavior only when *they* have been activated first. Similarly, the simultaneous existence of incompatible social norms is no longer a damaging criticism of normative accounts if we assume that the conflicting norms may coexist within the same society but that the one that will produce congruent action is the one that is temporarily prominent in consciousness.

Pursuing this last realization further, we can see that it also applies to the distinction between descriptive and injunctive norms. Although it is most frequently the case that what is done and what is approved in a social group are the same, this is often not the case. For instance, even though the majority of people who pass a sidewalk Salvation Army donation kettle might not give a contribution, it is likely that the majority would approve of someone who did. In situations of this kind, with clearly conflicting descriptive and injunctive norms, we would expect that focusing observers on what most people did or on what most people approved would lead to behavior change that is consistent only with whichever has become the now more salient type of norm.

II. Studying Littering in Natural Settings

One purpose of the present research program was to test our theoretical model as it applied to individuals' decisions to litter in public places. We chose littering because it allowed us to test our norm focus model on a behavior that was of practical importance. Although at first glance littering may appear to be a trivial problem that is more a mere annoyance than anything else, upon closer inspection it is clear that littering constitutes a large and growing social problem with considerable aesthetic, financial, and health-related costs. For example, in the state of California alone, litter has increased by 24% over a recent span of 15 years, requiring $100 million annually in clean-up costs (California Waste Management Board, 1988). Litter poses health threats, for both humans and wildlife, ranging from minor injury to death through water pollution, fire hazards, highway accidents, and rodent and insect infestations, as well as through thousands of injuries from discarded cans and broken bottles (Geller, Winett, & Everett, 1982). Clearly, then, littering is a social problem worthy of study.

In order to substantiate the need for the theoretical refinements presented in our norm focus model, two questions need to be answered: (1) Do behavioral patterns confirm our theorized distinction between descriptive and injunctive norms? and (2) is focus a critical mediator of which type of norm guides behavior? Depending upon how these questions are answered, there is also a third question of the practical implications and applications of our theoretical formulation. To attempt to converge upon the answers to these questions, we present a series of nine studies we have conducted that examine littering in public places.

Owing to this choice of public littering as our behavior of interest, we decided to conduct our studies in field settings where littering would occur naturally. Although people will litter in laboratory settings (e.g., Krauss, Freedman, & Whitcup, 1978), the external validity of such studies might be questioned. Given the stormy history surrounding the practical utility of normative explanations, we wanted to maximize our external validity in order to offer suggestions for litter-abatement programs. Thus we conducted the bulk of our research in field settings to increase our ability to generalize to such settings.

A. FOCUSING ON DESCRIPTIVE NORMS

We first turn our discussion toward the explication of the effects of focusing on the descriptive norms of a situation. One of the most commonly reported findings from studies of littering behavior is that individuals litter into an already littered environment at a greater rate than they do into an otherwise clean environment (see Geller *et al.*, 1982, for a review).[2] According to our focus theory, this occurs because individuals are to some degree focused on the descriptive norms present in the situation. Of course, our model is not the only one capable of explaining this data pattern. A social learning theorist (e.g., Bandura, 1977) might say that the effect is due to subjects' imitation of the behavior of those who have been in the environment before them. It could also be argued that the effect occurs because individuals perceive that their littering would do less damage in an already littered environment compared to a clean environment. Consequently, in order to show the utility of our theoretical refinements, we needed to develop a theoretical test that would predict effects for our model that were different from those predicted from the alternative accounts discussed above.

1. Study 1: Does Litter Always Beget More Littering?

In the first test of our theoretical model, we explored the effects of varying the saliency of the descriptive norm. We sought to increase the prominence of the

---

[2]In addition, gender differences in littering tendencies are often, but not always, reported. When there are gender differences, it is almost always the case that women littered less than men. Analyses of our data occasionally demonstrated gender differences. When these were encountered they are reported but are not discussed if they were not present.

descriptive norm regarding littering in our experimental setting by exposing subjects to a confederate who conspicuously dropped a piece of paper into the environment, thereby drawing their attention to the state of the environment and to its evident descriptive norm. We expected that if subjects were thereby focused on the state of the environment in a littered setting, they would litter at rates greater than those for control subjects, who were also exposed to the environment but not focused on evidence that many others had littered there. Conversely, in a clean environment, we expected to reduce littering among those subjects who we had focused on the state of the environment.

The form of this predicted cross-over interaction was important because, although consistent with our theoretical predictions, it could not be explained by either of the alternative accounts discussed previously. First, the imitation-based prediction is for an increase in littering in both clean and littered environments when the subject witnessed an unpunished litterer. Second, the prediction based on avoidance of damage to the environment is that littering should increase in both clean and littered environments after a confederate littered. Furthermore, the rate of increase in littering should be greater in the clean environment because the confederate's littering action would have markedly decreased the relative damage the subject's potential littering might have done. Thus, according to both of these alternative accounts, subjects should be more inclined to litter after seeing a confederate litter into a clean environment, not less inclined as we predicted.

Participants in this first study (Cialdini, Reno, & Kallgren, 1990, Experiment 1) were unobtrusively observed as they returned to their vehicles in a multilevel parking garage adjacent to a university-affiliated hospital. In the high-norm salience condition, shortly after a subject exited an elevator, a confederate who was walking toward the subject dropped a large handbill he or she was carrying approximately 4.5 m (5 yd) in front of the subject. In the low-norm salience condition, the confederate simply walked by the subject without a handbill to provide an equivalent degree of social contact. To manipulate the descriptive norm, on a 2-hour rotation the parking garage was either sprinkled with sundry litter (including a large number of handbills) to create a prolittering descriptive norm, or all traces of litter were carefully removed to create an antilittering descriptive norm. Upon arriving at their cars, subjects found a handbill, like the one dropped by the confederate, tucked under the driver's side wiper that read "THIS IS AUTOMOTIVE SAFETY WEEK. PLEASE DRIVE CAREFULLY." The dependent measure consisted of whether the subject dropped the flyer into the environment.

As may be seen in Fig. 1, the data patterns supported our experimental hypotheses. There was more littering in the littered environment than in the clean environment, and this pattern was accentuated by our descriptive norm focus manipulation. That is, the most littering occurred in the littered environment

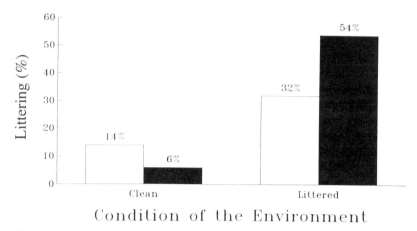

Fig. 1.   Percentage of subjects littering as a function of norm salience and the environmental condition in Study 1. (□), Model walks by; (■), model litters.

when subjects saw a confederate throw down a handbill, and the smallest proportion of subjects littered after having witnessed the confederate throw down the handbill in a clean environment. It is important to note once again that this latter effect is incompatible with both the imitation and damage to the environment alternate explanations but is consistent with our norm-focus model.

Although the predicted interaction was significant, neither of the simple effects within environmental condition was significant, suggesting that caution is warranted in drawing strong conclusions from these data. Thus, in the interest of generating enhanced confidence in our conclusions, a conceptual replication and extension was the next step.

2. Rethinking the Iron Eyes Cody Advertisement

Before discussing the next study, however, it would be appropriate to look back at the earlier described "Iron Eyes Cody" PSA, as the findings of Study 1 point to the reasons for our concern about the effectiveness of that advertisement. Recall that it depicted an Indian who shed a tear after encountering an array of litter—debris in the water and on the roadside, trash tossed from an automobile. No doubt the tear was a powerful reminder of the injunctive norm against littering in our culture. But accompanying the beneficial reminder was the potentially damaging message that many people *do* litter. Thus, the resultant impact of the injunctive norm *against* littering may have been undermined by the unintended presentation of a descriptive norm *for* littering. Moreover, that presentation occurred in a way that, according to the results of Study 1, may have been especially damaging. That is, the creators of the advertisement seem to have been correct in their decision to show an instance of someone (the passing motorist) actively littering the environment; but, they may have been mistaken in their decision to use an already littered environment, as that combination of circumstances produced the greatest littering in our data. In contrast, the combination of a littering other and an otherwise clean environment generated the least littering from our subjects.

Were we to advise the Keep America Beautiful organization on how to revise the Iron Eyes Cody advertisement, then, it would be to make the procedurally small but theoretically meaningful modification of changing the depicted environment from trashed to clean. Then, when the Indian cries, viewers would be focused on injunctive and descriptive norms working in concert to motivate the viewers against littering. Of course, it would be unwarranted to assume from the data of Study 1 that the *overall* impact of this advertisement has been negative. Our feeling is that, because it is so moving and memorable a piece, it has been a strong positive force. Nonetheless, it is interesting to wonder if its impact on viewers' littering actions could have been greater through a small change that would have put the presented injunctive and descriptive norms into line rather than into conflict with one another. Leaving the pragmatic issue of optimal litter-abatement tactics for the moment, let's return to a consideration of how to generate evidence pertinent to our conceptual model.

3. Study 2: Varying the Descriptive Norm for Littering

Dissatisfied that the simple effects in Study 1 were not significant, we conducted a replication and extension in order to detect the hypothesized decrease in littering when subjects were focused on the descriptive norm in a clean environment. This second study (Cialdini *et al.*, 1990, Experiment 2) was also designed to determine if the results from Experiment 1 were generalizable to other settings and other focus manipulations or whether they were due to some unique characteristics of our previous study. We reasoned that a lone piece of litter would, by its conspicuous nature, draw attention to the nearly pristine state of the environment. Thus, we expected subjects' littering would decrease when the amount of litter in the environment increased from zero to one piece because the single piece of litter would serve to focus subjects on the antilittering descriptive norm. As the number of pieces of litter in the environment increased beyond one, however, the perceived descriptive norm would change from antilittering to prolittering. As the descriptive norm changed in this fashion, we expected the littering rate would increase. Thus, we made a counterintuitive prediction that could be best described graphically as a checkmark-shaped relationship between amount of existing litter in the environment and the likelihood that subjects would litter into it.

To test these hypotheses, we observed the tendencies of adult visitors to an amusement park. At 1-minute intervals, the first adult to pass a confederate was given a handbill that read "DON'T MISS TONIGHT'S SHOW." Immediately afterward, upon rounding a corner, subjects were unobtrusively observed by a different experimenter as they walked down a path of approximately 55 m (60 yd) on which we had placed either 0, 1, 2, 4, 8, or 16 clearly visible handbills. All other litter had been removed from the walkway. In addition to whether or not subjects littered their handbill on the path, the subjects' latencies to litter were also recorded.

Preliminary analyses revealed a gender difference in littering rates that was consistent with that of previous studies that have detected a gender difference in littering behavior[2]; males tended to litter more than females (31 vs 19%). Gender, however, did not interact with any of the obtained effects described below, and thus will not be discussed further.

A visual inspection of Fig. 2a reveals a pattern of results that appears consistent with our predictions. Indeed, a planned comparison using trend weights for a check mark function (-2, -4, -1, 1, 2, 4) was significant. Despite the fact that littering decreased (from 18 to 10%) when one piece of litter was added to the environment, this planned comparison failed to reach conventional levels of significance. As may be seen in Fig. 2b, the results for the latency to litter measure were comparable to the frequency of littering results; the overall contrast was significant, and the contrast of zero to one piece was not.

While we were encouraged by the degree of corroboration our theorizing received from the empirical data to this point, we were nevertheless concerned by the lack of statistical significance we obtained in both studies for the reduction in littering in a clean environment when we focused people on the state of the environment. As is often the case when nonsignificance prevails, we had a *post hoc* explanation for this lack of significance; we may have bumped into a naturally occurring floor effect when we tried to reduce the already low littering frequency in clean environments (14% in Study 1 and 18% in Study 2) with our focus manipulations. Such an untested explanation was not satisfactory, however, as this hypothesized reduction in littering was a theoretically important effect.

4. Study 3: Varying Descriptive Norm Saliency

Given the theoretical importance of this effect, we were reluctant to rule out the ability of normative focus to reduce littering based on these nonsignificant results. Therefore, we conducted a conceptual replication (Cialdini *et al.,* 1990, Experiment 3) in which we made four changes: First, we chose an experimental situation, a college high-rise dormitory mailroom lobby, that allowed us to run a large volume of subjects in a relatively short period of time to increase our statistical power. Second, we limited our experimental conditions to three con-

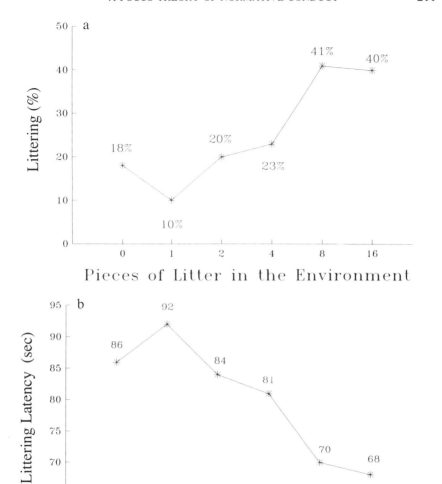

Fig. 2. (a) Percentage of subjects littering as a function of the number of pieces of litter in the environment in Study 2. (b) Mean latency (in seconds) to litter as a function of the number of pieces of litter in the environment in Study 2.

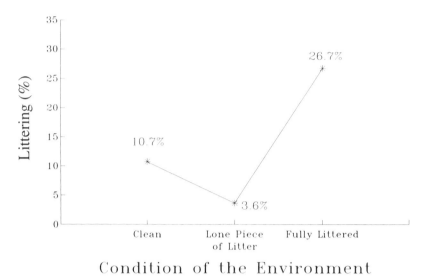

Fig. 3.   Percentage of subjects littering as a function of the amount of litter in the environment in Study 3.

ceptually important levels of litter (zero, one, and many pieces of litter in the environment). Third, we chose a single piece of litter that was particularly noisome and thus noticeable (a hollowed out watermelon rind heel) so we could push against the floor more firmly. Last, we restricted our sample to females to reduce the within-cell variability due to possible gender differences in littering.

Subjects were dorm residents who were alone when they opened their mailboxes and found a public service handbill. The floor of the lobby contained either no litter, the watermelon rind heel, or a plethora of litter, including the watermelon rind. An experimenter unobtrusively noted if a subject littered.

Figure 3 shows that the pattern of results were as expected. The quadratic trend was significant, as was the difference between the fully littered and unlittered environment litter rates. Moreover, the reduction in littering (10.7 to 3.6%) that occurred when we added one conspicuous piece of litter to an otherwise clean environment was significant.

5. Summary

In summary, we have consistently demonstrated thus far that one factor that motivates individuals' decisions to litter is the descriptive norm of the situation. That is, under control conditions, subjects litter more in littered environments (where the descriptive norm favors littering) than they do in clean environments, where the descriptive norm opposes littering. More important, when the saliency of these descriptive norms is increased, people tend to litter even more in littered environments and even less in clean environments. From a theoretical perspective, then, focusing people on the state of the environment (and thus the appropriate descriptive norm regarding littering) increases their norm-consistent behavior regardless of whether the behavior takes the form of littering or not littering. Having demonstrated this, we now turn our focus toward the behavioral influence of injunctive norms.

B. FOCUSING ON INJUNCTIVE NORMS

At the beginning of this article, we argued that norm theorists must be specific about whether they are referring to the descriptive or injunctive norm and which of these, if either, is salient. Up to this point we have only presented evidence of the effect of focusing attention on the descriptive norm. A demonstration that focusing on the injunctive norm against littering leads to injunctive norm-consistent behavior (decreased littering) would be theoretically important, as well as potentially important practically. If we are correct, focusing people on the injunctive norm, which is independent of the environmental conditions, should decrease littering in both littered and clean environments.

1. Study 4: Contrasting Injunctive and Descriptive Norms

In designing a test of these hypotheses concerning the injunctive norm, our first problem was developing a way that would allow us to focus people on clear social disapproval of littering in an experimentally malleable field situation where the descriptive norm indicated that littering was common there. Serendipity provided the answer. One of the experimental sessions of Study 1, wherein the parking garage was fully littered, occurred on an especially windy day, and all of the litter we had strewn about was blown into a rather tidy looking line along the leeward wall. We were perplexed because, even though there was much litter in the environment, when our confederate dropped a handbill onto the floor, virtually no subjects littered. As we talked about this apparent anomaly in our otherwise consistent data, it dawned on us that the line of litter looked like it could have been swept by human hands rather than by the wind. If that were true, we reasoned that subjects may have seen the seemingly swept litter as a clear disapproval cue for littering.

We recognized this as a way to arrange the experimental situation such that the descriptive norm indicated that one action was appropriate (littering is common in this environment), and the injunctive norm indicated that the opposite action was appropriate (one ought not to litter). Swept litter, we thought, would provide information to subjects that even though many people littered here (abundant litter), it ought not to be done (disapproval was strong enough that the litter had been swept up). Therefore, we arranged the environment to contain either swept or unswept litter, and we exposed a subject to a confederate who either did or did not drop a handbill in clear view of a subject in that environment (Cialdini *et al.*, 1990, Experiment 4). The experimental setting was the same as in Study 1.

When comparing low-salience (confederate walks by subjects) swept and un-swept conditions, we expected a small effect indicating less littering for the swept condition. Because of the contradictory normative messages present in the swept litter conditions, without a normative focus there was no theoretical speci-fication as to which type of norm would more strongly guide behavior. At the same time, however, we suspected that, because the swept piles of litter we had placed in the environment were relatively prominent features of the environment, subjects would probably litter less when litter was swept as opposed to when it was not swept.

Our main predictions, however, concerned the high-salience conditions, wherein subjects saw a confederate drop a piece of paper onto the floor. When the confederate littered into the environment thusly, we expected an increase in littering if the extant litter had not been swept (as found in Study 1) and a decrease if it had been swept into piles. In this latter condition, we reasoned that with the added attention drawn to the environment by our salience manipulation, even though their attention would be drawn to the litter in the environment (the descriptive norm), it would have been very hard for subjects not to have recog-nized that it was swept up litter (which should have brought the injunctive norm to bear). Consequently, these subjects were predicted to litter less. Thus, because little difference was expected between the low-salience conditions, we were predicting a magnitude interaction.

The results, depicted in Fig. 4, were consistent with our predicted interaction. Although a small and nonsignificant difference between the swept and unswept low-salience conditions occurred, a significantly larger difference appeared be-tween the high-salience conditions, resulting in a significant interaction. Thus, shifting subjects' focus from descriptive (unswept litter) to injunctive (swept litter) normative cues resulted in differing behavioral tendencies that were none-theless consistent with the type of normative information on which the subject had been focused.

Although we were encouraged that heightened normative focus resulted in greater amounts of both injunctive and descriptive norm-consistent behavior, the simple effects within environmental conditions were not significant. A normative focus did increase compliance with the prominent source of normative informa-tion, but it did not lead to significant shifts within the particular environmental conditions. It did appear, however, that we were able, to some extent, to reduce littering when we shifted subjects' attention to information that provided mixed descriptive and injunctive norm cues. Thus, the next reasonable step was to see if

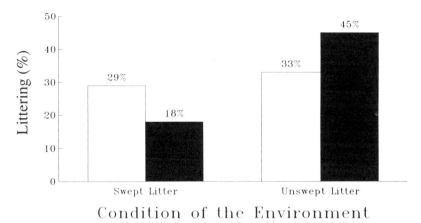

Fig. 4.   Percentage of subjects littering as a function of norm salience and the configuration of litter in the environment in Study 4. (□), Model walks by; (■), model litters.

littering could be reduced by focusing subjects in an uncontaminated way on the injunctive norm.

In addition to uncontaminating our injunctive norm cue, we also sought to change the nature of the norm-salience manipulation in our next study. A number of our studies have involved having a confederate throw down a handbill or having a solitary piece of litter in an otherwise clean environment. These manipulations may have resulted in subjects reacting negatively to the confederate (or the assumed cad who tossed down the solitary piece of litter). Subjects therefore may have desired to distance themselves from such an individual. To rule out such explanations of desired disassociation we performed a fifth experiment (Cialdini *et al.*, 1990, Experiment 5) in which we sought to develop a different focus manipulation, one that was not amenable to this type of explanation for reduced littering. To this end, we borrowed a manipulation from research conducted by cognitive psychologists.

2. Study 5: Priming Injunctive Norms

To focus people solely on the injunctive norm against littering in a way that was not amenable to disassociation-type explanations, we relied on the effect of cognitive priming (see Higgins & Bargh, 1987, for a review). That is, one concept (e.g., littering) has a greater probability of being activated when attention is drawn to a related concept (e.g., recycling) compared to when attention is drawn to an unrelated concept (e.g., fine arts). Furthermore, many explanations of priming effects invoke the concept of spreading activation, which posits that similar concepts are linked together in memory within a network of nodes and that activation of one concept results in the spreading of the activation along the network to other semantically or conceptually related concepts (Anderson, 1976, 1983; Collins & Loftus, 1975; McClelland & Rumelhart, 1981). If norms are stored in a network format, as suggested by Harvey and Enzle (1981), then varying the relatedness of activated norms to the target antilittering injunctive norm should result in systematic variations in the activation of the target norm. As the relatedness of the activated norm to the antilittering norm increases, the strength of activation of the target norm should also increase, and littering rates should decrease.

In selecting which other norms to activate, we considered not only the cognitive similarity between the selected norms and the antilittering norm but also the normativeness (likelihood that violation of it would meet with disapproval from others) of the selected norms. We based our selections on the results of the following scaling procedure. A total of 35 possible norms, including the antilittering norm, were presented to two separate classes of upper division psychology students. The first class rated the 35 possibilities as to their normativeness; the second class rated their conceptual similarity to the antilittering norm. Based on these ratings, we selected four norms that were comparable in perceived normativeness to the antilittering norm; however, one was identical to the antilittering norm (refraining from littering), one was close to the antilittering norm (recycling), another moderately close to the antilittering norm (turning out lights), and another was far from the antilittering norm (voting). We also selected a control issue that was nonnormative (the availability of museums).

Our experimental setting was a community library parking lot. We left the extant litter in place (there was a small amount of litter that was equivalent across all conditions). To manipulate focus on the various norms, we tucked flyers with norm-relevant statements under the driver's side windshield wiper of each car while the patrons were in the library. Upon returning to their cars, subjects found handbills with one of the following statements (similarity condition) on their windshields: "April is Keep Arizona Beautiful Month. Please Do Not Litter." (identical); "April is Preserve Arizona's Natural Resources Month. Please Recycle." (close); "April is Conserve Arizona's Energy Month. Please Turn Off Unnecessary Lights." (moderately close); "April is Arizona's Voter Awareness Month. Please Remember That Your Vote Counts." (far); and "April is Arizona's Fine Arts Month. Please Visit Your Local Art Museum." (control). We unobtrusively recorded littering of these handbills.

Preliminary analyses revealed a significant main effect for gender that was consistent with earlier reported gender effects; females littered less than males (14 and 22%, respectively). This gender effect did not interact with the effects of theoretical interest, and thus will not be discussed further.

As is clearly evidenced in Fig. 5, a significant linear trend was obtained, as predicted. This trend indicated that as the conceptual distance between the acti-

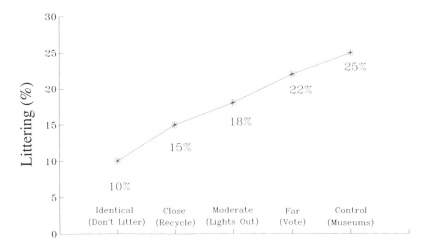

Distance from the Antilittering Norm

Fig. 5.   Percentage of subjects littering a handbill message as a function of its proximity to the injunctive norm against littering in Study 5.

vated norm or concept and the target antilittering norm increased, littering also increased. The specific norms were selected to provide a stepwise increase in the littering rates. As a result, the only significant comparison was that between the antilittering norm message (10%) and the control message (25%). This comparison, however, was the one of theoretical interest and supported our expectation that we could significantly reduce littering by simply shifting subjects' focus to the injunctive norm. The results of this study also ruled out the potential explanations that the reductions achieved in earlier studies were solely due to the subjects wishing to avoid negative association with the littering confederate.

3. Study 6: Perceptual Narrowing and Priming of Injunctive Norms

Bolstered by the results of Study 5, we returned once again to the question we had raised in Study 4; namely, would focusing subjects on the injunctive antilittering norm result in reduced littering in a littered environment where the descriptive norm condoned littering? We (Kallgren, Cialdini, & Reno, 1989) decided to address this question by using the priming technique employed in Study 5. In addition to the obvious difference of the present study being conducted in a littered rather than clean environment (Study 5), there was an additional difference. We attempted to strengthen the priming effect from Study 5 through perceptual narrowing that was generated by means of induced physical arousal.

Briefly, it has frequently been shown that arousal causes perceptual narrowing, that is, it reduces the range of cues that an organism attends to and uses (Easterbrook, 1959).

Because deciding to litter, or to take any other action that has a normative component, is multidetermined, we reasoned that if subjects were focused on a norm closely related to the antilittering norm and then mildly aroused, the salient normative information would remain in the foreground and the other nonnormative considerations would become less prominent in consciousness due to perceptual narrowing. The consequently increased salience of the related norm would also increase, via the process of spreading activation, the salience of the target antilittering norm. Consequently, the probability of the antilittering norm guiding behavior would increase. Moreover, we reasoned that aroused subjects would litter progressively more as they were focused on norms that were increasingly distant from the antilittering norm, or when they were not focused on normative issues at all. That is, the perceptual narrowing caused by the induced arousal would increase the saliency of target-norm-irrelevant information and reduce the likelihood that the antilittering norm would guide behavior.

Therefore, our predictions consisted of a main effect for the cognitive distance of the salient norm to the target norm (distance), and a cross-over interaction effect of distance and arousal/nonarousal (arousal). More specifically, we thought the pattern of this interaction would show progressively more littering as subjects who had been aroused were focused on norms that were increasingly distant from the target antilittering norm. However, we expected that this linear trend would not be present among nonaroused subjects, who would not be so focused on the normative information we gave them.[3]

Our experimental setting was an enclosed, heavily prelittered, three-story cement stairwell where we had precise control over the environment. We chose this setting because it was an environment where people were likely to litter (as opposed to a typical laboratory, where it would be more difficult to get subjects to litter), we could keep the amount of litter in the stairwell constant, we could exclude other people from the setting, and it provided a convenient way for us to arouse subjects—by having them walk down and up the stairs from the topmost landing where we conducted most of the experiment.

Our subjects were college students who participated for experimental credit in a study of a new (bogus) physiological measure. In reality, this was a cover story for giving our subjects paper towels they could litter. To focus subjects on a norm, after we had first taken a pulse reading, they read short diary excerpts in

---

[3]An alert reader will recognize an implication of this prediction for the results of Study 5: that we consider the subjects in that study, whose data did show a linear trend, to have been relatively aroused at the time they had the opportunity to litter. We make this presumption based on the fact that, before reaching their cars and the attached handbills, Study 5 subjects had emerged rather abruptly from a calm, quiet library environment and had traversed a busy public area that included a heavily trafficked street and parking lot.

which a norm was violated, the transgressor was chastised, and subsequently saw the error in her (for female subjects) or his (for male subjects) ways. The normative topics used in the diary excerpts were selected by the same criteria for topic selection used in Study 5. There were two topics for each distance from the antilittering norm: not writing graffiti and not polluting water (close); reusing containers and keeping one's stereo sound down at night (moderate); voting and returning library books on time (far). We also included a control condition with the topics of weather for a picnic and location of a picnic. Half of the subjects were assigned to sit quietly for 3 minutes, and half walked down and up the stairs three times (which took about 3 minutes). After sitting or exercising, pulse was again measured, the new bogus physiological measure was taken (a partial hand imprint of petroleum jelly and Wedgwood blue fingerpaint on a Petri dish), solvent was applied (in reality K-Y jelly), and subjects were reminded of the main point of the passage they had read while the alleged solvent loosened the goo. Subjects were then handed a small towel to wipe off their hand and told to exit via the door at the very bottom of the stairwell.

The dependent measure consisted of whether or not subjects littered the messy paper towel they were left holding, and if they littered it, where in relation to the bottom of the stairwell they littered. The information on where littering occurred was included as another measure of readiness to violate the littering norm. Although we opted for clarity's sake to present below only analyses of the measure of whether subjects littered, analyses based on the location measure were highly similar and slightly more powerful.

Preliminary analyses showed that subjects' pulse rates were elevated in our physical arousal condition. These preliminary analyses also showed that males violated the antilittering norm more than did females, but that gender did not interact with any other factor.

The data related to overall littering rates are presented in Fig. 6. Analysis yielded the predicted effects. There was a main effect for distance, and the overall linear trend was significant. As is evident in Fig. 6, there was also a significant interaction that was consistent with our predictions, except that the nonarousal control condition subjects violated the antilitter injunctive norm less than anticipated. For nonarousal conditions, no trend or comparison was significant. Within the arousal conditions, there was a significant linear trend indicating more littering with increasing conceptual distance from the antilittering norm, and the close and moderate distance conditions were significantly different from the control condition.

C. APPLIED CONSIDERATIONS

To this point, we have examined evidence from a variety of settings indicating that focusing individuals on descriptive or injunctive norms led to behavior that

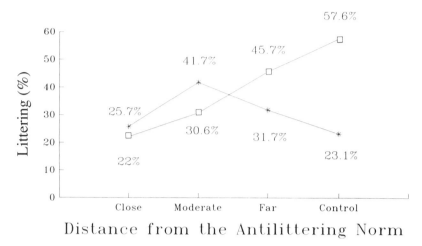

Fig. 6.   Percentage of littering behavior for arousal (□) and nonarousal (*) subjects by distance between the norm made salient and the antilittering norm.

was consistent with the dictates of the focused-upon norm. Such evidence fits well with the conceptual model that we have proposed. However, because littering is a social problem, it is appropriate to consider the practical implications of our data as well as their theoretical import.

For the first such implication, let's reexamine the results of Studies 1–3, which are consistent in demonstrating that the least littering occurred when subjects encountered a lone piece of litter in an otherwise clean environment. At first glance, this kind of result might seem to suggest that individuals seeking to retard the accumulation of litter in a particular environment should affix a single, prominent piece of litter there. More thoughtful consideration, however, suggests that such an approach would be inferior to beginning with a totally clean environment. Examination of Fig. 2a and b, showing the average likelihood and latency of littering among subjects in our amusement park study, illustrates the point. Subjects who encountered a perfectly clean environment tended not to litter there, leading to long delays before anyone despoiled it with a handbill. Once a single handbill appeared in the setting, subjects were even less likely to litter, generating even longer latencies before the second piece of litter appeared. At that point—with two pieces of litter visible in the environment—the descriptive norm began to change, and subjects' reluctance to litter into the setting began to deteriorate steadily, causing shortened littering latencies with each new addition of litter. Anyone wishing to preserve the state of a specific environment, then, should begin with a clean setting so as to delay for the greatest time the appearance of two pieces of litter there, as those two pieces are likely to begin a "slippery slope" effect that leads to a fully littered environment and to a perception that "everybody litters here." According to this logic, then, environments will be best able to retard littering if they are subjected to frequent and thorough litter pick-ups that return them to the optimal litter-free condition.

The second practical implication of our data comes from Studies 4–6, which showed the ability of injunctive norms to reduce littering. In each instance, procedures that focused subjects on the injunctive norm against littering brought littering rates down below control conditions; this was even the case, as in Studies 4 and 6, when the descriptive norms favored littering in that setting. This latter effect is instructive in that it suggests a practical advantage that injunctive norm-focus procedures may have over descriptive norm-focus procedures in reducing litter. Drawing an individual's attention to the descriptive norms of a situation should retard littering only in environments that are wholly or virtually unspoiled. Indeed, a focus on what others have done when the environment is widely littered could tend to increase littering there, as was seen in Studies 1 and 4. A descriptive norm-focus procedure, then, should have socially beneficial effects only in environments that do not need much help. The upshot is quite different, however, when the injunctive norm is made salient and when individuals, consequently, are focused on what others typically approve and disapprove rather than what they typically do in a situation. By making the injunctive norm against littering more prominent, we should see reduced littering no matter what the littered state of the ambient environment.

To test this prediction, we chose to use a different kind of injunctive norm-focus technique than we had used previously: We exposed subjects to a confederate who *picked up* a piece of litter. Reasoning that this display would focus subjects on the concept of social disapproval for littering in our society, we expected that—by drawing attention to the injunctive norm against littering—the procedure would suppress littering rates whether the environment was clean or littered. In counterpoint, as we had done in Studies 1 and 4, we exposed other subjects to confederate who threw down a piece of litter. We expected that they—having had their attention thus drawn to the state of the environment and to the dictates of the reigning descriptive norm there—would show suppressed littering rates only in an unlittered environment.

1. Study 7: Environmental Influences on the Effects of Norms

We selected as our experimental setting the one that we had used in Study 5: the local municipal library and its adjoining parking area. Subjects were library visitors who had left the library building and were returning to their cars in the main parking lot. That lot had either been cleaned by our experimental team of all visible litter or had been littered with a large number of handbills that read, "THIS IS AUTOMOTIVE SAFETY MONTH. PLEASE DRIVE CARE-FULLY." As subjects approached a roadway separating the library grounds from the parking area, they encountered a college-age experimental confederate

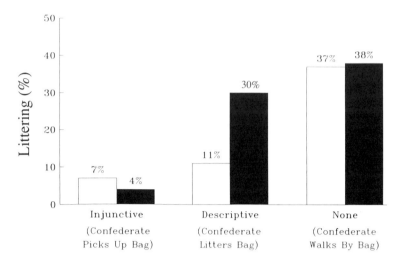

Norm Saliency

Fig. 7. Percentage of subjects littering by environmental condition and type of norm made salient in Study 7. (□), Clean environment; (■), littered environment.

who, before passing by, (1) threw down a fast food restaurant bag approximately 4.5 m (5 yd) in front of them, (2) picked up the same kind of bag at the same approximate distance from them, or (c) merely walked by, carrying nothing and picking up nothing in the process. Upon reaching their cars, subjects found an AUTOMOTIVE SAFETY MONTH handbill placed under the driver's side windshield wiper. Whether they deposited the handbill into the environment or placed it in the car with them (there were no trash receptacles nearby) constituted the measure of littering, which was assessed by a second experimental assistant from a hidden vantage point.

The results, depicted in Fig. 7, offer good support for our experimental hypotheses (unpublished data, Arizona State University). That is, subjects who saw another pick up the bag littered significantly less than the walk-by control subjects, regardless of the state of the environment. This was not the case, however, for subjects who saw another throw down the bag; they littered significantly less than control subjects only in the clean environment.[4] Thus, it appears that for

[4]Despite the generally confirmatory pattern of data for our experimental hypotheses, there was one way that the data did not fit our expectations. Extrapolating from the comparable conditions of Studies 1 and 4, we had anticipated that the subjects who saw another litter into a widely littered environment would litter more than would control subjects in such an environment. This did not occur, however, as these two sets of subjects did not differ in their littering rates. Although there are numerous differences between the present study and the earlier two, our favored explanation for the discrepancy is that, previously, subjects' littering involved the same type of litter (a handbill) as they saw the confederate discard, whereas in the present study the two types of litter were different (a

practical purposes there is an advantage to using techniques that create an injunctive rather than descriptive norm focus, in that injunctive norms—once activated—are more beneficial in their impact across the range of potential situations.

2. Transcendent Norms

The enhanced cross-situational robustness of an injunctive as compared to a descriptive norm focus may be even greater than the results of Study 7 suggest, however. That is, the advantage of an injunctive norm focus may not be limited to settings with societally harmful descriptive norms (e.g., fully littered environments; roads on which most drivers speed; precincts with low voter turnout). That advantage may apply, as well, to the likelihood of normative conduct in settings that are different from the one in which the relevant norm was evoked. Because the perception of what people do within a particular setting is a more situation-specific motivational construct than the perception of what people approve/disapprove in a society, it may be that the effect of focusing individuals on descriptive norm information (e.g., what another has done) will have less impact in a novel, second situation than will the effect of focusing subjects on injunctive norm information (e.g., what another has approved/disapproved). That is, descriptive norms are designed to tell us what makes for adaptive/effective behavior, which can be influenced and changed by many situationally based factors. Injunctive norms, on the other hand, are designed to tell us what others have been socialized to approve/disapprove in the culture, which is likely to change relatively little from situation to situation. Consequently, an injunctive norm focus should transcend situational boundaries to a greater extent than a descriptive norm focus.

It is our view, then, that not only will descriptive norm-salience procedures be relatively limited in their effect to the settings in which they occur but that, in contrast, injunctive norm-salience procedures will tend to remain effective even in relatively different settings. To test this hypothesis, we recognized the need to include norm-salience procedures of the descriptive and injunctive variety within the conditions of the same experimental design.

3. Study 8: The Impact of Norms across Environments

To generate a focus on what another has done, we chose to show subjects in the descriptive norm-salience conditions of Study 8 a confederate who was carrying a piece of litter (a fast food restaurant bag filled with paper wrappers and

---

handbill versus a bag). It seems possible that subjects who saw a handbill thrown into a littered environment had more specific normative information on which to base their own (handbill) littering behavior.

an empty soft drink can) and who disposed of it by throwing it into a trash container before passing a subject. Subjects in the injunctive norm-salience conditions, on the other hand, saw the same behavioral event as had occurred in the comparable conditions of Study 7—an approaching confederate *picking up* the bag and then continuing on past the subject. In addition, another set of (control) subjects saw a confederate who merely walked past them without carrying, disposing of, or picking up any litter in the process.

As in Study 7, the subjects were visitors to the local municipal library who had left the library building and were returning to their cars in a library parking lot. However, they encountered the confederate and his or her relevant action either on a path within a grassy, landscaped section of the property (different environment) or after they had proceeded into the asphalt-paved parking area (same environment); these areas had been cleaned of visible litter. We expected that seeing the confederate properly dispose of litter would provide descriptive norm information (what another has done) that would produce congruent behavior only if it occurred in the same setting in which subjects had to make their own littering decisions. However, we expected that seeing the confederate pick up litter would provide injunctive norm information (what another approves/disapproves) that would produce norm-congruent behavior across environments. To test these expectations, we watched what subjects did with an AUTOMOTIVE SAFETY WEEK handbill that they found attached to their windshields upon returning to their cars in the parking area.

As can be seen from Fig. 8, the results of the experiment generally confirmed

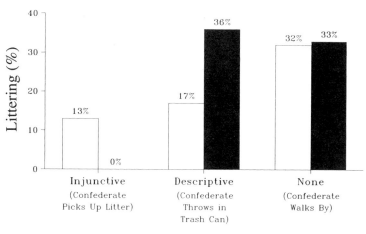

Fig. 8. Percentage of subjects littering by environmental similarity and type of norm saliency in Study 8. (□), Same environment; (■), different environment.

our hypotheses (unpublished data, Arizona State University). Subjects who encountered the confederate who picked up litter were less likely than controls to litter no matter where they had witnessed the confederate's action. This was not the case, however, for subjects who saw the confederate throw litter into a trash receptacle; they littered less than controls only when that event had occurred in the same setting as their own opportunity to litter.

D. PICKING UP CONCEPTUAL IMPLICATIONS FROM PRACTICAL APPLICATIONS

It seems clear from the findings of Studies 7 and 8 that one practical advantage of focusing individuals on injunctive versus descriptive norms is that the former are more robust in their impact across situations than the latter. Take, for example, the outcomes of Study 8. Our subjects who saw another refrain from littering (by using a litter receptacle) were affected by that display only in that particular setting, whereas our subjects who saw another disapprove of littering (by picking up litter) were affected by that display in a rather different setting as well. Our preferred explanation for this pattern of results is that (1) subjects were focused by the respective displays either on descriptive norm information or on injunctive norm information and that (2) injunctive norms are more likely to transcend situational boundaries because they orient individuals away from a concern with how others have behaved in a particular setting and toward a concern with what others approve/disapprove across the culture.

However, a close look at what subjects experienced in that experiment suggests that things may not be as clear-cut as we have implied. After all, subjects in *both* conditions saw another perform a behavior in a particular setting from which they could reasonably infer the other's disapproval of littering. Yet it was only when that behavior involved picking up another's litter that it was generally effective. We think this was the case because only that behavior clearly implicated the subjects' own littering action in the disapproval; the message from our confederate was unambiguous, "I find littering by others (our subjects included) objectionable." In this way, subjects were directly focused on a central feature of injunctive norms—*social sanctions* (e.g., disapproval) for counternormative behavior—thereby making the injunctive norm salient and generating powerful effects across situations. In contrast, subjects who saw litter thrown into a receptacle got a different message from the confederate, "I find littering objectionable within my own behavior," which did not remind them directly of social sanctions and, consequently, of injunctive norms. Instead, subjects may have remained focused on the descriptive norm information of what another had decided to do regarding littering in that setting.

A conceptual implication of our analysis, if correct, is that the concept of approval/disapproval needs sharpening in its relation to social norms. Another's demonstrated approval/disapproval for norm-related conduct may engage the full power of the relevant injunctive social norm in an observer only when the observer is actively made to think that the approval/disapproval would be applied to his or her relevant conduct. Thus, expressing disapproval for counternormative action (e.g., cigarette smoking in an elevator, excessive alcohol consumption) in one's own behavior by visibly refraining from the action should not bring to bear on observers the full salutary impact of the injunctive social norm; instead, that impact should flow from the visible expression of disapproval for the action *in others*. A key, then, to the effective activation of injunctive social norms is a focus on the applicability of *interpersonal* sanctions to the behavior *in question*.

It is not our position, however, that injunctive social norms function only when evaluating others are physically present to provide social sanctions. We concur with the developers (Cooley, 1902; Mead, 1934) and modern proponents (e.g., Schlenker, 1980) of symbolic interaction theory that people often seek to satisfy the expectations of imagined audiences, one of which—the generalized other—represents the generalized viewpoint of society. Thus, once focused on a representative of society who approves/disapproves of another's behavior, an observer is likely to conform to the societal rules for that behavior even when alone, as long as the focus remains. In this respect, injunctive social norms are somewhat similar to the concept of personal norms as explicated by Schwartz (1973, 1977; Schwartz & Howard, 1982), in that the possibility of direct social sanctions is not necessary for the stimulation of normative conduct.

According to Schwartz, personal norms are self-based standards or expectations for behavior that flow from one's internalized values and that are enforced through the anticipation of self-enhancement or self-deprecation. Thus, Schwartz differentiates personal norms from (injunctive) social norms by locating both the standards and the sanctions for action inside the self. A number of studies (see Schwartz, 1977, for a review) have demonstrated a significant relationship between measured personal norms and relevant behavior that is greater than the comparable relationship between the behavior and perceived social norms. What's more, the social norm measured in these studies provided no additional predictive component to that already provided by the personal norm measure. On the surface, these results would seem to indicate that personal norms represent the stronger influence on behavior. We hold a different view, however.

In keeping with our emphasis on attentional focus, we are convinced that both constructs are importantly generative of normative conduct, but which one has the greater impact on action in any given setting will depend on whether the actor is focused on internal or external standards and sanctions for that action. To investigate our contention, we performed a final experiment that was designed to test several hypotheses. First, we sought to demonstrate that, for at least a short time after subjects have been focused on social disapproval of a behavior—thereby activating the relevant injunctive social norm—they will behave consistently with the norm even when their behavior is not under direct social surveillance. Second, we wanted to test our view that others' evaluation of an individual will not result in conduct that is more consistent with the injunctive social norm unless the evaluation implies social approval/disapproval of the normative behavior in question. Finally, we wished to examine the hypothesis that a focus on internal standards and sanctions for a particular behavior would result in action that is consistent primarily with personal norms, whereas a focus on social standards and sanctions for the same behavior would result in action that is consistent primarily with (injunctive) social norms. To these ends, we returned to the stairwell setting used in Study 6 and once again assessed littering tendencies there.

Study 9: The Impact of Social and Personal Sanctions

Subjects were undergraduate students from the Introductory Psychology course at Arizona State University who, as part of an omnibus testing session during the first week of classes, had responded to a questionnaire designed to measure their personal norms toward littering. The measure, based on the personal norm for helping scales used in prior research by Schwartz, included 10 items asking about the extent to which subjects felt a personal obligation to refrain from littering in a variety of situations (see Table I). Subjects were classified as having a strong or weak personal norm toward littering on the basis of a median split done on the scores of experimental participants.

The subjects, who were seated in a deskchair on the top landing of a little-used $3\frac{1}{2}$-story stairwell in the psychology building, listened to pairs of tones presented over earphones while physiological measures were supposedly being taken to assess various "physiological correlates of auditory discriminations." One of these physiological measures required that a petroleum jelly paste be applied to one hand. At the completion of the experiment, subjects received a small paper towel from the experimenter to wipe the paste off the affected hand. The experimenter then exited the stairwell through a locked third floor door, leaving the subjects alone to exit by descending three flights of stairs to the ground floor door. After the subject had left, the experimenter returned and searched the stairwell to determine whether the subject had littered the paper towel on the way out. So as to demonstrate the power of (activated) personal norms and injunctive social norms over descriptive norms, in all instances we had previously littered the stairwell environment with a variety of litter, including a large number of paper towels.

Before the opportunity to litter, however, subjects experienced one of four experimental treatments while hearing the tones over their earphones. In the first,

TABLE I

PERSONAL NORM AGAINST LITTERING QUESTIONNAIRE ITEMS

My personal obligation to not litter is:

No personal
obligation 1 ----------- 2 ----------- 3 ---------- 4 ----------- 5----------- 6 -----------7 -----------8 ---------- 9
for me   Weak   Moderate   Strong   Very
                                                                                Strong

1. Do you feel a personal obligation to not litter when you are holding an empty soft drink can and there are no trash cans available?

2. Do you feel a personal obligation to not litter when you are holding a gum wrapper and there are no trash cans available?

3. Do you feel a personal obligation to stop and pick up a piece of scrap paper that you accidentally drop because you are in a hurry?

4. Do you feel a personal obligation to stop and pick up a piece of scrap paper that blows off a big stack of papers that you are carrying in both arms?

5. Do you feel a personal obligation to not litter when you are ill (fever, headache, muscle ache) and you would have to walk out of your way to reach a trash receptacle?

6. Do you feel a personal obligatoin to not litter when you are preoccupied with important things on your mind?

7. Do you feel a personal obligation to pick up a piece of paper you dropped when it is raining and you are getting soaked?

8. Do you feel a personal obligation to not litter when it is dark outside and nobody could have seen if you littered?

9. Do you feel a personal obligation to not litter even though you know a litter pickup crew will be coming to the area soon?

10. In general, do you feel a personal obligation to not litter?

the *simple external focus condition,* subjects watched a television monitor that displayed a set of geometric forms that changed every 10 seconds for 3 minutes. This served as our baseline condition. In the second, the *simple social focus condition,* subjects watched a television monitor picture of three researchers who appeared to be recording data from a computer screen. Subjects were told that the researchers (who were actually on videotape) were in an adjacent room monitoring the subjects' physiological responses to the tones. This condition was intended to focus subjects on a simple form of social evaluation that was not related to the normative behavior under consideration. Consequently, according to our earlier analysis, we should not expect it to influence littering rates. In the third, the *(injunctive) social norm focus condition,* subjects were treated exactly as in the simple social focus condition except that, along with the tones, they also heard two vignettes over their earphones. In one, a college student was admonished by a friend for writing graffiti on a wall. In the other, a college student was admonished by a friend for the improper disposal of a chemistry project. Recall that these were the vignettes used in Study 6 to activate the littering norm in subjects by virtue of the process of spreading activation. Accordingly, we expected that subjects in the (injunctive) social norm focus condition of Study 9 would have had their attention drawn indirectly but nonetheless effectively to the societal rule against littering and that their littering tendencies would be suppressed. In addition, we expected that this would be the case even for subjects with weak personal norms against littering. Finally, in the fourth, the *self-focus condition,* subjects saw on the monitor a closed circuit television picture of themselves. We anticipated that this would cause subjects to focus on internal standards and sanctions for behavior (Duval & Wicklund, 1972), thereby activating their personal norms. In this condition, we predicted that only those subjects with strong personal norms against littering would show a lowered littering rate.

The results shown in Fig. 9 supported all three of our predictions nicely (unpublished data, Arizona State University). Taking those predictions in reverse order, we found good evidence that focusing subjects on internal standards and sanctions for behavior would cause the relevant personal norm to predominate, but focusing subjects on social standards and sanctions for that behavior would cause the relevant (injunctive) social norm to predominate. It is clear that, among subjects who were focused on themselves, only those with strong personal norms against littering showed lowered littering rates relative to the externally oriented

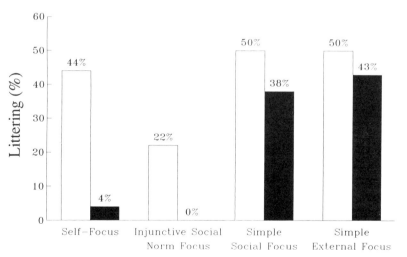

Fig. 9.   Percentage of subjects littering by personal norm level and focus of attention in Study 9. (□), Weak personal norm; (■), strong personal norm.

control subjects. In fact, the personal norm measure had little impact on behavior except for subjects who were oriented on normative considerations. As could be extrapolated from Schwartz's (1977) model, this impact was greatest among those focused inward; however, there was a smaller (nonsignificant) impact on subjects who were focused on social rules, suggesting that an injunctive social norm focus may have a weaker, reverberating effect upon individuals' personal norms as well. The most important difference in our data, however, between subjects focused on personal norms versus (injunctive) social norms is that the social norm-focused subjects showed significantly retarded littering tendencies regardless of their personal norm status. It was only in the (injunctive) social norm-focused condition that even the weak personal norm subjects suppressed their littering.

No such suppression occurred among the simple social focus-condition subjects. In line with our second prediction, social evaluation unrelated to the relevant normative behavior was not sufficient to influence that behavior. Finally, because subjects were alone with no chance of detection when making their littering decisions, the suppressed littering rates in the (injunctive) social norm-focus condition offer support for our first prediction that such a focus would be influential in the absence of the possibility of direct social sanctions.

III. Conclusions

Any integrated series of nine studies on an important aspect of human behavior is likely to produce a number of findings worthy of attention. It is our view that the results of our program of research converge to allow three main conclusions. First, despite earlier reasons for doubt, norms can be demonstrated to affect human action systematically and powerfully. Second, at least three distinct types of norms can be effective in this regard: social norms of the descriptive kind, which guide one's behavior via the perception of how most others would behave; social norms of the injunctive kind, which guide one's behavior via the perception of how most others would approve/disapprove of one's conduct; and personal norms, which guide one's behavior via the perception of how one would approve/disapprove of one's own conduct. Finally, at a given time, an individual's actions are likely to conform to the dictates of the type of norm that is currently focal, even when the other types of norms dictate contrary conduct.

From the last of these conclusions, we can derive one more main conclusion from our findings—this one more practical than conceptual. Anyone wishing to enhance the likelihood of socially beneficial behavior in others via norm activation would be well advised under most circumstances to use procedures that activate injunctive social norms. That is, of the three types of norms we have discussed, injunctive social norms—once activated—are likely to lead to bene-ficial social conduct across the greatest number of situations and populations. A descriptive social norm focus will be effective prosocially only when most indi-viduals already *do* behave in a socially desirable way; in situations where such desirable action is not the norm, a focus on what others do is likely to prove detrimental to societal goals. Likewise, orienting individuals to their personal norms will be societally advantageous only when the personal norms of the target individuals already fit with prosocial goals; here again, such an orientation could backfire among those individuals whose personal standards for their own conduct are not congruent with the societal standards. Thus, a billboard campaign de-signed to reduce excessive highway speeds by (1) creating a descriptive norm focus in passing motorists should be successful only on those stretches of road where speeding was not typically a problem; (2) creating a personal norm focus should be successful only among those passing motorists who don't prefer to exceed the speed limit; (3) focusing motorists on social disapproval of speeders should be successful across a wide variety of settings and drivers.

Although we feel that our research program has answered several important questions about norms and norm salience, we recognize that other questions remain. One such important question concerns the nature of the stimuli that are likely to lead to a norm's salience. On the one hand, one could say that the factors that enhance norm salience will be the same as those that have been shown to enhance the salience of any concept—the cognitive accessibility of the concept (Fazio, 1986), the recency and frequency of activation of the concept, its degree of connectedness with other salient concepts in the environment, etc. (see Fiske and Taylor, 1991, for a review of the evidence for these and other influ-ences on salience). On the other hand, because norms appear to occur in three distinct forms, one must be careful in specifying the particular type of norm that is being made salient by a given technique or mechanism. For example, we should expect that dispositional tendencies toward high or low self-monitoring (Snyder, 1987) would make injunctive and personal norms differentially accessi-ble and thereby differentially salient. That is, the low self-monitor, who tends to orient primarily to personal standards in the determination of his or her conduct, should find personal norms chronically more salient; whereas the high self-monitor, who tends to orient primarily to the approval of others in the determina-tion of his or her conduct, should find injunctive and (to a lesser degree) descrip-tive social norms more salient.

Another interesting but unexplored set of questions involves the relationships among the three types of norms that we have specified. It seems likely that there are perceived connections between each of these types of norms. For example, even though the connections are not logically necessary ones, there is normally a relationship between what most people do and what most people ap-prove/disapprove, just as there is normally a relationship between societal and individual standards of conduct. Thus far, these relationships have not played a central role in our research. That is, by focusing subjects on one or another type of norm, we have been able to stimulate the action of that particular kind of norm, without seeming to activate the other kinds. However, it strikes us as possible that we could simultaneously energize two related norm types if we focused subjects on one kind of norm and on its *connection* to another kind of norm. Once again, then, we are led to expect that the crucial ingredient in any attempt to predict an individual's norm-relevant behavior is the ability to localize that individual's focus of attention within an intricate normative mix. That undoubtedly dynamic mix should provide the opportunity for much further research.

References

Agostinelli, G., Sherman, S. J., Fazio, R. H., & Hearst, E. S. (1986). Detecting and identifying change: Additions versus deletions. *Journal of Experimental Psychology: Human Perception and Performance, 12,* 445–454.

Anderson, J. R. (1976). *Language, memory, and thought.* Hillsdale, NJ: Erlbaum.

Anderson, J. R. (1983). *The architecture of cognition.* Cambridge, MA: Harvard University Press.

Asch, S. E. (1956). Studies of independence and conformity: A minority of one against a unanimous majority. *Psychological Monographs, 70* (9, Whole No. 416).

Bandura, A. (1977). *Social learning theory.* Englewood Cliffs, NJ: Prentice-Hall.

Berkowitz, L. (1972). Social norms, feelings, and other factors affecting helping and altruism. In L. Berkowitz (Ed.), *Advances in experimental social psychology* (Vol. 6). New York: Academic Press.

Berkowitz, L., & Daniels, L. R. (1964). Affecting the salience of the social responsibility norm. *Journal of Abnormal and Social Psychology, 68,* 275–281.

California Waste Management Board (1988). *The California litter problem.* Sacramento, CA: Author.

Cialdini, R. B. (1988). *Influence: Science and practice* (2nd ed.). Glenview, IL: Scott, Foresman.

Cialdini, R. B., Reno, R. R., & Kallgren, C. A. (1990). A focus theory of normative conduct: Recycling the concept of norms to reduce littering in public places. *Journal of Personality and Social Psychology, 58,* 1015–1026.

Collins, A. M., & Loftus, E. F. (1975). A spreading-activation theory of semantic processing. *Psychological Review, 82,* 407–428.

Cooley, C. H. (1902). *Human nature and the social order.* New York: Scribner's.

Crutchfield, R. A. (1955). Conformity and character. *American Psychologist, 10,* 191–198.

Darley, J. M., & Latané, B. (1970). Norms and normative behavior: Field studies of social interdependence. In J. Macaulay & L. Berkowitz (Eds.), *Altruism and helping behavior* (pp. 83–102). New York: Academic Press.

Deaux, K., & Major, B. (1987). Putting gender into context: An interactive model of gender-related behavior. *Psychological Review, 94,* 369–389.

Deutsch, M., & Gerard, H. B. (1955). A study of normative and informational social influence upon individual judgment. *Journal of Abnormal and Social Psychology, 51,* 629–636.

Duval, S., & Wicklund, R. A. (1972). *A theory of objective self awareness.* New York: Academic Press.

Easterbrook, J. A. (1959). The effect of emotion on cue utilization and the organization of behavior. *Psychological Review,* **66,** 183–201.

Fazio, R. H. (1986). How do attitudes guide behavior? In R. M. Sorrentino & E. T. Higgins (Eds.), *The handbook of motivation and cognition.* New York: Guilford.

Fishbein, M., & Ajzen, I. (1975). *Belief, attitude, intention, and behavior.* Reading, MA: Addison-Wesley.

Fiske, S. T., & Taylor, S. E. (1991). *Social cognition* (2nd ed.). Reading, MA: Addison-Wesley.

Garfinkel, H. (1967). *Studies in ethnomethodology.* Englewood Cliffs, NJ: Prentice-Hall.

Geller, E. S., Winett, S., & Everett, P. B. (1982). *Preserving the environment.* New York: Pergamon.

Gouldner, A. W. (1960). The norm of reciprocity: A preliminary statement. *American Sociological Review,* **25,** 161–178.

Gruder, C. L., Romer, D., & Korth, B. (1978). Dependency and fault as determinants of helping. *Journal of Experimental Social Psychology,* **14,** 227–235.

Harvey, M. D., & Enzle, M. E. (1981). A cognitive model of social norms for understanding the transgression-helping effect. *Journal of Personality and Social Psychology,* **41,** 866–875.

Higgins, E. T., & Bargh, J. E. (1987). Social cognition and social perception. *Annual Review of Psychology,* **38,** 369–425.

Kallgren, C. A., Cialdini, R. B., & Reno, R. R. (1989). *Cognitive conditionals on social norm-behavior relations.* Paper presented at the meeting of the American Psychological Association, New Orleans, LA.

Kallgren, C. A., & Wood, W. W. (1986). Access to attitude-relevant information in memory as a determinant of attitude–behavior consistency. *Journal of Experimental Social Psychology,* **22,** 328–338.

Krauss, R. M., Freedman, J. L., & Whitcup, M. (1978). Field and laboratory studies of littering. *Journal of Experimental Social Psychology,* **14,** 109–122.

Krebs, D. L. (1970). Altruism: An examination of the concept and a review of the literature. *Psychological Bulletin,* **73,** 258–302.

Krebs, D. L., & Miller, D. T. (1985). Altruism and aggression. In G. Lindzey & E. Aronson (Eds.), *The handbook of social psychology* (3rd ed.). New York: Random House.

Marini, M. M. (1984). Age and sequencing norms in the transition to adulthood. *Social Forces,* **63,** 229–244.

McClelland, J. L., & Rumelhart, D. E. (1981). An interactive activation model of context effects in letter perception. *Psychological Review,* **8,** 375–407.

McKirnan, D. J. (1980). The conceptualization of deviance: A conceptualization and initial test of a model of social norms. *European Journal of Social Psychology,* **10,** 79–93.

Mead, G. H. (1934). *Mind, self and society.* Chicago: University of Chicago Press.

Mehan, H., & Wood, H. (1975). *Reality of ethnomethodology.* New York: Wiley.

Milgram, S., Bickman, L., & Berkowitz, O. (1969). Note on the drawing power of crowds of different size. *Journal of Personality and Social Psychology,* **13,** 79–82.

Millar, M. G., & Tesser, A. (1989). The effects of affective–cognitive consistency and thought on the attitude–behavior relation. *Journal of Experimental Social Psychology,* **25,** 189–202.

Miller, L. E., & Grush, J. E. (1986). Individual differences in attitudinal versus normative determination of behavior. *Journal of Experimental and Social Psychology,* **22,** 190–202.

Pepitone, A. (1976). Toward a normative and comparative biocultural social psychology. *Journal of Personality and Social Psychology,* **34,** 641–653.

Rutkowski, G. K., Gruder, C. L., & Romer, D. (1983). Group cohesiveness, social norms and bystander intervention. *Journal of Personality and Social Psychology,* **44,** 545–552.

Schaffer, L. S. (1983). Toward Pepitone's vision of a normative social psychology: What is a social norm? *Journal of Mind and Behavior,* **4,** 275–294.

Schlenker, B. R. (1980). *Impression management.* Monterey, CA: Brooks/Cole.

Schwartz, S. H. (1973). Normative explanations of helping behavior: A critique, proposal, and empirical test. *Journal of Experimental and Social Psychology,* **9,** 349–364.

Schwartz, S. H. (1977). Normative influences on altruism. In L. Berkowitz (Ed.), *Advances in experimental social psychology* (Vol. 10). New York: Academic Press.

Schwartz, S. H., & Fleishman, J. A. (1978). Personal norms and the mediation of legitimacy effects on helping. *Social Psychology,* **41,** 306–315.

Schwartz, S. H., & Howard, J. A. (1982). Helping and cooperation: A self-based motivational model. In V. Derlega & H. Grezlak (Eds.), *Cooperation and helping behavior.* New York: Academic Press.

Sherif, M. (1936). *The psychology of social norms.* New York: Harper.

Snyder, M. (1987). *Public appearances/private realities: The psychology of self-monitoring.* New York: Freeman.

Staub, E. (1972). Instigation to goodness: The role of social norms and interpersonal influence. *Journal of Social Issues,* **28,** 131–150.

Storms, M. D. (1973). Videotape and the attribution process: Reversing actors' and observers' points of view. *Journal of Personality and Social Psychology,* **27,** 165–175.

Triandis, H. C. (1977). *Interpersonal behavior.* Monterey, CA: Brooks/Cole.

Venkatesan, M. (1966). Experimental study of consumer behavior, conformity, and independence. *Journal of Marketing Research,* **3,** 384–387.

THE EFFECTS OF INTERACTION GOALS ON PERSON PERCEPTION

James L. Hilton

John M. Darley

Recently, there has been a resurgence of interest in understanding the impact that perceivers' goals have on person perception. The perceiver, having frequently been portrayed as an unconstrained, accuracy-seeking (although frequently not accuracy-finding) observer, is now seen as a goal- and event-driven interactant who must expend scarce cognitive resources to accomplish specific ends (e.g., Bargh, 1989; Fiske & Neuberg, 1990; Hilton, Darley, & Fleming, 1989; Miller & Turnbull, 1986; Srull & Wyer, 1986; Swann, 1984). In this article, we have several related goals. In the first half of the article we analyze why, historically, there has been relatively little interest in the influence that perceivers' goals have on person perception, and then we briefly review the literature that has led us and others to argue for a second look at the roles that these goals play in social perception. One conclusion that emerges from this review is that when perceivers' goals are taken into account, they often qualify our understanding of a variety of issues in the person perception literature (e.g., the correspondence bias, person memory, impression formation). But a stronger conclusion is also possible—that the neglect of perceivers' goals in much of the person perception literature has led to an image of the perceiver that is wrong at a fundamental level. In the second half of the article we try to support this stronger conclusion, as well as bring some order to the variety of perceiver goals that can be identified, by focusing on the pervasive effects that different categories of goals have on the outcomes of social interaction and perception. More specifically, we examine perceivers' goals in light of the degree to which they are likely to produce a concern with assessment and accuracy during the interaction.

ADVANCES IN EXPERIMENTAL
SOCIAL PSYCHOLOGY, VOL. 24

I. Historical Approaches to Perceivers' Goals and Person Perception

Within the impression formation literature, the emphasis that has been placed on perceivers' goals has varied considerably over the past 50 years. The new look theorists of the 1940s and 1950s (e.g., Bruner & Postman, 1948), for example, maintained that perception is rarely free from the motives, needs, and personality of the perceiver. They were intrigued by findings indicating that subjects were slow to recognize threatening words (Bruner & Postman, 1947), that poor children tended to overestimate the size of coins (Bruner & Goodman, 1947), and that subjects with different personalities emerged from the same situation with very different perceptions (Frenkel-Brunswik, 1949), because these results fit with their belief that in order to understand perception, one must understand the contribution that the perceivers' motivational states make to their final percepts. For new look theorists, understanding perceivers' goal states was an essential component of any theory of perception (e.g., Bruner, 1951, 1957; Jones & Thibaut, 1958).

However, as the theoretical underpinnings and empirical findings of the new look came under increasingly heavy attacks (for a review, see Erdelyi, 1974), there was a move to focus on more cognitive accounts of person perception—"cognitive" meaning, among other things, free of the taint of motivational factors. Asch (1946), for example, argued that his work on impression formation provided a necessary balance to the new look perspective. "The preoccupation with emotional factors and distortions of judgment has had two main consequences for the course investigation has taken. First, it has induced a certain lack of perspective which has diverted interest from the study of those processes which do not involve subjective distortions as the most decisive factor. Secondly, there has been a tendency to neglect the fact that emotions too have a cognitive side, that something must be perceived and discriminated in order that it may be loved or hated" (p. 260).

In order to address these issues, Asch developed what is now a familiar technique in which subjects are first presented with a list of traits, and are then asked to form an impression of a person described by those traits. Asch found that subjects had little trouble forming impressions under these conditions and that variations in the traits used could produce dramatic changes in the impressions formed. Indeed, problems like the change of meaning hypothesis (e.g., Hamilton & Zanna, 1974), the primacy effect (e.g., Anderson & Norman, 1964; Jones & Goethals, 1971), and the centrality of certain traits were sufficiently intriguing that literally hundreds of studies using variations on the Asch paradigm have been conducted since 1946.

Suffice it to say that Asch's influence on the impression formation literature has been tremendous (for reviews, see Fiske & Taylor, 1984; Jones, 1985). What is critical from the perspective of the current article, however, is that both methodologically and theoretically, Asch's argument has carried the day. Methodologically, investigators have tended to rely upon increasingly sophisticated versions of the Asch paradigm (Jones, 1985). Although reaction time measures have replaced subject protocols, the basic procedure developed by Asch is still the method of choice in many person perception experiments. More important, at the level of theory, psychologists have devoted enormous energies to the study of person perception with the guiding assumption that questions about motivational perturbations on ongoing perceptual and cognitive processes were to be set aside until a better understanding of those cognitive processes emerged.

A similar lack of concern with perceivers' goals also emerged in the attribution literature. Although both Heider's work on phenomenal causality (Heider, 1944, 1958) and Jones and Davis's (1965) work on correspondent inferences contained concepts that involved perceivers' goals (e.g., Heider's notion of egocentric cognition and Jones and Davis's notion of hedonic relevance), with the publication of Kelley's (1967) covariation model of attribution, attribution theories became less descriptive of what perceivers do and more prescriptive of what they should do. That is, attribution models became normative standards against which perceivers' performances could be compared. As the interest shifted, vast numbers of studies were conducted in which subjects' actual perceptual judgments were evaluated against the judgments prescribed by normative attributional rules. Moreover, as investigators attempted to understand these deviations, the preferred manner of explanation was to identify some cognitive mechanism (e.g., reliance upon availability or representativeness rather than consensus) that was responsible for the error. Indeed, there was general agreement that motivational accounts would be appealed to only as a last resort (Jones et al., 1972; Nisbett & Ross, 1980).

Thus, for reasons that were central to the internal logic of the approaches, the two dominant areas of person perception research were built upon studies in which the subject was cast in the role of passive perceiver—a perceiver generally free of goals other than providing the experimenter with an accurate image of the perceived. While much has been learned within this tradition about the cognitive structure and underpinnings of social perception, what has been slow to emerge has been an understanding of the ways in which the dynamic, goal-driven nature of social interaction shapes social perception (for similar conclusions, see Jones & Thibaut, 1958, and Swann, 1984). Indeed, the image that emerged from the research conducted during the 1960s and 1970s was of an observer, without interactive purposes, attempting to form accurate impressions of a target individual, without in any way being able to interact with that target, to extract desired information or test personality generalizations.

A. EARLY DEMONSTRATIONS OF THE
IMPORTANCE OF PERCEIVER GOALS

Although the dominant paradigms of the 1960s and 1970s did not focus attention on the goal-directed nature of social perception, during that time period two important lines of research emerged that demonstrated the importance of perceivers' goals. The first was Zajonc's (1960) work on cognitive tuning. Zajonc found that perceivers who were told that their task was to transmit information about a person to someone else formed impressions that were more unified and organized than were the impressions of perceivers who were told that their task was simply to receive information about another person. In other words, Zajonc found that a perceiver's openness to new information depended upon the communication goal that the perceiver had at the time that the information was encountered. Similarly, Cohen (1961) found that, relative to reception subjects, transmission subjects who encountered positive and negative information about a target were more likely to organize the information around either the positive or negative information rather than forming a more complicated impression incorporating both kinds of information.

The second line of research that demonstrated the importance of perceivers' goals was research that examined the impact that manipulations of outcome dependency had on the impressions perceivers formed of their interaction partners. Berscheid, Graziano, Monson, and Dermer (1976), for example, reasoned that if perceivers' outcomes were somehow dependent upon the target, they would pay closer attention to the target than if this were not the case. Outcome dependency was manipulated by leading some of the perceivers to expect a series of consequential social interactions with the target while leading other perceivers to expect no future interaction with the target. All subjects then watched a videotape of the target. Their results showed that when perceivers expected to spend time together with the target in a dating context, they paid more attention to the target, formed more favorable impressions of the target, and tended to remember more information about the target than when they were not dependent upon the target for their outcomes.

What studies like these demonstrated was the potential importance that manipulations of the interactive context between target and perceiver have for the resulting perceptions of the target by the perceiver. However, probably because they were not a sustained series of studies, offering a unified vision of how to conceptualize the possible differences in interaction contexts, this message was often difficult to hear or practice, and the goal perspective was slow to emerge in the social perception literature.

B. RECENT DEMONSTRATIONS OF THE GOAL-DIRECTED NATURE OF SOCIAL PERCEPTION

1. Research on Outcome Dependency

Recently, however, a number of investigators have begun to examine in a more systematic manner the roles that perceivers' goals play in impression formation. Fiske, Neuberg, and their colleagues (e.g., Fiske, Neuberg, Beattie, & Milberg, 1987; Neuberg, 1989; Neuberg & Fiske, 1987), for example, have conducted a series of investigations examining the effects that different interaction structures have on the impressions that perceivers form. In one study (Neuberg & Fiske, 1987, Study 1), subjects were led to expect to interact with a former mental patient. Half of the subjects were made outcome dependent upon the former patient by telling them that they would be competing as a team against other pairs of subjects and patients. The competition involved designing creative games, and the subjects were told that each member of the team that designed the most creative game would win a $20 prize. The other half of the subjects were in the not-outcome-dependent condition. These subjects were also told that they would be working with a patient to design creative games and that they would be eligible for a $20 prize. Unlike subjects in the outcome-dependent condition, however, these subjects were told that the prize would be based on each team member's individual contribution to the final product rather than upon the team's joint contribution. All subjects then received more information about the former mental patient. Half of the subjects received information that was neutral with regard to the stereotypic image of mental patients and half received information that was inconsistent with the stereotypic image of mental patients. All subjects' perceptions of the target were then examined.

The results of the study indicated that subjects who were outcome dependent were more influenced by the individuating information that they received about the patient, and relied less upon their stereotypes of mental patients than subjects who were not outcome dependent. Evidence obtained during a follow-up study (Neuberg & Fiske, 1987, Experiment 3) suggested that the reason the outcome-dependency manipulation had this effect was because it led perceivers who were outcome dependent to set accuracy as a goal for the interaction. Because their rewards depended upon the performance of the target, they were much more interested in determining what the target was really like than were subjects who were not outcome dependent.

Of course, not all interaction context manipulations that create what we would generally describe as "interdependencies" or "outcome dependencies" necessarily lead perceivers to pay closer attention to the individual characteristics of the target, and they do not always have the effect of creating perceptual accuracy as an interaction goal. Omoto and Borgida (1988), for example, found that when outcome dependency leads perceivers to become concerned with their self-presentations, the impressions that they form are sometimes less individuated than when they are not outcome dependent. Specifically, they found that white male subjects who learned that they would be dating a black female as part of their participation in the experiment formed more negative, stereotype-consistent impressions than did white male subjects who learned that they would be having a brief interaction with a black female, because the subjects who expected to date the black female began devoting greater attention to managing their self-presentations and less attention to forming an impression of their partner than did subjects who expected to interact in a more casual setting.

In summarizing much of this research, Fiske and Neuberg (1990) have recently proposed a continuum model of impression formation in which the perceivers' goals play a critical role in determining the extent to which the impressions that are formed deviate from expectancies that are derived from the category to which the target belongs. They argue that when the relationship between a perceiver and a target is sufficiently important to the perceiver, the perceiver will allocate sufficient attentional resources to the target to form an individuated impression. When, however, the relationship is not terribly important to the perceiver, the perceiver will tend to form a quick, less individuated impression that reflects knowledge that the perceiver has about the target's category rather than the knowledge that is available about the target as an individual. In other words, unless the target surpasses some minimal level of interest to the perceiver, the perceiver will default to a category-based impression of the target (Jones & McGillis, 1976) that reflects the general perceptions that the perceiver has of the salient categories to which the target belongs (e.g., women, academician, black, etc.) rather than a rich, individuated impression of the target.

2. Research on Accountability

Further evidence of the important role that perceivers' goals play during impression formation is also available from work by Tetlock and colleagues. Specifically, Tetlock and colleagues have conducted a number of studies examining the impact that making perceivers accountable (i.e., responsible) for the impressions they form has on these impressions. In these studies, some perceivers are simply asked to form an impression of a target while others are made accountable by telling them that they should be prepared to justify the impressions that they form of the target to someone else. The findings that typically emerge indicate that this simple manipulation leads perceivers to form more complex impressions of others and to avoid some of the biases that permeate social perception. Tetlock (1985), for example, found that perceivers who were made accountable were less likely to commit the fundamental attribution error. Similarly, Tetlock and Kim

(1987) found that perceivers who were made accountable formed more accurate, integrative, and complex impressions in the context of a personality prediction task, and Tetlock (1983) found that perceivers who were made accountable were less likely to fall prey to the primacy effect in an impression formation task than were perceivers who were not made accountable.

3. Research on Person Memory

Still further evidence of the important role that perceivers' goals have on person perception has emerged from the person memory literature. There, a number of studies have been conducted that have examined the influence that perceivers' goals have on the encoding and organizational processes involved in person memory (for a more complete review, see Srull & Wyer, 1986, 1989). For example, Hamilton and Katz (1975), in one of the first studies to examine the impact that perceivers' processing goals have on perceivers' memories for other people, found that subjects who were exposed to the same information, but who had different processing goals, had differential recall for the information. Specifically, they found that when subjects were instructed to read a set of behavioral statements, those who had been instructed to try to form an impression of a person who would engage in those behaviors remembered more of the behavioral statements than did subjects who were simply instructed to remember as many of the behavioral statements as possible. These results proved to be quite robust (Hamilton, Katz, & Leirer, 1980; Srull, 1981, 1983; Wyer, Bodenhausen, & Srull, 1984; Wyer & Gordon, 1982) and they suggest that the total amount of information that a perceiver can recall about a given target depends, in part, upon the goal the perceiver has at the time that the target is encountered.

There is also evidence that goals influence not only how much information is recalled, but how that information is organized and stored in memory. Wyer and Gordon (1982), for example, found that in comparison to perceivers who are simply instructed to memorize information about another person, perceivers who are instructed to form an impression of a person tend to be more likely to encode behaviors spontaneously in trait terms. Similarly, Srull (1983) found that perceivers in an impression formation set store the information about the target in a more integrated fashion than do perceivers in a memory set.

In another line of research, Mischel and colleagues (Hoffman, Mischel, & Mazze, 1981; Jeffery & Mischel, 1979) have found that the manner in which information about a target is organized depends upon the perceivers' information processing goals. They found that when subjects were instructed to read information about a target with an eye toward either remembering the information or empathizing with the target, subjects tended to organize the information primarily in terms of the target's goals (e.g., taking diet pills meant that the target's goal was to lose weight). However, when the subjects were instructed to read the information with an eye toward either forming a personality impression of the target or predicting the target's future behavior, they tended to organize the information in terms of the target's traits (e.g., certain behaviors led to inferences of the trait of dishonesty).

There is also evidence that the perceivers' processing task at the time of recall can influence the information that is recalled. Snyder and Cantor (1979), for example, had subjects read about a target who behaved in a variety of introverted and extroverted ways. After reading the information, subjects were asked to assess her suitability for one of two jobs. Half of the subjects were asked to determine whether she would be suitable for the rather introverted job of research librarian. The other half of the subjects were asked to determine whether she would be suitable for the extroverted job of real estate salesperson. Prior to making these assessments, however, all subjects were asked to write down all of the information that they could remember and considered relevant to making the assessment. Regardless of which of the jobs was in question, subjects tended to recall information that was consistent with the demands of the job and not recall information that was inconsistent with the demands of the job. Moreover, this confirmation bias was reflected in the subjects' assessments of her job suitability; regardless of which job was in question, subjects indicated that the target was suitable. [For an alternative account of the recall data, however, see Srull and Wyer (1986) and Wyer, Srull, Gordon, and Hartwick (1982).]

More recently, work by von Hippel (1990) suggests that whether perceivers' memories are driven primarily by memory of the original instance, or memory of the conceptual information that has been abstracted from the original instance, depends upon whether the perceivers' goal is to form an integrated impression of the material or not. [For discussions of the distinction between data-driven memory and conceptually driven memory, see Brooks (1978), Jacoby and Brooks (1984), and Roediger and Blaxton (1987).] Specifically, von Hippel has found that when perceivers process information about a meaningful social unit (e.g., behaviors from a single person), they have better conceptually driven memory (i.e., recognition memory) but worse data-driven memory (i.e., fragment completion) than when they process information about a meaningless social unit (e.g., behaviors from a random collection of people). In other words, when subjects expect information to be conceptually related, they attempt to integrate the information and abstract themes from the information. However, when they do not expect information to be conceptually related, they do not attempt to abstract common themes and process the information in a relatively raw form. As a result of these different processing goals, subjects who expect the information to be thematically related do better on memory measures that tap their memory for the concepts, while subjects who expect the information to be thematically unrelated do better on memory measures that tap their memory for the original instances.

Taken together, the work on outcome dependency, accountability, and person memory suggests that manipulations of interaction contexts that are likely to induce different perceiver goals are an important variable in the impression formation process. At some level, of course, this is a rediscovery of an old fact, demonstrated in the Berscheid *et al.* (1976) and Zajonc (1960) experiments cited earlier. But what is important about the recent work is that it is contained in several series of studies that embody the recognition that the purposes for which perceivers gather information matter greatly in the impressions that are formed. Indeed, the conclusion that emerges from this recent research is that without knowing a perceiver's goals, it is impossible to specify the kind of impression that will be formed of the target (Bargh, 1989).

II. Interaction Goals and Social Interaction

Having found evidence of a renaissance in research examining the impact that goals have on social perception, we now turn to the more difficult question of specifying how perceivers' goals influence person perception in fairly specific ways. Recently, we (Hilton *et al.*, 1989) have proposed a general model for social interaction that builds upon Jones and Thibaut's (1958) notion of interaction goals. More specifically, we have proposed that prior to initiating an interaction, interactants evaluate the goals that they have for the interaction in light of information that they have about both the situation (e.g., situational norms and resources) and their fellow interactants (i.e., expectancy information). The sources of these goals range along a continuum. At one end are the relatively permanent goals created by the interactants' needs and life circumstances. An individual driven by needs for achievement, for example, will bring competitive issues to many interaction situations. Similarly, someone whose life circumstances are dominated by a need to find a job will seek to fulfill that goal in many interactions. At the other end are the relatively transitory goals generated by circumstances specific to the interaction at hand. Someone who is waiting for a flight that has been delayed, for example, may seek out companionship to help pass the time. Someone who is attempting to make tight connections, on the other hand, probably will not set companionship as a goal. Based upon the evaluations the interactants perform, they then choose specific interaction tactics to employ during the interaction. The stranded passenger may attempt to strike up a conversation with a kindly looking gentleman. The unemployed dinner guest may try to work his plight into the dinner conversation. As the interaction unfolds, the interactants reassess the interaction in light of new information they acquire about both their fellow interactants and the situation. They then generate new interaction tactics to employ as the interaction proceeds. This process of evaluation and tactic generation continues until the interaction is terminated. [For a related analysis of the reactive nature of interaction strategies, see Bargh (1990).]

So far, we have concentrated most of our efforts on applying the interaction goals model to the literature on the self-fulfilling prophecy (Merton, 1948). From that literature, it is clear that expectations frequently lead to behavioral and/or perceptual confirmation. Teachers who expect students to excel during the coming year, for example, ask more challenging questions and elicit superior performances from their students (Rosenthal & Jacobson, 1968). Conversationalists who believe that their partners are attractive behave in socially desirable ways and elicit attractive behavior from their partners (Snyder, Tanke, & Berscheid, 1977). White interviewers create harsher interviewing conditions for black applicants than for white applicants and subsequently elicit less favorable performances from the black applicants (Word, Zanna, & Cooper, 1974).

But, expectations do not always lead to self-fulfilling prophecies. Not all expectations of intellectual achievement lead to improvement (Brophy, 1983; Jussim, 1986; Swann & Snyder, 1980). Not all expectations of attractiveness lead to attractive behavior (Bond, 1972; Snyder & Haugen, 1990). Not all stereotypes lead to confirmation (Hilton & Fein, 1989; Locksley, Hepburn, & Ortiz, 1982). Indeed, in an exhaustive review of the self-fulfilling prophecy literature, Rosenthal and Rubin (1978) found that only one-third of the studies examining the effects that expectancies have on interactions found evidence of behavioral confirmation.

According to the interaction goals analysis, however, self-fulfilling prophecies should occur only when perceiver's interaction goals combine with expectancy information to produce tactics that elicit behavioral confirmation from the target (see also Jones, 1986; Miller & Turnbull, 1986). For example, imagine that Sue, a woman who has recently moved to town, is about to have separate encounters with two people. The first person she will encounter is the building manager of a small apartment complex where she has just rented an apartment. The second person is a woman she is considering as a potential roommate. Imagine further that prior to interacting with either individual, she learns that each is rumored to be rude and to sometimes take advantage of others. What are the interaction goals that she is likely to formulate for each interaction? In the case of the building manager, her goal is probably to make it clear that she is not the kind of tenant who can be taken advantage of. In attempting to achieve this goal, she might choose to adopt a belligerent posture when negotiating with the building manager. She might, for example, go out of her way to demand that trivial repairs be made to the apartment before she moves in. Moreover, as a consequence of her actions, she may appear to the manager to be rude and he may respond in kind, thus confirming her initial expectations. In the case of the potential roommate, however, it seems likely that Sue will be more concerned with gaining an accurate assessment of the person than with convincing the person that she is not someone who can be stepped upon. Given that she is not yet committed to the roommate, we can imagine that she might look carefully at the potential roommate's behavior in an attempt to determine whether or not the rumors are true. Moreover, nothing about her strategy would seem to guarantee that the potential roommate will behaviorally confirm her expectations in quite the same way that the manager will confirm those expectations.

A number of studies provide both direct and indirect support for this view of the interaction. Indirect support comes from studies that have examined the effects that negative expectations have in different social contexts. Both Kelley and Stahelski (1970) and Snyder and Swann (1978), for example, found that when perceivers expected their opponents in a competitive game to be competitive, they behaved more competitively themselves. Bond (1972), Ickes, Patterson, Rajecki, and Tanford (1982), and Hilton and Darley (1985), on the other hand, found that when perceivers expected their conversational partners to be cold, they behaved less coldly themselves. While these results seem at first glance to be contradictory, they make sense if we assume that perceivers adopt interaction tactics on the basis of their interaction goals. Perceivers in both the Kelley and Stahelski and the Snyder and Swann studies were presumably interested in winning the game they were playing. With that as a goal, a reasonable strategy would be to behave competitively if one expected one's opponent to be competitive. Perceivers in the other three studies, however, were not interested in winning a game. Instead, they were presumably interested in having as pleasant a conversation as possible. Given pleasantness as a goal, a reasonable strategy for achieving that goal would be to compensate for the anticipated shortcomings of one's partner by behaving exceptionally warmly (Ickes et al., 1982).

More direct support for the interaction goals framework has been found in studies by Darley, Fleming, Hilton, and Swann (1988) and Neuberg (1989). Darley et al. examined the impact that perceivers' interaction goals have on the tactics that perceivers adopted during an interaction. All subjects were led to believe that they were participating in an interpersonal communication study, and that they would be interacting with a person who, they were told, might be the kind of person who "chokes" under pressure. Half of the perceivers were then placed in an interaction setting that made the goal of evaluating the target relevant, and half were placed in an interaction setting that made the goal of avoiding social awkwardness relevant. Orthogonal to this manipulation, half the perceivers interacted with a target who, if probed, provided evidence that was consistent with the expectancy, and half interacted with a target who, if probed, provided evidence that was inconsistent with the expectancy. Consistent with predictions, subjects in the potential partner conditions asked more expectancy-relevant questions and were more likely to discover the truth or fiction of the expectancy information than were subjects in the casual conversation conditions.

Conceptually similar results have been found by Neuberg (1989). Neuberg found that negative expectancy information had considerable impact on the impressions perceivers formed when they were given no particular motivation to be accurate. When, however, perceivers were specifically told that accuracy was very important, the negative expectancy information had little impact relative to the no-expectancy controls. Moreover, structural modeling suggested that these effects were mediated by the more penetrating, expectancy-relevant questions asked by subjects who were motivated to be accurate.

III. An Accuracy-Driven Classification of Interaction Goals

Although the interaction goal framework has been helpful in illuminating some of the complexities of the self-fulfilling prophecy, as it stands, the framework is not without problems. The first problem with the framework is that it is often difficult to specify the nature of the perceivers' interaction goals in ways that are consistent with respect to levels of abstraction. Obviously, at a concrete level of description it is possible to say that perceivers have as many goals as they have interactions. When someone is stopped for speeding, for example, his or her goal may be described as avoiding being issued a speeding ticket. Should we then move to a higher level of abstraction and refer to a class of "interactions determined by blame-avoiding goals"? As a matter of pragmatics, the answer partly depends on whether this is a class of interactions that has similar perceptual consequences for the interactants. If it is, then moving to a higher level seems appropriate. But if the interactions do not produce similar perceptual outcomes, then little is gained by moving to the more abstract level. [For recent examples of hierarchical models of goals, see Martin and Tesser (1989) and Vallacher and Wegner (1987).]

The second problem that emerges is that it is frequently the case that a person has more than one interaction goal. As a potential employer, for example, the person is not only concerned with assessing job applicants' aptitudes, he or she is also probably concerned with creating a favorable impression on the applicants and clearly communicating the demands that will come with the job. Similarly, when a person is preparing to attend a business lunch, he or she may seek to impress the company's clients while simultaneously using the lunch to pump competitors for information.

The problem that confronts us, then, is how to partition interaction goals in ways that preserve the insights that the interaction goals concept can bring to social perception without reducing social perception to a case-by-case analysis. Jones and Thibaut (1958) attempted to deal with this problem by breaking interaction goals into three sets: Causal-genetic sets, value-maintenance sets, and situation-matching sets. When perceivers are in a causal-genetic set they are attempting to determine what has caused their interaction partners to behave in a particular way. When perceivers are in a value-maintenance set they are attempting to determine what it is about their fellow interactants that makes perceivers want to approach or avoid them. When perceivers are in a situation-matching set they are attempting to determine what norms and social sanctions are appropriate for the current interaction.

Our own approach has been to focus primarily upon the extent to which the goals of the perceiver are likely to lead to an explicit concern with assessing what another person is like. On some occasions, forming an accurate perception is an interaction goal of the perceiver, and the situation allows for a reasonably discrete period of time to be devoted to that before the interaction begins. Putting this another way, some interaction goals lead perceivers to become explicitly concerned with determining what another person is like, and the situation allows for, or can be manipulated to allow for, that possibility. Evaluating someone for a job is a task that typically places a premium on accurate impression formation, at least in the domains that are thought to be relevant to the job. On other occasions, there is relatively little emphasis on arriving at any generalized representation of another person. Ordering dinner in a restaurant, for example, is a task that requires patrons to interact with members of the wait staff, but it places relatively little emphasis on discovering what the members of the wait staff are really like. For the sake of convenience, we will refer to the state in which perceivers find themselves when their interaction goals lead them to focus explicitly on impression formation as an ''assessment set.'' When people are in an assessment set, they weigh possibilities carefully, attempt to look at people from a variety of perspectives, and are concerned with arriving at correct impressions. They are as open to new information as they can ever be.

In contrast, we will refer to the state in which perceivers find themselves when their interaction goals lead them to form impressions rather incidentally as an ''action set.'' When people are in an action set they are busily working toward some fairly specific goal that is only incidentally related to impression formation. Moreover, they are concerned with processing new information and arriving at accurate impressions only to the extent that these endeavors will help them achieve that goal.

That there may be some utility in distinguishing between assessment sets and action sets is suggested by several theorists in the social psychological literature. For instance, a number of theorists have suggested that a perceiver's openness to new information changes over time. Bruner (1957), for example, argued that perceivers are initially quite open to information relevant to a perceptual hypothesis, but that as the perceiver gathers increasing amounts of information relevant to the hypothesis, the openness to subsequent information decreases. Similarly, Jones and Gerard (1967), argued that there exists a "basic antinomy between openness to change and the desire to preserve a pre-existing view or conviction" (p. 227). Unlike Bruner, however, Jones and Gerard argued that the organism's openness to change depends upon where in the decision process the organism is. Specifically, they argued that prior to making a decision the organism is relatively open to new, unexpected information. After arriving at a decision, however, the organism is much less receptive to new information.

More recently, Heckhausen and Gollwitzer (1987; Gollwitzer & Heckhausen, 1987) have made a distinction that is similar to the basic antinomy of Jones and Gerard in their work stemming from Heckhausen's (1986) Rubicon model of action. According to Heckhausen and Gollwitzer, predecisional individuals operate in a deliberative mind set in which they actively consider the positive and negative consequence associated with the pending decision. In contrast, postdecisional individuals operate in an implemental mindset in which they are no longer open to information that runs counter to their decision, but instead focus only on the information necessary for implementing the decision (e.g., when and where to act on the decision).

Along somewhat similar lines, Higgins and Bargh (1987) concluded their review of the person memory literature by noting that perceivers' goals play a critical role in determining whether perceivers incorporate inconsistent information in the impression they maintain. Specifically, Higgins and Bargh argue that perceivers will consider and remember inconsistent information only if they have the goal of forming an impression of the person. Once the goal of forming the impression has been satisfied, perceivers are less likely to incorporate and remember inconsistent information. In other words, when perceivers are testing impressions rather than forming impressions, they are unlikely to incorporate inconsistent information.

A. ASSESSMENT SETS

1. Factors Leading to Assessment Sets

But what determines when a person will be in an assessment set rather than an action set? Sometimes, assessment sets are induced directly. A search committee is charged with finding the best available person for a departmental position. A customs inspector is charged with determining which people may be smuggling drugs. A jury is charged with determining the guilt or innocence of the defendant. In each of these cases, there is an overt concern with accurately assessing the target's personality. Similarly, in many experiments the experimenter tells subjects that they should try to arrive at an accurate impression of the target (e.g., Neuberg, 1989; Shapiro & Hilton, 1988).

At other times, however, the assessment set is induced indirectly. A perceiver who learns that his fate is tied to the fate of another, for example, may become concerned with arriving at an accurate impression of the person because an accurate impression will allow him to better predict the other person's behavior and, consequently, better predict his own fate (Berscheid *et al.*, 1976). Similarly, when perceivers are told that they will be held accountable for the impressions they form, these instructions may lead them to weigh carefully the information that is available about the target (Tetlock, 1983). Conversational demands (Grice, 1975) can also influence the set perceivers adopt. Transmission instructions (Cohen, 1961; Zajonc, 1960), for example, lead perceivers to focus on telling a simple, integrated story, perhaps at the expense of accuracy and detail.

In still other instances, the unfolding of events may trigger an assessment set. A gifted student may, for example, do poorly on an exam. Or a typically passive friend may lash out in anger during an argument. Considerable evidence now suggests that when perceivers are surprised (i.e., when their expectations for a person or situation are violated), they begin to process attributionally relevant information more elaborately (e.g., Hastie, 1984; Lau & Russell, 1980; Pyszczynski & Greenberg, 1981; Wong & Weiner, 1981) and to pay greater attention to the target's expectancy-relevant behaviors (Bargh & Thein, 1985; Erber & Fiske, 1984; Hilton, Klein, & von Hippel, in press; White & Carlston, 1983). Hilton *et al.* (in press), for example, found that when perceivers encounter expectancy-consistent information, they devote relatively little attention to the perceptual task and form relatively simple impressions of the target. In contrast, when perceivers encounter expectancy-inconsistent information, they devote considerable attention to the task and form complex, multifaceted impressions of the target. In other words, as perceivers encounter expectancy-inconsistent information they often begin evaluating the target in a much more deliberate, and often effortful, way than when the target behaves in expectancy-consistent ways.

Finally, the unfolding of events will sometimes conspire to make perceivers suspicious of the target's motives. People may become suspicious, for example, when an employee compliments his boss on her taste in fashion, or when a woman suddenly develops a romantic interest in an elderly man of considerable wealth. When perceivers become suspicious, they begin to wonder why a person is behaving in a particular way. Does a compliment reflect the complimenter's genuine enthusiasm, or does it reflect his desire to ingratiate? Does a woman's affectionate behavior toward a wealthy octogenarian reflect love, or does it reflect greed? Moreover, once suspicious, perceivers are often quite willing to suspend their judgments of the suspect until information can be obtained that can disambiguate the suspect's motives. Fein, Hilton, and Miller (1990), for example, found that when perceivers were suspicious of a target's motives, they refrained from making dispositional inferences. Indeed, suspicious perceivers successfully avoided falling prey to the correspondence bias (Gilbert & Jones, 1986; Ross, 1977). More generally, as perceivers become suspicious of the target's motives, they will often expend considerable cognitive resources in a deliberate attempt to determine the true motive(s) of the target.

2. Distinctions among Assessment Sets

Recall that when people are in an assessment set they are explicitly concerned with forming impressions of their fellow interactants. Perceivers in an assessment set are interested in knowing what their fellow interactants are like, because assessors think that this is a guide to how they are likely to behave, or because some specific interaction goal has caused them to derive this set. In a review of the accuracy literature, Swann (1984) distinguishes between global accuracy and circumscribed accuracy. Global accuracy refers to the perceivers' ability to predict someone's behavior independent of the specific situation in which the behavior occurs, the audience that is present, or the time at which the behavior occurs. Circumscribed accuracy refers to the perceivers' ability to predict how someone will behave in the perceivers' presence, in a limited number of situations, and in a fairly constrained period of time. Swann argues that although perceivers are not terribly good at achieving high levels of global accuracy, they are extremely good at achieving high levels of circumscribed accuracy. Moreover, Swann argues that from the standpoint of pragmatics, circumscribed accuracy is often sufficient for the perceivers' needs. A similar distinction can be drawn with regard to assessment sets. Sometimes, perceivers who are in an assessment set are concerned with assessing their fellow interactants' general personalities, other times the interaction context gives them more specific interaction goals which lead to a desire for an assessment of the other in a circumscribed domain.

It is instructive to attempt to think of examples of situations in which a general assessment set is created. One situation that seems likely to lead to a general assessment set is when a perceiver meets someone for the first time, and it is clear that there may be many future meetings. Upon meeting a new roommate, for example, a person might try to figure out whether the roommate will be smart, kind, humorous, outgoing, etc. Similarly, when a new soldier arrives in the barracks, or when an academic department hires a new assistant professor, there may be considerable attention given to getting to know the new person.

But it seems to us that these interactions are rare. Instead, most of the time when perceivers are in an assessment set, they are attempting to assess their fellow interactants with some more specific purposes in mind. When a baseball scout watches a young pitcher, for example, she is attempting to determine if the pitcher has potential. In other words, the scout is in an assessment set, in that she is explicitly concerned with forming an impression of the pitcher's ability, but she is only concerned with forming an impression of the pitcher on dimensions that she thinks will predict his success at the game. Similarly, in a pickup tennis game, we want to pick an opponent who is reasonably matched in skills to ours. Sitting next to somebody on a plane, we wonder if he has the wherewithal to carry on an interesting conversation. Deciding among undergraduates on which to advise, we want to know which has the intelligence and self-discipline to carry through a project.

Indeed, even in the ''general'' instances we cited above, some specificity guides the assessment; the college student wants to know how the other will be as a roommate, the members of the platoon want to know how the draftee will be as a comrade in arms, and the department wants to know what the faculty member will be like as an intellectual and social colleague. In other words, even though the perceivers in each of these situations want to know the answers to many questions, the anticipated social interaction setting confers more importance to certain questions than to others.[1]

A similar point can be made concerning the effects that expectancy disconfirmation will have on assessment sets. We earlier noted that expectancy disconfirmation during an interaction is one of the things that is likely to trigger an assessment set. Here, too, the assessment sets in which perceivers find themselves are likely to be narrowly focused. If, for example, a perceiver encounters someone that he expects to be hostile, but who acts very pleasantly, he may reassess his impression of the target, but the reassessment will, at least initially, be rather limited. Specifically, the perceiver can entertain two hypotheses—that his expectations were wrong about the person; or that his expectations may still be right, but that there are strong situational demands that are leading the person to behave in a nonhostile fashion. Few of us, for example, would be convinced that an accused murderer is not violent simply because he does not behave violently in court. Moreover, if the perceiver has insufficient evidence to decide between these two options, the strength of the prior expectancy competes with the plausibility of the various situational pressures.

Following Swann (1984), we propose to call assessment sets that lead to a concern with assessing a fellow interactant's general personality characteristics and abilities *global assessment sets* and to call assessment sets that lead to a concern with assessing fairly specific characteristics of a fellow interactant *circumscribed assessment sets*. When perceivers are in a global assessment set, they are explicitly concerned with discovering what their fellow interactants are like on many dimensions. When perceivers are in a circumscribed assessment set,

---

[1]It is interesting to notice that, in modern assessment theory, the assessor is very concerned with knowing in advance exactly what are the purposes to which the assessment will be put. There has been a movement away, amply supported by the literature on the success of clinical predictions, from a model in which one first forms a general impression of an individual, and then derives specific predictions from that general model.

they are equally concerned with explicitly figuring out what their fellow interactants are like, but their concern is limited to a relatively small number of dimensions made salient by their goals for the interaction.

3. Assessment Sets and Perceptual Accuracy

One reason for distinguishing between global assessment sets and circumscribed assessment sets is that perception in the case of circumscribed assessment should be more "accurate," in several limited but important senses, as compared to global assessments. First, we would offer the generalization that there should be a higher degree of consensus among perceivers about circumscribed rather than global assessments. Second, allowing ourselves a blanket "all other things being equal," we would expect circumscribed assessments to converge better with the self-reports of the target individual on the same dimensions. Third, in those instances when a criterion can be offered that the field would accept as instantiating "truth," we would suggest that the perceivers would be nearer that criterion if the interaction goals that induced the search were circumscribed rather than global. However, we also ought to add that these convergences cannot be expected to be complete. Different people can hold different templates about what dimensions are important for a job, and thus can come to a very different assessment of the same individual for that job. Alternatively, similar social situations may arouse different interaction goals in different individuals. Paired with another, you and I may have different goals to be achieved with that other. I may seek to bring him to like me, you to bring him to subordinate himself to you. We would then assess very different qualities of the other, and come to very different overall assessments of him.

An interesting second-order possibility arises concerning the relationships between circumscribed evaluation goals and perceptual accuracy. What happens to the accuracy of perception when a person has evaluated another on certain dimensions, and then is asked to judge that person on other dimensions? As perceivers, we may emerge from an encounter in a social setting that imposed only certain limited assessment goals with the unexamined feeling that we do know about the other's personality in general. We may be willing to articulate a very general image of the other's "whole personality." What remains to be examined is the degree to which the general impression is conditioned by the specific impressions that were dictated by the original interaction goals. One of the most psychologically interesting questions that arises from an interaction goals analysis concerns what is "learned" about a target individual on dimensions not relevant to the assessment goals set up by original interaction situation. It might be that these new dimensions are filled in from the implicit personality theory of the perceiver, but filled in with some (misplaced) confidence; the confidence stemming from the fact that the perceiver knows that he has had extensive interaction with the target. Thus we are suggesting that there might be an ''overgeneralization error'' which involves the tendency to think we know everything about an individual when we only know some things. One consequence of this is that a perceiver is likely to be inaccurate in judging dimensions of the target that were not relevant to the initial interaction.

B. ACTION SETS

1. Factors Leading to Action Sets

Although we have spent a considerable amount of time discussing assessment sets, it is important to remember that in many interactions perceivers may be relatively unconcerned with determining what their fellow interactants are like. Indeed, based on an intuitive examination of our day-to-day doings, we suggest that action sets are far more common than assessment sets, and that within action sets there is considerably more variability than within assessment sets. In part, this reflects our belief that most of the time people are doing and perceiving rather than perceiving and doing. And, quite often, they may be doing many things at once. In other words, most of the time people form impressions incidental to the attainment of specific interaction goals rather than as the result of deliberately attempting to assess their fellow interactants. A harried usher urges people to keep moving in an attempt to get everyone seated before the performance begins. An anxious student asks her instructor to extend the deadline for an assignment. In each case, the person may form a vivid impression of his or her fellow interactants. The usher may think that the members of the audience are slow and cumbersome. The student may see her instructor as stern and unreasonable. But in each case, these impressions emerge incidental to the task at hand. Putting this still another way, social perception is generally subordinate to social action.

But how can we maintain that perceivers are frequently unconcerned with attempting to figure out what their fellow interactants are like? Do not all social interactions require people to know what their fellow interactants are like in order that they may better predict their fellow interactants' behaviors? For several reasons, the answer is frequently ''no.''

First, people often find themselves in situations where the norms that govern the behaviors of others are sufficiently constraining that there is little need to know what the other person is like as an individual in order to predict how the person will behave. When we interact with a bus driver, loan officer, or waitperson, for example, we can usually predict how the person will behave even before we have met them: As passengers we can expect to be taken to our destination; as loan applicants we can expect to be listened to seriously; and, as customers in a restaurant we can expect to receive the food that we order. Similarly, the bus driver can expect us to ride to our destination quietly, the loan officer can request us to provide her with personal information that we would not normally share with others (e.g., income and debt load), and the waitperson can expect to be paid for the meal that we order. All of this can occur without anyone needing to know what the other person is like because the roles that each interactant occupies constrains and orders the behavior. (Indeed, this may be why the waitperson's greeting of, "Hi, I'm Bill and I will be your waiter tonight," is sometimes jarring—it seems to imply that more information is needed before the interaction can proceed.)

Second, social interaction is, among other things, a process of negotiation, and, as various authors have noted (e.g., Athay & Darley, 1981; Goffman, 1959), one of the commodities up for negotiation is the personalities of the interactants. An example may convey this point. Let us suppose that punctuality is important to me in a relationship that I am beginning with you. This may be because punctuality is a trait I value in all others, or because there is something in the particular nature of our relationship that causes punctuality to be important (e.g., perhaps we will be carpooling). Certainly to assess your punctuality may be a goal in the beginning stages of our relationship. However, I am also likely to engage in various interaction tactics designed to shape your actions toward punctuality, and to get you to commit yourself to being a punctual person in our relationship. If punctuality is a general issue for me, I will seize a chance to disclose to you how the early circumstances of my life made it so—perhaps a story of being left waiting by a parent in a strange place and being accosted by strangers, or being the recipient of criticism from coaches or teachers because an unpunctual parent was always dropping me off late to practice sessions or music lessons. If punctuality concerns arise because of the particular nature of our relationship, I will tell stories about being in a carpool with an unpunctual person, and how awful that was, or emphasize the degree to which people in my office depend on my arriving on time, or how the rituals that I use to prepare for my midmorning lecture require timely arrival.

The reason that we refer to this interaction as a process of negotiation is because while I am making my concerns clear, the other person is also making his clear. He may be telling stories about how anxious it made him to drive with a nervous person who kept pointing out road hazards and stepping on imaginary brake pedals. The deal here is clear. For him, I become a phlegmatic passenger, even if my usual inclination is toward nervous passengerhood. For me, he becomes punctual.

To the extent that perceivers are successful in negotiating their fellow interactants' personalities, it is less critical to suppose that there is ever a time at which they consciously take stock of their fellow interactants. Indeed, recent research by Gilbert and colleagues (Gilbert, Pelham, & Krull, 1988) suggests that because of the cognitive demands that social interaction places on perceivers, perceivers frequently rely upon impressions that are formed in a semiautomatic fashion rather than upon impressions resulting from a more controlled, deliberate consideration of the evidence (see also Bargh, 1989; Bargh & Thein, 1985). Moreover, even if perceivers become aware of the constraints that their negotiations have placed on their fellow interactants, research on the fundamental attribution error (Ross, 1977) and perceiver-induced constraint (Gilbert & Jones, 1986) suggests that perceivers will rarely take this information into sufficient account in the impressions they form.

Because perceivers who are in action sets are concerned with perception only incidentally, and because they frequently underestimate the extent to which they are responsible for the behavior of their fellow interactants (Kelley & Stahelski, 1970; Gilbert & Jones, 1986), then one implication that action sets have for our understanding of social perception is that expectancy effects should be relatively more robust when perceivers are in action sets. In a relatively direct test of this proposition, Shapiro and Hilton (1988) had subjects play a game patterned after the noise weapon game of Snyder and Swann (1978). In this game, the subjects are told they are competing against another subject and that their task is to react as quickly as possible each time they see a light by pressing a reaction-time button. They are also told that on some trials they will have access to a noise weapon that can be used to impede their opponent's performance but that on other trials their opponent will have access to the noise weapon and can use it to impede their performance. Snyder and Swann found that the introduction of a hostile expectancy led perceivers to behave in a more hostile fashion (i.e., make greater use of the noise weapon) and to elicit more hostile behavior in return.

Half of the subjects in the Shapiro and Hilton (1988) study were given information indicating that their opponent was hostile and half were given no such information. Independent of this expectancy manipulation, all of the subjects' sets were manipulated. Half of the subjects were placed in an action set by telling them that their goal in the interaction was to win the game. The other half were placed in an assessment set by telling them that their goal was to use the game and the noise weapon as a way of finding out what kind of person their interaction partner was. Thus, half of the conditions were designed to replicate the Snyder and Swann experiment while the remaining half were designed to place subjects in an assessment set. All subjects subsequently played against a confederate who responded to their hostile moves with a matching strategy.

Consistent with predictions, when the subjects were in an action set the expectancy had a strong influence. Subjects who expected their partners to be hostile made greater use of the noise weapon and emerged from the interaction believing quite confidently that their partner was indeed hostile. When subjects were in an assessment set, however, the expectancy information had very little effect. Subjects who expected their partners to be hostile were no more likely to use the noise weapon, nor were they likely to emerge from the interaction believing that their partner was hostile.

Conceptually similar results have been found by Hilton, Fein, and von Hippel (1990). Hilton *et al.* allowed subjects to participate in face-to-face interactions. Half of the subjects were randomly designated as targets and half were designated as perceivers. Prior to interacting, half of the perceivers were given information indicating that their interaction partner might have a cold personality and half were given no such information. All subjects were then told that during the experiment they would be playing a game much like the popular "Newlywed Game" found on television. After learning about the game, subjects were asked to spend a few minutes writing a brief outline of their favorite game show and were left alone with each other for 10 minutes. The subjects were given no particular instructions concerning how they should spend the time once they had completed their outlines. Following this initial period, the subjects were asked to fill out a preliminary evaluation of their partners. Once these evaluations were finished, the subjects learned that in the game they would be playing, the perceiver's task would be to predict how the target would react to a variety of situations. The subjects were then given 10 minutes together in which the perceiver could interview the target in preparation for the game. Following this preparation period, the subjects were again asked to fill out an evaluation of their partners.

Hilton *et al.* (1990) predicted that during the initial interaction, perceivers should have been in an action set. After all, their primary task at that point was to write a brief outline of their favorite game show. During the second interaction, however, the primary task of the perceivers should have been to try to figure out what their partners were like, given that they were told that winning the game would require them to be able to predict their partners' behavior to a variety of situations. In other words, during the second interaction subjects should have been in an assessment set. Consistent with predictions, perceivers' initial ratings of their partners exhibited the typical expectancy confirmation effect. Perceivers who expected their partners to be cold rated them as colder than did perceivers who did not have the cold expectancy. The expectancy confirmation effect was eliminated, however, by the second interaction.

Although both the Shapiro and Hilton (1988) and Hilton *et al.* (1990) results are consistent with the notion that a person in an action set often ignores the influence of the processes generated by that set, and infers that the interactant has personality traits congruent with the actions elicited, a number of questions remain. First, to what degree is it generally true that perceivers in action sets form personality dispositions about the interactants that are consistent with the dimensions of behavior that the interactant displayed in the encounter? For example, the role-driven constraints that operate on waitpersons typically ensure that they are cheerful and enthusiastic in their interactions with customers. After encountering a cheerful waitperson, do we as customers then conclude that the person is dispositionally cheerful and enthusiastic? Or, if prior to a guest lecture by a European scholar we remind our class to behave with the visible standards of respect that we think that person expects, do we then conclude that the class is dispositionally respectful if they show respect to the scholar?

Second, do we form general impressions of the other's personality that transcend the action dimensions that the other person displays in their behavior in our interaction? Because in action sets we are sometimes so consciously focused on producing certain behaviors from the interactants, do we not realize at least that we bent our energies to produce those actions even from those who did not have the sorts of personalities that would naturally lead to those behaviors, and thus not infer that the complete range of their personalities were inferable from their constrained behaviors?

Although relatively little research has addressed these two questions, a study by Swann, Pelham, and Roberts (1988) suggests that under certain conditions perceivers do recognize the roles that they play in producing a target's behavior. Specifically, Swann et al. had subjects play a game simulation of the nuclear arms race. Half of the subjects were given the goal of convincing their opponents that they would not hesitate to initiate a first strike (offensive set), while the remaining half were given the goal of simply matching their actions to their opponents' actions (defensive set). Swann et al. reasoned that the offensive goal would lead subjects to view themselves as causal agents and to see themselves as influencing their opponents' behaviors. In contrast, they reasoned that the matching goal would lead subjects to see their opponents as the causal agents in the interaction. Consistent with this reasoning, Swann et al. found that the offensive goal led subjects to "chunk" the interaction in "self-causal" units and to refrain from making dispositional inferences about their opponents.

A third question concerns the inferential mechanisms that operate in action sets. That is, assuming that there are certain conditions under which we make "unwarranted" inferences from behaviors that we induce in action sets, what inferential mechanisms produce these conclusions? Are they, to use a currently broadly used concept, "automatic" in nature? Alternatively, are they subject to some sorts of control? One way of concretizing the question is to ask whether the perceiver interactant, knowing that he or she has constrained the behavior of the other individual, becomes alert to a particular class of clues that the interactant could emit that signals that the behavior is done for constrained reasons? Recent research by Fleming and Darley (1989, in press) suggests that this is so. They had subjects observe an actor reading aloud an essay that supported a particular side of a controversial issue. Consistent with research on the correspondence bias, subjects tended to attribute an attitude to the actor that was consistent with the position advocated in the essay, even when the subjects were aware that the actor had been assigned to read that particular essay. More importantly, however, the subjects also demonstrated considerable sensitivity to the constraints inherent to the situation facing the actor and searched for clues that could reveal the actor's true attitudes on the issue. For example, if a frown flickered across the actor's face prior to reading the essay, the subjects attributed counteressay attitudes to the reader. In contrast, if the actor smiled just before reading the essay, subjects inferred essay-consistent attitudes that were equal in extremity to the attitudes inferred from essays that were freely chosen by the actor. These results suggest that, under the right conditions, perceivers will actively search for cues that can reveal the constraints that are operating in a particular interaction.

2. Action Sets and Perceptual Accuracy

The perspective that emerges from the current analysis is one that makes the notion of perceptual accuracy somewhat more problematic than it was before. Or, to put it more precisely, it seems to make it more beside the point. If individuals in action sets are creating the personalities of their fellow interactants by these negotiating processes, then the image of the individual assessing certain characteristics of the other before entering an interaction becomes less applicable.

Does this perspective, carried to its logical extreme of personality as a product of social negotiation, discredit the utility of the concept of social perception? We think not, for one direct and one more complex reason. First, the direct reason: our sense is that the two processes of social perception and personality negotiation "live side by side" in real social interactions. Our perceptions of our fellow interactants often cue us to the specific arenas in which to carry out our negotiations with them. If we perceive that the other individual is a conservative, for instance, we are given a vocabulary in which we can make our needs for punctuality clear and salient. We may also be able to infer our fellow interactants' goals, which will cue us to what incentives we have to offer them, which will, in other words, enable us to construct the personalities we will have for them. Thus even within a negotiation of personality through social interaction model, processes of perception of the characteristics of the other still have a major role to play.

Next, the more indirect reason: although it is probably the case that we, as perceiver interactants, play a larger and more active role in shaping the actions of others than we are aware of, it is still the case that our vocabulary for describing other individuals has the vocabulary of social perception and social accuracy built into it. We generally describe others in terms of a vocabulary of personality that does not leave much room for the insight that we shaped the actions from which we infer the personality of the other. In other words, we think in person perception terms, even when a large mixture of social interaction processes have colored the inputs to our person perception decisions.

IV. Summary

At the broadest level, the analysis that we are proposing is intended to serve as a reminder that social perception is critically dependent upon the goals that perceivers have for the interaction. Moreover, in many interactions, these goals may have very little to do with forming an impression, much less an accurate impression, of their fellow interactants. Stated this way, this is something that "everybody knows" (e.g., see Jones & Thibaut, 1958; Swann, 1984). Yet it is not a perspective that has gained sufficient recognition at a deep level. In the typical person perception experiment, the perceiver is someone who knows that he or she is participating in a person perception experiment and who, consequently, is likely to be in an assessment set and exhibit a relatively high level of concern with global accuracy. While this is certainly a goal that perceivers may adopt in their daily interactions, it is only one goal, and one that we believe occurs with surprisingly little frequency in the real world.

Indeed, it is our sense that we psychologists have inadvertently backed into assuming that the goals we create in our perceivers when they know that they are the subjects of psychological experiments are the goals typical of all interaction situations. Instead, experiments are one of the few things that we can think of that trigger a global assessment set. Most of the time people are not terribly concerned with figuring out what their fellow interactants are like, except as that occurs incidental to their other goals. Moreover, when people are in an assessment set, they are usually concerned with assessing their fellow interactants on a fairly limited number of dimensions.

Implicit in this belief is a methodological message. As noted above, a number of what we might call second generation person perception studies have appeared in which the goals of the perceiver are explicitly manipulated, and the effects of these manipulations are then observed on the perceivers' subsequent impressions. While the results of these studies have successfully demonstrated the important roles that perceivers' goals can have on the impressions they form, there is a sense in which even these studies underestimate the roles that these goals have. After all, in the typical study the information that is available to the perceivers is held constant. But in social interactions, perceivers' goals not only influence how they process the information that is available, they also are likely to influence what information becomes available. A perceiver who is about to play tennis with someone will spend time and resources finding out what the person's tennis ability is likely to be. A perceiver who is about to ask another person out on a date will spend time and resources finding out what the person is going to be like as a dinner companion. Notice that the impressions that the two perceivers form could be radically different, even when the target is the same person. In other words, one of the recommendations that comes out of the current analysis is that we need to move to what we might call a "third generation" of studies, in which we allow the goals of the perceiver to actually influence the course of the interaction.

As an example of this kind of "third generation" study, we are struck by the research done by John Holmes and associates on the development of trust in close relationships. Whether or not one's potential partner in a close relationship is trustworthy is certainly a central concern of participants. But how do people assess their partners' trustworthiness? What Holmes and colleagues have shown is that the establishment of mutual trust is a process in which aspects of social perception are inextricably intertwined with processes of social negotiation and interaction.

Initially, interactants start out with an agenda that seems to be a social percep-tual one—they seek to determine whether the other is predictable. Then, if predictability is established, they seek to determine whether that predictability can be attributed to the possession of a set of traits that can be referred to as the "dependability prototype," which includes honesty, reliability, cooper-ativeness, and benevolence (Rempel, Holmes, & Zanna, 1985). As the interac-tion progresses, however, a number of individual differences enter into determin-ing the interactants' behaviors and attributions. Of particular interest are those that lead to different interaction strategies. Miller, Lefcourt, Holmes, Ware, and Saleh (1986), for example, found that individuals with a high locus of internal control were more likely to make their own feelings and needs clear in the relationship. By making these needs clear, these individuals also made obvious to the other person the particular dimensions that they were using to evaluate the person and the relationship. Thus, they created for themselves the possibility of clearly assessing the other's commitment to the relationship. In contrast, low-control subjects, who left their needs more imprecisely specified, faced the problem of attributing the others' failures to meet their needs either to not understanding those needs, or to a lack of commitment to the relationship.

Notice that as the relationship progresses, the definition of trust alters. People are first concerned with assessing trust as a general prototype. As the relationship continues, people begin to assess their partners not in terms of general trust-worthiness, but rather in terms of how trustworthy their partners are with respect to commitment to this particular relationship. Often, the question that the interac-tants try to answer is whether the other person is equally committed to the relationship. Thus, each person focuses on whether his or her self-disclosures, or other contributions to the relationship, are matched by the other person. For this phase of the interaction, "these concerns about equal involvement motivate

people to focus on the balance in patterns of social exchange in their relationships'' (Holmes & Rempel, 1989, p. 195). Later, as this level of trust is
established, concerns over short-term reciprocity diminish.

To us, this research serves as a vivid reminder of the interconnectedness of
social perception and social interaction. The trustworthiness of the other changes
meaning during the interaction, and is explicitly assessed in response to the
interactional moves of the partners. Although freeing up perceivers in these sorts
of ways (i.e., looking both at how their perceptions change and how their
strategies change) certainly complicates experimental procedures and sometimes
muddies the precision with which we can measure the internal cognitive processes at work, it has the important advantage of giving us a more complete
understanding of the broad influences that interaction goals can have on person
perception.

At another level, the analysis we have been proposing has implications for the
concept of accuracy in person perception. For a number of reasons that we and
others have elucidated (e.g., Cronbach, 1955; Funder, 1987; Kruglanski, 1989;
Swann, 1984), the concept of accuracy is a surprisingly slippery notion. In the
current article we have made a general distinction between perceivers who are in
an assessment set versus those who are in an action set. When perceivers are in
an action set, they are concerned with accomplishing certain goals, and they tend
to treat their fellow interactants as objects whose roles in the interactions are
largely instrumental. They tend to form simple, category-based impressions of
their fellow interactants rather than integrated, individuated impressions. Moreover, while perceivers who are in action sets may be quite capable of predicting
how their fellow interactants may behave in the current interaction, they will not
be terribly accurate in predicting how their fellow interactants will behave when
the situation or role constraints change. An instructor who concludes that his
students have a finely developed sense of humor because they laugh at his jokes
in class may be surprised to find that they don't laugh at similar jokes outside of
class.

In contrast, when perceivers are in an assessment set, they are explicitly
concerned with figuring out what their fellow interactants are like. Occasionally,
an assessment set will manifest itself as a general concern with determining what
the other person is like on multiple dimensions. More often, however, an assessment set will manifest itself as a concern with determining what the other person
is like on the relatively few dimensions that are relevant to the perceivers' goals.
Based on Swann's analysis of accuracy and pragmatics, it seems likely that
perceivers who are in a global assessment set will be more likely to attain high
levels of global accuracy, while those in a circumscribed assessment set will be
more likely to attain high levels of circumscribed accuracy.

Finally, the current analysis raises one last question with regard to accuracy.
Specifically, do we always assess others on conventional personality terms? As

we saw in the literature review, it would be a mistake to assume that all contexts that created assessment sets always triggered a desire to assess the other's personality, as conceptualized on trait terms. Mischel and colleagues (Hoffman, Mischel, & Mazze, 1981; Jeffery & Mischel, 1979) have demonstrated that certain sets direct attention toward determining the other's goals rather than traits. A college coach looking over a recruit, for example, may be interested in assessing her sports skills, but also a particular definition of her personality, stressing coachability, motivation to excel, team loyalty, and so on. The important point is this: even when an individual is motivated to do a very general assessment of another person, that assessment will not always be a "personality assessment," as that is conventionally conceptualized. These and other questions that have been regarded as settled in a social perception literature that does not incorporate the goal-directed nature of social interaction become opened again when social perception is encased in social interaction.

Acknowledgments

The preparation of this article was facilitated by National Science Foundation Grants BNS-8717784 and BNS-8707412 to James L. Hilton and John M. Darley, respectively. Any opinions, findings, and conclusions or recommendations expressed in this article are those of the authors and do not necessarily reflect the views of the National Science Foundation. We gratefully acknowledge the assistance of John Bargh, Nancy Cantor, John Fleming, Dale Miller, Mark Snyder, and Bill Swann, who commented on earlier drafts of the article.

References

Anderson, N. H., & Norman, A. (1964). Order effects in impression formation in four classes of stimuli. *Journal of Abnormal and Social Psychology, 69,* 467–471.

Asch, S. E. (1946). Forming impressions of personality. *Journal of Abnormal and Social Psychology, 41,* 258–290.

Athay, M., & Darley, J. M. (1981). Toward an interpersonal action-centered theory of personality. In N. Cantor & J. F. Kihlstrom (Eds.), *Personality, cognition, and social interaction.* Hillsdale, NJ: Erlbaum.

Bargh, J. A. (1989). Conditional automaticity: Varieties of automatic influence in social perception and cognition. In J. S. Uleman & J. A. Bargh (Eds.), *Unintended thought.* New York: Guilford.

Bargh, J. A. (1990). Auto-motives: Preconscious determinants of social interaction. In E. T. Higgins & R. M. Sorrentino (Eds.), *Handbook of motivation and cognition* (Vol. 2). New York: Guilford.

Bargh, J. A., & Thein, R. D. (1985). Individual construct accessibility, person memory, and the recall–judgment link: The case of information overload. *Journal of Personality and Social Psychology, 49,* 1129–1146.

Berscheid, E., Graziano, W., Monson, T., & Dermer, M. (1976). Outcome dependency, attention, attribution, and attraction. *Journal of Personality and Social Psychology, 34,* 978–989.

Bond, M. H. (1972). Effect of an impression set on subsequent behavior. *Journal of Personality and Social Psychology, 24,* 301–305.

Brooks, L. R. (1978). Non-analytic concept formation and memory for instances. In E. Rosch and B. Lloyd (Eds.), *Cognition and categorization.* Hillsdale, NJ: Erlbaum.

Brophy, J. (1983). Research on the self-fulfilling prophecy and teacher expectations. *Journal of Educational Psychology, 75,* 631–661.

Bruner, J. (1957). On perceptual readiness. *Psychological Review, 64,* 123–152.

Bruner, J. S. (1951). Personality dynamics and the process of perceiving. In R. R. Blake and G. V. Ramsey (Eds.), *Perception—An approach to personality.* New York: Ronald Press.

Bruner, J. S., & Goodman, C. C. (1947). Value and need as organizing factors in perception. *Journal of Abnormal and Social Psychology, 42,* 33–44.

Bruner, J. S., & Postman, L. (1947). Emotional selectivity in perception and reaction. *Journal of Personality, 16,* 69–77.

Bruner, J. S., & Postman, L. (1948). Symbolic value as an organizing factor in perception. *Journal of Social Psychology, 27,* 203–208.

Cohen, A. R. (1961). Cognitive tuning as a factor affecting impression formation. *Journal of Personality, 29,* 235–245.

Cronbach, L. J. (1955). Processes affecting scores on "understanding of others" and "assumed similarity." *Psychological Bulletin, 52,* 177–193.

Darley, J. M., Fleming, J. H., Hilton, J. L., & Swann, W. B., Jr. (1988). Dispelling negative expectancies: The impact of interaction goals and target characteristics on the expectancy confirmation process. *Journal of Experimental Social Psychology, 24,* 19–36.

Erber, R., & Fiske, S. T. (1984). Outcome dependency and attention to inconsistent information. *Journal of Personality and Social Psychology, 47,* 709–726.

Erdelyi, M. H. (1974). A new look at the new look: Perceptual defense and vigilance. *Psychological Review, 81,* 1–25.

Fein, S., Hilton, J. L., & Miller, D. T. (1990). Suspicion of ulterior motivation and the correspondence bias. *Journal of Personality and Social Psychology, 58,* 753–764.

Fiske, S. T., & Neuberg, S. L. (1990). A continuum of impression formation, from category-based to individuating processes: Influences of information and motivation on attention and interpretation. In M. P. Zanna (Ed.), *Advances in experimental social psychology* (Vol. 23, pp. 1–74). San Diego, CA: Academic Press.

Fiske, S. T., Neuberg, S. L., Beattie, A. E., & Milberg, S. J. (1987). Category-based and attribute-based reactions to others: Some informational conditions of stereotyping and individuating processes. *Journal of Experimental Social Psychology, 23,* 399–427.

Fiske, S. T., & Taylor, S. E. (1984). *Social cognition.* Reading, MA: Addison-Wesley.

Fleming, J. H., & Darley, J. M. (1989). Perceiving choice and constraint: The effects of contextual and behavioral cues on attitude attribution. *Journal of Personality and Social Psychology, 56,* 27–40.

Fleming, J. H., & Darley, J. M. (in press). Mixed messages: The multiple audience problem and strategic social communication. *Social Cognition.*

Frenkel-Brunswik, E. (1949). Intolerance of ambiguity as an emotional and perceptual personality variable. *Journal of Personality, 18,* 108–143.

Funder, D. C. (1987). Errors and mistakes: Evaluating the accuracy of social judgment. *Psychological Bulletin, 101,* 75–90.

Gilbert, D. T., & Jones, E. E. (1986). Perceiver-induced constraint: Interpretations of self-generated reality. *Journal of Personality and Social Psychology, 50,* 269–280.

Gilbert, D. T., Pelham, B. W., & Krull, D. S. (1988). On cognitive busyness: When person perceivers meet persons perceived. *Journal of Personality and Social Psychology,* **54,** 733–740.

Goffman, E. (1959). *The presentation of self in everyday life.* New York: Doubleday.

Gollwitzer, P. M., & Heckhausen, H. (1987). *Breadth of attention and the counter-plea heuristic: Further evidence on the motivational vs. volitional mind-set distinction.* Unpublished manuscript, Max-Planck-Institut für psychologische Forschung, Munich.

Grice, H. P. (1975). Logic and conversation. William James Lectures, Harvard University, 1967. In P. Cole and J. L. Morgan (Eds.), *Studies in syntax* (Vol. 3, pp. 352–411). New York: Academic Press.

Hamilton, D. L., & Katz, L. B. (1975, August). *A process-oriented approach to the study of impressions.* Paper presented at the meeting of the American Psychological Association, Chicago.

Hamilton, D. L., Katz, L. B., & Leirer, V. O. (1980). Organizational processes in impression formation. In R. Hastie, T. M. Ostrom, E. B. Ebbesen, R. S. Wyer, D. L. Hamilton, & D. E. Carlston (Eds.), *Person memory: The cognitive basis of social perception* (pp. 121–153). Hillsdale, NJ: Erlbaum.

Hamilton, D. L., & Zanna, M. P. (1974). Context effects in impression formation: Changes in connotative meaning. *Journal of Personality and Social Psychology,* **29,** 649–654.

Hastie, R. (1984). Causes and effects of causal attribution. *Journal of Personality and Social Psychology,* **46,** 44–56.

Heckhausen, H. (1986). Why some time out might benefit achievement motivation research. In J. H. L. van den Bercken, E. E. J. De Bruyn, & T. C. M. Bergen (Eds.), *Achievement and task motivation* (pp. 7–39). Lisse, The Netherlands: Swets & Zeitlinger.

Heckhausen, H., & Gollwitzer, P. M. (1987). Thought contents and cognitive functioning in motivational vs. volitional states of mind. *Motivation and Emotion,* **11,** 101–120.

Heider, F. (1944). Social perception and phenomenal causality. *Psychological Review,* **51,** 358–374.

Heider, F. (1958). *The psychology of interpersonal relations.* New York: Wiley.

Higgins, E. T., & Bargh, J. A. (1987). Social cognition and social perception. *Annual Review of Psychology,* **38,** 369–425.

Hilton, J. L., & Darley, J. M. (1985). Constructing other persons: A limit on the effect. *Journal of Experimental Social Psychology,* **21,** 1–18.

Hilton, J. L., Darley, J. M., & Fleming, J. H. (1989). Self-fulfilling prophecies and self-defeating behavior. In R. Curtis (Ed.), *Self-defeating behaviors: Experimental research and practical implications* (pp. 41–65). New York: Plenum.

Hilton, J. L., & Fein, S. (1989). The role of typical diagnosticity in stereotype-based judgments. *Journal of Personality and Social Psychology,* **57,** 201–211.

Hilton, J. L., Fein, S., & von Hippel, W. (1990). Unpublished data, University of Michigan, Ann Arbor.

Hilton, J. L., Klein, J. G., & von Hippel, W. (in press). Attention allocation and impression formation. *Personality and Social Psychology Bulletin.*

Hoffman, C., Mischel, W., & Mazze, K. (1981). The role of purpose in the organization of information about behavior: Trait-based versus goal-based categories in person cognition. *Journal of Personality and Social Psychology,* **40,** 211–225.

Holmes, J. G., & Rempel, J. K. (1989). Trust in close relationships. *Review of Personality and Social Psychology,* **10,** 187–220.

Ickes, W., Patterson, M. C., Rajecki, D. W., & Tanford, S. (1982). Behavioral and cognitive consequences of reciprocal versus compensatory responses to preinteraction expectancies. *Social Cognition,* **1,** 160–190.

Jacoby, L. L., & Brooks, L. R. (1984). Nonanalytic cognition: Memory, perception and concept learning. In G. H. Bower (Ed.), *The psychology of learning and motivation: Advances in research and theory* (Vol. 18). Orlando, FL: Academic Press.

Jeffery, K. M., & Mischel, W. (1979). Effects of purpose on organization and recall of information in person perception. *Journal of Personality, 47,* 397–419.

Jones, E. E. (1985). Major developments in social psychology since 1930. In G. Lindzey & E. Aronson (Eds.), *Handbook of social psychology* (Vol. 1, pp. 47–107). New York: Random House.

Jones, E. E. (1986). Interpreting interpersonal behavior: The effects of expectancies. *Science, 234,* 41–46.

Jones, E. E., & Davis, K. E. (1965). From acts to dispositions: The attribution process in person perception. In L. Berkowitz (Ed.), *Advances in experimental social psychology* (Vol. 2). New York: Academic Press.

Jones, E. E., & Gerard, H. B. (1967). *Foundations of social psychology.* New York: Wiley.

Jones, E. E., & Goethals, G. R. (1971). Order effects in impression formation: Attribution context and the nature of the entity. In E. E. Jones, D. E. Kanouse, H. H. Kelley, R. E. Nisbett, S. Valins, & B. Weiner (Eds.), *Attribution: Perceiving the causes of behavior.* Morristown, NJ: General Learning Press.

Jones, E. E., Kanouse, D. E., Kelley, H. H., Nisbett, R. E., Valins, S., & Weiner, B. (Eds.). (1972). *Attribution: Perceiving the causes of behavior.* Morristown, NJ: General Learning Press.

Jones, E. E., & McGillis, D. (1976). Correspondent inferences and the attribution cube: A comparative reappraisal. In J. H. Harvey, W. J. Ickes, & R. F. Kidd (Eds.), *New directions in attribution research* (Vol. 1). Hillsdale, NJ: Erlbaum.

Jones, E. E., & Thibaut, J. (1958). Interaction goals as bases of inference in interpersonal perception. In R. Tagiuri & L. Petrullo (Eds.), *Person perception and interpersonal behavior.* Stanford, CA: Stanford University Press.

Jussim, L. (1986). Self-fulfilling prophecies: A theoretical and integrative review. *Psychological Review, 93,* 429–445.

Kelley, H. H. (1967). Attribution theory in social psychology. *Nebraska Symposium on Motivation, 15,* 192–238.

Kelley, H. H., & Stahelski, A. J. (1970). Social interaction basis of cooperators' and competitors' beliefs about others. *Journal of Personality and Social Psychology, 16,* 66–91.

Kruglanski, A. W. (1989). The psychology of being "right": The problem of accuracy in social perception and cognition. *Psychological Bulletin, 106,* 395–409.

Lau, R. R., & Russell, D. (1980). Attributions in the sports pages. *Journal of Personality and Social Psychology, 39,* 29–38.

Locksley, A., Hepburn, C., & Ortiz, V. (1982). Social stereotypes and judgments of individuals: An instance of the base-rate fallacy. *Journal of Experimental Social Psychology, 18,* 23–42.

Martin, L. L., & Tesser, A. (1989). Toward a motivational and structural theory of ruminative thought. In J. S. Uleman & J. A. Bargh (Eds.), *Unintended thought.* New York: Guilford.

Merton, R. K. (1948). The self-fulfilling prophecy. *Antioch Review, 8,* 193–210.

Miller, D. T., & Turnbull, W. (1986). Expectancies and interpersonal processes. In M. R. Rosenzweig & L. W. Porter (Eds.), *Annual review of psychology* (Vol. 37, pp. 233–256). Palo Alto, CA: Annual Reviews.

Miller, P. C., Lefcourt, H. H., Holmes, J. G., Ware, E. E., & Saleh, W. (1986). Marital locus of control and marital problem solving. *Journal of Personality and Social Psychology, 51,* 161–169.

Neuberg, S. L. (1989). The goal of forming accurate impressions during social interactions: Attenuating the impact of negative expectancies. *Journal of Personality and Social Psychology,* **56,** 374–386.

Neuberg, S. L., & Fiske, S. T. (1987). Motivational influences on impression formation: Outcome dependency, accuracy-driven attention, and individuating processes. *Journal of Personality and Social Psychology,* **53,** 431–441.

Nisbett, R. E., & Ross, L. (1980). *Human inference: Strategies and shortcomings of social judgment.* Englewood Cliffs, NJ: Prentice-Hall.

Omoto, A. M., & Borgida, E. (1988). Guess who might be coming to dinner?: Personal involvement and racial stereotyping. *Journal of Experimental Social Psychology,* **24,** 571–593.

Pyszczynski, T. A., & Greenberg, J. (1981). Role of disconfirmed expectancies in the instigation of attributional processing. *Journal of Personality and Social Psychology,* **40,** 31–38.

Rempel, J. K., Holmes, J. G., & Zanna, M. P. (1985). Trust in close relationships. *Journal of Personality and Social Psychology,* **49,** 95–112.

Roediger, H. L., III, & Blaxton, T. A. (1987). Retrieval modes produce dissociations in memory for surface information. In D. S. Gorfein and R. R. Hoffman (Eds.), *Memory and cognitive processes: The Ebbinghaus Centennial Conference,* Hillsdale, NJ: Erlbaum.

Rosenthal, R., & Jacobson, L. (1968). *Pygmalion in the classroom.* New York: Holt, Rinehart & Winston.

Rosenthal, R., & Rubin, D. B. (1978). Interpersonal expectancy effects: The first 345 studies. *Behavioral and Brain Sciences,* **3,** 377–415.

Ross, L. (1977). The intuitive psychologist and his shortcomings: Distortions in the attribution process. In L. Berkowitz (Ed.), *Advances in experimental social psychology* (Vol. 10, pp. 173–220). New York: Academic Press.

Shapiro, J., & Hilton, J. L. (1988). *The impact of interaction goals on expectancy confirmation.* Paper presented at the 60th Annual Meeting of the Midwestern Psychological Association, Chicago.

Snyder, M. (1984). When belief creates reality. In L. Berkowitz (Ed.), *Advances in experimental social psychology* (Vol. 18). Orlando, FL: Academic Press.

Snyder, M., & Cantor, N. (1979). Testing hypotheses about other people: The use of historical knowledge. *Journal of Experimental Social Psychology,* **15,** 330–342.

Snyder, M., & Haugen, J. A. (1990). *Why does behavioral confirmation occur? A functional perspective on the role of the perceiver.* Unpublished manuscript, University of Minnesota, Rochester.

Snyder, M., & Swann, W. B. (1978). Behavioral confirmation in social interaction: From social perception to social reality. *Journal of Experimental Social Psychology,* **14,** 148–162.

Snyder, M., Tanke, E. D., & Berscheid, E. (1977). Social perception and interpersonal behavior: On the self-fulfilling nature of social stereotypes. *Journal of Personality and Social Psychology,* **35,** 656–666.

Srull, T. K. (1981). Person memory: Some tests of associative storage and retrieval models. *Journal of Experimental Psychology: Human Learning and Memory,* **7,** 440–463.

Srull, T. K. (1983). Organizational and retrieval processes in person memory: An examination of processing objectives, presentation format, and the possible role of self-generated retrieval cues. *Journal of Personality and Social Psychology,* **44,** 1157–1170.

Srull, T. K., & Wyer, R. S. (1986). The role of chronic and temporary goals in social information processing. In R. M. Sorrentino & E. T. Higgins (Eds.), *Handbook of motivation and social cognition* (pp. 503–549). New York: Guilford.

Srull, T. K., & Wyer, R. S., Jr. (1989). Person memory and judgment. *Psychological Review,* **96,** 58–83.

Swann, W. B. (1984). Quest for accuracy in person perception: A matter of pragmatics. *Psychological Review,* **91,** 457–477.

Swann, W. B., Pelham, B. W., & Roberts, D. C. (1988). Causal chunking: Memory and inference in ongoing interaction. *Journal of Personality and Social Psychology, 53,* 858–865.

Swann, W. B., & Snyder, M. (1980). On translating beliefs into action: Theories of ability and their application in an instructional setting. *Journal of Personality and Social Psychology, 38,* 879–888.

Tetlock, P. E. (1983). Accountability and complexity of thought. *Journal of Personality and Social Psychology, 45,* 74–83.

Tetlock, P. E. (1985). Accountability: A social check on the fundamental attribution error. *Social Psychology Quarterly, 48,* 227–236.

Tetlock, P. E., & Kim, J. I. (1987). Accountability and judgment processes in a personality prediction task. *Journal of Personality and Social Psychology, 52,* 700–709.

Vallacher, R. R., & Wegner, D. M. (1987). What do people think they're doing? Action identification and human behavior. *Psychological Review, 94,* 3–15.

von Hippel, W. (1990). *The effect of schemata on memory for instances.* Unpublished doctoral dissertation, University of Michigan, Ann Arbor.

White, J. D., & Carlston, D. E. (1983). Consequences of schemata for attention, impressions, and recall in complex social interactions. *Journal of Personality and Social Psychology, 45,* 538–549.

Wong, P., & Weiner, B. (1981). When people ask ''why'' questions, and the heuristics of attributional search. *Journal of Personality and Social Psychology, 40,* 650–663.

Word, C. O., Zanna, M. P., & Cooper, J. (1974). The nonverbal mediation of self-fulfilling prophecies in interracial interaction. *Journal of Experimental Social Psychology, 10,* 109–120.

Wyer, R. S., Bodenhausen, G. V., & Srull, T. K. (1984). The cognitive representation of persons and groups and its effect on recall and recognition memory. *Journal of Experimental Social Psychology, 20,* 445–469.

Wyer, R. S., & Gordon, S. E. (1982). The recall of information about persons and groups. *Journal of Experimental Social Psychology, 18,* 128–164.

Wyer, R. S., Srull, T. K., Gordon, S. E., & Hartwick, J. (1982). Effects of processing objectives on the recall of prose material. *Journal of Personality and Social Psychology, 43,* 674–688.

Zajonc, R. B. (1960). The process of cognitive tuning in communication. *Journal of Abnormal and Social Psychology, 61,* 159–167.

STUDYING SOCIAL INTERACTION WITH THE ROCHESTER INTERACTION RECORD

Harry T. Reis
Ladd Wheeler

Suppose you were given the task of describing in some detail the differences in social life between two categories of people—males and females, the lonely and the not lonely, the beautiful and the plain, or college students and young marrieds. "In some detail" would probably mean that you would want to know if one group had more social interactions than the other, or more dyadic interactions, or more opposite-sex interactions, or longer interactions, or more enjoyable interactions, or more intimate interactions, or a larger number of partners, and so forth. The list could get very long as you considered the problem. Deciding what you wanted to know, however, would be the easy part of the task; getting to know it would be much tougher. Barring following each person around and observing his or her behavior, your first thought would be to construct a questionnaire. Such a questionnaire, however, would assume an almost computer-like respondent, one who had entered details of all interactions and had the necessary software to retrieve and report them with great accuracy. This is clearly not realistic, and we say more about that below. There is, however, a method to approximate this ideal sequence. This method is called the Rochester Interaction Record (RIR).

For the past quindecennial, we and our colleagues and students at Rochester have worked with the RIR, a diary procedure for assessing and characterizing patterns of social interaction in everyday life. By social interaction, we refer to all situations involving two or more people in which the behavior of each person is in response to the behavior of the other. Conversation is not necessary, although in practice most interaction involves talk. The RIR is designed to be a flexible tool for providing information about various features of social participation, be they objective (e.g., amount of contact, number of different partners) or subjective (e.g., perceived intimacy, enjoyment). It is further intended to serve

269

ADVANCES IN EXPERIMENTAL
SOCIAL PSYCHOLOGY, VOL. 24

both descriptive and hypothesis-testing functions. Thus, the obtained data can be used to describe and compare persons on a broad variety of interaction parameters, or to evaluate theoretically driven propositions outside the experimental laboratory.

The RIR is one of several new methods for examining the nature and impact of daily life experience (Tennen, Suls, & Affleck, in press). Whereas prior methods have focused on major life events or personal interpretations of past experience, this approach is concerned with the multitude of "small events" that compose everyday activity and thought. Our presumption is that there are important and unique understandings of human social behavior to be obtained through the study of social phenomena as they are manifested in ongoing, spontaneous social life. As a consequence, daily event-recording procedures, such as the RIR, and laboratory experimental methods are best considered complementary strategies in programmatic research. In laboratory studies, one finds out how people behave in situations in which we as experimenters place them; in daily life-event studies, one learns which situations people place themselves into, and how they react in those situations. Later in this article we present several examples of the theoretical advantages offered by this dual approach.

In this article, we provide a brief overview of the RIR, as well as its rationale, usages, and limitations. We seek to orient the reader and potential researcher to the technique, and to furnish an overview of the various procedural and psychometric concerns that have guided our work. Because we believe that theoretically useful conclusions are the *sine qua non* of methodological innovation in the behavioral sciences, we will also describe some of the findings that have emerged from studies using the RIR and related instruments, both in our own studies and in the work of others.

This article has five major sections. The first two sections describe the rationale for the RIR, including comparison with traditional methods in interaction research. In the next segment, we present the technique itself in terms of its essential procedural and data analytic details. A discussion of reliability and validity issues is included in this section. The fourth part of this article provides an overview of studies that we and others have conducted with the RIR. Finally, we discuss the application of the RIR and related methods to other problems in social psychology.

I. Why a Diary Procedure?

The RIR was first applied to study the changes in interaction patterns that occur during the first year of college (Wheeler & Nezlek, 1977). Although various attitudinal and behavior summary questionnaires existed (for example, those used in the famous Michigan studies), none appeared adequate for the purpose of describing in precise detail ongoing patterns of spontaneous social activity in everyday life. The potential benefits of such an instrument were apparent. For one, it could be used to paint a vivid and highly detailed portrait of a person's social interaction. (It has always seemed odd to us that despite the field's facility with elegant theories of the myriad components of social interaction, we could not answer such elemental questions as "How much do people socialize?" and "Are most interactions enjoyable?") Second, if the various components could be measured precisely and distinguishably, then it would be possible to develop and evaluate theories about the nature and pattern of social interaction in everyday life. Third, and most appealing to us as traditionally trained experimental social psychologists, these data could be used to test, within the flow of spontaneous, everyday behavior, hypotheses about variables presumed to affect social participation (e.g., gender, physical attractiveness, personality traits) or be affected by it (e.g., loneliness, health, self-consciousness).

Questions about social interaction are certainly not new to the behavioral sciences. Two general strategies have traditionally been utilized in this research: self-report questionnaires and behavioral observation. We next discuss weaknesses in these methods that led us to develop the diary approach.

A. SELF-REPORT QUESTIONNAIRES

In the first approach, subjects are asked, via standardized questionnaires, to report their social experiences during a specific, recent time interval, typically anywhere from the past week to the past year. For example, in a study of social activity in the elderly, Lemon, Bengtson, and Peterson (1972) had subjects answer the question "How often do you get together with your close friends (neighbors, relatives)?" to provide estimates of interaction frequency. In another study, designed to validate measures of social and emotional loneliness, Russell, Cutrona, Rose, and Yurko (1984) asked subjects a variety of questions, such as how often they had been on a date in the past 2 weeks, how many friends they currently had, and how satisfying their current relationships were, compared to 1 year ago. Such measures can be useful as descriptions of people's global perceptions of their social activity, but because the rating process requires them to filter and aggregate events that span extended time periods and multiple occasions and partners, they should not be viewed as descriptions of actual social interaction (Huston & Robins, 1982). Instead, they are best seen as personalized impressions of social activity that have been percolated, construed, and reframed through various perceptual, cognitive, and motivational processes.

There are three stages through which subjects must proceed to arrive at global impressions of the sort most questionnaires require, all of which are liable to substantial distortion: *selection* of representative events and/or partners, *recall* of the characteristics of those events, and *aggregation* across multiple events. Here we briefly review the relevance of each of these problems to the distinction between standard questionnaires and diary methods. A more detailed discussion of cognitive biases relevant to questionnaire construction is provided by Schwarz (1990).

1. Selection

Selection poses potential problems for several reasons. For one, instructions rarely indicate whether subjects should describe all social interactions or a more narrowly defined set. Without explicit instructions to the contrary, subjects often assume particular criteria for delimiting the domain of events that seem to matter most: emotional significance, enjoyability, purely social (as opposed to task) functions, or formal (versus spontaneous) occurrence, for example. Moreover, even well-specified criteria for inclusion can be misunderstood by subjects, or produce idiosyncratic interpretations (Belson, 1981).

Another, more important reason why selection biases can affect responses to global questionnaires concerns people's difficulty in storing and retrieving detailed information about repetitive and often mundane events in long-term memory. Within the social cognition literature, many studies have demonstrated that the most available exemplars—instances that easily come to mind—influence judgments more strongly than less available events (e.g., Fazio, 1986; Tversky & Kahneman, 1982). Undoubtedly, certain social interactions are likely to be more cognitively available than others—a traumatic argument, an extremely intimate conversation, a recent meeting, a newly acquired or lost love, or a betrayed trust. It is improbable that the events being described are selected randomly or representatively (Halverson, 1988), especially when the time period subjects are asked to describe is lengthy. Instead, memorable, recent, and frequent events are more likely to be reported.

Characteristics of the questionnaire-administration situation may also influence the selection of events to be described. Mood and mood-related cognitions may affect memory retrieval, such that mood-congruent events are more likely to be recalled than mood-incongruent events (Blaney, 1986; Gilligan & Bower, 1984; Isen, 1984). This is true even when mood is induced by extraneous factors. Ehrlichmann and Halpern (1988) asked subjects to recall incidents cued by various words. Subjects were more likely to recall happy incidents when the room was filled with a pleasant odor; when the odor was unpleasant, they were more likely to recall unpleasant incidents.

Indeed, the mere act of asking questions may influence event selection. Consider a study by Goodhart and Peters (1986). To activate memories of socially supportive interactions, subjects were instructed to think about and evaluate previous situations in which they had received tangible or self-esteem support from friends. Subsequently, various self-descriptive questionnaires were administered. Compared to a control group, the priming task induced lower self-esteem and feelings of self-control and positive affiliation, especially among females. Presumably, raising these events to conscious awareness made salient feelings of dependency, thereby diminishing perceptions of self-efficacy. Questionnaires can, depending on their focus, nonrandomly call particular past interactions to attention, altering subsequent recollections and assessments. More generally, research on the self-referencing effect—namely the phenomenon that having to decide whether given words refer to the self or not enhances later recall of those words, especially when they apply to the self (e.g., Rogers, Kuiper, & Kirker, 1977)—suggests that questionnaires can, by virtue of their format or timing, selectively influence subsequent recall of social activity.

These findings suggest that people's recollections of which social events did and did not take place within a specified interval may exhibit considerable inaccuracy. An extensive program of research into recall accuracy has been conducted by Bernard and Killworth and their colleagues (e.g., Bernard & Killworth, 1977; Bernard, Killworth, & Sailer, 1982; Killworth & Bernard, 1976). Their research focused on whether people remember who they talk to, as well as on moderating variables that might increase or decrease accuracy. For example, in a 1982 study, 57 scientists who were part of an existing computer-network communication system were asked with whom they had communicated, and how often, during specified intervals of 1 to 30 days occurring between 1 day and 2 months ago. Objective information was available from the networking records. Of partners listed during the interviews, 30% had not actually been in communication with the subject. Furthermore, subjects had forgotten 66% of those partners who had actually communicated with them. When asked to name their most frequent communication partner, 52% of subjects chose the wrong person. As might be expected, maximum error rates were obtained for shorter target intervals assessed at least 2 weeks afterward (note that most questionnaires utilize time periods exceeding 2 weeks), but even longer intervals of relatively recent vintage (e.g., 1 week of communication assessed 1 week later) produced inaccuracy rates not substantially lower than the study means.[1]

[1]A recent paper by Kashy and Kenny (1990) questions the conclusiveness of this program of research. These authors argue that the results of Bernard and colleagues are confounded, given that they used aggregate data and did not partition the variance into actor, partner, and relationship components. In reanalyses of the original data, Kashy and Kenny found differential results for these three components. They found that people were not very accurate when estimating how frequently they interacted in general (the actor component). Only when estimating relative interaction with a specific partner (the relationship component) were accuracy coefficients significant. Thus, while their results qualify the conclusions of Bernard and co-workers, they support our inference that generalized estimates of interaction frequency tend to be inaccurate.

A similar study with questionnaire data conducted by Conrath, Higgins, and McClean (1983) in three independent organizational settings found that, when subjects were asked to estimate how much they had interacted with particular others, only about 27% of their recollections were reciprocal (i.e., cited by both partners). There is also evidence that recall accuracy decreases linearly over time (Skowronski, Betz, Thompson, & Shannon, 1990). The implication of this work is that people often find it difficult to remember spontaneously just which interactions have actually happened. As we shall describe later, the RIR, like other daily self-reporting methods, greatly lessens such inaccuracy by obtaining subjects' reports soon after the event itself, before the event has been forgotten and precluding (or at least minimizing) retrieval-related biases.

2. Recall of Content

As for accuracy in recalling the content of social interactions, the literature in human social cognition is replete with demonstrations of biases in recollections of past occurrences, some due to heuristic, schematic, and other systematic memorial processes, some attributable to random forgetting, and still others based on motivated distortions such as selective perception, defense mechanisms, or dissonance reduction. [For extensive reviews of this evidence, see Fiske and Taylor (1984), Haan (1977), Markus and Zajonc (1985), Nisbett and Ross (1981), and Ross (1989).] Note we speak here not of individual differences in the interpretation of given social events, but rather of the manner in which those interpretations might differ at a later assessment from their standing at the time of occurrence.

Transitory factors such as mood can significantly alter the impressions a subject "remembers." For example, Schwarz and Clore (1983) found that subjects induced to experience positive moods at the time of appraisal reported higher life satisfaction and happiness than subjects induced to experience negative moods. And Forgas, Bower, and Krantz (1984) demonstrated that both the evaluation and recall of social interaction activity are influenced by mood at the time of recall. Moreover, even methodological details, such as the format of a questionnaire, can affect remembrances. For example, Schwarz and colleagues have shown in several studies that response scales requiring subjects to place themselves among low-frequency alternatives (i.e., "never" to "several times a week") produce significantly lower estimates of event occurrence than scales using high-frequency response alternatives (i.e., "less than once a week" to "several times a day"). Thus, even reports of discrete, easily defined, and distinguishable events (among other examples, their subjects were asked to recall the frequency of sexual intercourse) are subject to considerable potential for systematically biased recollection.

This is not to deny the essential importance of the individual in giving meaning to her or his social experiences (Duck & Pond, 1989). Individuals possess motives, traits, fears, and desires that affect impressions of interactions with others. Because many of the most interesting and consequential features of social life intrinsically involve deeply personal construals—for example, intimacy, joy, hurt, security, control—independent objective appraisals, even if they were possible to obtain, would be unlikely to capture fully the individual's experience of a given event. (Although, to be sure, the discrepancies between personal and independent assessments represent an important source of information about the person and relationship.) The problem with retrospective questionnaires is that they involve yet further reinterpretations over time, thereby obscuring *in vivo* interactional experience. Reconstructions of this sort are important in their own right, but because they are based on derivative processes that operate subsequent to, and independent of, the event itself, they first require understanding of interactional experience as it occurs.

Sometimes, interpretational biases in the recollection of prior personal history can obscure the meaning of empirical results. For example, the prototypical question "How many close friends do you see regularly?" requires subjects to decide just how close a close friend ought to be, and how often is regularly enough. Memory of past interactions must then be searched for events that either correspond with or contradict these standards, and these events must then be evaluated in the light of present circumstances. This process offers considerable potential for distortion, compared to what contemporaneous records might reveal. Such distortion is not necessarily random, however. Ross (1989) has demonstrated that people's reconstructions of their personal history are guided by implicit theories of the self, such that the content of remembrances is more likely to resemble current views about the self than actual past events. For example, McFarland, Ross, and DeCourville (1989) had women keep daily records about their menstrual symptoms for 4 to 6 weeks. Two weeks later, they were asked to recall their symptoms on a day they were menstruating. These ratings resembled their personal theories about their menstrual symptoms (assessed via questionnaire) better than their self-reported symptoms did. Ross (1989) interprets these results, as well as similar findings from other studies, as indicating that people invoke implicit theories of the self to "decide" what their past standing on any particular variable was.

Note that McFarland *et al.* (1989) used a daily diary to establish true accounts of subjects' symptoms against which retrospections were compared. Because global questionnaires almost universally require retrospection, it seems likely that they will verify subjects' self-conceptions, which may or may not yield accurate assessments of their ongoing activity. Returning to the prototypical question posed in the preceding paragraph, suppose a significant correlation were obtained between this item and psychological well-being. It would be tempting to conclude that unhappy people are socially isolated. However, their view of themselves as unhappy might just as well have led some people to see their friends as distant and infrequent visitors, despite having socialized just as often and perhaps as intimately as happy persons do (Meehl, 1945). Obviously, it is most important in such research to distinguish these causal alternatives from one another, a task to which daily diary techniques are well suited.

3. Aggregation

Another set of difficulties inherent in global questionnaires concerns the aggregation process. Simply stated, we do not know how people combine data from multiple interactions to arrive at singular global impressions. In our studies, the average college student reports approximately seven interactions lasting 10 minutes or longer per day. Summarizing social activity over a typical month would therefore require consolidating data from 210 individual events. Many heuristics are possible: simple arithmetic averages (as, we suspect, researchers sometimes assume); averages weighted by factors such as relationship closeness, time duration, emotional intensity, historical noteworthiness, or temporal immediacy; selection of the most available or vivid event; and so on. Of course, even given the existence of a systematic rule, it is unlikely that people will apply it with much precision. Thus, aggregate ratings are likely to diverge substantially from composites that are computed independently from individual-event data. (We later present data on this point.)

Support for the notion that the aggregation process may be skewed by atypical events is provided by Hedges, Jandorf, and Stone (1985). They had subjects report their momentary mood four times a day: 9 AM, 1 PM, 4 PM, and 7 PM. Then, around 10 PM, the same subjects were asked to report their overall mood for that day. Peak momentary mood reports resembled overall daily moods more than the daily average, computed over the four momentary reports, did. The implication is that, when trying to summarize their day, subjects were more swayed by extreme momentary moods than by true averages of ongoing moods. Less intense events are simply more likely to be forgotten or ignored, a conclusion consistent with research on the availability heuristic (Tversky & Kahneman, 1982).

Diary methods that use computer aggregation to summarize event-by-event records avoid these problems (Csikszentmihalyi & Larson, 1987; Wheeler & Reis, in press). These procedures have another related advantage, namely that molecular data may be less susceptible to bias than global ratings are. In a recent study by Ritter and Langlois (1988), women playing with babies were rated on traits such as relaxation, competence, sensitivity, and support, either with their facial features visible or with these features occluded, thereby obscuring their attractiveness. The same videotapes were used in both conditions. When these traits were assessed on global rating scales, a strong attractiveness bias emerged. When molecular codes for specific holding, kinesthetic, caregiving, and play activities (codes that in the literature have been related closely to these general traits) were examined, no such bias appeared. Thus, molecular codes were less susceptible to bias than global ratings were, presumably because these categories concern concrete behaviors and therefore require minimal integration and judgment by raters. This conclusion is similar to one offered by Shrauger and Osberg (1981) in a different domain. To facilitate accuracy in self-assessment, they suggest phrasing questions in terms of specific, well-defined behaviors and absolute criteria.

Event-by-event records are similar to molecular codes in that they require subjects to evaluate a specific, concrete circumstance, rather than to infer general trends across a series of events. They should therefore be less subject to biases and distortions. This is true for both objective (e.g., how many interactions with what sex persons took place) and subjective (e.g., how pleasant and supportive were one's interactions) variables. If dispositional and motivational factors affect the manner in which social memory is processed (as has been demonstrated repeatedly; see Ross, 1989; Snyder & Ickes, 1985; Taylor & Brown, 1988, for reviews), responses to global questionnaires are likely to represent biased reports of subjects' experiences. Of course the process of interpreting social experience is important to investigate in its own right (Duck & Pond, 1989) and is often the researcher's primary target. However, this process cannot be fully identified without comparison of the filtered, retrospective recollection against an objective, contemporaneous account. Thus, as a molecular method, the RIR embodies an ideal tool for evaluating the role of dispositional and motivational factors in the process of digesting everyday experiences into global impressions.

B. BEHAVIORAL OBSERVATION

Another approach traditionally used in investigations of interaction and relationship phenomena involves direct behavioral scrutiny. These methods have been described in detail by Weick (1985) and Ickes and Tooke (1988). Typically, subjects are observed, often in a laboratory but sometimes elsewhere (e.g., at home or in schools), and their interaction is recorded, either obtrusively or surreptitiously, by live coders or on videotape, a method that facilitates detailed coding and analysis. Two paradigms predominate: (1) observation of particular relationship types, such as marital partners, parents and their children, or friendship pairs (e.g., Gottman, 1979; Gottman & Parker, 1986) or (2) observation of a single individual's activity in a fixed and conceptually interesting setting, such as work or school (Homans, 1950; Josephson, 1987). These techniques are undoubtedly useful, as evidenced by the rich body of knowledge they have produced. Nevertheless, three issues compromise their utility for characterizing fully the nature and extent of everyday social life.

1. It is likely that the behavior of subjects represents optimal rather than typical performance, especially when they are aware of being observed. Impression management, social desirability, and politeness rules all impel behaviors that, away from the inspecting eyes of presumably insightful researchers, might take very different forms. In such settings people often assume that their social or personal adequacy is being evaluated and, consequently, seek to do their best. For example, shy college students participating in a study of conversations might try to assert themselves more forcefully so as to avoid being perceived negatively. Similarly, domineering husbands or fathers might repress angry and avoidant responses in problem-solving interactions, knowing that an expert in family relations was watching. [Procedures in which subjects are unaware of being observed, such as the Dyadic Interaction Paradigm (Ickes & Tooke, 1988), preclude this problem.]

Another, more subtle way in which laboratory observations differ from spontaneous social activity is in the mandated existence of that interaction in the first place. In everyday life, people must decide whether or not to interact, weighing the anticipated rewards and costs against other alternatives (solitude, work, study, etc.). Furthermore, schedules, distance, fatigue, and other mundane details often inhibit socializing. Participation in a laboratory study precludes noninteraction as an alternative; subjects are present, usually to receive an extrinsic reward, such as experimental credit or money. Data about the frequency of socializing and the choice of interaction over substitute activities, which can highlight important predilections in real-life social participation, are by definition unattainable from this sort of research. For example, Larson, Raffaelli, Richards, Ham, and Jewell (1990) found that although depressed fifth to ninth graders experienced other people as less friendly and wanted to be alone more often, they did not actually spend more time alone than nondepressed youths.

2. Unless observations are conducted unobtrusively in the setting in which those behaviors naturally occur, it is likely that the research milieu will influence the behaviors that are displayed (Weick, 1985). The psychological laboratory, for example, even when comfortably outfitted, is replete with cues that elicit formal, polite, and perhaps introspective behavior rather than casual, unbounded informality (Ickes, 1983). Settings generally affect the nature of social interaction, of course (Altman, 1975; Barker, 1968); barrooms, fraternity houses, family dinners, departmental meetings, and encounter groups evoke varied moods, goals, scripts, and expectations that affect social interaction.

It is not generally acknowledged by interaction researchers that the setting in which an observation is conducted might be responsible, at least as a moderator variable, for results that are obtained, even though treatises on observational methodology often assign paramount importance to this factor. Weick (1985, p. 569), for example, includes the phrase "in relation to their naturally occurring contexts" as one of seven criteria for defining systematic observation, arguing that all such research must "specify contexts where people do and do not perform this activity" (p. 569). Although the patterns of interaction and social interdependence that have emerged from laboratory observations unquestionably provide useful information, comparable data generated from naturalistic settings are needed to fill out the picture of human interaction that emerges. Further discussion of the impact of the laboratory on spontaneous social behavior is provided by Ickes (1983).

An incidental finding by Snyder, Berscheid, and Glick (1985) supports this logic. Male subjects were asked to select one of two potential partners for a date: an attractive woman with an undesirable personality or an unattractive woman with a desirable personality. When the meeting was scheduled to take place in a local bar/restaurant, high self-monitors chose attractive partners, whereas low self-monitors preferred dates with desirable personalities. When the date was planned for a laboratory room, however, no differences occurred, apparently because the laboratory setting involves scrutiny by an experimenter and therefore invokes different sorts of concerns.

3. In that most observational studies focus on particular relationship types (e.g., spouses, strangers, playmates, or co-workers), they tend not to be informative about the breadth of interaction, nor about the generalizability of interaction processes and components across different relationships. Many important questions are included in this omission. Are an individual's interaction styles consistent in a traitlike fashion, or do they vary across partners? Does the receipt of social support in one relationship lessen its impact in other relationships? Are different needs satisfied by different relationships? Questions that extend beyond a given situation or a particular relationship require multiple observations in multiple settings, a costly, time-consuming, and largely impractical research strategy. On the other hand, self-reported event records can be adapted readily to provide such information.

II. A Brief Taxonomy of Event-Recording Methods

The RIR is one of several methods for the self-recording of daily life events. Although these methods are relatively new to social-personality researchers, they have a long history within two separate subdisciplines, behaviorism and indus-trial/organizational (I/O) psychology. Beginning with Lindsley (1968), behav-iorists have used such devices as portable wrist counters and paper-and-pencil logs to record the frequency of various events in everyday life. These events could include positively valued behaviors, such as smiling, and negatively val-ued behaviors, such as cigarette smoking. The general purpose of these records was to provide an objective and salient account of the frequency with which target events occur, so that behavior modification techniques might be used to alter their frequency. Within I/O psychology, observation and recording of workers' activities within fixed time periods is a long-established tradition (Weick, 1979), which was extended to self-reporting by Hinrichs (1964). Wheel-er and Reis (in press) offer a somewhat more extensive history of these methods.

Self-recording of daily events became more widely popularized in the 1970s, in large part through the independent development of the Experience Sampling Method (ESM) (Csikszentmihalyi, Larson, & Prescott, 1977) and the RIR (Wheeler & Nezlek, 1977). In the ESM, subjects carry electronic pagers or portable, preprogrammed beepers, and are signaled at several randomly selected points during the day. When cued, subjects complete a brief questionnaire de-scribing their current activities, thoughts, and impressions. [Interested readers are referred to Csikszentmihalyi and Larson (1987), Hormuth (1986), and Larson and Csikszentmihalyi (1983) for more detailed descriptions.)] The RIR, in con-trast, requires subjects to complete a record form whenever social interactions lasting 10 minutes or longer have occurred.

These methods, along with several other daily event-recording techniques (see, in particular, Robinson, 1987), led to a profusion of different procedures, each of them sharing the general goal of assessing daily life events through ongoing, contemporaneous self-reports, but differing in procedural details, re-search design, and specific content. Wheeler and Reis (in press) have recently suggested a taxonomy for classifying these methods based primarily on sampling units. This taxonomy highlights not only the advantages and disadvantages of each particular strategy but also the general range of phenomena to which such methods can be applied.

1. *Interval-contingent recording*: Participants report their experiences at some regular, predetermined interval. Typically, these intervals are chosen to demark theoretically or logically meaningful units of time or activity (e.g., at the end of each day or after every meal). This is the oldest and most widely used method of daily event self-recording. Examples include daily accounts of stressful experi-ences (Bolger, DeLongis, Kessler, & Schilling, 1989), descriptions of mood at four (Hedges *et al.*, 1985) and five fixed points each day (Campbell, Chew, & Scratchley, in press), and daily reports of headaches (Blanchard *et al.*, 1990).

2. *Signal-contingent recording*: In this paradigm, subjects are instructed to describe their activities whenever signaled by the researcher (e.g., through

beepers or telephone calls). Signal intervals can be fixed, random, or a combination of both (in which signals are randomly generated within fixed blocks of time). The ESM, described above, is a prototypical example of signal-contingent recording. Most of these studies use between six and nine signals per day, each randomly and unpredictably spaced within a predetermined interval. This technique has been used to study adolescent experience (Csikszentmihalyi & Larson, 1984), the daily life of ambulatory chronic mental patients (Delespaul & de-Vries, 1987), motivational effects on academic achievement (Wong & Csikszentmihalyi, in press), and intimacy motivation (McAdams & Constantian, 1983).

3. *Event-contingent recording*: This method requires a report from participants every time an event meeting some predetermined definition has occurred. The frequency of the relevant events, and hence subjects' reports, is usually variable. The key here is in the unambiguous definition of events requiring a report, so that *all* such events are described, as well as timeliness in completing the record as soon after the event as possible. This paradigm has been used to study various features of social interaction (in the RIR studies described subsequently), conversations (Duck, Rutt, Hurst, & Strejc, in press), and fluctuations in self-esteem (Hoyle, 1990). Event sampling might also be applied to other discrete events, such as by requiring reports after every use of drugs or alcohol; every marital conflict or fight between siblings; every headache or meal; or every sexual episode.

COMPARISON OF THE THREE PARADIGMS

Interval-contingent methods are usually chosen when researchers wish to examine the prevalence of certain events in daily life (e.g., stressors, headaches), or when they want to characterize everyday experience across some time period (e.g., daily mood). The longer the interval, and the more changeable and ephemeral the behavior in question, however, the more likely it is that retrospection biases will influence the data. Diary methods are expressly designed to minimize such distortion, so that interval-contingent methods should be used only when the time between the event and its description is short, or when the phenomenon itself is easily remembered. A major advantage of this method, on the other hand, is its simplicity. Subjects need only complete the instrument at the appointed time [which experimenters might even control, as by telephoning subjects once a day (Stone, Kessler, & Haythornthwaite, in press)]. Also, especially when equal time intervals are used, interval-contingent methods readily lend themselves to spectral analysis.

Signal-contingent and event-contingent recording reduce the likelihood of forgetting or reappraisal by requiring reports that are close in time to the event. Furthermore, if the signaling schedule is random, signal-contingent methods have the considerable advantage of avoiding systematic bias introduced by assessing behavior or feelings at fixed times. (People may always feel lethargic after dinner, for example.) This makes the method most desirable for assessing the prevalence of different sorts of daily events—for example, socializing versus studying or alert versus lethargic states—or for comparing the nature of relatively common events. On the other hand, the rarer the event in question, the less useful this method is, since the chance of the signal and event coinciding are diminished. As a consequence, signal-contingent recording renders infeasible the study of variation within a class of even moderately rare events. If one wanted to compare interactions with best friends and romantic partners, it is unlikely that more than a few episodes within a week would be obtained from random signals. Alternatively, data would have to be collected for a prohibitively long time before an acceptable database was achieved. Moreover, because the psychometric advantages of event diaries stem from the assessment of many events within a category, it seems unlikely that signal-contingent sampling will produce a sufficient number of episodes to yield high reliability and confidence regarding generalizability. With even rarer events—for example, feelings and practices regarding sexual activity or alcohol use—the necessity of focusing directly on the events of interest becomes clear. Also, by including all relevant events, there is little chance that significant episodes will be omitted, either because of the respondent's own deliberations or because of signaling happenstance.

Hormuth (1986) has criticized event-contingent sampling on the grounds that it "permits subjects to anticipate many of the behaviors that will be measured, giving rise to a greater possible problem with behavioral reactivity" (p. 263). Subjects in our studies with the event-contingent RIR report minimal interference, however (see below). It seems unlikely that subjects would modify their social behavior for the sake of our ratings, since it would be far simpler merely to alter their ratings (a form of behavioral reactivity equally feasible with both methods). Although participants in a signal-contingent study may not be able to predict the exact moment of notification, the relative frequency of signals per day, as well as their dispersion, facilitate awareness of the assessment process and anticipation of the behaviors to be described. This awareness is also coupled with heightened chances for public self-consciousness. Although both paradigms are intrusive, event-contingent recording is less intrusive than signal-contingent recording because subjects are typically required to complete the questionnaire after an event occurs, and no one has to know about this but themselves. (Although beeper signals are often audible, some ESM studies allow subjects to switch them to silent vibrate mode.) Signal-contingent methods have also been criticized for sacrificing control over and information about the specific activities that are being described (Davison, Robins, & Johnson, 1983; Singer & Kolligian, 1987).

We therefore believe that the choice between signal-contingent and event-contingent sampling ought to rest with the researcher's goals. In general, event-contingent sampling is preferable when (1) researchers are interested only in a limited domain of human activities, such as eating, socializing, or studying; (2) those events can be defined clearly for subjects; and (3) it is important to obtain a large number of events, so that variation within the category may be studied. On the other hand, signal-contingent sampling is preferable when (1) researchers are interested in the relative distribution of human behavior across different activities; and (2) when comparison of different domains is of prime interest.

III. The Rochester Interaction Record

The RIR was designed to allow researchers to examine in detail the nature and extent of an individual's participation in everyday social life. Because its intent is to permit discrimination among, and characterization of, the many types of social events that people encounter, it relies on event-contingent sampling. For a specified interval, typically 1 to 2 weeks, respondents are asked to complete a brief, fixed format record after every social encounter lasting 10 minutes or longer. A standard set of questions is used in each study, but the format is intended to be flexible enough to allow researchers to assess whichever dimensions interest them. From these records, summary indices are computed, aggregated, and subdivided according to theoretical and psychometric concerns. In our most recent studies, we have focused on two sets of variables. The first set includes five quantitative variables—number of interactions per day, average interaction length, time per day, number of different others, and dispersion across different partners. The second set consists of seven qualitative variables—perceived intimacy, self-disclosure, other-disclosure, pleasantness, satisfaction, initiation, and influence. Each of these variables is averaged across all interactions, as well as within categories based on composition: same sex, opposite sex, mixed sex, and group (see subsequent section for definitions of these terms). Indices can also be calculated for different types of relationships (e.g., close friends vs acquaintances, dyads), or for specific significant others, such as spouses, best friends, or co-workers.

Our procedures alleviate many of the problems described earlier. Selection bias is not relevant, because subjects are asked to describe all social encounters. Recall bias is minimized by having subjects complete the records shortly after the interaction. Aggregation occurs by computer according to the researcher's criteria, eliminating distortion inherent in subjective, imprecise appraisals. In that the database is composed entirely of interactions within people's natural everyday settings, encompassing all of the constraints and facilitators typical in social life, the obtained records are likely to be representative of that person's usual social activity (at least to the extent that any 2-week slice can be representative of a longer interval). Finally, because all interactions are assessed, the findings are not limited to particular relationships.

An additional advantage of the RIR stems from its ability to provide detailed, accurate, and differentiated information. Accuracy is enhanced over other available methods because the contemporaneous diary-like format of the RIR minimizes many biases common to questionnaire research, as described earlier. This is not to suggest that all data gathered via the RIR are "objective" (in the sense that a team of well-trained observers would, if capable of following subjects throughout their daily lives, produce identical ratings). Some constructs, such as intimacy and satisfaction, are properly conceptualized in subjective terms. That is, they depend on the unique perceptions of the person doing the interacting, as she or he personally experiences that interaction (Duck & Pond, 1989; Markus & Zajonc, 1985; Reis & Shaver, 1988). Even so, subjective ratings are likely to be estimated more precisely with the RIR than with global questionnaires. This is because the RIR records subjective interpretations and evaluations at or near the time of interaction, one interaction at a time, thereby minimizing additional distortion and subjectivity brought on by selection, recall, and aggregation of many interactions over an extended period of time. For those variables that can be assessed objectively, such as the amount of social time, RIR-based ratings are likely to be more accurate than methods requiring greater cognitive activity from subjects.

The ability of the RIR to discriminate among the various features of social participation is also an important part of its rationale. Discriminability is an important yet often unaddressed issue in self-report methods. People often have difficulty distinguishing interaction parameters from one another, especially when their assessments are retrospective summaries. For example, perceptions of closeness and enjoyment might be hard to separate in the aggregate. Moreover, hedonic tone is by far the dominant dimension characterizing emotional experience in relationships (Attridge & Berscheid, 1990), so that ratings of positivity versus negativity in lay accounts might swamp other descriptors. Recording events separately not only provides the psychometric advantages of a large database of repeated measurements, it also increases researcher's ability to determine which facets of social participation are related to a given outcome, and, with equal importance, which factors are not related. That is, it allows researchers to establish both convergent and discriminant validity (Campbell & Fiske, 1959).

In its methodological format, the RIR is essentially a microanalytic approach. That is, it is designed to permit the study of patterns of social interaction by focusing in detail on their constituent elements. This strategy has been used increasingly in observational studies of marital and friendship dyads (Gottman, 1989), but is less common with self-report data. RIR data are not limited, however, to examination of "micro" acts, as the examples we later provide will show. In fact, the RIR is well suited for crossing the bridge between microacts and macromotives. Holmes (1981) has argued that higher order (i.e., general) attitudes and dispositions over time control behavior in relationships. But, as Holmes and Gottman both point out, we know little about how these general macromotives are operationalized in everyday interpersonal behaviors. By aggregating over many such events, the RIR provides portraits of daily social activity that investigators can then relate to measures of higher order attitudinal and dispositional factors. For example, one might discover that people high in passionate love for their partners have a greater frequency of highly intimate interactions with them. Studies of this sort have the potential to answer important questions about the processes by which global motives, feelings, and traits come to affect social behavior and relationships.

A. PROCEDURES

Although the hallmark feature of the RIR is its use of standardized, fixed format records, its content is intended to be flexible and responsive to the researcher's theoretical interests. Figure 1 presents a sample RIR that we have used in several studies. Its components and scales were chosen to assess constructs relevant to particular processes and hypotheses in that research. Thus, for example, keeping track of partners' initials allowed us to determine how many different interaction partners subjects had, an important question in our physical attractiveness research (Reis, Nezlek, & Wheeler, 1980; Reis et al., 1982). The social integration scale was included in a recent study of adults to test hypotheses

```
Date _____     Time _____ a.m.____   Length: _____ hrs. _____ mins.
                                        p.m.____
Initials:    _____ _____ _____      If more than 3 others:

Sex:         _____ _____ _____      No. of females _____   No. of males _____

Intimacy:    ...............superficial  1  2  3  4  5  6  7  meaningful

I disclosed: .............very little   1  2  3  4  5  6  7  a great deal

Other disclosed: .........very little   1  2  3  4  5  6  7  a great deal

Social integration: did not feel like   1  2  3  4  5  6  7  felt like part of
                    part of a group                          a group

Quality:     .................unpleasant 1  2  3  4  5  6  7  very pleasant

Satisfaction: .....less than expected    1  2  3  4  5  6  7  more than expected

Initiation:  ..............I initiated   1  2  3  4  5  6  7  other initiated

Influence:   .........I influenced more  1  2  3  4  5  6  7  other influenced more

Nature:  Job    Task    Pastime    Conversation    Date
```

Fig. 1.   Rochester Interaction Record.

comparing the relative impact of social networks and primary close relationships (Reis, 1989).

Other researchers have modified the RIR more substantially. Hays (1989), for example, added scales to assess specific benefits and costs received in social interaction, so that social exchange predictions regarding differences between close and casual friendships could be tested. Cutrona (1986) had subjects identify whether their interactions were help oriented and, if so, what sort of helpful activity took place (e.g., expressed caring or concern, gave advice). DePaulo, Kirkendol, Epstein, Wyer, and Hairfield (1990) had subjects complete a Deception Record every time they told a lie, rating its spontaneity, seriousness, and the target's reaction, as well as their reason for telling the lie. Sometimes, the basic record format has been modified so extensively that all that remains is the common strategy of using standardized, objective records for all interactions of a given sort. One such example is the Iowa Communication Record, developed by Duck *et al.* (in press) to examine the content, focus, and format of conversations. Such elaborations and metamorphoses are entirely consistent with our belief in the value of event-contingent sampling for studying social events.

In our studies, we have found that 1 to 2 weeks is the optimal record-keeping duration. Shorter periods can be prejudiced by atypical days, especially because at least among college students, each day of the week has a characteristic structure (e.g., particular classes, jobs, Saturday night dates) affecting social activity. Intervals longer than 2 weeks would probably tax subjects too greatly, lessening the quality of their data. In another context, Huston and Robins (1982) concluded that 9 days gave a satisfactory and representative sampling of day-to-day marital functioning. It is important to choose time periods that do not include important special events, such as major holidays or examination periods. Although these events might be constant across subjects, individual reactions may differ (for example, some students go home for holidays, others don't), compromising the assumption that the underlying social opportunities are reasonably equivalent for all participants.

In this type of research, subjects must be cooperative, motivated, and at least somewhat interested in the research itself. Because the process at times can be tedious and intrusive, they must see some purpose, not only to their own participation but to the research project as well. (We have found that the stated need to establish scientifically valid parameter estimates regarding basic facets of social life—"How much do people socialize?"—often strikes a resonant chord.) Thus, our solicitations typically focus on two features: the inherent appeal of more closely examining one's social life, and a minimal but nontrivial extrinsic reward (e.g., $20 or a semester's worth of experimental credit). The aim is to provide enough reward to make the exchange feel equitable to subjects, but not so much that unmotivated subjects will enroll solely to receive the reward.

It is also important to maintain a collaborative, trusting relationship with subjects. Indeed, for this reason, we refer to our subjects as "co-investigators." One can easily imagine the fears and anxieties that diary keepers might have about sharing very personal records; without any objective check on the accuracy of their diaries, they might alter their records in response to those fears. It is therefore particularly critical that subjects be given strong assurances regarding the complete confidentiality of their data. We give all subjects the option of withdrawing any time and taking their diaries with them (an option that no subjects have yet exercised). Furthermore, it is also productive to answer subjects' questions as fully as possible without jeopardizing specific hypotheses. (Most participants are sufficiently naive about interaction concepts that broad generalizations usually suffice.) The openness and candor of the investigators provide a good model for participants. Methods for establishing such relationships are discussed in greater length by Nezlek, Wheeler, and Reis (1983).

Two additional steps are taken to ensure the accuracy of the database. First, in both written and oral instructions, subjects are instructed to complete each RIR as soon as possible after the interaction in question, but certainly no less than once or twice a day. Scratch sheets are provided as memory aids. To encourage reliability, subjects are asked to hand in completed records and pick up blank forms every 2 or 3 days (although this requirement is not feasible if subjects are not on site daily). Second, at the conclusion of the record-keeping period, subjects are interviewed by the researcher or an assistant. They are encouraged to voice their reactions to the study, and, especially, to note inaccuracies in their records (without penalty). Most subjects report that they enjoy maintaining the records, and that they have been reasonably accurate (mean ratings approximate 2.5 on 7-point scales, with 7 representing "highly inaccurate"). Subjects generally report omitting between 5 and 10% of their interactions, but without systematic bias as to nature or content. Typically, about 3 to 5% of respondents indicate that they have been substantially inaccurate. They are thanked for their honesty, and their data are eliminated.

Subjects are asked to complete one record for every interaction that lasts 10 minutes or longer. The 10-minute time limit is imposed for two reasons, one theoretical, the other practical. First, we intend the database to incorporate the more meaningful social events that occur in a person's life, and we believe (supported by pilot data) that, for the most part, very brief social contacts rarely meet this criterion. Second, requiring subjects to describe every encounter would pose too burdensome a task. Indeed, it could lead to substantial inaccuracy in the recording process. The 10-minute cutoff is therefore a compromise between the ideal and reality.

Interactions are defined as

> any situation involving two or more people in which the behavior of each person is in response to the behavior of the other person.
>
> A conversation is the most obvious example of an interaction, but there are many other

sorts of interactions as well. Merely being in the presence of another person is not enough by itself. For example, watching television and not talking to the person next to you is not an interaction. In order to count as an interaction, you must be responding to each other, such as by talking about what you are watching. Any social activities that involve mutual responding count: work, hanging out, conversing, doing things together, etc.

Keep the records for every interaction that lasts 10 minutes or longer. It does not matter where the interaction occurs, be it at home, at work, on the street, etc. It is vital that you keep the record every day, all the time. Record job activities to the extent that you and your co-workers are responding to one another for 10 minutes or longer. Record phone calls, if they last for at least 10 minutes.

The various components of the record are defined only to the extent necessary to guarantee clarity. Subjects are not told how specific interactions should be represented, and, in fact, our interest in their personal interpretations is emphasized. They are told that intimacy is not necessarily equivalent to sexual activity. The difference between pleasantness (reaction to an interaction) and satisfaction (expectations about an interaction) is explained. The distinction between jobs (regular work that requires interaction), tasks (doing something), pastime (shared, unfocused activity), conversations, and dates (any activity you would call a "date") is also discussed.

Subjects are asked to identify their interaction partners with a unique set of initials for each partner. We suggest using code initials if they are concerned about preserving anonymity and confidentiality (especially if their friends are also study participants). During the post-record-keeping interview, we inquire about their role relationship with each set of initials, depending on the aims of that study: best friends, romantic partners, confidants, parents, work supervisors, etc. These codes permit sorting according to particular types of relationships (e.g., best friends vs superficial acquaintances).

Once completed, the RIRs are entered into a computer file and aggregated into theoretically relevant categories. FORTRAN programs are available for this purpose (Nezlek & Wheeler, 1984), although most statistical software packages can readily perform the necessary sorting and summarizing (e.g., the SPSS-X Aggregate Program; Lin, 1990a). Typically, four categories have predominated in our analyses: same sex (up to three others of the subject's sex), opposite sex (up to three others of the opposite sex), mixed sex (two or three others, one of each sex), and group (more than three others). The cutoff of four to define a group is derived from group size research (e.g., Asch, 1956; Wilder, 1977), which has shown that the incremental effects of additional group members decrease greatly above three others. Role-based groupings, such as all interactions with romantic partners, best friends, and confidantes, are also useful. Of course, other content groupings (e.g., all dyadic interactions, all work-related interactions, all high self-disclosure interactions), specific role groupings (e.g., parent–child interactions, supervisor–supervisee interactions), and role-task combinations (e.g., comparing interactions with one's romantic partner at work versus at home) are also feasible.

B. RELIABILITY AND VALIDITY

Because RIR composite variables average across events that inherently vary in the degree to which various characteristics are present, standard measures of internal consistency are not appropriate indicators of reliability. That is, in computing the reliability of trait or ability inventories, one assumes that items have been sampled randomly from the universe of all possible items, and that if each item were a perfect indicator of the trait in question, individuals ought to score equivalently on all items (correcting for mean and variance differences). In contrast, interaction data properly should vary. For example, some relationships are more intimate than others, and even within the same relationship some interactions are more intimate than others. Because there is no reason to expect or desire consistency across interactions (items), standard reliability indices are problematic.

Nonetheless, the 2-week record-keeping period is assumed to represent a stable and generalizable estimate of social life, so some degree of consistency ought to appear. Split-half correlations were computed for 2 weeks of interactions reported by 113 subjects (Reis, 1989). For each variable, separate composites were computed for even and odd days and then correlated with each other. Two standard quantitative indices, frequency and length, each yielded intraclass correlations of .85. Among the subjective RIR scales, correlations were as follow: intimacy, .89; self-disclosure, .92; other-disclosure, .88; social integration, .95; quality, .79; satisfaction, .76; initiation, .62; and influence, .75.[2]

Three studies allowed comparison of RIRs from interacting partners. The first (Wheeler & Nezlek, 1977) included several pairs of college roommates, permitting checks on reported interactions with each other. Intraclass correlations were computed on the number of interactions per day reported with each other, separating data for males and females, and for the fall and spring semesters of the academic year. These values ranged from .67 to .84. The Reis *et al.* (1982) data set contained 17 roommate pairs, for whom the comparable intraclass correlation was .81. In a third study (Hodgins & Zuckerman, 1990), the intraclass correla-

---

[2]These results hold theoretical interest aside from their psychometric implications. That is, they suggest that people's interaction patterns may exhibit traitlike stability over time. Although previous studies have shown stability in personality traits relevant to socializing—such as need affiliation, intimacy motivation, and sociability—evidence for continuities in the behavioral manifestations of these traits is much more sparse. Later we report a more extensive study relating to this possibility.

tion for 55 roommate pairs was .84 for the mean number of interactions with each other and .67 for the average length of those interactions. These figures indicate substantially high levels of mutual reporting, suggesting that errors of inclusion or exclusion were rare.

Another indication of accuracy stems from interviews. In the five most comprehensive studies we have conducted (Reis, 1989; Reis *et al.*, 1980; Reis, Senchak, & Solomon, 1985; Wheeler & Nezlek, 1977; Wheeler, Reis, & Nezlek, 1983), the following means (*M*) were obtained.

1. Degree of difficulty in recording interactions (1 = no difficulty, 7 = very much difficulty), M = 2.75, 3.21, 3.41, 3.13, 3.00
2. Perceived accuracy (1 = very accurate, 7 = very inaccurate), M = 2.62, 2.47, 2.46, 2.84, 2.47
3. Did such accuracy increase or decrease as the study progressed? (1 = decreased, 2 = no change, 3 = increased), M = 2.17, not available (na), 2.11, 2.16, na.
4. Subject's guess of the percentage of interactions not recorded, M = 9.7, 5.6, 5.9, 8.2, 6.5
5. Extent to which the record keeping interfered with interactions (1 = no interference, 7 = a great deal of interference), M = 1.36, 2.06, 1.41, 1.83, 1.64
6. Number of interactions recorded of less than 10 minutes, M = na, 0.37, 1.03. na, 0.99

Cutrona (1986), Hoyle (1990), Milardo, Johnson, and Huston (1983), and Sullivan, Nezlek, and Jackson (1990) report similar interview data, as do Hodgins and Zuckerman (1990), who collected these data anonymously. These self-reports are not objective measures of accuracy. However, to the extent that one might reasonably expect them to reveal difficulties, they indicate that subjects experienced few problems with the records and believed them to be accurate.

Validity studies are difficult in that objective criteria against which to compare the various qualitative scales are not easily defined; features such as intimacy and satisfaction reside largely in the mind of the beholder. Nevertheless, to the extent that consensual agreement can be established, the generalizability of RIR data would be enhanced. Reis, Senchak, and Solomon (1985) videotaped 26 male and 28 female subjects conversing with their best friend about a meaningful topic. Immediately afterward, they completed an RIR form for that interaction. The videotapes were rated for intimacy by seven female graduate students in education and psychology who were unacquainted with the subjects or the purpose of this research. RIR self-ratings and the mean judge rating correlated .62 ($p <$ .001) for female subjects, and .47 ($p <$ .02) for male subjects. It is important to remember that subjects had been asked to discuss a meaningful topic, thereby restricting the range of intimacy scores and, in all likelihood, attenuating the obtained correlations. Thus, the degree of correspondence between RIR ratings of intimacy and independent judges' assessments is considerable.

In another study (Whitbourne & Reis, 1982), subjects who had already completed the RIR were classified as to their intimacy status level, using an interview format developed by Tesch and Whitbourne (1982) based on Erikson's (1950) theorizing. As the theory predicts, those classified as Isolates had significantly fewer opposite-sex interactions for less time per day and reported significantly lower intimacy levels in both same- and opposite-sex interactions (all p values $<$ .05) than those who had already achieved Intimacy status or who were further along in this process.

It may also be helpful to mention several psychometric studies examining different event-sampling methods. Conrath *et al.* (1983) had subjects keep diary records of 100 consecutive interactions, as well as complete a global questionnaire afterward. When the degree to which two individuals concurred was calculated, results showed that the diary method fared significantly better than the questionnaire ($p < .001$). Furthermore, diary records tended to be more accurate when interactions exceeded 90 seconds (Higgins, McClean, & Conrath, 1985). Csikszentmihalyi and Larson (1987) present extensive reliability and construct validity information regarding the Experience Sampling Method, including data revealing substantial stability over time for activity frequencies and psychological states (e.g., affect, arousal).

C. COMPARISON OF THE RIR WITH GLOBAL QUESTIONNAIRES

A guiding principle of our work has been the assertion that detailed diaries provide information different from global questionnaires. "Different" does not imply better; rather, different measures speak to different conceptual perspectives, each of which may be illuminating in its own right. The RIR (and related techniques) is intended to yield detailed, objective accounts of everyday social activity. Global questionnaires, in contrast, assess such activity as filtered through the various cognitive and motivational processes described earlier. Both types of information are needed, and, in fact, comparison of global impressions with RIR data is an appropriate and informative way of identifying and delineating this filtering process (see McFarland *et al.*, 1989, for a good example). What is most important is that the two types of information not be mistaken for each other (Meehl, 1945).

Because gathering data with the RIR is obviously more tedious and labor intensive than with global questionnaires, it must pass muster on three criteria: (1) It must in fact provide different information than global questionnaires do; (2)

the data must be more accurate, in the sense of faithfully characterizing ongoing social activity; and (3) this information must repay the researcher by supporting unique findings and theoretical insights. In order to address the first of these criteria, Reis (1989) asked subjects to answer a series of general questions about the quantity, quality, and distribution of their social activity immediately after they had completed a set of RIR diaries. These responses were then correlated with the RIR indices to which they might reasonably be expected to pertain. As shown in Table I, these correlations ranged from null to strongly significant, but even in the latter instances, more than three-quarters of the variance was left unaccounted. It is heartening that most of these correlations were significant; recollections and interpretations should, after all, be grounded substantially in

TABLE I
CORRELATIONS OF SELECTED RIR AND QUESTIONNAIRE ITEMS

1.	How many close friends do you have at the university?			
	With number of different male partners	$r =$	.17	
	With number of different female partners		.13	
2.	How much time have you spent alone?			
	With time per day spent interacting	$r =$	$-.26$	
3.	How frequently have you done things alone as opposed to with a friend?			
	With total interaction frequency	$r =$	.24	
	With total time spent interacting	$r =$	.23	
4.	How often have you done things with your friendship group?			
	With frequency of all interactions	$r =$	.35	
	With frequency of same-sex interactions	$r =$	.33	
	With frequency of group interactions	$r =$	.38	
5.	How often have you participated in group activities?			
	With frequency of group interactions	$r =$	.17	
6.	Satisfaction with quality of social friendship group:			
	With overall pleasantness; satisfaction	$r =$	.25;	.19
	With same-sex pleasantness; satisfaction	$r =$	.24;	.18
	With oppositie-sex pleasantness; satisfaction	$r =$	.20;	.12
	With best friend pleasantness; satisfaction	$r =$	.29;	.24
7.	Satisfaction with number of friends at the university:			
	With number of male partners	$r =$	.08	
	With number of female partners	$r =$	.30	
	With same-sex pleasantness; satisfaction	$r =$	.16;	.13
	With opposite-sex pleasantness; satisfaction	$r =$	.15;	.15
	With best friend pleasantness; satisfaction	$r =$	.28;	.28
	With romantic partner pleasantness; satisfaction	$r =$	.07;	.05
8.	How often have you gone on a planned date?			
	With frequency of romantic partner interactions	$r =$	.48	
9.	Satisfaction with quality of dating relationship:			
	With romantic partner pleasantness; satisfaction	$r =$	.08;	.04
10.	Satisfaction with number of dates in the past 2 months:			
	With romantic partner frequency	$r =$	.34	
	With romantic partner pleasantness; satisfaction	$r =$	$-.09;$	$-.15$

actual events. The discrepancies nevertheless indicate that different information is provided by each sort of measure.

This brings us to the second criterion: accuracy. Which account better reflects the facts of social participation? Although this question cannot be answered absolutely without a truly independent, objective criterion (such as having observers surreptitiously keep track of subjects' social activity for 2 weeks), there are several reasons why the RIR should be preferred. For one, as described earlier, the vicissitudes of selection, recall, and aggregation will likely exert greater influence on retrospections that consolidate many exemplars over more time than on singular, contemporaneous ratings. For another, the recording conditions and instructional set of the RIR stress objectivity. Most global questionnaires, in contrast, ask subjects for "their own personal view" simply because personal experience is the intended construct. Thus, whatever their utility, RIR data would seem the more trustworthy representations of social activity. Several studies have already been cited in support of enhanced accuracy of diary methods over other techniques (for further discussion, see Duck, 1991; Ericsson & Simon, 1980; Huston & Robins, 1982; Singer & Kolligian, 1987).

The final criterion, uniqueness of findings, is perhaps the most contentious. Global questionnaire methods have always played, and doubtlessly will continue to play, a valuable role in the development of empirically based knowledge about social interaction. Yet, even in this context, RIR-type data can play an important role in providing new insights. Suppose a researcher was trying to establish the precise social deficiencies responsible for feelings of loneliness. One might administer simultaneously the UCLA Loneliness Scale (Russell, Peplau, & Cutrona, 1980), the RIR, and a series of general questions about social life. In all likelihood, questions like "How much time do you spend alone?" would probably correlate as well or better with Loneliness scores than RIR total time spent interacting would. After all, this question and the UCLA scale score share several sources of variance—including method factors and dispositional variables that lead to systematically biased recollections—that are not shared with RIR indices. But a significant correlation between the general item and loneliness should not be considered firm evidence that interaction quantity is deficient among lonely persons; alternative explanations deriving from their shared variance are also possible. It might be the case, for example, that loneliness predisposes people to see their social activity, regardless of its prevalence, as insufficient. On the other hand, a significant correlation between the amount of time per day spent interacting, as gauged by the RIR, and reports of loneliness reveals with greater certainty that lonely people do in fact interact less (for whatever reason).

This is indeed what our research has shown (Wheeler *et al.*, 1983). Prior research (Russell, 1982) found a correlation of .41 between the aforementioned "time alone" item and loneliness; our study found correlations of $-.38$ (females) and $-.46$ (males) between time per day with female partners and loneliness. Further analyses revealed that this effect was likely due to the higher intimacy level of interactions involving at least one female, providing useful specification of the obtained time correlation. We do not believe it would be appropriate to draw such conclusions from global questionnaire ratings.

Two other brief illustrations taken from the results listed in Table I might help emphasize this point. First, although item 2 (How much time have you spent alone?) correlated reasonably well with total interaction time, it correlated best with time spent in group interaction ($r = -.32$) as opposed to the various other composition categories. In that the sample was mostly first and second year students, this result supports the salience and value placed on large group interactions in the mind of younger college students (Astin, 1987; Wheeler & Nezlek, 1977). Second, item 9, concerning perceived satisfaction with dating relationships, correlated better with romantic partner intimacy (.32), self-disclosure (.34), and other-disclosure (.43) than it did with pleasantness (.08) or satisfaction (.04). This would seem to indicate that global perceptions of satisfaction are more closely tied to intimacy than to ongoing levels of satisfaction, a point related to a theoretical model we have proposed elsewhere (Reis, 1990).

In conclusion, the advantages of the RIR stem from its ability to provide data that are more accurate and better specified than global self-report questionnaires are. By portraying social participation more precisely, the RIR permits researchers to rule out many alternative explanations, thereby pinpointing the correlates of social interactions with considerably greater theoretical precision. Ultimately, it is this factor that justifies the extra effort that RIR data collection and tabulation require.

IV. Research Overview: Findings Generated
by the RIR and Related Techniques

The conceptual and methodological justifications for the RIR discussed so far tell only half the story. The RIR is advantageous for researchers only to the extent that it speaks to theoretically interesting issues in a novel, unique, or empirically superior fashion. To illustrate the RIR's effectiveness in this regard, we next provide a brief synopsis of several studies that have used the RIR to good conceptual account.

A. ADAPTATION TO A NEW
SOCIAL ENVIRONMENT

In a series of well-known experiments, Schachter (1959) showed that fear may increase people's desire to affiliate with others. This finding has been replicated many times, in both laboratory and natural (e.g., during blackouts) experiments (although, to be sure, certain situational or dispositional variables may attenuate or even reverse this tendency). These studies generally use fear-arousing situations that are one-shot, involuntary, temporary, or otherwise detached from the stream of ongoing, voluntarily chosen daily interactions. Thus, the question remains whether people would show similarly heightened desires for affiliation when the source of anxiety is pervasive, continuous, and embedded in real-life activity.

Wheeler and Nezlek (1977) obtained relevant data by examining changes in social interaction during the transition to college. For students who attend a university away from home, this transition can be quite stressful, since their comfortable, secure, home social environment is exchanged for a new academic and social life, new friends, and a new domicile. Therefore, one would expect an increase in socializing early in the year, followed by a decrease once the new environment becomes familiar. Wheeler and Nezlek had 58 first year students complete an early version of the RIR (see Fig. 1) at the end of their first month at college (fall) and 1 month before the end of their first year (spring). They found clear evidence of the expected decrease in socializing, but only for females: They dropped from 389 to 323 minutes per day, whereas males remained steady at 338 and 337 minutes per day. [Recall that Schachter's (1959) original subjects were females.] Further analyses indicated that the drop for females was most evident in interactions with subjects' same-sex best friend. The authors interpret these (and related) data as indicating females' greater reliance on their same-sex best friends as coping resources during a stressful transition. In part, this may be due to the higher intimacy level of women's same-sex interaction when compared with men's, a robust finding that has emerged in all of our RIR studies. Males apparently relied on other, less socially involved means of coping with the transition to college, consistent with other research showing that women both receive and give higher levels of emotional support (Vaux, 1985). As a result, males showed few significant changes in their interaction patterns from fall to spring.

B. LONELINESS

Our research on loneliness (Wheeler et al., 1983) is a good example of a study in which the RIR provides higher quality evidence and better differentiated results than alternative methods. Validation studies for the well-known UCLA scale reported significant correlations between this scale and global self-report items such as "How often have you done something with a friend?" ($r = -.28$) and "How many close friends do you have?" ($r = -.44$; see Russell, 1982; note that similar results have been reported for other loneliness scales).

There are several problems with interpreting these correlations as evidence for the specific social deficits inherent in the experience of loneliness. First, the loneliness scale itself is made of similar items, and one is almost bound to find some correlation for purely methodological reasons. Second, some aspects of social activity are probably more closely related to loneliness than others, but it is not clear that general impressionistic questions can distinguish them. Although loneliness is typically characterized as a discrepancy between desired and actual social activity (Peplau & Perlman, 1982), it is important to identify the specific deficiencies that are most likely to be problematic. Third, because loneliness as a psychological state might motivate subjects to underestimate their social contacts and the meaningfulness of those contacts, a significant correlation might not mean that lonely people in fact socialize less or less meaningfully. Cognitive distortion of this sort would be important to document, but this can be done only by having objective accounts of social participation against which to compare. And barring constant observation by independent observers, event-contingent self-recording is probably as objective as we can get.

To identify the specific interaction correlates of loneliness, Wheeler *et al.* (1983) had 96 college seniors keep the RIR for 2 weeks. Immediately afterward, they filled out the UCLA Loneliness Scale. Two general results were obtained. First, for both sexes, the amount of interaction with female, but not male, partners was strongly related to loneliness. For example, as noted previously in Section III,C, time per day spent socializing with women correlated $-.38$ ($p <$ .05) for female subjects and $-.46$ ($p < .01$) for male subjects; the comparable correlates for interaction with male partners were $-.06$ and .15 (both *ns*), respectively. Second, levels of intimacy were significantly related to loneliness in both sexes, for partners of both sexes (*r* values range from $-.33$ to $-.48$, all *p* values $< .05$). Because interactions involving at least one female tend to be significantly more intimate than interactions involving males alone (a finding that has been replicated in all of our studies), these results were interpreted as indicating that the lack of intimacy in social interaction is the fundamental deficiency related to loneliness.

These differential results are an important part of the rationale for the RIR. It would be difficult to argue that method or motivationally based biases were responsible for finding significant correlations for interaction with women partners but not men partners. Differentiability on the criterion variable side is also useful to note. That is, different outcomes should, and do, relate to different interaction variables. In that vein, Reis, Wheeler, Kernis, Spiegel, and Nezlek (1985) found that although total visits to the University Health Service were predicted by poor interaction quality, visits for socially communicated illnesses, such as flus and viruses, were more prevalent among subjects who interacted more often.

C. THE IMPACT OF PHYSICAL ATTRACTIVENESS
ON SOCIAL PARTICIPATION

Two early studies in our research program were concerned with the impact of physical attractiveness on social participation (Reis *et al.,* 1980, 1982). Although much research to that point had demonstrated that attractive persons are perceived to enjoy better social lives, nearly all of this evidence derived from studies in which subjects (1) gave first impressions of strangers about whom little information was available, (2) described the social characteristics of someone whose attractiveness was known, which might therefore bias their ratings, or (3) evaluated their own experiences on global questionnaires. Because attractiveness is known to have strong effects on self- and other-perception (Berscheid & Walster, 1974; Hatfield & Sprecher, 1986), we felt that it would be important to determine how the social life of attractive and unattractive individuals actually differs (as opposed to how people *think* they might differ).

In the first study (Reis *et al.,* 1980), 35 male and 36 female first-year college students kept the RIR for four 10-day periods spread across the academic year. We obtained consensual attractiveness ratings by having their photographs rated by a large number of students at another university. Among males, the average correlations across the four periods between attractiveness and social behavior were impressive: With number of different females interacted with, $r = .50$; with number of opposite-sex interactions per day, $r = .54$; with percentage of opposite-sex interactions, $r = .56$; with average length of opposite-sex interactions, $r = .44$; with total opposite-sex time per day, $r = .57$. For females, none of these correlations approached significance (nor were curvilinear trends evident). The greater time that attractive males spent with females came at the expense of socializing with other males. That is, attractive males were not just heavy socializers in general—they simply interacted more with females.

Had we conducted this study with standard methods, such as by asking subjects how popular they were with the opposite sex or how many dates they had, we probably would not have obtained these results, but rather would likely have found a stronger relationship for females than for males between attractiveness and opposite-sex contact (cf. Feingold, 1990). There is a cultural belief that attractiveness is a more important asset for females, and subjects, having at least some idea how attractive they are, would probably respond in line with the cultural belief. Some support for the cultural belief was obtained, however, from the RIR measure of interaction quality. For both sexes, but especially for females, attractiveness was associated with significantly high levels of rated pleasantness.

The mundane task of recording interactions bypasses the cultural belief. This belief is, in fact, so strong that we felt compelled to replicate the study using seniors rather than first year students. Our reasoning was that, from an evolution-ary perspective, attractiveness ought to be a more important asset for whatever sex is in a more competitive "mating and dating" situation (Buss, 1988). Among freshmen, males are in a more competitive situation because age–dating norms dictate that they compete for a smaller group of first year females with all other undergraduate males and perhaps graduate students. (This university also enrolled 60% male students at that time.) Freshman females are in a relatively less competitive situation. Among seniors, however, the situation is reversed. Given that females are less likely to date younger males than the reverse, senior females have an unfavorable sex ratio, whereas senior males have a larger pool of eligibles.

In the senior study (Reis et al., 1982), data were collected for one 2-week period during the first semester. And, once again, we found that physical attrac-tiveness predicted the social behavior of males but not of females. Male correla-tions with attractiveness were $r = .49$ for number of different females interacted with, $r = .45$ for number of opposite-sex interactions per day, and $r = .48$ for percentage of interactions that were opposite sex. Unlike the freshman study, however, average length of opposite-sex interaction was not related to males' attractiveness. Correlations for females again did not approach significance. Thus, we replicated in a quite different group a result that contradicts cultural beliefs, thereby discounting the sex-ratio explanation. We also replicated the significant correlation between attractiveness and interaction pleasantness among females ($r = .41$), although the comparable effect for males was not significant.

In this study, we also sought to identify mediating variables by giving subjects several questionnaires of interaction-relevant traits. As might be expected, at-tractive males were more assertive (on the Dating and Assertiveness Question-naire) and lower in fear of rejection by the opposite sex. Both of these charac-teristics related to opposite-sex interaction in the expected way, and partialing them from the correlation between attractiveness and opposite-sex social contact reduced the size of these correlations but did not eliminate them. Attractive females were *lower* on assertiveness and *lower* on trust in the opposite sex, suggesting that this trait difference might counteract any advantage based on appearance.

These results suggest that the impact of attractiveness on everyday social experience is different—and more complex—than cultural beliefs, as well as research from other paradigms, indicate. Of course, the RIR assesses all social contact, and it is possible that the cultural belief applies more circumspectly to romantic attraction. That would be an important qualification to identify, since it suggests a person × situation interaction in the impact of physical attractiveness.

D. DEVELOPMENTAL TRENDS
IN SOCIAL PARTICIPATION

Although most theories of life-span development posit changes in the nature and goals of social participation at different stages of life (Whitbourne & Weinstock, 1979), there has been little empirical work directly examining these changes. One reason for the absence of such studies concerns the inherent difficulty of interpreting age-related changes in self-reported descriptions of social activity. People evaluate their social behavior according to age-related norms and personal desires. For example, loneliness in a 10-year-old person is likely linked to different circumstances than in a 40-year-old person. Another reason is that questionnaires that ask people to retrospect over long periods in their lifetimes often yield responses that are affected by the various recall biases discussed earlier.

In a recent study (Reis, 1989), we used the RIR to examine changes in social interaction from the college years to age 30. Early adulthood is a period in which establishing intimate adult relationships is thought to represent a critical developmental goal (e.g., Erikson, 1950; Levinson, 1978). This interval is also of interest from the perspective of coping, since the move away from a residential college to adult life includes one of life's most abrupt and complete transitions: at graduation, social networks, work and financial responsibilities, and physical locations change dramatically, necessitating new adaptations. Further, the impact of the situational environment also changes markedly. In residential colleges, physical settings and tasks all facilitate spontaneous interaction; privacy, if desired, must be sought out. In adulthood, living arrangements are typically more private, so that social contact must be sought actively and usually scheduled. These factors make the comparison between college and adult social life intrinsically interesting.

The RIR is well suited to this comparison, since it requires participants to report all of their interactions in a concrete, standard fashion. One hundred thirteen subjects, all between the ages of 26 and 31, kept the RIR for 2 weeks. All had participated in a prior RIR study as college students, so that their college-age interaction data were already available for longitudinal comparisons. Three results were most striking. First, looking at interaction quantity, the amount of daily interaction decreased significantly, from an average of 341 to 278 minutes. Significant and substantial decreases were evident in same-sex and group interactions (same sex: from 130 to 76 minutes per day; group: from 86 to 36 minutes per day). On the other hand, opposite-sex interactions, and especially interactions with opposite-sex best friends (usually romantic partners), *increased* significantly, from 92 to 116 minutes per day. These results are consistent with theorizing about the importance of groups and same-sex friends in late adolescence (Sullivan, 1953), as well as common sense assumptions about the heightened role of male–female dyads in adulthood.

Second, interaction intimacy increased significantly in all categories: for example, on the RIR 1–7 scale, in same-sex interaction from 3.68 to 4.00; and in opposite-sex interaction from 4.10 to 4.35. The fact that this increase appeared in all categories suggests that the trend reflects a developmental shift in social preferences or abilities. Although this shift is consistent with Erikson's (1950) theorizing, its breadth implies that the shift is not merely limited to the union with a heterosexual partner, but rather pertains to wider patterns of social engagement. It is important to note that this increase was *not* due to generalized increases in positivity over time. Ratings of interaction satisfaction *decreased* from college to adulthood, especially so in opposite-sex interactions. Thus, while socializing became more intimate in adulthood, it was also less enjoyable. The implication may be that, compared to social life in college, adult socializing emphasizes closeness and commitment (e.g., conflict, "serious" conversations, relationship maintenance), and is focused to a lesser extent on recreation and other pleasurable activities. Further longitudinal research is needed to see if this divergence continues into middle adulthood.

Third, we were also interested in whether individuals' interaction patterns demonstrated relative stability from college to early adulthood. For these analyses, correlations were computed separately for those individuals who had participated in their college RIR study as first year students or as seniors. For the senior group, strong continuity was shown. For example, the correlations between their college and young adult data were $r = .32$ ($p < .05$) for the total number of interactions, $r = .59$ ($p < .001$) for mean intimacy, and $r = .52$ ($p < .001$) for mean satisfaction. For the first year group, the comparable correlations were $r = .42$ ($p < .001$) for the total number of interactions, $r = .16$ (*ns*) for mean intimacy, and $r = .27$ ($p < .05$) for mean satisfaction. Given that these correlations span interaction records collected between 6 and 11 years apart, they present strong evidence for viewing interaction patterns as a stable characteristic of an individual's adaptation to his or her social environment.

E. NONVERBAL DECODING ABILITY AND DYADIC INTERACTION

Hodgins and Zuckerman (1990) used the RIR to test the hypothesis that nonverbal decoding ability increases emotional sharing between friends. Prior studies had shown correlations between several measures of nonverbal decoding sensitivity and self-reports of relationship quality. However, Hodgins and Zuckerman preferred to examine RIR reports about specific, concrete interactions, since global ratings might be affected by variables external to the interaction exchange itself. On the basis of the Interpersonal Perception Task (Constanzo & Archer, 1989), 31 female and 24 male roommate pairs were classified into dyads who were both high on decoding ability (HH), dyads who were both low (LL), and dyads who were mixed (HL). For 2 weeks, they kept the RIR, which was modified somewhat by the addition of scales on involvement, support given, and support received; these, combined with the usual scales of self- and other-disclosure, produced a factor of "emotional sharing."

As predicted, females had more emotional sharing than males, and HH pairs had more emotional sharing than HL or LL pairs. However, this latter effect was due entirely to males. Females had high levels of emotional sharing regardless of the decoding ability composition (on a 1–7 scale, the female means were as follow: HH, 4.38; HL, 4.24; LL, 4.49). Among males, only HH roommate pairs had high levels of emotional sharing (the corresponding means were 4.60, 3.73, and 3.43). Importantly, the other RIR-based scales they reported did not differ as a function of nonverbal skill matching, suggesting that decoding effects in social interaction may be limited to emotional sharing.

Hodgins and Zuckerman (1990) interpret this result in terms of sex-role orientations. The traditional female role emphasizes emotional sharing, whereas the male role does not, so that only dyads involving females or two nonverbally sensitive males enjoyed relatively high levels of emotional sharing. In other words, roommate pairs with at least one male *low* in decoding ability were lower in emotional sharing, suggesting that this quality of interaction depends partly on reciprocated decoding skills. This result is reminiscent of the Wheeler *et al.* (1983) loneliness findings, described above, in which meaningfulness of interactions with males and time spent with females predicted a lack of loneliness for both sexes. We interpreted those results as indicating that females generally inject meaningfulness into interactions, but only some males, namely those high in expressive (feminine) skills and interests, do. The Hodgins and Zuckerman findings are entirely consistent with that interpretation.

F. INTERDEPENDENCE IN CLOSE AND CASUAL FRIENDSHIPS

An elusive question for researchers studying relationships concerns the manner in which individual and independent interactions contribute to the development of relationships (Duck & Sants, 1983; Reis & Shaver, 1988). Retrospections about this process might differ importantly from contemporaneous accounts, suggesting the value of a diary approach. Hays (1989) modified the RIR to test several hypotheses derived from interdependence theory postulates about the maintenance and growth of friendships. To do so, Hays had 65 college students use the modified RIR to describe all interactions (regardless of length) with two particular partners—a close friend and a casual friend—within a 1-week interval. Rating scales were added to the RIR to assess benefits/rewards received (fun, task help, emotional support, intellectual stimulation, and useful information/advice), costs incurred (wasting time, irritation, boredom), and the perceived impact of the interaction on this relationship (i.e., feeling closer/more positively versus less close/more negatively).

Three tenets of interdependence theory were considered in this research. First, Clark and Mills (1979; Clark, 1985) have argued that exchange processes are more strongly operative in casual relationships than in close relationships. Consistent with this notion, Hays found that rewards and costs accounted for 46% of the variance in perceived impact on the relationship for causal friends, but only 27% for close friends. Hays's second set of analyses asked whether rewards and costs were equally relevant in both types of relationships. In a study of married and regularly dating adults, Rusbult, Johnson, and Morrow (1986) found that rewards but not costs were associated with relationship satisfaction and commitment. However, they had no available contrast group of casual relationships, nor did they look at individual interactions. Hays found that benefits received were strongly correlated with perceived impact in close friendships ($r = .49$, $p < .001$), but costs experienced were not ($r = -.23$, ns). On the other hand, with casual friends, both benefits received ($r = .39$, $p < .01$) and costs incurred ($r = -.55$, $p < .001$) were related to perceived impact. Thus, it would appear that cost notions are more important in less close relationships, an important theoretical qualification to interdependence theory.

Finally, Hays (1989) wanted to determine which particular classes of benefit and cost best distinguished between close and casual friends. For benefits, the results indicated that emotional support and information/advice were more common in close than casual friend interactions, whereas fun, task help, and intellectual stimulation did not significantly differentiate these relationships. In terms of costs, there were no significant differences. Thus, it seems that emotional support and information/advice are the hallmark of interaction with close versus casual friends.

G. DIFFERENCES IN SOCIAL PARTICIPATION ACROSS CULTURES

Cross-cultural psychologists have recently become interested in studying how the value differences between cultures are reflected concretely in the manner of social interaction characteristic of these cultures. Global questionnaires are a useful means of assessing cultural values, but given the difficulties described earlier, they are not optimal for providing independent accounts of social activity. Because of its emphasis on everyday social interaction and event-by-event records, the RIR is well suited to this task. As a result, we have recently conducted cross-cultural comparisons of interaction data collected via translations of the RIR (see Fig. 2) from individuals in the United States, Hong Kong, and Jordan (Haddad, Reis, & Lin, 1990; Wheeler, Reis, & Bond, 1989). In each

Your name _____

Date_____ Beginning Time_____ Length:_____hours_____minutes

Initials and sex: (1)_____M,F (2)_____M,F (3)_____M,F

If more than 3 others:# of Males _____ # of Females_____

Compatibility: Very compatible 1 2 3 4 5 6 7 Very incompatible
　"夾"　　　十分"夾"　　　　　　　　十分不"夾"
I disclosed: Very little 1 2 3 4 5 6 7 Very much
我傾吐了　　十分少　　　　　　十分多
Other disclosed: Very little 1 2 3 4 5 6 7 Very much
其他人傾吐了　　十分少　　　　　　十分多
Quality: Unpleasant 1 2 3 4 5 6 7 Pleasant
質素　　不愉快　　　　　　　　愉快
Satisfaction: Less than 1 2 3 4 5 6 7 More than
滿意　　　　expected　　　　　　expected
　　　　比預期為低　　　　　比預期為高
Initiation: I initiated 1 2 3 4 5 6 7 Other initiated
發起　　我發起　　　　　　其他人發起
Influence: I influenced 1 2 3 4 5 6 7 Other influenced
影響　　我作出影響　　　　其他人作出影響
Nature: Paid work Task Recreation Chatting
性質　有薪工作 事務　娛樂　　閒談

التاريخ : _____ الوقت : قبل الظهر _____ المده : ساعه _____
_____ بعد الظهر _____ دقيقــــه _____
العدد : ذكور _____ اناث : _____

	٧	٦	٥	٤	٣	٢	١	
ذو معنـــى	٧	٦	٥	٤	٣	٢	١	القيمه المعنويه : سطحـــــي
بقدر كبير جدا	٧	٦	٥	٤	٣	٢	١	اغنيت عن نفسي : بقدر قليل جدا "
بقدر كبير جدا	٧	٦	٥	٤	٣	٢	١	اغنى الاخر عن نفسه : بقدر قليل جدا "
مستمتـــــعجـــدا	٧	٦	٥	٤	٣	٢	١	الاستمتاع : غير ممتـــع
اكبر مما متوقع	٧	٦	٥	٤	٣	٢	١	الرضى : اقل مما هو متوقع
بادر الاخــــر	٧	٦	٥	٤	٣	٢	١	المبادره : بادرت انـــا
اثر الاخر اكثر	٧	٦	٥	٤	٣	٢	١	التأثير : اثّرت انا اكثر
حديـــث	تضنية وق_____		مهمـــة					طبيعة التفاعل : وظيفـــة

Fig. 2. Chinese and Arabic versions of the RIR.

culture, a sample of college students kept the RIR for 2 weeks. Although cross-cultural samples can never be equivalent, the samples were chosen to be as comparable as possible along dimensions such as age, academic level, and educational goals.

These studies focused on two cultural value variables. The first, collectivism–individualism, is discussed by Hofstede (1980) and Triandis, Bontempo, Villareal, Asai, and Lucca (1988). In collective cultures, behavior is determined by goals and attitudes shared with one's group (typically family). Attachment to the group is strong, conformity and loyalty to the group are stressed, and socializing tends to be limited to one's group. In individualistic cultures, on the other hand, behavior is influenced mostly by personal goals and beliefs, and strong emphasis is placed on autonomy, sociability, and individual rights. Moreover, individualists move freely and easily from one social contact to another. Jordan and Hong Kong are collective cultures, whereas the United States is an individualistic culture. This led to the prediction that Americans will have more interactions, but proportionately fewer group interactions, than the other two cultures. This hypothesis was supported. Americans averaged 6.9 interactions lasting approximately 346 minutes per day, whereas the corresponding figures for the Chinese were 3.7 interactions lasting 214 minutes per day, and 4.7 interactions lasting 216 minutes per day for Jordanians (culture p values $<$ .0001). Furthermore, the percentage of group interaction was 29% in Hong Kong and 26% in Jordan, compared to only 17% in the United States.

The second cultural variable addressed in this research, namely attitudes toward heterosexual social contact, modified these trends. In traditional Arabic cultures, opposite-sex contact is discouraged; whereas in Western cultures, particularly among young adults, it is prized. Thus, we expected and found that opposite-sex interaction was significantly more prevalent in the United States (averaging 1.87 interactions for 103 minutes per day) than in Jordan (averaging 0.55 interactions for 25 minutes per day). Even when the overall base rate of interaction was controlled, opposite-sex contact was more frequent in the United States than in Jordan: 27% versus 12% of all interactions. Hong Kong fell in between these extremes (0.90 interactions for 55 minutes per day).

Collectivism–individualism and heterosexual attitudes also led to interesting subjective differences among the cultures. Because persons in collectivist cultures focus on close relationships more than on superficial acquaintanceships (Triandis *et al.*, 1988), we expected higher interaction intimacy in Hong Kong and Jordan than in the United States. This trend should be qualified, however, by the gender composition of the interaction. In all of our studies of American subjects, males' same-sex interaction has been significantly less intimate than that of females (Reis, 1989; Reis *et al.*, 1980; Wheeler & Nezlek, 1977; Wheeler *et al.*, 1983) because both sexes rely on females for expressive interaction and intimacy. In a culture such as Jordan, which restricts access between the sexes and which places greater reliance on same-sex relationships for psychological closeness, this sex difference ought to disappear. Table II displays the relevant means, summed over the two RIR disclosure scales. There was a significant culture difference, such that over all interactions, intimacy was highest in Hong Kong ($M = 8.24$), followed by Jordan ($M = 8.18$) and the United States ($M = 7.25$; $p < .001$). This effect was qualified by culture $\times$ sex interactions in the same-sex, mixed sex, and group categories (p values $< .005$). It can be seen in

TABLE II
INTERACTION INTIMACY RATINGS[a]

	United States		Hong Kong		Jordan	
	Male	Female	Male	Female	Male	Female
Same sex	6.57	8.22	8.20	8.63	8.40	8.20
Opposite sex	7.69	8.03	8.77	8.54	8.55	8.41
Mixed sex	6.07	7.19	7.78	8.02	8.56	7.94
Group	5.36	6.48	7.54	7.27	8.37	7.42

[a]Values expressed are means summed over two RIR disclosure scales.

Table II that whereas among Americans, females' intimacy exceeded that of males, among Jordanians the pattern was reversed. The conceptual importance of this reversal is in demonstrating that gender differences in interaction intimacy are a function of culture norms and socialization practices, rather than biologically or evolutionarily based imperatives (cf. Reis, Senchak, & Solomon, 1985).

One other finding from this research bears note. Overall interaction quality (the sum of pleasantness and satisfaction) was highest in the United States ($M = 9.42$), followed by Hong Kong ($M = 9.20$) and Jordan ($M = 8.75$; the three culture means differ at $p < .001$). This is consistent with the Triandis et al. (1988) notions about the importance of hedonic tone in individualistic cultures. The appreciably lower Jordanian mean might denote the impact of political and economic tension on individual socializing. Gender effects were similar to those for intimacy, but weaker.

These results demonstrate that the RIR can be used to quantify and test hypotheses about theoretically interesting differences between cultures, a potentially productive research direction that has heretofore received little attention (Wheeler & Reis, 1988).

H. THE DYADIC WITHDRAWAL HYPOTHESIS

Several theorists in the marriage and family area have argued that as dating partners become more involved with each other their outside social contacts diminish (e.g., Boissevain, 1974; Huston & Burgess, 1979). Presumably, this is due to limitations in the amount of time and energy available for social interaction, as well as normative sanctions against relationships that compete with the primary monogamous bond. Milardo et al. (1983) decided to examine this issue in a short-term longitudinal study. They argued that reports based on global questionnaires might be misleading, since members of developing relationships might perceive that others are becoming less significant because of their de-creased psychological reliance on them, rather than due to any drop in actual interaction with them. Event-based diary records bypass this alternative explanation.

Milardo *et al.* (1983), had 89 college students keep a modified version of the RIR for two 10-day periods, separated by 95 days. In cross-sectional analyses, people involved in the later stages of courtship interacted with outsiders less often for less time than people in early courtship stages. The only exception was interaction with kin, which showed no correlation with courtship stage. Longitu-dinal analyses were partly consistent with this trend. Over time, for those couples whose courtship progressed, interaction with intermediate friends and acquain-tances decreased, whereas interaction with kin and best friends remained stable. Conversely, interaction with all types of partners increased for those couples whose courtship regressed or ended.

Lin (1990b) replicated and extended these results using data from the sample described in Section IV,D. Lin's subjects also completed the Relationship Close-ness Inventory (Berscheid, Snyder, & Omoto, 1989), a measure that opera-tionalizes the Kelley *et al.* (1983) conceptualization of closeness and interdepen-dence. As predicted, the study showed that the more interdependent couples were, the less they interacted with others. This trend was somewhat stronger for interaction with casual friends ($r = -.43$ between closeness and time per day) than for interaction with best friends ($r = -.29$). Moreover, couple closeness predicted decreases in interaction intimacy ($r = -.39$) and quality ($r = -.29$) with casual friends, but not at all with best friends ($r = -.03$ and $-.05$, respectively).

The implication of these results is that social withdrawal by members of close heterosexual relationships emphasizes reduction in relatively superficial contacts with others, supporting the interpretation that "the dyadic withdrawal hypoth-esis" represents selective use of limited social time and energy rather than relatively nonselective, broad-based decreases in all sorts of social activity. Together, the Milardo *et al.* (1983) and Lin (1990b) studies provide clear evi-dence that the progression of dating and marital relationships to deeper, more interdependent stages involves simultaneous withdrawal from the outside social network. Moreover, the degree of withdrawal is itself a function of how close the individual and those outsiders are.

V. Other Applications of the RIR
and Related Approaches

As we have tried to document above, we believe that the RIR is a powerful tool for assessing the quantity and quality of people's social activity in everyday life. Its benefits stem directly from the event-contingent, self-recording approach, which eliminates many of the sources of distortion that plague other self-report methods. As such, the data that are obtained provide a more accurate and more detailed characterization of ongoing social interaction than other methods do. Given these advantages, it is appropriate to note that there are many other problems in psychology to which the RIR methodology might profitably be applied. Below we briefly describe some of these applications, in the hope that they will facilitate the work of others.

Modifications of the RIR may take either of two directions: changing the rating scales and dimensions, or recording different event types (or both). The RIR was designed to be flexible enough to allow researchers to ask varied questions, and the particular scales that we have used were chosen to meet specific theoretical goals. To address different sorts of theoretical questions, different scales should be used. For example, researchers interested in social support might include scales of support given and received (cf. Cutrona, 1986; Sullivan et al., 1990), perhaps detailed further corresponding to the support subtypes commonly discussed in that literature (e.g., instrumental, emotional, group belonging). Investigators studying the affective consequences of social interaction might use scales representing different emotions. Those interested in conflict and conflict resolution might include scales addressing the nature of everyday disagreements and how people cope with them. And environmentally oriented researchers might record the specific locations in which interactions take place so as to examine territory and place effects (as some already have; see, for example, Duck & Miell, 1986; Hays, 1989; Wheeler & Nezlek, 1977).

The event-contingent basis of the RIR might also be adapted to events other than social interaction. Duck et al. (in press) have developed the Iowa Communication Record, which subjects use to describe in detail their conversations. Wheeler and Miyake (1990) have recently begun work with the Rochester Social Comparison Record, a diary procedure in which subjects provide basic data every time they are aware of comparing themselves with someone else. The information on each record includes the dimension of comparison (e.g., appearance, academic performance), the direction of comparison (upward, with similar others, or downward), the subject's relationship with the target of comparison (close friend, stranger, etc.), and mood before and after comparison. The purpose is, of course, to test hypotheses about social comparison processes using data derived from spontaneous, naturally occurring events.[3]

[3]For example, 30% of comparisons were upward, 43% were downward, and 27% were at the same level. This varied, however, with the comparison dimension and the relationship to the comparison target. For example, same-level comparisons were relatively more frequent with close friends; downward comparisons were relatively more frequent with ordinary friends; and upward comparisons were relatively more frequent with acquaintances and strangers. In addition, preexisting negative mood led more often to upward comparison than to downward comparison, supporting a selective affect–cognition priming model in which dysphoria primes negative thoughts about the self (Forgas, Bower, & Moylan, 1990) rather than a motivational self-enhancement model.

It is relatively easy to imagine other research areas that might benefit from the RIR paradigm. Some concern events that are intrinsically engaging in their own right. For example, one might have subjects complete an event record after every sexual encounter, both to examine affective correlates of sexual activity, and to obtain information about sexual practices such as "safe sex" and alcohol use.[4] Or, in a more clinical vein, event ratings might be obtained after every headache, after every encounter with a phobia object, or after every "binge and purge" episode. The RIR can also be used with special populations. Buunk (1988), for example, used a variant of the RIR to examine interactions of police officers with their peers and superiors.

The RIR might also be adapted to events and processes more common in the social psychological literature. Subjects might, for example, categorize their interaction partners as in group or out group, so that naturally occurring interactions within each of these categories could be compared. Another example comes from the attribution for success and failure literature, which has been limited to laboratory tasks, one-time real-life events, or global questionnaires. Instead, subjects might complete an event record after every receipt of performance-evaluative feedback. Similarly, to complement the existing literature on attitude change, an event record might be completed after every attempt to change someone's attitude (or otherwise influence them). In this instance, the scales might conceivably assess the familiar three factors (source, message, and audience characteristics), as well as other dimensions tied to particular theoretical frameworks.

---

[4]These two examples suggest potential new advantages to the RIR and related techniques. In many studies of states (e.g., mood, sexual arousal) and substances (e.g., alcohol) that alter mental processes, people are asked to describe their past behavior, or to predict how they would behave in a given situation. Often in such work the person is in a different state of mind when answering questions about their behavior than when the behavior itself is enacted. For example, subjects are sometimes asked to describe their behavior while intoxicated, or how they would respond to a sexually arousing situation. Accounts and predictions provided while in a neutral, baseline state (as is typical in surveys and interviews) may be inaccurate because social perception and cognition in the situations being studied are influenced markedly by thought-altering agents, such as alcohol, strong emotions, and sexual arousal. On the other hand, if subjects' accounts and predictions were obtained while in the relevant mental state, their reports would reflect some of the same influences that affect the target behaviors. In other words, if an agent such as alcohol affects social thought (as it does; see Steele & Josephs, 1990), it is possible that the most accurate self-reports and self-predictions would be obtained when the person was intoxicated. If this line of reasoning is correct, there would be considerable advantages to collecting data before the person's mental state had changed. This might be accomplished by having subjects complete event-records during or shortly after whatever events are of interest (e.g., moderate drinking, sexual excitement, drug use). Of course, it would be impractical to expect subjects to complete an event-record in some of these instances. Still, many of these situations may prove more tractable to such research procedures than seems apparent, and the potential advantages of this approach over traditional alternatives suggests that they be attempted.

As one example of these possibilities, we would offer the recent work by Hoyle (1990). Hoyle was interested in the manner in which the self-focusing characteristics of social interaction affect momentary self-esteem. After every 10-minute or longer social interaction, Hoyle's subjects rated their feelings about themselves in four domains: task competence, appearance, social confidence, and "stage presence." They also described the situational context along several dimensions (e.g., whether the interaction was public or private). Among the findings were the following: Interactions that subjects initiated themselves left them feeling more task competent, but not more positive in other ways; interactions with some degree of conflict also enhanced feelings of task competence but not the other domains; interactions that took place in public tended to enhance self-esteem along all dimensions except task competence.

The RIR also shows promise for investigating social interaction effects at different levels of analysis. As Kashy (1990) has noted, each RIR rating derives from four sources of variance: person, partner, day, and interaction. Nearly all of the studies we have discussed are confined to examining person effects (e.g., how does one person's pattern of interaction differ from another's?). There are important questions awaiting empirical attention at other levels of analysis, however, and the RIR seems potentially useful in this regard. For example, how does interaction with different types of partners differ? How much consistency in interaction patterns exists from one day to the next? Within a single interaction, how does one partner's self-disclosure relate to the other's self-disclosure, and is this relation moderated by closeness? Kashy (1990) has recently proposed a set of procedures for decomposing RIR data into the four sources of variance noted above, and we believe these procedures open an important new direction for researchers using self-reported event diaries and logs.

In none of this do we wish to imply that the RIR, or other naturalistic procedures for self-recording daily events, should substitute for laboratory-based studies, especially those that feature manipulation of independent variables. Standard laboratory practices are admirably powerful tools for testing hypotheses under controlled, and usually well-circumscribed, conditions. Many questions are appropriately addressed with these methods, and we do not believe it would be desirable for social psychologists to adopt the RIR approach in their stead. Nevertheless, the generalizability and external validity of many laboratory manipulations have been questioned, and it is important for the field to begin testing hypotheses about the nature and prevalence of its favored constructs in everyday life. Thus, the RIR adds a method to our research armamentarium for precisely testing hypotheses with data collected from the ongoing stream of everyday social behavior. True, naturalistic research of this sort sacrifices much of the internal validity for which experimental methods are properly celebrated. But the enhanced generalizability of a relatively nonreactive "in-stream" approach gives the RIR and other daily event-recording strategies unique and powerful advantages, so much so that the two strategies are best considered to be complementary, and perhaps even a necessity in programmatic research.

A FEW OTHER APPLICATIONS

Aside from its use in theoretically oriented research, three other possible applications of the RIR bear note. First, the RIR might be used as an outcome measure in intervention and other clinically oriented studies (e.g., Christensen, Arkowitz, & Anderson, 1975; Johnson, Christensen, & Bellamy, 1976). For example, before and after RIR data sets might be used to see if social skills training can ameliorate the experience of loneliness or shyness, or to determine whether intercultural training groups can enhance spontaneous social contact between different ethnic or cultural groups. Kirchler (1988) has used the RIR to describe differences between happily and unhappily married couples in their interaction with each other. As one indicator of therapeutic change, such data might be compared to similar records collected after marital counseling. For that matter, the RIR might provide useful fodder for therapy, as the ESM has (Massimini, Csikszentmihalyi, & Carli, 1987). As we argued earlier, retrospective accounts of social experience are often the product of considerable reinterpretations. By having accurate records available, patients might become more aware of these processes, which can serve as a stimulus for evaluating, and potentially changing, relationships with others.

Second, in that the RIR (and similar techniques) is the best available method for obtaining accurate information about social interaction, it might be used to provide validity standards against which other techniques can be evaluated. The McFarland et al. (1989) study mentioned earlier is a good example of the use of daily event records to provide objective behavior accounts, although they did not seek to establish the validity of another method. However, Lippa and Donaldson (1990) did, in order to establish the validity of a computer-based measure of behavioral consistency. Lin (1990b) is also using the RIR to assess the accuracy of the quantitative components of the Closeness Scale recently developed by Berscheid et al. (1989).

Third, by its very nature, the RIR is well suited to supplying detailed descriptive information about social interaction. In our studies of Rochester college students, for example, we have consistently found that the average student socializes about 6 hours per day, that same-sex interactions are about twice as frequent as opposite-sex interactions, and that most interactions are relatively pleasant and satisfying (see Nezlek et al., 1983, for a summary). Descriptive comparisons can be used inductively to suggest explanations and generate hypotheses for further research. Moreover, descriptive research is important in its own right (Ossorio, 1981). As Deaux (1978) noted, full conceptual understanding of human social behavior requires knowing not only which antecedents produce which consequences, but also how frequently these circumstances occur. Descriptive studies are especially valuable in the early stages of research (Gottman, 1989), particularly when the area is phenomenon centered, as opposed to theory or paradigm centered. In other words, researchers need to know what the key parameters are before they can be comprehensively accounted for.

VI. Conclusion

The vast array of new research technologies that has become available in the past two decades has given researchers extensive new opportunities for operationalizing the multimethod approach to behavioral science first advocated by Campbell and Fiske (1959). Event-contingent self-recording methods such as the RIR fill a unique niche in our repertoire of research tools, offering a potent and flexible strategy for studying social behavior as it naturally and spontaneously occurs in everyday life. Wider adoption of these methods, especially in concert with existing, complementary procedures, has the potential to add an important new perspective to social psychology's bank of empirical data and theoretical constructs. With this aim in mind, we hope that other researchers will find ways of adapting these methods to their own problems. Such an approach can only enrich our understanding of human social behavior.

Acknowledgments

The research described in this article has profited immeasurably over the years from the efforts and suggestions of many collaborators and students. John Nezlek was centrally involved in all of the early RIR studies, and without his contributions none of this research would have been possible. We are also grateful to Yi-Cheng Lin, Michael Kernis, Nancy Spiegel, Michael Bond, Yasmin Haddad, Elizabeth Sementilli, Marilyn Senchak, Beth Solomon, and Laura Robinson for their many contributions. Elizabeth Whitehead deserves our thanks for keeping much of this research under control, and David Landy made several helpful suggestions in the initial development of the RIR. Caryl Rusbult, Laurie Jensen, William Graziano, and Mark Zanna provided valuable comments for revising this manuscript. To all of these individuals, we wish to express our deep gratitude.

Finally, our research has been facilitated by grants from the National Science Foundation, the Public Health Service, the Center for Naval Analysis, and the University of Rochester. We are also grateful to them.

References

Altman, I. (1975). *The environment and social behavior.* Monterey, CA: Brooks/Cole.

Asch, S. E. (1956). Studies of independence and submission to group pressure: I. A minority of one against a unanimous majority. *Psychological Monographs,* **70** (9, Whole No. 417).

Astin, A. (1987). *The American freshman: Twenty year trends, 1966–1985.* Los Angeles: UCLA Graduate School of Education.

Attridge, M., & Berscheid, E. (1990). *The positivity and intensity characteristics of selected emotion terms.* Unpublished manuscript, University of Minnesota, Minneapolis.

Barker, R. G. (1968). *Ecological psychology: Concepts and methods for studying the environment of human behavior.* Stanford, CA: Stanford University Press.

Belson, W. A. (1981). *The design and understanding of survey questions.* Aldershot, England: Gower.

Bernard, H. R., & Killworth, P. D. (1977). Informant accuracy in social-network data II. *Human Communication Research,* **4**, 3–18.

Bernard, H. R., Killworth, P. D., & Sailer, L. (1982). Informant accuracy in social-network data V. An experimental attempt to predict actual communication from recall data. *Social Science Research,* **11**, 30–66.

Berscheid, E., Snyder, M., & Omoto, A. M. (1989). The Relationship Closeness Inventory: Assessing the closeness of interpersonal relationships. *Journal of Personality and Social Psychology,* **57**, 792–807.

Berscheid, E., & Walster, E. H. (1974). Physical attractiveness. In L. Berkowitz (Ed.), *Advances in experimental social psychology* (Vol. 7, pp. 158–215). New York: Academic Press.

Blanchard, E. B., Appelbaum, K. A., Radnitz, C. L., Michultka, D., Morrill, B., Kirsch, C., Hillhouse, J., Evans, D. D., Guarnieri, P., Attanasio, V., Andrasik, F., Jaccard, J., & Dentinger, M. P. (1990). A controlled evaluation of thermal biofeedback and thermal biofeedback combined with cognitive therapy in the treatment of vascular headache. *Journal of Consulting and Clinical Psychology,* **58**, 216–224.

Blaney, P. H. (1986). Affect and memory: A review. *Psychological Bulletin,* **99**, 229–246.

Boissevain, J. (1974). *Friends of friends. Networks, manipulators and coalitions.* Oxford, England: Blackwell.

Bolger, N., DeLongis, A., Kessler, R. C., & Schilling, E. A. (1989). Effects of daily stress on negative mood. *Journal of Personality and Social Psychology,* **57**, 808–818.

Buss, D. M. (1988). Love acts: The evolutionary biology of love. In R. J. Sternberg & M. L. Barnes (Eds.), *The psychology of love* (pp. 100–118). New Haven, CT: Yale University Press.

Buunk, B. (1988, July). *Companionship and support in organizations: A microanalysis of the stress-reducing features of social interaction.* Paper presented at the 4th International Conference on Personal Relationships, Vancouver, British Columbia, Canada.

Campbell, D. T., & Fiske, D. W. (1959). Convergent and discriminant validation by the multitrait–multimethod matrix. *Psychological Bulletin,* **56**, 81–105.

Campbell, J. D., Chew, B., & Scratchley, L. S. (in press). Cognitive and emotional reactions to daily events: The effects of self-esteem and self-complexity. *Journal of Personality.*

Christensen, A., Arkowitz, H., & Anderson, J. (1975). Practice dating as a treatment for college dating inhibitions. *Behaviour Research and Therapy,* **13**, 321–331.

Clark, M. S. (1985). Implications of relationship type for understanding compatibility. In W. Ickes (Ed.), *Compatible and incompatible relationships* (pp. 119–140). New York: Springer-Verlag.

Clark, M. S., & Mills, J. (1979). Interpersonal attraction in exchange and communal relationships. *Journal of Personality and Social Psychology,* **37**, 12–24.

Conrath, D. W., Higgins, C. A., & McClean, R. J. (1983). A comparison of the reliability of questionnaire versus diary data. *Social Networks, 5,* 315–322.

Constanzo, M., & Archer, D. (1989). Interpreting the expressive behavior of others: The interpersonal perception task. *Journal of Nonverbal Behavior, 13,* 225–245.

Csikszentmihalyi, M., & Larson, R. (1984). *Being adolescent.* New York: Basic Books.

Csikszentmihalyi, M., & Larson, R. (1987). Validity and reliability of the experience-sampling method. *The Journal of Nervous and Mental Disease, 175,* 526–536.

Csikszentmihalyi, M., Larson, R., & Prescott, S. (1977). The ecology of adolescent activity and experience. *Journal of Youth and Adolescence, 6,* 281–294.

Cutrona, C. E. (1986). Behavioral manifestations of social support: A microanalytic investigation. *Journal of Personality and Social Psychology, 51,* 201–208.

Davison, G. C., Robins, C., & Johnson, M. K. (1983). Articulated thoughts during simulated situations: A paradigm for studying cognition in emotion and behavior. *Cognitive Therapy Research, 7,* 17–40.

Deaux, K. (1978). *Patterns of self-disclosure in natural social interaction.* Unpublished manuscript, Purdue University, West Lafayette, IN.

Delespaul, P. A. E. G., & deVries, M. W. (1987). The daily life of ambulatory chronic mental patients. *The Journal of Nervous and Mental Disease, 175,* 537–544.

DePaulo, B. M., Kirkendol, S. E., Epstein, J. E., Wyer, M., & Hairfield, J. (1990). *Everyday lies.* Unpublished manuscript, University of Virginia, Charlottesville.

Duck, S. (1991). Diaries and logs. In B. M. Montgomery & S. W. Duck (Eds.), *Studying interpersonal interaction* (pp. 141–161). New York: Guilford.

Duck, S., & Pond, K. (1989). Friends, Romans, countrymen, lend me your retrospections: Rhetoric and reality in personal relationships. In C. Hendrick (Ed.), *Close relationships.* Newbury Park, CA: Sage.

Duck, S., Rutt, D. J., Hurst, M. H., & Strejc, H. (in press). Some evident truths about conversation in everyday relationships: All communications are not created equal. *Human Communication Research.*

Duck, S. W., & Miell, D. E. (1986). Charting the development of personal relationships. In R. Gilmour & S. W. Duck (Eds.), *The emerging field of personal relationships* (pp. 133–143). Hillsdale, NJ: Erlbaum.

Duck, S. W., & Sants, H. K. A. (1983). On the origin of the specious: Are personal relationships really interpersonal states? *Journal of Social and Clinical Psychology, 1,* 27–41.

Ehrlichmann, H., & Halpern, J. N. (1988). Affect and memory: Effects of pleasant and unpleasant odors on retrieval of happy and unhappy memories. *Journal of Personality and Social Psychology, 55,* 769–779.

Ericsson, K. A., & Simon, H. A. (1980). Verbal reports as data. *Psychological Review, 87,* 215–251.

Erikson, E. (1950). *Childhood and society.* New York: Norton.

Fazio, R. H. (1986). How do attitudes guide behavior? In R. M. Sorrentino & E. T. Higgins (Eds.), *Handbook of motivation and cognition: Foundations of social behavior* (pp. 204–243). New York: Guilford.

Feingold, A. (1990). Gender differences in effects of physical attractiveness on romantic attraction: Comparison across five research domains. *Journal of Personality and Social Psychology, 59,* 981–993.

Fiske, S. T., & Taylor, S. E. (1984). *Social cognition.* Reading, MA: Addison-Wesley.

Forgas, J. P., Bower, G. H., & Krantz, S. E. (1984). The influence of mood on perceptions of social interactions. *Journal of Experimental Social Psychology, 20,* 497–513.

Forgas, J. P., Bower, G. H., & Moylan, S. J. (1990). Praise or blame: Affective influences on attributions for achievement. *Journal of Personality and Social Psychology, 59,* 809–819.

Gilligan, S. G., & Bower, G. H. (1984). Cognitive consequences of emotional arousal. In C. E. Izard, J. Kagan, & R. B. Zajonc (Eds.), *Emotions, cognition, and behavior.* Hillsdale, NJ: Erlbaum.

Goodhart, D., & Peters, K. A. (1986). *The give and take of friendship: The effects of reciprocity and social support on psychological well-being.* Unpublished manuscript, University of Illinois at Urbana, Champaign.

Gottman, J. (1989, May). Award address presented at the Iowa Network on Personal Relationships Conference, Iowa City, IA.

Gottman, J. M. (1979). *Marital interaction: Experimental investigations.* New York: Academic Press.

Gottman, J. M., & Parker, J. G. (1986). *Conversations of friends.* New York: Cambridge University Press.

Haan, N. (1977). *Coping and defending: Processes of self-environment organization.* New York: Academic Press.

Haddad, Y., Reis, H. T., & Lin, Y.-C. (1990). *A cross-cultural comparison of social interaction in three cultures.* Unpublished manuscript, University of Rochester, Rochester, NY.

Halverson, C. F. (1988). Remembering your parents: Reflections on the retrospective method. *Journal of Personality, 56,* 435–444.

Hatfield, E., & Sprecher, S. (1986). Mirror, mirror . . . The importance of looks in everyday life. Albany, NY: State University of New York Press.

Hays, R. B. (1989). The day-to-day functioning of close versus casual friendships. *Journal of Social and Personal Relationships, 6,* 21–37.

Hedges, S. M., Jandorf, L., & Stone, A. A. (1985). Meaning of daily mood assessments. *Journal of Personality and Social Psychology, 48,* 428–434.

Higgins, C. A., McClean, R. J., & Conrath, D. W. (1985). The accuracy and biases of diary communication data. *Social Networks, 7,* 173–187.

Hinrichs, J. R. (1964). Communication activity of industrial research personnel. *Personnel Psychology, 17,* 193–204.

Hodgins, H., & Zuckerman, M. (1990). The effect of nonverbal sensitivity on social interaction. *Journal of Nonverbal Behavior, 14*(3), 155–170.

Hofstede, C. (1980). *Culture's consequences: International differences in work-related values.* Beverly Hills, CA: Sage.

Holmes, J. G. (1981). The exchange process in close relationships. Microbehavior and macromotives. In M. J. Lerner & S. C. Lerner (Eds.), *The justice motive in social behavior.* New York: Plenum.

Homans, G. C. (1950). *The human group.* New York: Harcourt, Brace.

Hormuth, S. E. (1986). The sampling of experiences *in situ. Journal of Personality, 54,* 262–293.

Hoyle, R. H. (1990). *Social interaction and the focus of self-attention.* Unpublished manuscript, University of Kentucky, Lexington.

Huston, T. L., & Burgess, R. L. (1979). The analysis of social exchange in developing relationships. In R. L. Burgess & T. L. Huston (Eds.), *Social exchange in developing relationships.* New York: Academic Press.

Huston, T. L., & Robins, E. (1982). Conceptual and methodological issues in studying close relationships. *Journal of Marriage and the Family, 44,* 901–925.

Ickes, W. (1983). A basic paradigm for the study of personality, roles, and social behavior. In H. Reis (Ed.), *New directions for methodology of social and behavioral science.* San Francisco, CA: Jossey-Bass.

Ickes, W., & Tooke, W. (1988). The observational method: Studying the interaction of minds and bodies. In S. Duck (Ed.), *Handbook of personal relationships: Theory, research and interventions* (pp. 79–97). Chichester, England: Wiley.

Isen, A. M. (1984). Toward understanding the role of affect in cognition. In R. S. Wyer, Jr., & T. K. Srull (Eds.), *Handbook of social cognition* (pp. 179–236). Hillsdale, NJ: Erlbaum.

Johnson, S. M., Christensen, A., & Bellamy, G. T. (1976). Evaluation of family intervention through unobtrusive audio recordings: Experiences in bugging children. *Journal of Applied Behavior Analysis, 9,* 213–219.

Josephson, W. L. (1987). Television violence and children's aggression: Testing the priming, social script, and disinhibition predictions. *Journal of Personality and Social Psychology, 53,* 882–890.

Kashy, D. A. (1990). *Levels of analysis of social interaction diaries: Separating the effects of person, partner, day, and interaction.* Unpublished manuscript, University of Connecticut.

Kashy, D. A., & Kenny, D. A. (1990). Do you know whom you were with a week ago Friday? A reanalysis of the Bernard, Killworth, and Sailer studies. *Social Psychology Quarterly, 53,* 55–61.

Kelley, H. H., Berscheid, E., Christensen, A., Harvey, J. H., Huston, T. L., Levinger, G., McClintock, E., Peplau, L. A., & Peterson, D. R. (1983). *Close relationships.* San Francisco, CA: Freeman.

Killworth, P. D., & Bernard, H. R. (1976). Informant accuracy in social network data. *Human Organization, 35,* 269–296.

Kirchler, E. (1988). Marital happiness and interaction in everyday surroundings: A time-sample diary approach for couples. *Journal of Social and Personal Relationships, 5,* 375–382.

Larson, R. W., & Csikszentmihalyi, M. (1983). The experience sampling method. In H. Reis (Ed.), *New directions of naturalistic methods in the behavioral sciences.* San Francisco, CA: Jossey-Bass.

Larson, R. W., Raffaelli, M., Richards, M. H., Ham, M., & Jewell, L. (1990). Ecology of depression in late childhood and early adolescence: A profile of daily states and activities. *Journal of Abnormal Psychology, 99,* 92–102.

Lemon, B. W., Bengtson, V. L., & Peterson, J. A. (1972). An exploration of the activity theory of aging: Activity types and life satisfaction among in-movers to a retirement community. *Journal of Gerontology, 27,* 511–523.

Levinson, D. (1978). *The seasons of a man's life.* New York: Random House.

Lin, Y.-C. (1990a). *Aggregating Rochester Interaction Record data.* Unpublished manuscript, University of Rochester, Rochester, NY.

Lin, Y.-C. (1990b). *Dyadic withdrawal hypothesis: A reexamination.* Unpublished manuscript, University of Rochester, Rochester, NY.

Lindsley, O. (1968). A reliable wrist counter for recording behavioral rates. *Journal of Applied Behavior Analysis, 1,* 77–78.

Lippa, R., & Donaldson, S. I. (1990). Self-monitoring and idiographic measures of behavioral variability across interpersonal relationships. *Journal of Personality, 58,* 465–479.

Markus, H., & Zajonc, R. B. (1985). The cognitive perspective in social psychology. In G. Lindzey & E. Aronson (Eds.), *Handbook of social psychology* (3rd ed., Vol. 1, pp. 137–230). New York: Random House.

Massimini, F., Csikszentmihalyi, M., & Carli, M. (1987). The monitoring of optimal experience: A tool for psychiatric rehabilitation. *The Journal of Nervous and Mental Disease, 175,* 545–549.

McAdams, D. P., & Constantian, C. A. (1983). Intimacy and affiliation motives in daily living: An experience sampling analysis. *Journal of Personality and Social Psychology, 45,* 851–861.

McFarland, C., Ross, M., & DeCourville, N. (1989). Women's theories of menstruation and biases in recall of menstrual symptoms. *Journal of Personality and Social Psychology, 57,* 522–531.

Meehl, P. E. (1945). The dynamics of 'structured' personality tests. *Journal of Clinical Psychology*, **1**, 296–303.

Milardo, R. M., Johnson, M. P., & Huston, T. L. (1983). Developing close relationships: Changing patterns of interaction between pair members and social networks. *Journal of Personality and Social Psychology*, **44**, 964–976.

Nezlek, J., & Wheeler, L. (1984). RIRAP: Rochester Interaction Record Analysis Package. *Psychological Documents*, **14**(6), 2610.

Nezlek, J., Wheeler, L., & Reis, H. T. (1983). Studies of social participation. In H. T. Reis (Ed.), *Naturalistic approaches to studying social interaction* (pp. 57–73). San Francisco, CA: Jossey-Bass.

Nisbett, R., & Ross, L. (1981). *Human inference: Strategies and shortcomings of social judgment.* Englewood Cliffs, NJ: Prentice-Hall.

Ossorio, P. G. (1981). Outline of descriptive psychology for personality theory and clinical applications. In K. E. Davis (Ed.), *Advances in descriptive psychology* (Vol. 1). Greenwich, CT: JAI Press.

Peplau, L. A., & Perlman, D. (1982). Perspectives on loneliness. In L. A. Peplau & D. Perlman (Eds.), *Loneliness: A sourcebook of current theory, research and therapy* (pp. 1–18). New York: Wiley.

Reis, H. T. (1989). *The impact of social interaction on health during the transition to adult life.* (Final Report to the National Science Foundation, Grant Number BNS-8416988)

Reis, H. T. (1990). The role of intimacy in interpersonal relations. *Journal of Social and Clinical Psychology*, **9**, 15–30.

Reis, H. T., Nezlek, J., & Wheeler, L. (1980). Physical attractiveness in social interaction. *Journal of Personality and Social Psychology*, **38**, 604–617.

Reis, H. T., Senchak, M., & Solomon, B. (1985). Sex differences in the intimacy of social interaction: Further examination of potential explanations. *Journal of Personality and Social Psychology*, **48**, 1204–1217.

Reis, H. T., & Shaver, P. (1988). Intimacy as an interpersonal process. In S. Duck (Ed.), *Handbook of personal relationships: Theory, research and interventions* (pp. 367–389). Chichester, England: Wiley.

Reis, H. T., Wheeler, L., Kernis, M. H., Spiegel, N., & Nezlek, J. (1985). On specificity in the impact of social participation on physical and psychological health. *Journal of Personality and Social Psychology*, **48**, 456–471.

Reis, H. T., Wheeler, L., Spiegel, N., Kernis, M. H., Nezlek, J., & Perri, M. (1982). Physical attractiveness in social interaction: II, Why does appearance affect social experience? *Journal of Personality and Social Psychology*, **43**, 979–996.

Ritter, J. M., & Langlois, J. H. (1988). The role of physical attractiveness in the observation of adult–child interactions: Eye of the beholder or behavioral reality? *Developmental Psychology*, **24**, 254–263.

Robinson, J. P. (1987). Microbehavioral approaches to monitoring human experience. *The Journal of Nervous and Mental Disease*, **175**, 514–518.

Rogers, T. B., Kuiper, N. A., & Kirker, W. S. (1977). Self-reference and the encoding of personal information. *Journal of Personality and Social Psychology*, **35**, 677–688.

Ross, M. (1989). Relation of implicit theories to the construction of personal histories. *Psychological Review*, **96**, 341–357.

Rusbult, C. E., Johnson, D. J., & Morrow, G. D. (1986). Impact of couple patterns of problem solving on distress and nondistress in dating relationships. *Journal of Personality and Social Psychology*, **50**, 744–753.

Russell, D. (1982). The measurement of loneliness. In L. A. Peplau & D. Perlman (Eds.), *Loneliness: A sourcebook of current theory, research and therapy* (pp. 81–104). New York: Wiley.

Russell, D., Cutrona, C. E., Rose, J., & Yurko, K. (1984). Social and emotional loneliness: An examination of Weiss's typology of loneliness. *Journal of Personality and Social Psychology,* **46,** 1313–1321.

Russell, D., Peplau, L. A., & Cutrona, C. E. (1980). The revised UCLA loneliness scale: Concurrent and discriminant validity evidence. *Journal of Personality and Social Psychology,* **39,** 472–480.

Schachter, S. (1959). *The psychology of affiliation.* Stanford, CA: Stanford University Press.

Schwarz, N. (1990). Assessing frequency reports of mundane behaviors: Contributions of cognitive psychology to questionnaire construction. In C. Hendrick & M. S. Clark (Eds.), *Research methods in personality and social psychology* (pp. 98–119). Newbury Park, CA: Sage.

Schwarz, N., & Clore, G. L. (1983). Mood, misattribution, and judgments of well-being: Informative and directive functions of affective states. *Journal of Personality and Social Psychology,* **34,** 513–523.

Shrauger, J. S., & Osberg, T. M. (1981). The relative accuracy of self-predictions and judgments by others in psychological assessment. *Psychological Bulletin,* **90,** 322–351.

Singer, J. L., & Kolligian, J., Jr. (1987). Personality: Developments in the study of private experience. *Annual Review of Psychology,* **38,** 533–575.

Skowronski, J. J., Betz, A. L., Thompson, C. P., & Shannon, L. (1990). *Social memory in everyday life: The recall of self-events and other-events.* Unpublished manuscript, Ohio State University, Newark.

Snyder, M., Berscheid, E., & Glick, P. (1985). Focusing on the exterior and the interior: Two investigations of the initiation of personal relationships. *Journal of Personality and Social Psychology,* **48,** 1427–1439.

Snyder, M., & Ickes, W. (1985). Personality and social behavior. In G. Lindzey & E. Aronson (Eds.), *The handbook of social psychology* (3rd ed., Vol. 2, pp. 883–947). New York: Random House.

Steele, C. M., & Josephs, R. A. (1990). Alcohol myopia: Its prized and dangerous effects. *American Psychologist,* **45,** 921–933.

Stone, A. A., Kessler, R. S., & Haythornthwaite, J. A. (in press). Methodological considerations in the measurement of daily events and experiences. *Journal of Personality.*

Sullivan, H. H. (1953). *The interpersonal theory of psychiatry.* New York: Norton.

Sullivan, L. A., Nezlek, J., & Jackson, L. A. (1990). *Social interaction and emotional support: Reciprocity and sex differences.* Unpublished manuscript, Michigan State University, East Lansing.

Taylor, S. E., & Brown, J. D. (1988). Illusion and well-being: A social psychological perspective on mental health. *Psychological Bulletin,* **103,** 193–210.

Tennen, H., Suls, J., & Affleck, G. (in press). Special issue. *Journal of Personality.*

Tesch, S. A., & Whitbourne, S. K. (1982). Intimacy and identity status in young adults. *Journal of Personality and Social Psychology,* **43,** 1041–1051.

Triandis, H. C., Bontempo, R., Villareal, M. J., Asai, M., & Lucca, N. (1988). Individualism and collectivism: Cross-cultural perspectives on self-ingroup relationships. *Journal of Personality and Social Psychology,* **54,** 323–333.

Tversky, A., & Kahneman, D. (1982). Judgment under uncertainty: Heuristics and biases. In D. Kahneman, P. Slovic, & A. Tversky (Eds.), *Judgment under uncertainty* (pp. 3–20). New York: Cambridge University Press.

Vaux, W. A. (1985). Variations in social support associated with gender, ethnicity, and age. *Journal of Social Issues,* **41,** 89–110.

Weick, K. E. (1979). *The social psychology of organizing* (2nd ed.). Reading, MA: Addison-Wesley.

Weick, K. E. (1985). Systematic observational methods. In G. Lindzey & E. Aronson (Eds.), *The handbook of social psychology* (3rd ed., Vol. 1, pp. 567–634). New York: Random House.

Wheeler, L., & Miyake, K. (1990, June). *Social comparison in everyday life.* Paper presented at the Second Annual Convention of the American Psychological Society, Dallas.

Wheeler, L., & Nezlek, J. (1977). Sex differences in social participation. *Journal of Personality and Social Psychology, 35,* 742–754.

Wheeler, L., & Reis, H. T. (1988). On titles, citations, and outlets: What do mainstreamers want? In M. H. Bond (Ed.), *The cross-cultural challenge to social psychology* (pp. 36–40). Beverly Hills, CA: Sage.

Wheeler, L., & Reis, H. T. (in press). Self-recording of events in everyday life. *Journal of Personality.*

Wheeler, L., Reis, H. T., & Bond, M. H. (1989). Collectivism–individualism in everyday social life: The middle kingdom and the melting pot. *Journal of Personality and Social Psychology, 57,* 79–96.

Wheeler, L., Reis, H., & Nezlek, J. (1983). Loneliness, social interaction, and sex roles. *Journal of Personality and Social Psychology, 45,* 943–953.

Whitbourne, S. K., & Reis, H. T. (1982). *Intimacy status and social interaction.* Unpublished manuscript, University of Rochester, Rochester, NY.

Whitbourne, S. K., & Weinstock, C. S. (1979). *Adult development: The differentiation of experience.* New York: Holt, Rinehart & Winston.

Wilder, D. A. (1977). Perception of groups, size of opposition, and social influence. *Journal of Experimental Social Psychology, 13,* 253–268.

Wong, M. M., & Csikszentmihalyi, M. (in press). Motivation and academic achievement: The effects of personality traits and the quality of experience. *Journal of Personality.*

SUBJECTIVE CONSTRUAL, SOCIAL INFERENCE, AND HUMAN MISUNDERSTANDING

Dale W. Griffin

Lee Ross

To construe an action, person, situation, or event, according to the *Shorter Oxford Dictionary,* is "to interpret or put a construction on" it, and a prototypical use of the term is "to construe silence as an affront." The example is well-chosen, for silence itself has no unique meaning. It could be construed as an indication of another person's deliberate attempt at insult; but it alternatively could be construed as an indication of the other's great sorrow, or great respect, or great embarrassment. Thus although silence itself exists as an objective phenomenon, construal by the perceiver is required to bridge the gulf between the objective world of stimuli and the subjective world of experience.

I. Construal Processes and Psychological Inquiry

The process of subjective construal is fundamental to psychological inquiry at all levels of analysis. Even at the most molecular level of analysis, we find that the study of sensory perception is the study of how the organism, faced with the blooming, buzzing confusion of sensory input, constructs one particular coherent reality from the set of possible alternatives. Neisser (1976, p. 76) makes the point clearly when noting that "Stimuli themselves cannot possibly have meaning because they are merely patterns of light or sound or pressure. The meaning must be supplied by the perceiver *after* the stimuli have been registered." At a more intermediate level of analysis, we find the study of concept formation and categorization to be an investigation of the conscious and unconscious strategies that people use in discerning, systematizing, and utilizing regularities in their experience. As Barsalou (1987, p. 101) explains, "Rather than being retrieved

319

as static units from memory to represent categories, concepts originate in a highly flexible process that retrieves generic and episodic information from long-term memory to construct temporary concepts in working memory.'' And of course, at the highest or most molar level of analysis, in the study of culture and society, the emphasis on subjective reality is inescapable. As Geertz (1973, p. 52) eloquently argues, ''We become individual under the guidance of cultural patterns, historically created symbol systems of meaning in terms of which we give form, order, point, and direction to our lives.''

This chapter examines some social psychological implications of human subjectivity—implications of the fact, and perhaps more importantly the insight, that people are governed not by the passive reception and recognition of some invariant objective reality, but by their own subjective representations and constructions of the events that unfold around them. We begin by reviewing the history of the subjective–objective distinction, first in some traditional theoretical and methodological concerns of social psychology, and then in somewhat later, more applied, discussions of human motivation. We next turn to social cognition, a research area that has held center stage in our field for most of the past two decades. Our particular focus will be the problem of situational construal and its contribution to the difficulties of predicting social actions and making inferences or attributions about social actors. Finally, we examine the role of construal processes and construal biases in social misunderstanding and conflict, concluding with an attempt to spell out some of the implication of our analysis for the task of conflict resolution.

Throughout, we will be explicating and defending two theses. The first and more familiar thesis is simply that construal processes are variable and uncertain, and as such that they contribute heavily to the variability and unpredictability of a wide range of social responses. The second and less familiar thesis is that social perceivers fail to recognize, or at least fail to make adequate inferential allowance for, these ''vagaries'' of construal. We argue that people characteristically make attributions and other social judgments and decisions predicated on a kind of naive realism, one that overestimates both the accuracy of their own construals and the degree to which other people's construals are congruent with their own.

A. THE SUBJECTIVIST TRADITION
IN SOCIAL PSYCHOLOGY

Today, as the intellectual community struggles with the implications of hermeneutics and deconstructionism, both to our understanding of art and literature and to central tenets of the humanities and social sciences, Jerome Bruner's famous 1957 statement that the perceiver must, in seeking to understand an event, ''go beyond the information given'' does not seem particularly controversial either in its central message or in its implications. But Bruner's general insistence on the importance of active cognitive processes, and other later point-ed critiques of the simple-minded, purely "objective," and associationist ap-proaches to conditioning and learning (e.g., Bandura, 1965; Garcia & Koelling, 1966; Miller, Galanter, & Pribram, 1960), marked the beginning of the end of behaviorism's reign in mainstream North American experimental psychology. Provoked partly by the powerful new computer metaphor, partly by the awk-wardness and seeming circularities of behaviorist formulations, and partly by the renewed interest in human as opposed to animal learning, the return of "men-talism" to academic psychology was sweeping and unabashed (Neisser, 1967). Cognitivists in virtually every area of psychology turned their attention to the processes by which people bring their prior knowledge, expectations, needs, and wishes to bear in extracting meaning from, and assigning meaning to, the partic-ular stimulus confronting them. Renewed interest in "schemas" (Bartlett, 1932; Piaget, 1936), and increasingly frequent references to "scripts," "frames," "mental models," and other tools of construal became characteristic of the new cognitive psychology and marked its increasing interplay with the rapidly devel-oping field of artificial intelligence (e.g., Schank & Abelson, 1977).

The story of construal within social psychology itself goes back still further. Even in the heyday of behaviorism, that is, beginning with the enormously influential writings of Watson in the 1920s through the ensuing decades when mainstream experimental psychology was dominated by such learning theorists as Clark Hull and B. F. Skinner, leading social psychologists insisted on assign-ing a central role to subjective mental life. The Gestalt notion of an active perceiver, working to create a meaningful "whole" out of a complex and disor-ganized array of stimuli, always trying to make sense out of his or her experi-ence, guided the discussion of social perception in Solomon Asch's celebrated 1952 text. Indeed an even earlier social text by Krech and Crutchfield (1948, p. 94) offered the following, decidedly modern-sounding constructionist conten-tion: "There are no impartial 'facts'. Data do not have a logic of their own that results in the same perceptions and cognitions for all people. Data are perceived and interpreted in terms of the individual perceiver's own needs, own emotions, own personality, own previously formed cognitive patterns." Both Asch's and Krech and Crutchfield's arguments, in turn, owed an obvious (and clearly ac-knowledged) debt to Kurt Lewin's (1935) "field theory," which emphasized the extent to which individual events are interpreted as part of meaningful sequences organized in terms of the current goals of the organism. These arguments owed a similar debt to Thomas and Znaniecki's (1918) even earlier discussions empha-sizing the importance of the actor's "definition of the situation."

The central role assigned to subjective interpretation in the work of Solomon Asch merits special emphasis (see also Ross, 1989; Ross & Nisbett, 1991). Most important, and controversial, was Asch's "change of meaning" or "change in the object of judgment" hypothesis, a hypothesis that figured prominently in his discussions both of impression formation and of attitude change. According to Asch (1946), the apparently disproportionate impact of "central" trait descriptors and evaluation dimensions such as *coldness* versus *warmth* results not just from the heavy weight we give to them in our evaluation of the relevant target person, but also from their impact on the meaning assigned to other evidence about that person. Thus a seemingly straightforward descriptor like *intelligent* has a very different connotation—indeed has a very different meaning—when construed in the light of a global impression organized around the central trait of coldness as opposed to warmth. The intelligence of someone described as cold connotes a sharp-edged, cutting brilliance, devoid of human compassion. By contrast, the intelligence of someone described as warm suggests something far more sympathetic, a kind of wisdom marked by the capacity to integrate divergent viewpoints and solve human problems.

The effect of a message source on its persuasive impact was similarly recast in construal terms. Americans agree with the statement "A little rebellion . . . is a good thing" when it is attributed to Thomas Jefferson, but reject the same statement when attributed to V. I. Lenin, Asch (1948, 1952) argued, not because of conditioned positive or negative reactions to the different sources, or even because of their desire to associate themselves with or disassociate themselves from those sources. Rather, Asch insisted, the statement in general and the notion of rebellion in particular mean different things in the two instances—in the former conjuring up the image of honest tradesmen and farmers struggling to throw off the yoke of foreign oppression, in the latter suggesting that of bloodthirsty zealots struggling to replace the old brand of authoritarianism with tyranny of their own.

In an even earlier paper, Asch (1940) offered a similarly cognitive interpretation of conformity, one that challenged the purely motivational account emphasized by more conventional theorists. In particular, Asch pointed out that in conforming to the expressed views of their peers about some object of judgment, people may not be trying to curry favor, avoid disapproval, or otherwise derive any comforts of like-mindedness. Rather, people may conform because their peers' expressed views serve to define, or even to change, the object of judgment itself. By way of illustration, Asch conducted an informal study in which subjects were first exposed to the judgments of a group that ranked politicians either very low or very high in intelligence, then were called upon to offer rankings of their own. As anticipated, subjects in the two groups came to define the object "politician" in a way that was consistent with the expressed group standard (citing examples such as "ward bosses," "Tammany Hall," and "local underlings" in the former case, but examples such as "senators," "national politicians," or "statesmen" in the tradition of Jefferson or Lincoln, in the latter case). In light of such construals, the willingness of subjects to join their peers in ranking politicians either at the bottom or the top of the occupational list hardly constituted evidence that they were "giving in" or "currying favor" or "avoiding disapproval" (especially given that the subjects had no reason to expect that they would ever meet the previous raters). Indeed, their "conformity" seemed quite logical—or at least eminently defensible should they be called upon to justify their views to themselves or to anyone else.

Social psychologists trained in the Group Dynamics tradition of Kurt Lewin were similarly aware of the potential ambiguity of social behaviors and events, and the significance of such ambiguity. Leon Festinger began his original 1954 presentation of "social comparison" theory by postulating that where objective assessment is lacking, people look to "social reality"—that is, to the attitudes and abilities of their peers—in their endeavor to define what is good or bad, true or false, success or failure. Stanley Schachter (Schachter & Singer, 1962), in his two-factor theory of emotion, went even further, arguing that social cues are used not only to assess one's opinions and abilities, but also to label one's visceral states and emotional reactions.

Researchers who followed in the cognitive dissonance tradition likewise recognized, both implicitly and explicitly, the importance of subjective construal. As methodologists, they went to great pains (and a lot of pretesting) to craft elaborate manipulations and "cover stories" to guarantee that the experimental situation they contrived would create precisely the subjective experience and hold precisely the meaning for subjects necessary for the testing of the relevant theory (Aronson, 1990; Carlsmith, Ellsworth, & Aronson, 1976). As theorists, they sought to demonstrate that the impact of a reinforcer may depend less on its objective magnitude than on its role in the subject's ongoing attempts to justify their behavior and find subjective consistency or coherence among their beliefs, attitudes, and actions. In particular, they showed that "small" incentives offered for espousing a given opinion could, in some circumstances (i.e., where subjects could not adequately justify or explain the discrepancy between their public espousal and their private opinions), prove more effective than "large" incentives in leading subjects to internalize the opinions they expressed (Festinger & Carlsmith, 1959; Linder, Cooper, & Jones, 1967).

B. SUBJECTIVIST APPROACHES TO MOTIVATION

The dissonance researcher's cunning demonstrations led many theorists to think more deeply about the processes by which people explain or "attribute" their own behavior—and about the nonobvious motivational consequences of such explanations. Bem's (1967, 1972) self-perception theory, although initially intended as a nonmotivational alternative to dissonance theory, was similarly provocative in this regard, for it suggested the possibility that rewarding a given behavior might sometimes decrease rather than increase its attractiveness to the actor, and might thereby reduce rather than increase the likelihood of its future occurrence. Perhaps the best known study of this sort was one conducted by Lepper, Greene, and Nisbett (1973). These investigators reasoned that if children undertook a novel task while expecting to be rewarded for their efforts, even a task that they normally would have found quite interesting and enjoyable, they might infer that they had engaged in the relevant task in order to obtain the promised reward and therefore come to deem the behavior in question as less attractive or enjoyable in its own right. In other words, they would come to view such behavior as the "means to an end" they desired, rather than as an attractive "end in itself" and would thereafter, unless a similar prospect for an extrinsic as opposed to intrinsic reward was at hand, show relatively little inclination to engage in the task "for its own sake."

The results obtained by Lepper et al. confirmed this surprising hypothesis about the potentially detrimental effects of tangible performance incentives. Preschool children who were offered a "good player award" to draw with magic markers—something children had done with great relish in the absence of any extrinsic incentive during an earlier test period—showed relatively little interest in the markers when they subsequently were introduced as an ordinary classroom activity. By contrast, children who had neither anticipated nor received a "good player" award for playing with the markers showed no such decrease in subsequent interest. Nor, we should note, did children who had not anticipated any reward for their play but had received one anyway—as a kind of "bonus." Anticipated reward, it appears, had changed the children's interpretation of the magic marker activity from something highly reinforcing in its own right to something that one does in order to get reinforced. In short, the children's subjective construal of their activity had been altered; "play" had been turned into "work" (see also Lepper & Greene, 1979).

Over the ensuing years, the broader implications of the dissonance, self-perception, and attribution theory results have become increasingly clear to applied practitioners (e.g., Langer & Rodin, 1976; Seligman, 1975). These theories, especially attribution theory, have spurred researchers on health and education to worry a great deal about the patients', or the students', perceptions about the causes and implications of what they do, and what happens to them. Indeed, it has become increasingly clear that any attempts at social control— from the promises, threats, and reinforcement contingencies introduced by parents, teachers, or employers, to the grander social interventions that policy makers introduce to treat the ills of communities—may change the meaning of the relevant actors' behaviors and thus have subtle but profound cognitive and motivational consequences for actors, change agents, and observers alike. An abundance of studies have shown the positive affective and behavioral consequences of feeling personally efficacious, as opposed to feeling that one's fate (especially negative aspects of one's fate) depend upon factors that are beyond one's personal control. At the same time, the recipe for depression, inertia, and continued failure or at least underachievement has become all too clear—that is, the conviction that the determinants of one's success or failure are not only unalterable through greater effort or better strategy, but also global (as opposed to specific) in their applicability, and personal (i.e., ability related) as opposed to situational in their origin (Dweck, 1975; Fosterling, 1985; Garber & Seligman, 1980; Weiner, 1980, 1986).

The insights gained from attribution research hold important lessons both for those who seek to change society and for those who doubt the wisdom, or despair about the possibility, of such social intervention. Political "liberals" must learn to recognize the potentially negative motivational and attributional consequences of well-intended interventions if those interventions undermine people's feelings of personal freedom, efficacy, and responsibility. And political conservatives must learn that although "throwing money at problems" will not solve them, interventions in our schools and communities can have positive rather than negative social consequences, provided that the interventions are psychologically sophisticated in conception, design, execution, and evaluation (see Ross & Nisbett, 1991, pp. 284–285).

II. Construal Processes and Contemporary Research

The lessons of Asch, Bruner, and other early cognitivists have not been lost on contemporary researchers in social psychology. We will briefly sketch out a few selected examples of current research—i.e., social labeling effects, attitude–behavior consistency, judgment and decision making, and cognitive approaches to individual differences—simply underscoring in each area the role that "vagaries of construal" play in producing the relevant phenomena.

A. SOCIAL LABELING EFFECTS

The modern counterpart of Asch's "object of judgment" argument is to be found in studies dealing with the determinants and effects of social categorization. We see that the label given to particular behaviors or particular situations can be affected by subtle cues in the social environment, and that such labels can in turn have far-reaching effects on people's overt responses.

Recall, for example, the famous studies of bystander intervention conducted by Latané and Darley (1968, 1970), in which subjects confronting a potential intervention situation proved more likely to render assistance when they were (or perceived themselves to be) alone rather than one of a group. In interpreting this effect, the investigators concluded that two separate factors had been relevant. Groups showed relatively low intervention rates, they argued, in part because the presence of peers diluted each bystander's personal feelings of responsibility to intervene. But intervention in group situations was further attenuated, they maintained, because the presence of peers who did not immediately intervene changed the subjects' construal of the situation. That is, the same objective social stimulus (e.g., a choking cry for help, or the sound of collapsing boxes followed by low moans or even "smoky fumes" wafting into the rooms from a vent), when experienced in the presence of peers who simply ignored the situation or otherwise failed to act, was defined as less of an emergency, or as a situation in which intervention would seem less appropriate and less likely to be effective. The same analysis, of course, could be applied to real-world intervention failures of the sort that originally inspired the Latané and Darley research. That is, when individuals are confronted with a potential intervention situation that presents some ambiguity, either about the nature of the situation or about the appropriateness of particular responses to that situation, they are apt to look to each other for guidance in resolving such ambiguity. And when the most salient information they provide each other is their common reluctance to act quickly and decisively, the result may be the tragic one that inspired Latané and Darley—that is, victims of illness, accident, or assault whose chances for help are diminished rather than increased by the fact that there are many potential Good Samaritans instead of one.

People's construal of, and responses to, a particular event are guided not only by the response or nonresponse of their peers but also by the cognitive scripts, schemas, or analogies that they choose, or are somehow prompted to employ. An interesting demonstration in this vein was provided in a study by Tom Gilovich (1981), in which subjects were asked to render judgments about the wisdom of American intervention in a hypothetical international conflict. As they did so, however, the relative salience or availability of the two familiar and evocative "scripts" or scenarios from twentieth century history was subtly manipulated—one script was the "appeasement" or "Munich conference" script provided by the prelude to World War II, and the other was the "gradual escalation" or "foreign entanglements" script provided by America's ill-fated involvement in the Vietnam War. (We should note, parenthetically, that as we prepare this chapter the Persian Gulf crisis is again leading proponents of forceful and immediate military intervention to invoke the former of these scripts, whereas those who reject military initiatives and favor patient diplomacy invoke the latter.) Gilovich cued the World War II script by describing a hypothetical, modern-day invasion in terms of a "Blitzkrieg invasion" that resulted in refugees fleeing to a neutral country in boxcars. The "Vietnam" script was invoked by describing the same invasion in terms of a "quick strike invasion" resulting in refugees' flight to a neutral country in small boats. Subjects in the two relevant conditions were also shown a map with contours and labels evoking associations either to Europe or Indochina. As expected, subjects induced to invoke the World War II script were significantly more in favor of direct United States intervention (as opposed to working through the United Nations) than were subjects induced to invoke the Vietnam script, even though there were no between-condition differences in the subjects' explicit ratings of the similarity of the situation in question to Vietnam versus World War II.

The role of momentarily activated category labels has been the target of one of the most active areas of contemporary social cognition research, that is, the study of "priming effects" (see reviews by Higgins & Bargh, 1987; Srull & Wyer, 1986). In a typical priming experiment subjects first are incidentally exposed to a category label (e.g., "hostile" or "independent") and then (in an apparently unrelated task) allowed to show the effects of such priming in the way they choose to construe or interpret an ambiguous stimulus event. The object of the experiment is the demonstration that the same objective behaviors will be construed differently depending on which particular label has been primed. For example, Srull and Wyer (1979) asked subjects to construct grammatical sentences out of a series of words—sentences that were designed to be either kindness related or hostility related. Then, in a second and ostensibly independent study, the subjects were given a short vignette and asked to form an impression of the person described. The vignette described a series of events that were ambiguous with respect to either hostility or kindness (for example, an ambiguously hostile event was "refusing to pay the rent until the landlord repainted the apartment"). As the investigators predicted, their subjects' impressions of the stimulus person were strongly influenced by the particular trait label that had been primed in the earlier task. As Bargh (1988) noted, the world seems like a very different place depending on whether one has just finished the biography of Machiavelli or of Mother Teresa.

One particularly provocative and important priming study, conducted by Patricia Devine (1989), dealt with the ubiquitous phenomena of racial prejudice. Devine's thesis was that every member of a society, prejudiced and nonprejudiced alike, knows the components of shared stereotypes, and that these stereotypes are automatically activated upon the thought or the sight of a member of the stereotyped group. What determines the presence or absence of overt displays of prejudice, according to Devine, is the exercise of conscious control to resist the influence of the automatically activated stereotypes. In pursuit of this thesis, Devine showed that the subliminal presentation of priming words associated with, and presumably able to activate, the stereotype of a black American (e.g., "jazz" and "cotton") induced subjects to interpret the behavior of an actor in a vignette as more violent and aggressive—despite the fact (or, Devine would argue, at least in the case of nonprejudiced individuals, because of the fact) that the race of this actor was deliberately unspecified. The implications of this finding are disturbing indeed. Cognitive and emotional responses to the actions of particular individuals may be shaped by stereotypes and other schemas that are in turn triggered, without our awareness, by cues and associations that we would recognize to be logically irrelevant and probably would actively resist, if we were aware of the connection being made (see Uleman and Bargh, 1989, for further discussions).

The power of semantic priming effects, we should note, is not some hothouse product of clever laboratory manipulations. Public relations consultants and propagandists have long recognized the denotative *and* connotative power of labels to shape public perception and policy. As we write at the inception of the Persian Gulf crisis we see propagandists on both sides struggling to control the semantics of the debate, for example in choosing between the term "hostages" and the term "detainees" (or even "guests") to describe the Americans and other foreign nationals prevented from leaving Iraq. As in earlier foreign policy crises and issues (where propagandists used labels like *freedom fighters* versus *terrorists,* or *police actions* versus *invasions,* or *surgical strikes* versus *bombing raids*) the propagandists seek to do more than evoke overall positive or negative affective responses. They hope that the labels in question will encourage us to go beyond the information given to make additional inferences and form associations consistent with the connotations of those labels (for example, to proceed from the label *freedom fighters* to images and associations involving virtuous, self-sacrificing patriots, or to proceed from the label *terrorists* to images and associations involving cruel, anomic psychotics), thereby heightening our sympathy or distaste, and influencing our political actions accordingly. Closer to home, the labels that opposing spokespersons use to frame public debate about abortion, public funding of medical costs, and preferential hiring of minorities (i.e., reproductive *freedom* versus *murder* of the *unborn child,* health *insurance* versus *socialistic* medicine, *affirmative* action versus *discrimination* against non-minorities) similarly are attempts to manipulate our political judgments and behavior by manipulating the way we go beyond the information given to construe the relevant objects of judgment.

B. ATTITUDE–BEHAVIOR CONSISTENCY

In the early 1930s sociologist R. T. LaPiere, traveling across the United States in the company of a young Chinese couple, found that despite the widely recognized bigotry of the times, only one of the more than 200 hotels and restaurants they visited refused service to the group. By contrast, when the investigator wrote to such establishments inquiring whether they accepted "members of the Chinese race as guests" over 91% of those who responded claimed they would refuse them service. This dramatic demonstration of apparent attitude–behavior inconsistency has been the subject of controversy ever since. Critics have called attention to various methodological flaws that diminish the study's value as a test of the link between attitudes and actions; defenders have insisted that the discrepancy observed between verbal response and actual behavior simply was too great to be dismissed on methodological grounds. Our present concern, however, is not this controversy per se. (Although we cannot resist pointing out that the study, and its intent, has itself been the object of construal biases. LaPiere's critique was aimed not at assumptions of attitude behavior consistency, but at the use of one-shot questionnaire measures.) Rather, our concern is one particular objection raised to LaPiere's study.

This objection, summarized in a number of social psychology textbooks (e.g., Berkowitz, 1975, p. 291), goes to the heart of the construal problem. Critics point out that when the proprietors of the hotels and cafes responded to the relevant written inquiries they presumably had in mind a very different image of their prospective guests than the well-dressed, westernized couple they were ultimately to confront. The proprietors, accordingly, were not guilty of any inconsistency, only of having failed to construe the situation accurately (and, perhaps, of having been guided in their construal by dubiously accurate stereotypes). The more general theoretical point is that attitude measures—even candid self-reports of private beliefs—will predict behavior toward a given social object or class of objects only insofar as the respondents' construals of these objects at the point of attitude assessment are congruent with their construals at the point of action. This is a very important caveat, one that has been pursued in separate lines of research by Charles Lord and by Russ Fazio.

Lord, Lepper, and Mackie (1984) began by noting that attitude questionnaire items (and indeed questions about any hypothetical objects of judgment) generally prompt the individual to construct a concrete cognitive representation or "prototype" of the object of judgment. Only to the extent that the actual object of judgment corresponds to the particular "prototype" constructed or construed by the individual, they argued, are the expressed attitudes of the individual likely to have predictive value. In support of this argument Lord *et al.* first measured subjects' attitudes towards two different campus groups—male members of a particular "eating club," and male homosexuals—and then separately measured each subject's perceptions of the "typical" members of these two groups. Later, subjects were presented with a personality description of a member of one of these groups, a description designed by the experimenters to be either a complete or partial match to the particular subject's prototype for members of the relevant group. As the investigators had anticipated, the specific behavioral intentions subjects expressed toward the "target person" in question were predicted by their attitudes only when that description completely matched their prototype; otherwise, the link between subjects' expressed attitudes and their behavioral intentions (and presumably, also their overt behavior) was very weak indeed.

Lord, Fein, Lepper, and Desforges (1990) extended this analysis to consider subjects' responses not only to social groups but to social issues and policies as well. Specifically, they demonstrated that a subject's response to a particular case of welfare fraud or to a particular murder case was again predictable from his or her general attitudes only if the details of the welfare scenario or murder case matched that subject's prototypes. In other words, Lord and colleagues illustrated that the "problem" of subjective representation or construal is far more than an artifactual source of attitude–behavior "inconsistency" in studies of the sort pioneered by LaPiere. Rather, it is central to our understanding of the role that attitudes and beliefs play in social life. Moreover, the uncertainty of construal is not simply a source of error variance to be "averaged out" in attitude assessment through use of multiple items or methods of measurements. This uncertainty is an important phenomenon to be addressed in any attempt to understand, predict, or control social behavior (see also Ross & Nisbett, 1991).

A rather different attempt to address the link between attitudes and behavior is offered by the work of Russ Fazio. Attitudes should predict behavior, Fazio (1986, 1990) contends, only when they are cognitively "accessible" to the actor at the moment of action and thereby likely to bias his or her interpretation of the object of judgment. In pursuit of this contention, it was found that in the 1984 presidential election, political attitudes predicted voting behavior most successfully for those whose political attitudes were "chronically accessible," that is, for those who were relatively fast in responding to whether or not they were favorably disposed toward Ronald Reagan (Fazio & Williams, 1986). For those with highly accessible attitudes toward Reagan, voting behavior correlated above .9 with relevant attitudes; for those with low accessibility attitudes by contrast, the correlation dipped below .7. This result occurs, the investigators contend, because easily accessible attitudes "come to mind" and guide selective perception so one continues to "see" the candidates' positions in a manner congruent with one's political preferences. Congruent with this "biased assimilation" account, voters with highly accessible attitudes also showed higher correlations between their attitudes and their perceptions of the televised debates. (See Volume 23 in this series for a comprehensive review of Fazio's theory.) In Fazio's work, as in that of Lord, uncertain situational construal has moved from being something to be explained away to being a central explanatory principle.

C. JUDGMENT AND DECISION MAKING

Long a normative and prescriptive discipline, the study of judgment and decision making has in recent years acquired an increasingly psychological and descriptive flavor (e.g., Bell, Raiffa, & Tversky, 1988). With the change in emphasis has come a greater concern with people's subjective representation of the decision problems they face. Increasingly, decisions and judgments are described in terms of the "mental models" (Johnson-Laird, 1983; Kahneman & Tversky, 1982a), "scenarios" (Kahneman & Tversky, 1982a), "simulations" (Kahneman & Tversky, 1982b), or "story models" (Pennington & Hastie, 1986, 1988) used by the decision maker. Two essential insights are offered by this new subjectivist or constructionist approach. First, changes in problem presentation that result from seemingly inconsequential (and usually normatively irrelevant) changes in the manner of presenting or "framing" information may have major effects on subsequent judgments. Second, people's preferences, values, and utilities cannot be treated as fixed features of the task or problem at hand; rather, they are often uncertain and variable, constructed "on the fly" in response to particular superficial features of the problem or the eliciting situation (see Slovic, Griffin, & Tversky, 1990, for illustrations and further discussion).

The importance of problem representation and its relation to issues of construal is convincingly demonstrated by two research programs in the domain of legal psychology. One such program, conducted by Nancy Pennington and Reid Hastie (1986, 1988), required mock jurors to watch videotapes of legal testimony and then write down what they remembered and surmised about the evidence they had heard. Through extensive, painstaking content analysis of these written materials, Pennington and Hastie were able to conclude that the jurors organized the trial evidence into a coherent story, adding the actors' intentions and connecting episodes to the given evidence and, where necessary, even altering inconsistent evidence to make the story "fit" into a proper narrative structure. The investigators then showed that the essential features of the "stories" constructed by subjects (specifically, the extent to which the story suggested guilt or innocence) predicted juror's decisions better than any formal models of evidence evaluation and integration. This correlational study was followed with an experiment that presented all subjects with the same information and testimony, but manipulated the order of information presentation such that either a pro-defense or pro-prosecution version of the story was easier to construct. As predicted, this manipulation significantly influenced the jurors' decisions about the innocence or guilt of the defendant—despite the fact that the relevant facts and evidence upon which the decisions were to be based were held constant.

In related research, Casper and colleagues (e.g., Casper, Benedict, & Kelly, 1988) have examined how construal of the "facts" of a criminal case can be influenced in a way that makes it easier for constitutional protections against unreasonable search and seizure to be violated. In their experiments, Casper et al. presented subjects with an account of a drug arrest but varied the outcome of an illegal search that accompanied the arrest. As predicted, those subjects who were informed that the illegal search turned up drugs were not only less punitive to the police officers who conducted the search, they also interpreted the relevant facts differently. Specifically, subjects who were informed that "340 small plastic bags of heroin'' were found in the illegal search (and then asked to disregard this knowledge) assumed the police officers to have been more certain of the accused's guilt, and to have been more experienced, than did subjects who believed that no drugs were found or subjects who were left uncertain of the outcome. Subjects, in short, proved unwilling or unable to make allowance for the extent to which the "tainted evidence" exerted a continuing influence on their construal of other facts and evidence.

D. INDIVIDUAL DIFFERENCES AND CONSTRUAL

Personality theorists dissatisfied with traditional "trait" approaches, from George Kelly (1955) to more contemporary investigators (see Cantor & Kihlstrom, 1987), have maintained that an understanding of individual differences in behavior depends on an understanding of differences in the way particular individuals or groups construe important features of the environment. Contemporary researchers, as we noted in our earlier discussions of construal and motivation, have focused particular attention on issues of perceived internal versus external control—that is, differences in attributional style that prompt individuals to see their social world as a place where personal capacity or effort overcome or, alternatively, are overcome by situational forces and constraints. These individual differences in "helplessness" or "mastery," in turn, have been linked to a variety of important outcomes in education, health, and even occupational success (e.g., Fosterling, 1985; Rodin, 1986; Wilson & Linville, 1982). We cannot undertake a review here of the many important attempts that have been designed to explore individual differences in the knowledge structures and information-processing strategies that people bring to the task of social construal. We can, however, cite two very recent lines of work that illustrate again how issues of construal continually come to the fore when we address topics of traditional concern to personality researchers. The first relates to familiar problems of using questionnaire self-assessment to predict overt behavior; the second relates to the problem of self-esteem and self-enhancement biases.

As we noted in discussing LaPiere's famous study of attitude–behavior inconsistency, questionnaire items generally oblige respondents to "go beyond the information given"—that is, to resolve ambiguities and fill in details wherever items are expressed in general or imprecise terms. A pilot study by one of the present authors (Griffin, 1990) suggests that what appear to be individual differences in a standard personality trait may in fact be individual differences in the way subjects construe the relevant assessment items. In this study, students who scored either extremely high or extremely low on a scale designed to measure the trait of social anxiety (Buss, 1980) were asked to specify, via forced choice measures, the situation that came to mind when they considered each item on the relevant assessment scale. This simple procedure revealed significant differences in the construal or "meaning" of the items by the two groups. For example, students classified by the scale as highly socially anxious not only were more likely to agree with the scale item "large groups make me nervous," they were also more likely to construe such groups as "rowdy, close-knit strangers" rather than as "peaceful and accepting acquaintances."

The follow-ups demanded by this pilot study are obvious, and potentially quite important to our understanding of the value, and limitations, of the relevant assessment instrument and others like it. First, we must determine the extent to which the respondents scoring at opposite ends of the continuum in question continue to differ in assessing their social anxiety (or whatever trait is being assessed) when the items seek to minimize the latitude for such construal differences. Second, and more important, we must seek to determine whether ambiguous or nonambiguous items do the better job of predicting behavior—that is, whether individual differences in the way items are construed constitute a source of "noise" to be eliminated by removing ambiguity, or a valuable clue about the way people "high" versus "low" with respect to the relevant trait differ in their response to ambiguous stimuli—not only in dealing with ambiguous hypothetical descriptions but in anticipating and interpreting ambiguous real situations as well.

The second line of "in-progress" research that we shall cite here has been conducted by David Dunning and colleagues. This research proceeds from the assumption that ambiguity inherent in social labels, and latitude in construal of abilities, may provide an opportunity for people to maintain relatively high levels of self-esteem, both "in general" and with respect to particular ability domains or dimensions. Thus, for example, most adults might be able to define themselves as good parents by defining or operationalizing the notion of a "good parent" in terms that are congruent with their own particular credentials. A busy working mother might define a good parent as someone who provided "quality time" and gave her children "space to develop on their own," whereas a father who has chosen to stay at home might give heavy weight to mundane everyday demands and opportunities that are best met by a parent who is "always there." It is worth noting how such self-serving biases can operate without any systematic distortion of evidence or other violations of normative standards of inference (see also Kunda, 1990). In order to maintain the glow of healthy self-regard, people need only give themselves the "benefit of the doubt" in deciding on the nature and weighting of the criteria to be used in their self-assessment.

What Dunning's research (e.g., Dunning, Meyerowitz, & Holzberg, 1989) showed specifically was that the amount of ambiguity or room for construal in a given trait term predicts the extent to which people will be able to rate themselves positively on that term. Thus, whereas ambiguous positive traits (e.g., idealistic or sensible) led to mean self-ratings that were significantly greater than the midpoint of "average," equally desirable but less ambiguous positive traits (e.g., athletic and punctual) led to self-ratings that were not significantly greater than average. Furthermore, within the domain of ambiguous traits, the tendency for self-ratings to be higher than the midpoint of "average" disappeared when subjects were given simple, behavioral definitions of a trait by the experimenter. Indeed, when subjects were forced to use the concrete but "idiosyncratic" operational definitions given by a peer to whom they were yoked in the research design, subjects offered mean self-ratings that were significantly below average.

Again, it is worth emphasizing that no self-deception or distortion of evidence need occur in this nonzero sum pursuit of self-esteem. People need only to choose criteria and construals judiciously (or, alternately, to allocate their efforts and resources in a way that helps them to develop those capacities necessary to satisfy their own idiosyncratic standards, whatever their origin). Motivational processes appear not to operate in any simple, crude, or even reliable fashion to "guarantee" high self-esteem either in general or with respect to particular domains. However, they do drive us to exploit ambiguity when it can be used to give ourselves the "benefit of the doubt" (see also Kunda, 1990).

III. Egocentric Construal: The Failure to Make Allowance for Uncertainty

In introductory sections of this article we argued that the study of situational construal—that is, the study of individual, group, and societal constructions of social meaning—lies at the heart of both classic and contemporary social psychology. The guiding insight of the researcher and theorist has concerned the inherent variability and unpredictability of the construal process itself, and therefore the inherent variability and unpredictability of whatever judgments and behaviors follow from such construals. In this section we defend a more specific, but less self-evident, thesis. We contend that people are guilty of a kind of naive realism or egocentrism, one that gives them neither the insight nor encouragement necessary to make adequate inferential allowance for the constructed (and hence variable and uncertain) nature of their situational construals. We contend that this failure, no less than the variability and uncertainty of the construal process itself, accounts for important sources of human misunderstanding and significant shortcomings in social judgment, prediction, and attribution.

A. AN ILLUSTRATION: HEARD VERSUS UNHEARD MELODIES

An elegant, albeit somewhat metaphorical, demonstration of our thesis about peoples' failure to distinguish their private perceptions from the objective nature of stimuli was recently conducted by Elizabeth Newton (1990) in dissertation research carried out at Stanford University. Subjects in Newton's studies were assigned to one of two roles: "tappers" or "listeners." Each tapper was given a list of 25 well-known songs (not made available to the listener), ranging from "America the Beautiful" to "Rock around the Clock," and asked to choose one song and tap out the rhythm to a listener sitting across the table. After doing so, the tapper was asked to assess the likelihood that his or her listener would successfully identify the title of the song, and also to estimate the proportion of students in general who would be able to do so if given the same opportunity. The listener's job was first to identify the tune as best he or she could, and then to estimate the proportion of his or her peers who would succeed or fail in the same task.

To anticipate Newton's results, and appreciate their significance, it is helpful to pause for a moment to consider the differing subjective experiences of the two participants (or, better still, to try out the two roles for oneself). First, imagine yourself as the tapper. As you tap rhythmically on the table in communicating the opening bars of the catchy tune you have chosen (let's say "Yankee Doodle" or "Auld Lang Syne") you inevitably experience much more than your own tapping. Rather than impoverished knocks on the table, you "hear" the tune and the words to the song; indeed you are apt to hear (so Newton's tappers report, and we have found for ourselves in trying out the tappers' task) a full orchestration, complete with rich harmonies between strings, winds, brass, and human voice. Now imagine you are the listener. For you, there are no notes, words, chords, or instruments; you hear only an aperiodic series of taps. Indeed, you are unable even to tell how the brief, irregular moments of silence between taps should be construed—that is, whether each is a sustained note, a musical "rest" between notes, or a simple pause as the tapper contemplates the "music" to come next.

Such is the difference in perspectives. If tappers can make adequate allowance for the difference between their own richly embellished internal representations and the impoverished, ambiguous stimuli being presented to listeners, then they should recognize the difficulty of the listeners' task. But if, as postulated, they cannot make such allowances, they are doomed to be grossly overconfident in estimating the likelihood of correct identifications of their tune. Newton's results provided resounding support for the "nonallowance" thesis. Senders' estimates of the probability of correct recognition ranged from 10 to 95%, with an average of 50%. Audience members, however, correctly identified only 3 out of 120 songs, a "hit rate" of 2.5%.

To ensure that these overestimates were due not to the tappers' bravado or general inclination to be overly optimistic, but rather to their inability to make allowance for the differences between their own and their listeners' private experiences, Newton looked at the estimates of yet another group of participants. This group consisted of listeners, told in advance the name of the tune to be tapped. Like the tappers, these "informed" listeners were able to supply for themselves the full, private, orchestrated richness of melody, harmony, and emotional associations, and like the tappers they grossly overestimated the ability of naive listeners to guess the title of the song being tapped. Like the tappers, they expected roughly 50% listener accuracy, rather than the 2.5% actually found. Only the naive listeners themselves (and subsequent participants who heard the tapping without being asked personally to guess the song's identity) provided an appropriately low estimate of the actual hit rate. We invite the reader to try this as a parlor game or in-class demonstration. There are few experiments about which we feel as confident in predicting the results.

It is worth emphasizing the two insights needed, but apparently not present, for the tappers to make appropriate estimates of the listener's success rates. First, they had to recognize the extent to which their own subjective experience of the auditory stimuli in question differed from the experience of the naive listeners. Second, they had to make adequate allowance for this difference in subjective experiences when called upon to make their estimates of listeners' performances. As Newton's results show, tappers clearly could neither meet the challenge nor appreciate the difficulty of transcending their own subjective, highly "constructed" experience.

Our claim that people egocentrically fail to make allowance for the uncertainty and intersubjective variability of construal is somewhat akin to the Piagetian claim that young children are egocentric and unable to adopt others' perspectives in their understanding of the physical world. Such children cannot escape the conviction that their own visual perspective defines what is "really there," and that their own view will be shared by all other observers. To be sure, adults do eventually learn that different visual perspectives provide different views of the same physical world, and that one's own knowledge is not right and the other wrong. However, as we will argue in the next few sections of the article, adults never entirely overcome the problems of egocentric construal. Gustav Ichheiser (1951), another prominent social psychologist who, like Solomon Asch, long ago defied the behaviorist tenor of his times, offered the following story to emphasize these limits to adult insight:

> A friend is visiting your city for the first time and he wants to gain a general view of the city. You take him first to the north end where there is a tall tower with a view commanding the whole area. Then you take him to a similar spot at the south end. At that point your friend exclaims with great amazement, "How very strange! The city looks quite different from here!" Now, what is your reaction? Something of shock, for you rightly assume that every normal adult understands that things in physical space look different from differing points of view. . . . Now, the really strange thing is that what every normal person understands by himself as far as things in *physical* space are concerned, most people do not understand, and even do not want to understand, as far as phenomena in *social* space are concerned. And any attempt to explain the relativity of social perspectives, and its full implications, usually meets with strong psychological resistance. (p. 311)

We will return to this failure again, when we discuss problems of conflict and conflict resolution. Issues look different to opposing partisans, who think their own perceptions—and emotional reactions—are the only "natural" ones (i.e., the ones dictated by the nature of the issue, independent of what the perceiver himself or herself brings to the issue).

B. PERCEPTIONS OF FALSE CONSENSUS

Egocentrism in construal, and the failure to make allowance for it, may play a role in a well-documented social perception bias, the so-called "false consensus effect" (Ross, Greene, & House, 1977). This bias involves the tendency for people to overestimate the commonness, and normativeness, of their own beliefs and choices. The specific finding of Ross et al. was that in a survey of preferences and beliefs, and in both simulated and actual behavioral dilemmas, the subjects who made a given choice estimated the commonness of that choice to be greater than did subjects who made the opposite choice. The participants in these studies showed similar biases in their attributions, rating choices that corresponded to their own as less revealing of personal dispositions (presumably because those choices were attributed to situational forces and constraints) than choices that differed from their own.

To begin to appreciate the role that construal processes played in these results, consider the task faced by subjects in one of the relevant studies who were presented with the following vignette and then asked to predict their own behavior and that of their peers.

> As you are leaving your neighborhood supermarket a man in a business suit asks whether you like shopping in that store. You reply quite honestly that you do like shopping there and indicate that in addition to being close to your home the supermarket seems to have very good meats and produce at reasonably low prices. The man then reveals that a videotape crew has filmed your comments and asks you to sign a release allowing them to use the unedited film for a TV commercial the supermarket chain is preparing.

In considering this scenario, we suggest, subjects were apt to "go beyond the information given" by filling in the details necessary to form a specific image, or construal, of the situation. Their predictions about their own behavior, in turn, would depend on these added context and content details—for example, the clothes they were wearing, the manner of the interviewer, even their mood and the amount of time pressure they were under. Furthermore, the predictions they made about the responses of their peers, and also the attributions they made about peers who agreed or refused to sign the release, would depend upon the same construals.

The original Ross et al. (1977) article claimed that such construal processes and biases might be one of the mechanisms underlying the false consensus phenomenon but provided no actual evidence to support their claim. Indirect evidence, however, has subsequently been provided by Tom Gilovich (1990). Reasoning that if variability in construal, and inadequate allowance for such variability, played a role in the false consensus effect, then those response items and scenarios offering the greatest latitude for construal differences should show the largest false consensus effects, Gilovich reexamined the Ross *et al.* data. As predicted, those items rated by an independent panel of judges to be more ambiguous and subject to variable interpretation proved to the ones that had yielded the greatest differences in consensus estimates. Gilovich then proceeded to offer a more direct demonstration of the link between a response item's "latitude for construal" and the size of the false consensus produced by that item. For example, Gilovich asked two groups of subjects whether they preferred the color "aqua" to the color "tan." Members of one group were given only the color names (which obviously could be construed differently by different subjects), whereas members of a second group were given specific swatches of the two colors (stimuli that left little or no room for any construal differences). As predicted, there was a significant false consensus effect for subjects choosing between the color names but no differences at all in consensus estimates for the actual color swatches.

Emboldened by these successes, Gilovich (1990) went on to further probe the differential construal interpretation of the false consensus effect. In a cleverly designed study Gilovich asked college student subjects first to indicate whether they personally preferred "1960s music" or "1980s music," and second to estimate the proportion of college students who would share this view. He then asked these subjects to stipulate some of the specific musical groups of the two eras that they "had in mind" when they expressed their preference. This design allowed Gilovich to test the differential construal hypothesis in two steps. First, a panel of judges rated the construals (i.e., the specific groups and music that the fans of the two eras specified they "had in mind" in expressing their personal preferences). As predicted, these ratings showed that the 1960s fans' construals of the two musical eras specified an objectively (or at least consensually) more appealing "object of judgment" for the earlier era whereas the 1980s fans' construals specified a more appealing object of judgment for the later era. Gilovich then gave the specific exemplars of 1960s music and 1980s music to two "second-generation" groups of subjects (i.e., subjects who had never been asked to express a general preference with respect to the music of the two eras) and asked them to choose between them. Again, as predicted, these second-generation subjects showed a strong tendency to make choices that reflected the construals of their first-generation counterparts. In a real sense, therefore, first generation subjects did not err in assuming that others would share their responses to the relevant objects of judgment; rather, they erred in not recognizing, or not allowing for the fact, that the objects in question were subject to construal, and that others could, and would, construe these objects differently.

C. OVERCONFIDENCE IN PREDICTIONS ABOUT PEERS AND ABOUT SELF

We have proposed that people tend to automatically and idiosyncratically "fill in" the details of social stimuli, and that they treat these constructions as if they were both objective and shared with others. In a series of papers with various colleagues we first suggested, and later attempted to demonstrate, the relevance of these tendencies to the phenomenon of overconfident behavioral prediction.

The first paper in this series (Dunning, Griffin, Milojkovic, & Ross, 1990) dealt with the task of social prediction. Our principal finding was that subjects, across several different types of prediction items and tasks, proved to be highly overconfident. That is, regardless of the type of prediction item (e.g., responses to hypothetical dilemmas, responses to contrived laboratory situations, or simple habit inventories) and regardless of the amount and source of information available about the target of their prediction (e.g., predictions about roommates, predictions about strangers interviewed by the subject, or predictions about anonymous targets shown in photographs), achieved levels of accuracy remained far below the levels required to justify the subjects' expressed confidence levels.

In one study, for example, male undergraduate students were asked to predict the responses of their roommates to a series of questions such as which magazine subscription their roommate would choose (between *Playboy* and the *New York Review of Books*), his probable response upon finding a $5 bill on the floor of the dining hall ("pocket it" or "turn it in"), and the self-rated quality of his typical lecture notes ("neat" or "messy"). Overall, subjects expected to be correct on about 78% of their predictions (compared to a "chance" rate of 50%); however, when the actual accuracy rates were computed, by comparing subjects' predictions to the self-reports of their roommates, only about 68% of their predictions proved to be correct.

In another study, subjects were allowed to interview a target individual prior to making predictions about the behavior of that individual. Some of these prediction items dealt with actual behavior observed during the target's participation (for each of these items, subjects were given a detailed account of the situation that confronted the target.) For example, the experimenter deliberately called the target person by the wrong first name and then observed whether the target person corrected him. He also offered the target person a chance to comb his or her hair before posing for a photograph, and then observed whether the offer was accepted or refused. In this study, subjects again were fairly confident of their ability to predict the target person's response based upon the interview information (average confidence was about 77%, or 27 percentage points better than "chance"), but their achieved accuracy was dramatically lower, a little under 60%, or less than 10 percentage points better than chance.

Additional analysis of all studies further revealed that although relatively higher confidence levels were associated with relatively higher rates of accuracy, the gap between anticipated and achieved accuracy was greatest (as one might expect from the imperfect correlation between confidence and accuracy) when subjects were most confident in their success. Relatively high levels of confidence also proved unrealistic to the extent that subjects knowingly or unknowingly went "against" the relevant response base rates—that is, predicted that particular targets would idiosyncratically differ from the consensus of their peers.

In a pair of follow-up studies, Vallone, Griffin, Lin, and Ross (1990) extended the domain of enquiry from social prediction to self-prediction. Newly arrived Stanford undergraduates were asked to predict their own future actions and outcomes (as well as those of their roommates) over the weeks and months of their freshman year. Every type of prediction item studied, from academic choices and outcomes (e.g., Where will I study? What major will I choose? What courses will I drop?) to social and leisure activities (e.g., Will I end up close friends with my roommate? Will I take part in the dorm play? Will I go to San Francisco once a week?) again revealed marked overconfidence. And again, the gap between confidence levels expressed and rates of accuracy achieved was widest precisely when confidence itself was greatest and/or when subjects' predictions went against the relevant behavioral base rates. Moreover, although subjects were more accurate, overall, in predicting their own actions and outcomes than those of their roommates, the discrepancy between subjective certainty and objective accuracy was virtually identical in both cases. In other words, even in predicting the behavior of the person whose attributes and past experiences they knew best—that is, themselves—subjects were considerably overconfident. Furthermore, the degree of their overconfidence was greatest precisely when they assumed that their self-knowledge allowed them to "go against the base rate," that is, to predict that their behavior would differ from that of their peers (and, presumably, from the dictates of the situational pressures and constraints that govern the behavior of people in general).

The overconfidence effect in personal and social prediction obviously cannot be traced to a single cause or underlying mechanism. Like the false consensus effect, and like most other robust phenomena involving errors and biases in human inference or judgment, it almost certainly is multiply determined, and probably also overdetermined. That is, the phenomenon is apt to reflect the joint impact of many different processes that may be sufficient to produce the phenomena in at least some contexts, without being necessary to do so in other contexts. Our own interpretation of overconfidence in social prediction, as it happens, focused initially not on problems of construal but on the inveterate dispositionism that we believed to be characteristic of social perceivers. But further reflection, and the magnitude of the overconfidence effect for self-predictions, prompted us to explore other possible mechanisms relating to the problem of situational construal.

There are, in fact, two different aspects to the construal problem as it relates to behavioral prediction. First, to predict an actor's response to a given situation—even the response of an actor whom one knows very well and whose behavior one has observed in a wide variety of previous situations—one generally must either know or correctly infer the details of that situation, that is, the features of content and context that determine the relative attractiveness of the available response alternatives. Second, beyond knowing the "objective" features of the situation, one must discern or anticipate the meaning of the situation from the private perspective of the actor. Uncertainty about objective features of the situation and/or their subjective construal by the actor increases the difficulty of prediction and the likelihood of error. And failure to recognize and/or make adequate allowance for such uncertainty promotes overconfident social prediction, both in the context of our present laboratory research and, more important, in everyday social experience as well.

Consider, for example, the construal task subjects in the Dunning et al. (1990) study faced in predicting how a particular individual, even one about whom they had a great deal of information, would respond to just one of the specified situations—that is, the situation obliging the target individual simply to decide whether or not to comb his hair before having his picture taken in the context of an ongoing experiment. Clearly, the target person's decision would depend, at least in part, on many unspecified, indeed unknowable, details relating to the immediate situation (i.e., the experimenter's tone of voice, the state of disarray of the individual's hair, the imagined use of the picture, the press of later appointments, even the interpretation that the individual thinks the experimenter will place on his grooming decision). Any mistakes in "filling in" these details about objective and subjective factors on the part of the subject offering the relevant prediction, it was contended, would increase the likelihood of error. And failure to recognize and make allowance for the possibility of error-producing misconstruals would likely result in confidence levels that could not be justified by actual rates of predictive success.

It is worth reemphasizing that construal problems by no means disappear when it is one's own behavior that is being predicted. For example, subjects in the Vallone et al. (1990) study faced the problem of predicting whether or not they would act in their dorm play during the upcoming year. To the extent that one must guess details about the specific situations one will face (How many of one's friends will be taking part? What other obligations and time commitments will one be facing? Will there be competition for parts, or will there be a part for everyone who seeks one?) and/or the way one personally will experience these situations, misconstruals become inevitable. And again, it is the failure to make adequate allowance for such uncertainty that makes one susceptible to overconfidence and the potential costs one pays for overconfidence, costs that range from mild social embarrassment to misuse of one's resources and ill-advised neglect of measures that would insure oneself against error.

The overconfidence studies described thus far provided evidence consistent with the theoretical arguments that we have advanced about naive realism and the failure to allow for the vagaries of the construal process. But such evidence is neither direct nor definitive. In an attempt to provide more direct and persuasive evidence, Griffin, Dunning, and Ross (1990) undertook a series of studies that manipulated the status of the subjects' situational construals, such that it was reasonable in some conditions but unreasonable in others for subjects to assume the accuracy of their construals. The purpose of the study was to determine whether the confidence subjects expressed in their predictions about behavior would be influenced by the subjects' "construal" condition.

The first Griffin *et al.* (1990) study conducted to test this line of reasoning dealt exclusively with self-predictions. Subjects in the various construal conditions were called upon to make predictions about the amount of time or the amount of money they would spend in a specified set of circumstances (e.g., the amount of time they personally would talk during a 60-minute round-table discussion with four peers on the issue of abortion, or the amount of money they would spend during an end-of-the-quarter celebration in San Francisco). In all conditions, furthermore, details about context or situation were described in rather modest detail, leaving lots of room for variable interpretation or construal, and in all conditions subjects were asked not only to make specific "best guess" estimates about their own behavior but also to furnish appropriate confidence intervals around their predictions.

What varied in the different conditions were the instructions subjects received about the status of their situational construals. In the control condition, no mention was made of construal. In the uncertain construal condition, subjects were simply asked to specify their particular construal of contextual or situational details and then, with no guidance about the potential accuracy or inaccuracy of their construals, they were invited to provide the relevant estimate and confidence interval. In the certain construal condition, subjects were similarly asked to specify each situational construal; however, in contrast to the procedure followed in the control or uncertain construal condition, subjects in this certain construal condition were then told that in furnishing their estimates they were to assume that their situational construals were "exactly correct." In other words, they were invited to make their reconsidered predictions and confidence intervals conditional on the accuracy of their prior situational construals.

The results for these three self-prediction conditions, assessed using both within-subject and between-subject comparisons, can be summarized very succinctly. Confidence intervals were unaffected by the three construal manipulations. That is, simply making it explicit to subjects that their predictions were predicated upon their situational construals (which might or might not be accurate) did not increase the width of the confidence intervals they offered. More important, stipulating to subjects that they should assume their construals to be completely accurate (i.e., that no allowance had to be made for the uncertainty inherent in the process by which they filled in gaps in information, resolved ambiguity, or otherwise went "beyond the information given") did not decrease their confidence intervals. Our interpretation for this result, of course, is that subjects in the "uncertain" and the "certain" construal conditions alike (as well as those in the control condition) furnished predictions and offered confidence estimates that failed to make the logically warranted allowance for the possibility of inaccurate construal.

The fourth experimental condition in the initial Griffin *et al.* (1990) experiment becomes important in the light of these findings and the interpretation we have offered for them. It showed that subjects can and will make allowance for the possibility of misconstrual, provided this possibility is demonstrated with sufficient force and clarity. In this fourth condition, subjects were again invited to specify their situational construals; but, before being asked to provide predictions and confidence intervals, they were told explicitly to suggest respects in which the actual situation might differ from their initial construal of it (that is, to furnish *alternative* construals). In this condition, at last, the subjects seemed to recognize the implications of the uncertain status of the situational construals at which they had arrived, and to increase the width of their confidence intervals substantially. Follow-up investigation revealed that subjects widened their confidence intervals only to the extent that their alternative construals implied different outcomes. Whereas subjects who offered essentially redundant construals did not change their expressions of certainty, subjects who considered very diverse construals widened their confidence intervals to reflect their uncertainty.

D. OVERCONFIDENCE AND LAY DISPOSITIONISM

The failure to make adequate inferential allowance for uncertain construal also plays a role in the problem of lay dispositionism, the systematic bias whereby social perceivers overlook situational explanations for observed actions and outcomes, and prematurely infer distinguishing personality traits and exaggerate their role in determining behavior. This inferential bias, recognized long ago by Lewin (1936), Heider (1944, 1958), and Ichheiser (1949), has been labeled the "fundamental attribution error" (Ross, 1977), or "correspondence bias" (Jones, 1990), and is commonly explained in terms of a general tendency of perceivers to underweight the importance of situational forces and constraints. However, our present analysis leads us to assert that inappropriate trait inferences owe as much to construal failures as they do to the simple underweighting of the situation. Specifically, such overly extreme trait inferences may occur because people fail to recognize the degree to which seemingly exceptional actions and outcomes inform us not that the relevant actors are exceptional in their personal dispositions but rather that we have misconstrued the relevant stimulus situation. That is, when behavior disconfirms our expectations and we have evidence that we need to revise our understanding, we usually change our mind about the actor, not about our construal of the situation.

To illustrate this "construal interpretation" of misguided lay dispositionism, consider a set of pilot studies undertaken by Ross and Penning (1985). Subjects in each of these studies were asked to make predictions about the behavior of a specific actor in a specific situation, a situation that was easy to imagine, yet left plenty of room for construal. After subjects made their behavioral predictions and reported their detailed construals of the relevant situation, they were informed that their predictions were, in fact, wrong. When these subjects were subsequently asked to report what could be inferred from the actors' (surprising) responses, they overwhelmingly favored dispositional explanations and inferences to situational ones. In other words, they were disposed to "recompute" the person—that is, to abandon the assumption that the person was probably quite average and to begin searching for dispositions that would explain the apparently exceptional behavior in question. What observers are insufficiently disposed to do, it seems, is to recompute the nature of the situation—that is, to consider ways in which the situation (either the objective situation or the person's subjective construal of it) might have been different from what they had assumed, different especially in ways that would make the relevant behavior less surprising and less reflective of extreme personal dispositions.

A final study in the previously discussed paper by Griffin et al. (1990) dealt explicitly with the problem of overly extreme trait inferences. Subjects in the four conditions of this study all were called upon to make dispositional inferences about a peer who purportedly had behaved in an "extreme" fashion (i.e., the individual had monopolized a group discussion of abortion by talking for 45 minutes out of the 75 minutes allotted). Consistent with the results of their other studies, they found that subjects exhibited as little conservatism (i.e., made just as extreme and confident trait assessments) when they did so under conditions where their situational construals (and/or their guesses about the relevant actor's construals) were of indeterminate accuracy as they did under conditions where the complete accuracy of such construals had been stipulated, and where their trait assessments were, in fact, contingent on that accuracy. Once again, only an explicit invitation to furnish alternative, highly divergent construals could induce subjects to become more conservative. Only then were they inclined to make adequate inferential allowance for the general uncertainty of their construals, and for the specific possibility that they had somehow misconstrued the situation by failing to imagine features of the objective or experienced situation that might have accounted for the extremity of the actor's response.

The general contention underlying this set of studies was that people typically generate a single construal of an ambiguous or incompletely specified situation and then make judgments as if their situational construals corresponded to perfect situational knowledge. The results of Griffin *et al.* (1990), like those of Gilovich (1990) and Newton (1990), suggest that people do not ever fully overcome the egocentrism that Piaget claimed to be characteristic of the immature social perceiver. In a range of judgment and prediction tasks, people seem unable to recognize, or at least unable to make appropriate allowance for, the fact that their subjective representations and constructions are neither isomorphic with reality, nor reliably shared by their peers. Instead, people illustrate a distinct lack of attributional conservatism, or, in cases where the dispositional inferences made on the basis of one's initial construal of the action and situation would be negative, a failure of attributional charity (see Ross & Nisbett, 1991).

Our multiple construal results also tempt us to speculate about the sources of, and remedies for, human disagreement and conflict. If we were willing to exercise constraint in drawing strong conclusions about behavior or judgments that differ from our own, if we were willing in such cases to look longer and harder for objective situational factors and subjective construals that could account for such divergence in responses, in short, if we acted more like the subjects in our multiple construal condition—we might find it easier to resolve conflict and communicate with our opponents. Are conflict and ill-will heightened because antagonists fail to recognize and/or make adequate inferential allowance for uncertainties and divergences in the construal of past events, present proposals, and existing social and political contexts? Can multiple construal (or related) manipulations induce the kind of attributional charity required for antagonists to develop mutual respect and trust? These questions form the basis of the final section of our article.

IV. Egocentric Construal in Social Misunderstanding

We tend to resolve our perplexity arising out of the experience that other people see the world differently than we see it ourselves by declaring that these others, in consequence of some basic intellectual and moral defect, are unable to see things 'as they really are' and

to react to them 'in a normal way'. We thus imply, of course, that things are in fact as we
see them and that our ways are the normal ways. (Ichheiser, 1949, p. 39)

Our discussion of the vagaries of social construal, and of related inferential
and attributional shortcomings, has clear and important implications for our
understanding of social conflict and for the problems of dispute resolution. Once
again, our working assumption is that people, in this case groups of partisans, are
guided by different construals of information and events, and unable to make
appropriate inferential or attributional allowance for such differences.

In part, our thesis has already been anticipated in our earlier discussion of the
false consensus effect, and the contention that people generally are insufficiently
conservative in the inferences they form about those who make choices opposite
to their own. Underlying, or at least exacerbating, many social conflicts, we
believe, are similar failures of "attributional charity." Adversaries form judgments about each other that would be appropriate if, but only if, those on the
"other side" really were confronting the same "object of judgment" but nevertheless persisting in judgments and courses of action (presumably because of
self-interest, ideological blinders, stupidity, or stubbornness) that seemed man-
ifestly inappropriate to that object of judgment. As the quotation from Ichheiser
(1949) implies, our contention is far from original. Ichheiser, and even earlier,
Asch (1940), explicitly suggested that what appear to be disagreements about
moral standards may frequently be disagreements about the nature of the case or
problem to which the parties' (often largely shared) moral standards are being
applied. We are essentially updating and elaborating this argument by claiming
that adversaries may fail to appreciate the "room for construal" that exists with
respect to the issues under contention, and thus the degree to which "reasonable" people could disagree with each other in assigning responsibility for the
problem and in proposing fair and effective remedies.

A. CONSTRUING CRIME AND PUNISHMENT

A provocative discussion of the role that construal processes can play in social
policy disputes is to be found in a report to the Canadian Department of Justice
prepared by Anthony Doob and Julian Roberts (reported in Doob & Roberts,
1984). Commissioned to study "public attitudes toward, and beliefs about, the
criminal justice system," the particular task undertaken by these two psychologists was to illuminate and explore the Canadian public's widely shared senti-
ment that the courts were too lenient in the sentences they imposed.

Through surveys and polling techniques, Doob and Roberts discovered that
the public's subjective perceptions and assumptions about crimes and criminals
were highly discrepant from the "objective" statistics offered by the govern-

ment. Respondents greatly overestimated the overall prevalence of violent crime and the frequency with which paroled prisoners commit violent crimes. They also believed (incorrectly) that the murder rate had increased since the abolition of capital punishment. In other words their disapproval of supposedly lenient sentencing policies, and their dismay about violent crime and its perpetrators, were far more congruent with their perceptions and assumptions than with the objective facts. The investigators' analyses exploring the link between people's attitudes toward sentencing and their construals of the crime problem drove this point home. The belief that sentences were too lenient was associated with higher estimates of the proportion of crimes involving violence and with lower estimates of the proportion of people going to prison for various offenses. Also, respondents who believed sentences were too lenient were more than twice as likely as other respondents to have had violent rather than nonviolent offenders in mind when answering opinion questions about sentencing policy in general. In short, "harsh" and "lenient" respondents were making different judgments not about some fixed, agreed upon set of crimes and criminals but about different crimes and criminals.

In light of these findings it is interesting to note what happened when Doob and Roberts's (1984) respondents were exposed to an actual case—one selected precisely because the sentence imposed on the offender had been relatively lenient given the particular offense (i.e., manslaughter) for which he was convicted. When presented only with the category of the offense and asked if the imposed sentence was "too harsh," "too lenient," "about right," or if they "would need more information in order to evaluate the sentence," 80% of those sampled judged the sentence to be too lenient and only 13% indicated that they would "need more information." By contrast, when the respondents were presented with a 500-word summary of the details of the case, only 15% judged that the sentence was too lenient. Indeed, when details of the case were specified rather than left for the respondents to construe for themselves, the proportion of respondents who judged the sentence as too harsh jumped from 0 to 45%.

The reader will be troubled, but in light of our earlier discussion perhaps not surprised, by the fact that so few subjects indicated that they "needed more information" before they could evaluate the sentence (and, apparently, that so few treated the apparent leniency of the sentence for manslaughter as a cue that the details of the case might have been somewhat exceptional.) Moreover, this failure to reserve judgment, especially in light of the seeming discrepancy between the magnitude of the punishment and the crime, was not due to any inability of subjects to imagine or recognize the significance of extenuating circumstances. When asked specifically if there "might be some circumstance" that would justify that sentence, 82% of those who had readily characterized the sentence as "too lenient" responded affirmatively. Such a finding underscores the message of the previously discussed Griffin *et al.* (1990) study on "multiple construal." That is, even when people have no basis for assuming their construals of some specific issue, event, or other object of judgment are correct (indeed, when their intuitions and standards have seemingly been violated in a way that invites them to consider the possibility that their construals are wrong), they make little if any allowance for this uncertainty in their judgments and inferences. Instead, they need special prompting (for example, an explicit invitation to consider alternative construals) to do what they would be well advised to do spontaneously—that is, to moderate the strength of construals that substitute uncertain conjecture for certain fact.

The report by Doob and Roberts (1984) went on to explore the particular role wittingly or unwittingly played by the media in shaping public dissatisfaction. When respondents were given an actual newspaper article to read about a case, one chosen specifically because it had been seized upon by the media as an example of "soft" sentencing, some 63% of them judged the sentence cited in the article to be too lenient. By contrast, when respondents were exposed to a summary of the actual court documents, only 19% judged the sentence in question to be too lenient. The authors (p. 277) appropriately concluded that "policy makers should not interpret the public's apparent desire for harsher penalties at face value; they should understand this widespread perception of leniency is founded upon incomplete and frequently inaccurate news accounts," or in other words, that the public's perceptions and desires are founded upon widespread misconstrual—and widespread failure to make allowance for the possibility of such misconstrual.

B. BIASED ASSIMILATION
AND ATTITUDE POLARIZATION

Although some disagreements can be resolved by providing more detailed accounts of the "object of judgment," many disagreements cannot be overcome so easily. Indeed, construal problems may still present themselves even when the same "objective" stimulus is presented to both sides. For, as we have noted throughout this article, facts do not always speak for themselves—often, people must go "beyond the information given" to fill in unspecified details, to infer links among causes, consequences, and correlates, and to find some overall meaning or moral. This requirement for subjective interpretation gives rise to differences in construal and consequent misunderstanding. In fact, in everyday social disputes between individuals, groups, or nations, the exacerbating factor often is not the absence of relevant information, but the presence of information that is complex, ambiguous, and mixed in its implications.

A number of studies have suggested that partisans respond to mixed, ambiguous evidence not by moderating their judgments (as virtually all normative standards would dictate) but by becoming more certain and extreme in their views. One mechanism underlying this "attitude polarization" effect was demonstrated in a classic study by Hastorf and Cantril (1954). In this study, Princeton and Dartmouth fans both viewed the same film of a hard-fought gridiron struggle between their respective teams. As a result of some particularly rough tackles, the Princeton quarterback was forced to the sidelines with a broken nose. Despite the constancy of the objective stimulus, the opposing partisans' assessments suggested two very different games. The Princeton fans' assessments suggested a continuing saga of Dartmouth atrocities and occasional Princeton retaliations whereas the Dartmouth fans' assessments suggested a hard-hitting contest in which both sides contributed equally to the violence. In particular, the Princeton students counted twice as many Dartmouth "fouls" as did the Dartmouth students. Each side, in short, "saw" a different game. And each side thought the "truth" in what they saw ought to be apparent to any objective observers of the same events.

Thirty-five years after the classic Hastorf and Cantril (1954) study, Lord, Ross, and Lepper (1979) extended this examination of the consequences of "biased assimilation" to the evaluation of social science data. When partisans are faced with mixed evidence relating to the efficacy or desirability of a particular social policy, they not only have the opportunity to construe particular pieces of evidence (like the football fans who selectively interpreted rough treatment of a star player either as brutal assault or hard-nosed play) they also have the opportunity to judge the *validity* and *relevance* of that evidence. Lord *et al.* reasoned that if partisans would respond to mixed "scientific" evidence by accepting supporting evidence at face value and attacking or explaining away disconfirming evidence, then two consequences would result. First, partisans would rate those studies whose results supported their own positions to be more convincing and well done than those studies yielding opposite results—even when the objective merits of the relevant research designs and empirical evidence were held constant. Second, partisans who have had the opportunity to contrast the "sound research" supporting their side with the "slipshod pseudoscience" supporting the other side would come away from viewing mixed evidence even *more* convinced that their own views are correct. Through the mechanisms of biased assimilation, Lord *et al.* predicted, the two sides would come to be even farther apart, or more polarized, in their views.

The authors tested their predictions by recruiting both proponents and opponents of capital punishment and asking them to read a mixed package of evidence about the deterrent effect of the death penalty. As predicted, both sides took comfort from the evidence in support of their position and had no trouble seeing the flaws in the evidence for the opposing view. In the end, both sides came away with their views on capital punishment strengthened and further polarized (and, we would argue, with an increased doubt about the open-mindedness and good faith of those on the "other side" who, so it seemed to them, failed to accept the plain lesson of the "objective evidence"). This "biased assimilation" phenomenon has been replicated and extended by Houston and Fazio (1989), who showed that it occurs primarily (and perhaps exclusively) for people whose attitudes are highly accessible.

C. BIASED PERCEPTIONS AND PERCEPTIONS OF BIAS

The same mechanisms that lead opposing partisans to find support for their respective positions in mixed or ambiguous evidence can lead them to perceive hostility or bias in any third party that attempts to present an even-handed assessment of issues or propose an even-handed settlement. That is, both partisan groups will deem the discrepancy between their own view of how things "really are" and the more moderate, two-sided view presented or implied in the effects of the third party, as evidence of that party's bias.[1]

To test this reasoning, Vallone, Ross, and Lepper (1985) presented pro-Israeli and pro-Arab student partisans (as well as some "neutral" students) with excerpts from television news coverage of the "Beirut massacre" of 1984. Whereas the most knowledgeable of the neutrals rated the broadcast summaries as being relatively unbiased, the partisans' evaluations were very different. On measure after measure there was virtually no overlap in the evaluations offered by the two partisan groups. Pro-Arab and pro-Israeli viewers alike were convinced that the other side had been favored by the media, that their own side had been treated unfairly, and that these biases in reporting had reflected the self-interests and ideologies of those responsible for the program. There was also evidence, reminiscent of Hastorf and Cantril's (1954) findings discussed earlier, that the two partisan groups in a sense "saw" different programs. Whereas viewers supportive of Israel claimed that a higher percentage of the specific facts and arguments presented were anti-Israel than pro-Israeli, viewers hostile to Israel offered the

---

[1]Critics and commentators often note that the perception of media bias in the study by Vallone, Ross, and Lepper (1985) appears to contradict the general principle of biased assimilation (Lord *et al.*, 1979) whereby partisan perceivers find more support for their position in mixed or ambiguous evidence than normative standards (or disinterested assessors) would deem reasonable. The answer offered by Vallone *et al.* is clear enough, to wit, the very process of finding consistent support for one's views in reality gives rise to the perception that neutral or even-handed assessments are discrepant from reality in a manner that is systematically biased against one's own side. In a sense, the phenomenon demonstrated by Vallone *et al.* represents the triumph of cognitive biases over motivational ones. For it is the partisans' inability to see the media offerings as they would wish them to be—that is, to notice and remember what is congruent, to ignore or forget what is incongruent, and to interpret ambiguous information favorably—that leads them to impugn the media's coverage and those responsible for it.

opposite assessment. Both sides, furthermore, believed that neutral viewers of the program would be swayed in the direction of the "other side."

The same conceptual analysis applied to partisan evaluations of news coverage can also be applied to partisan evaluations of proposed plans to deal with problems that the media cover. Imagine how the pro-Arab and pro-Israeli viewers in the hostile media study would have evaluated the efforts of some "nonpartisan" group that tried to fix blame, suggest punishments, or propose measures to avoid such tragedies in future. Better still, imagine how they would respond not to third party initiatives but to proposals offered by the other side. Any proposal that seems equitable and forthcoming to the partisan group offering it would likely seem inequitable and self-serving to the partisan receiving it—both because the two sides are apt to differ in what they believe to be "fair" (in the light of their divergent views of history and what the important issues are) and because they are apt to differ in the way they construe the specific terms and overall balance of the proposal itself. There is, however, an additional construal bias that comes into play in bilateral negotiation, one that constitutes a further barrier to conflict resolution. For as we shall now discuss, the very act of offering a proposal can change the way it is construed and evaluated.

D. REACTIVE DEVALUATION OF COMPROMISES AND CONCESSIONS

A series of studies by Stillinger, Epelbaum, Keltner, and Ross (1990) tested the thesis that the act of offering a compromise or concession causes it to be devalued in the eyes of the recipient. One such "reactive devaluation" study took advantage of a conflict between the Stanford University administration and various campus groups demanding that Stanford divest itself of all holdings in American companies doing business in South Africa. The particular focus of the study was on student responses to various compromise proposals that would have stopped short of total divestiture but nevertheless signaled the University's opposition to the racist apartheid policies of the South African regime. Two such compromise proposals were of particular interest: One was a proposal that the University immediately divest itself of stockholdings in companies that had been specifically linked to the South African military, to the police, or to apartheid practices in the work place (that is, a proposal for "partial" divestiture); and an alternative proposal that the University specify a 2-year deadline for major reforms in the apartheid system, after which total divestiture would follow if the reforms in question had not occurred (that is, a proposal for a "deadline"). When students were simply told (accurately) that the university was considering both proposals, along with many others, the two proposals were rated to be about equally satisfactory and significant. When the students were led to believe that the university was about to ratify one of these two compromise proposals, however, the reactive devaluation phenomenon was apparent. That is, when the university was purported to be ready to enact the partial divestiture plan a clear majority rated this concession to be less satisfactory and significant than the nonoffered alternative of a deadline for total divestiture. Conversely, when students were told that the university was about to propose a deadline plan, the clear majority rated this plan as less satisfactory and significant than a plan for immediate, albeit only partial, divestiture.

The final chapter in this research story was written a few months later, when the university at last decided to take action against apartheid by approving a plan rather similar to (but somewhat more comprehensive than) the partial divestment plan that had been attributed to it in the earlier study. As it happened, the investigators learned the details of this plan before it was made public. Accordingly, they were able to measure the partisan students' evaluations of its provisions twice, first before the announcement, when it could be described as merely one of several hypothetical possibilities, and then after the public announcement, when it was no longer hypothetical. As predicted, the students' ratings of the university's plan decreased significantly from the first evaluation to the second; and also as predicted, partisans soundly criticized the university's plan as "token" and "too little too late."

The mechanism initially proposed to underlie reactive devaluation was very simple, and closely linked to our discussion of construal biases. Our adversary's willingness to offer a particular compromise is apt to change our view both of the adversary's situation ("our boycott must really be working"; or "they must not have as much support as we thought") and of the terms of the compromise ("that missile system they're proposing to scrap if we'll reciprocate is probably obsolete"; or "they seem awfully anxious to get our tanks out of sector Z, we must be even more of a threat to them than we thought"). Furthermore, any ambiguities or omissions in proposed terms are apt to be seen as dangerous, perhaps deliberately wrought, "loopholes" that the other side is likely to exploit. In short, and in language familiar to two generations of social psychologists, the compromise or concession in question is to be received coolly by the other side not so much because of a change in their "judgment of the object" being proposed as because of a change in "the object of their judgment."[2]

---

[2]It is worth noting the apparent, yet ultimately elusive, relation of this phenomenon to the theory of cognitive dissonance (Aronson, 1990; Festinger, 1957). In one sense, reactive devaluation is yet another prediction derivable from dissonance theory and related consistency theories. That is, *ceteris paribus,* it is dissonance producing to see the terms offered by a foe in positive terms, and dissonance reducing to construe, or if necessary reconstrue, them and the context in which they are offered, in a fashion congruent with our hostility to our foe (and congruent with our belief about that foe's hostility toward us). However, the availability of a given set of terms, and more importantly the act of accepting them, creates dissonance-reducing pressures in the opposite direction—that is, toward

Subsequent research and conceptual analysis have begun to suggest other mechanisms that might play a role in the reactive devaluation phenomena. It has become increasingly clear (Kahneman & Tversky, 1979; Tversky & Kahneman, in press) that people are inclined to attach greater value to "losses" than "gains," and hence to see an "even-handed" proposal of trade concessions as disadvantageous, once the concessions to be ceded are seen as losses and the concessions to be received are seen as gains. There are even some intriguing hints that people may respond to concessions offered or received by changing the relative importance they attach to different needs, values, or desiderata—increasing their appetite for whatever is denied them, and losing their taste for whatever is made readily available.

Regardless of underlying mechanisms, however, the potential consequences of reactive devaluation are all too apparent (see Ross & Stillinger, in press). The party offering the compromise proposal is bound to be disappointed, and even resentful, when its proposal meets a cool reception and its concessions are dismissed as trivial or even self-serving. The party responding coolly, in turn, is apt to be similarly chagrined when its response produces not reciprocation but accusations of bad faith. What both sides fail to recognize, of course, is the extent to which the other side is responding to a subjectively different, and decidedly less appealing, proposal.

E. MISCONSTRUAL AND MISATTRIBUTION

We have elaborated some ideas and some research findings consistent with the notion that partisans, on occasion, simply fail to recognize that those on the other side see the world differently than they do. This oversight, in turn, can lead them to make erroneous attributions about each others' personal qualities in general, and moral standards in particular. If such partisans recognized that differences in opinion can be the product of differing construals rather than different values or standards, there is reason to imagine that disagreements would become less hostile and less personal. Or as Gustav Ichheiser—who anticipated much of this analysis some 50 years ago—mused, "if people who do not understand each other at least understand that they do not understand each other, then they understand each other better than when, not understanding each other, they do not even understand that they do not understand each other" (1949, p. 37).

---

attaching greater value to what one has received and accepted, and less value to what one has ceded. Very much the same kind of analysis can be made about the biased assimilation phenomenon of Lord *et al.* (1979) and the biased media phenomenon of Vallone *et al.* (1985). In each case, we see the relevance of dissonance processes, yet at the same time are faced with the longstanding problem of knowing exactly when, and where, and how, dissonance will be reduced, tolerated, or even enhanced in the service of some broader motivational or cognitive desideratum.

Our own reflections on this problem, however, combined with some new data collected by Robinson, Keltner, and Ross (1990), have made us question whether the postulation, or even the recognition, of divergent construals on the part of the other side is sufficient to reduce animosity or negative stereotyping. Indeed, we would contend that under some circumstances opposing partisans may appreciate or even exaggerate the magnitude of such differences yet be led by their naive realism to persist in negative inferences and attributions about their adversaries. The data that inform our conceptual analysis come from studies of partisans in two different social policy disputes, capital punishment and abortion rights (Robinson *et al.*, 1990). Although the relevant studies provided some examples of the classic failure of antagonists to recognize that they are construing issues differently or responding to a "different object of judgment," underestimation of such differences was less common than overestimation. The reason for this construal error by the Robinson *et al.* subjects was quite clear. The partisans generally overestimated the other side's tendency (and, often, their own side's tendency as well) to construe issues in whatever manner would be most congruent with its ideological stance.

In some, perhaps many, cases such suspicions are no doubt well founded. Individuals do tend to interpret the world in ways that are sympathetic to their own self-interests and ideology. It is no error to assume that others see the world through a filter colored by their own value-laden assumptions. The folly lies simply in the failure to recognize that one's own views or constructions of reality can be similarly subject to distortion. Questionnaire items employed by Robinson *et al.* (1990) dealing with the basis for beliefs made this aspect of naive realism quite clear. Partisans generally felt that whereas their own beliefs follow from their understanding of facts and arguments, the other side's beliefs dictate their interpretations of facts and arguments. The lessons learned and taught by social scientists in the laboratory and the field—that each of us constructs our own reality, and that we must both be aware of the vagaries of the construal process and charitable in our interpretation of perspectives and beliefs that differ from our own—are very difficult to grasp, and perhaps even more difficult to apply.

As we ponder the implications of these lessons, we find ourselves returning to the metaphor underlying Newton's (1990) "simple" demonstration. Individually and collectively, we are obliged to recognize that although we hear the other side's public words, we often cannot hear their private melodies—and that they share the same disability. Psychologists, we should note, generally prefer visual metaphors to auditory ones, so we close our discussion accordingly. To ease conflict in our increasingly heterogeneous communities, and in our ever smaller global village, we must struggle to see reality through our neighbors' and even our adversaries' eyes, and to make charitable attributions when we cannot.

Acknowledgments

The research reported in this paper was supported by a Social Sciences and Humanities Research Council of Canada grant to the first author and National Institute of Mental Health Grant 44321 to the second author. We are grateful to Robyn Dawes, David Dunning, Tom Gilovich, Mark Lepper, Michael Ross, Amos Tversky, and Mark Zanna for helpful comments on this chapter and/or the research it reports.

References

Aronson, E. (1990). *The return of the repressed: Dissonance theory makes a comeback.* Western Psychological Association Presidential Address, Reno, NV.

Asch, S. E. (1940). Studies in the principles of judgments and attitudes: II. Determination of judgments by group and by ego standards. *Journal of Social Psychology,* **12,** 433–465.

Asch, S. E. (1946). Forming impressions of personality. *Journal of Abnormal and Social Psychology,* **41,** 258–290.

Asch, S. E. (1948). The doctrine of suggestion, prestige, and imitation in social psychology. *Psychological Review,* **55,** 250–277.

Asch, S. E. (1952). *Social psychology.* New York: Prentice-Hall.

Bandura, A. (1965). Vicarious processes: A case of no-trial learning. In L. Berkowitz (Ed.), *Advances in experimental social psychology* (Vol. 2, pp. 3–57). New York: Academic Press.

Bargh, J. A. (1988). Automatic information processing: Implications for communication and affect. In L. Donohew, H. Sypher, & E. T. Higgins (Eds.), *Communication, social cognition, and affect* (pp. 9–32). Hillsdale, NJ: Erlbaum.

Barsalou, L. W. (1987). The instability of graded structure: Implications for the nature of concepts. In U. Neisser (Ed.), *Concepts and conceptual development: Ecological and intellectual factors in categorization.* New York: Cambridge University Press.

Bartlett, F. C. (1932). *Remembering: A study in experimental and social psychology.* Cambridge, England: Cambridge University Press.

Bell, D. E., Raiffa, H., & Tversky, A. (1988). *Decision making: Descriptive, normative, and prescriptive interactions.* Cambridge, England: Cambridge University Press.

Bem, D. J. (1967). Self-perception: An alternative interpretation of cognitive dissonance phenomena. *Psychological Review,* **74,** 183–200.

Bem, D. J. (1972). Self-perception theory. In L. Berkowitz (Ed.), *Advances in experimental social psychology* (Vol. 6, pp. 2–62). New York: Academic Press.

Berkowitz, L. (1975). *A survey of social psychology.* Imprint, IL: Dryden.

Bruner, J. S. (1957). Going beyond the information given. In H. Gruber, K. R. Hammond, & R. Jesser (Eds.), *Contemporary approaches to cognition* (pp. 41–69). Cambridge, MA: Harvard University Press.

Buss, A. H. (1980). *Self-consciousness and social anxiety.* San Francisco, CA: Freeman.

Cantor, N., & Kihlstrom, J. F. (1987). *Personality and social intelligence.* Englewood Cliffs, NJ: Prentice-Hall.

Carlsmith, J. M., Ellsworth, P. C., & Aronson, E. (1976). *Methods of research in social psychology.* Menlo Park, CA: Addison-Wesley.

Casper, J. D., Benedict, K., & Kelly, J. R. (1988). Cognitions, attitudes and decision-making in search and seizure cases. *Journal of Applied Social Psychology*, **18**, 93–113.

Devine, P. G. (1989). Stereotypes and prejudice: Their automatic and controlled components. *Journal of Personality and Social Psychology*, **56**, 5–18.

Doob, A. N., & Roberts, J. V. (1984). Social psychology, social attitudes, and attitudes toward sentencing. *Canadian Journal of Behavioural Science*, **16**, 269–280.

Dunning, D., Griffin, D. W., Milojkovic, J., & Ross, L. (1990). The overconfidence effect in social prediction. *Journal of Personality and Social Psychology*, **58**, 568–581.

Dunning, D., Meyerowitz, J. A., & Holzberg, A. D. (1989). Ambiguity and self-evaluation: The role of idiosyncratic trait definitions in self-serving assessments of ability. *Journal of Personality and Social Psychology*, **57**, 1082–1090.

Dweck, C. S. (1975). The role of expectations and attributions in the alleviation of learned helplessness. *Journal of Personality and Social Psychology*, **31**, 674–685.

Fazio, R. H. (1986). How do attitudes guide behavior? In R. M. Sorrentino & E. T. Higgins (Eds.), *Handbook of motivation and cognition* (pp. 204–243). New York: Guilford.

Fazio, R. H. (1990). Multiple processes by which attitudes guide behavior: The MODE model as an integrative framework. In M. P. Zanna (Ed.), *Advances in experimental social psychology* (Vol. 23, pp. 75–109). San Diego, CA: Academic Press.

Fazio, R. H., & Williams, C. J. (1986). Attitude accessibility as a moderator of the attitude-perception and attitude–behavior relations: An investigation of the 1984 presidential election. *Journal of Personality and Social Psychology*, **51**, 505–514.

Festinger, L. (1954). A theory of social comparison processes. *Human Relations*, **7**, 117–140.

Festinger, L. (1957). *A theory of cognitive dissonance*. Stanford, CA: Stanford University Press.

Festinger, L., & Carlsmith, J. M. (1959). Cognitive consequences of forced compliance. *Journal of Abnormal and Social Psychology*, **58**, 203–210.

Fosterling, F. (1985). Attributional retraining: A review. *Psychological Bulletin*, **98**, 495–512.

Garber, J., & Seligman, M. (1980). *Human helplessness: Theory and applications*. New York: Academic Press.

Garcia, J., & Koelling, R. A. (1966). Relation of cue learning to consequence in avoidance learning. *Psychonomic Science*, **4**, 123–124.

Geertz, C. (1973). *The interpretation of cultures*. New York: Basic Books.

Gilovich, T. (1981). Seeing the past in the present: The effect of associations to familiar events on judgments and decisions. *Journal of Personality and Social Psychology*, **40**, 797–808.

Gilovich, T. (1990). Differential construal and the false consensus effect. *Journal of Personality and Social Psychology*, **59**, 623–634.

Griffin, D. W. (1990). *The role of construal in measuring and maintaining individual differences*. Unpublished manuscript, University of Waterloo, Waterloo, Ontario.

Griffin, D. W., Dunning, D., & Ross, L. (1990). The role of construal processes in overconfident predictions about the self and others. *Journal of Personality and Social Psychology*, **59**, 1128–1139.

Hastorf, A., & Cantril, H. (1954). They saw a game: A case study. *Journal of Abnormal and Social Psychology*, **49**, 129–134.

Heider, F. (1944). Social perception and phenomenal causality. *Psychological Review*, **51**, 358–373.

Heider, F. (1958). *The psychology of interpersonal relations*. New York: Wiley.

Higgins, E. T., & Bargh, J. A. (1987). Social cognition and social perception. *Annual Review of Psychology*, **38**, 369–425.

Houston, D. A., & Fazio, R. H. (1989). Biased processing as a function of attitude accessibility: Making objective judgments subjectively. *Social Cognition*, **7**, 51–66.

Ichheiser, G. (1949). Misunderstanding in human relations: A study in false social perception. *American Journal of Sociology (Supplement)*, **55**(2).

Ichheiser, G. (1951). Misunderstandings in international relations. *American Sociological Review*, **16**, 311–315.

Ichheiser, G. (1970). *Appearances and realities: Misunderstandings in human relations*. San Francisco, CA: Jossey-Bass.

Johnson-Laird, R. N. (1983). *Mental models: Towards a cognitive science of language, inference, and consciousness*. New York: Cambridge University Press.

Jones, E. E. (1990). *Interpersonal perception*. New York: Freeman.

Kahneman, D., & Tversky, A. (1979). Prospect theory: An analysis of decision under risk. *Econometrica*, **47**, 263–291.

Kahneman, D., & Tversky, A. (1982a). On the study of statistical intuitions. In D. Kahneman, P. Slovic, & A. Tversky (Eds.), *Judgment under uncertainty: Heuristics and biases* (pp. 493–508). New York: Cambridge University Press.

Kahneman, D., & Tversky, A. (1982b). The simulation heuristic. In D. Kahneman, P. Slovic, & A. Tversky (Eds.), *Judgment under uncertainty: Heuristics and biases* (pp. 201–210). New York: Cambridge University Press.

Kelly, G. A. (1955). *A theory of personality: The psychology of personal constructs*. New York: Norton.

Krech, D., & Crutchfield, R. S. (1948). *Theory and problems of social psychology*. New York: McGraw-Hill.

Kunda, Z. (1990). The case for motivated reasoning. *Psychological Bulletin*, **108**, 480–498.

Langer, E. J., & Rodin, J. (1976). The effects of choice and enhanced personal responsibility for the aged: A field experiment in an institutional setting. *Journal of Personality and Social Psychology*, **34**, 191–198.

Latané, B., & Darley, J. M. (1968). Group inhibition of bystander intervention in emergencies. *Journal of Personality and Social Psychology*, **10**, 215–221.

Latané, B., & Darley, J. M. (1970). *The unresponsive bystander: Why doesn't he help?* New York: Appleton-Century-Crofts.

Lepper, M. R., & Greene, D. (1979). *The hidden costs of reward: New perspectives on the psychology of human motivation*. Hillsdale, NJ: Erlbaum.

Lepper, M. R., Greene, D., & Nisbett, R. E. (1973). Undermining children's intrinsic interest with extrinsic reward: A test of the overjustification hypothesis. *Journal of Personality and Social Psychology*, **28**, 129–137.

Lewin, K. (1935). *A dynamic theory of personality*. New York: McGraw-Hill.

Lewin, K. (1936). *Principles of topological psychology*. New York: McGraw-Hill.

Linder, D. E., Cooper, J., & Jones, E. E. (1967). Decision freedom as a determinant of the role of incentive magnitude in attitude change. *Journal of Personality and Social Psychology*, **6**, 245–254.

Lord, C. G., Fein, S., Lepper, M. R., & Desforges, D. M. (1990). *The role of attitude prototypes in attitudes toward social policies: When attitudes predict actions*. Unpublished manuscript, Texas Christian University, Fort Worth, TX.

Lord, C. G., Lepper, M. R., & Mackie, D. (1984). Attitude prototypes as determinants of attitude–behavior consistency. *Journal of Personality and Social Psychology*, **46**, 1254–1266.

Lord, C. G., Ross, L., & Lepper, M. R. (1979). Biased assimilation and attitude polarization: The effects of prior theories on subsequently considered evidence. *Journal of Personality and Social Psychology*, **37**, 2098–2109.

Miller, G. A., Galanter, E., & Pribram, K. H. (1960). *Plans and the structure of behavior*. New York: Holt, Rinehart & Winston.

Neisser, U. (1967). *Cognitive psychology*. Englewood Cliffs, NJ: Prentice-Hall.

Neisser, U. (1976). *Cognition and reality*. San Francisco, CA: Freeman.

Newton, L. (1990). *Overconfidence in the communication of intent: Heard and unheard melodies*. Unpublished doctoral dissertation, Stanford University, Stanford, CA.

Pennington, N., & Hastie, R. (1986). Evidence evaluation in complex decision making. *Journal of Personality and Social Psychology*, **51**, 242–258.

Pennington, N., & Hastie, R. (1988). Explanation-based decision making: Effects of memory structure on judgment. *Journal of Experimental Psychology: Learning, Memory, and Cognition*, **14**, 521–533.

Piaget, J. (1936). *La naissance de l'intelligence chez l'enfant*. Neufchâtel, France: Delachau & Niestle.

Robinson, R. J., Keltner, D., & Ross, L. (1990). *Misconstruing the views of the other side: Real and perceived differences in three ideological conflicts*. Unpublished manuscript, Stanford University, Stanford, CA.

Rodin, J. (1986). Aging and health: Effects of the sense of control. *Science*, **233**, 1271–1276.

Ross, L. (1977). The intuitive psychologist and his shortcomings: Distortions in the attribution process. In L. Berkowitz (Ed.), *Advances in experimental social psychology* (Vol. 10, pp. 173–220). New York: Academic Press.

Ross, L. (1978). Afterthoughts on the intuitive psychologist. In L. Berkowitz (Ed.), *Cognitive theories in social psychology* (pp. 385–400). New York: Academic Press.

Ross, L. (1989). Recognizing construal processes. In I. Rock (Ed.), *The legacy of Solomon Asch* (pp. 77–96). Hillsdale, NJ: Erlbaum.

Ross, L., Greene, D., & House, P. (1977). The false consensus effect: An egocentric bias in social perception and attribution processes. *Journal of Experimental Social Psychology*, **13**, 279–301.

Ross, L., & Nisbett, R. E. (1991). *The person and the situation: Perspectives of social psychology*. New York: McGraw-Hill.

Ross, L., & Penning, P. (1985). *The dispositionist bias in accounting for behavioral disconfirmation*. Unpublished manuscript, Stanford University, Stanford, CA.

Ross, L., & Stillinger, C. (in press). Barriers to conflict resolution. *Negotiation Journal*.

Schachter, S., & Singer, J. E. (1962). Cognitive, social and physiological determinants of emotional state. *Psychological Review*, **69**, 379–399.

Schank, R. C., & Abelson, R. P. (1977). *Scripts, plans, goals, and understanding*. Hillsdale, NJ: Erlbaum.

Seligman, M. E. P. (1975). *Helplessness: On depression, development, and death*. San Francisco, CA: Freeman.

Slovic, P., Griffin, D. W., & Tversky, A. (1990). Compatibility effects in judgment and choice. In R. Hogarth (Ed.), *Insights in decision making: A tribute to Hillel J. Einhorn* (pp. 5–27). Chicago: University of Chicago Press.

Srull, T. K., & Wyer, R. S., Jr. (1979). The role of category accessibility in the interpretation of information about persons: Some determinants and implications. *Journal of Personality and Social Psychology*, **37**, 1660–1672.

Srull, T. K., & Wyer, R. S. (1986). The role of chronic and temporary goals in social information processing. In R. M. Sorrentino & E. T. Higgins (Eds.), *Handbook of motivation and cognition* (pp. 503–549). New York: Guilford.

Stillinger, C., Epelbaum, M., Keltner, D., & Ross, L. (1990). *The reactive devaluation barrier to conflict resolution*. Unpublished manuscript, Stanford University, Stanford, CA.

Thomas, W. I., & Znaniecki, F. (1918). *The Polish peasant in Europe and America: Monograph of an immigrant group*. Boston: Badger.

Tversky, A., & Kahneman, D. (in press). Loss aversion in riskless choice. *American Economic Review*.

Uleman, J. S., & Bargh, J. A. (1989). *Unintended thought.* New York: Guilford.

Vallone, R. P., Griffin, D. W., Lin, S., & Ross, L. (1990). The overconfident prediction of future action and outcomes by self and others. *Journal of Personality and Social Psychology,* **58,** 582–592.

Vallone, R., Ross, L., & Lepper, M. R. (1985). The hostile media phenomenon: Biased perception and perceptions of media bias in coverage of the Beirut massacre. *Journal of Personality and Social Psychology,* **49,** 577–585.

Weiner, B. (1980). *Human motivation.* New York: Holt, Rinehard & Winston.

Weiner, B. (1986). *An attributional theory of motivation and emotion.* New York: Springer-Verlag.

Wilson, T., & Linville, P. (1982). Improving the academic performance of college freshmen: Attribution therapy revisited. *Journal of Personality and Social Psychology,* **42,** 367–376.

INDEX

A

Absolute annihilation, terror management theory and, 101, 106

Accessibility, self-interest and, 7–10

Accountability, person perception and, 240–241, 243

Accuracy-driven classification, person perception and, 246–248
action sets, 253–259
assessment sets, 248–253

Accuracy seeking, person perception and, 235

Accurate knowledge, terror management theory and, 98

Action readiness, mood and persuasion and, 192

Action sets, person perception and, 247, 253–259

Adaptation
normative conduct and, 223
self-interest and, 3
social interaction study and, 294–295, 300
terror management theory and, 101

Adaptive coping strategy, terror management theory and, 116

Affect, mood and persuasion and, 162
mood at exposure, 171
mood at time of judgment, 179
theoretical approaches, 163–164, 166, 168
theoretical implications, 187, 190–195

Affirmative action, self-interest and, 31–32

Age, self-interest and, 55

Agenda-setting effect, self-interest and, 8

Aggregate-level data, self-interest and, 17–19

Aggregation, self-report questionnaires and, 272, 276–277, 283–284, 293

Aggression, terror management theory and, 119–120

Annihilation
absolute, terror management theory and, 101, 106
terror management theory and, 142, 147

Anxiety
construal processes and, 332–333
social interaction study and, 295
terror management theory and, 96, 142, 144, 147, 149
architecture, 101–103
cultural anxiety buffer, 87–100
cultural anxiety buffer, breakdown of, 133–136
cultural worldview, 126, 128
maintenance of sense of value, 122, 124
research directions, 137–139
self-esteem, 105
self-esteem, correlational literature on, 114–118
self-esteem maintenance, 108–114
summary statement, 106

Arguments, mood and persuasion and, 167
mood at exposure, 169–171, 173–177
mood at time of judgment, 181–182
peripheral cues, 184, 186

Arousal
mood and persuasion and, 168, 189–190
normative conduct and, 218–219
terror management theory and, 110–111, 119

Assessment sets, person perception and, 247–253, 255–256, 259, 261

Associationists, construal processes and, 321

Associations, construal processes and, 328

Attention
mood and persuasion and, 166, 176
self-interest and, 79

Attentional focus, normative conduct and, 226, 229

CONTENTS OF OTHER VOLUMES